Left Lives in Twentieth Century Ireland

Volume 2

edited by

Francis Devine

and

Kieran Jack McGinley

A WATCHWORD PAPERBACK

Umiskin
Press

Contents

Dedication

In Memoriam

Caroline Byrne Birmingham – member, Trinity College Dublin SIPTU Library Section and staunch advocate for part- time and job-sharing staff missed by husband Kieran and children Rory & Lauren

David Fitzpatrick – Emeritus Professor of History and former member, *Saothar* Editorial Advisory Board

Seán Garland – former Workers' Party President, political and social activist

Sean Hare – retired SIPTU recruiter in the Library TCD, mainly at the Santry Book Repository

Dympna Harper – former Irish Labour History Society Trustee and member of FWUI and SIPTU, National Executive Councils representing AnCo/FÁS staff

Alan MacSimóin – historian and long-time activist in the SIPTU Education Branch and wider community

Alf Mac Lochlainn – Emeritus Academic Librarian, National University of Ireland Galway and long-standing ILHS member

Sylvia Meehan – first Head, Employment Equality Agency; Association of Secondary Teachers' Ireland and ICTU Women's Committee activist; and life-long campaigner for equality and human rights

Jer O'Leary – actor on stage and screen, banner artist, activist in ITGWU/SIPTU Health Services. On stage and street he became the personification of Big Jim Larkin.

Above: Dónal Ó Cofaigh (Secretary, Fermanagh Council of Trade Unions) and Jim Quinn at the launch of Labouring Beside Lough Erne in Enniskillen in February 2019

Below: Howard Thornton, Chair, Fermanagh & Omagh District Council with Officers and members of Fermanagh Council of Trade Unions at the launch of Labouring Beside Lough Erne

Foreword

On the closure of Watchword publishing, it was obvious that a need for the not-for-profit model of publishing labour history remained. Biographical works associated with the trade union movement and cultural endeavours were still needed. Umiskin Press's first imprint was the title *Dear Madam*, the written reflections of the late Dermot Sweeney, mainly through the medium of the *Irish Times*. That slim volume was funded by Dermot's workmates in the Trinity College Dublin Library and was a gift to his family to remember a man who was nothing if not controversial in his views, politics and speech. It was mainly organised by my colleague Tony Carey.

Umiskin Press has been happy to receive a number of commissions from trade unions and trades councils that have lightened the financial burden on its Principal. In this regard, I wish to thank most sincerely SIPTU, UNITE, ICTU and Fermanagh Council of Trade Unions who have hosted and part financed some of our ongoing work. Specifically, I wish to pay credit to Joe O'Flynn, SIPTU General Secretary, for making the Cois Life Bar and Connolly Room available to Umiskin for launches and to Jimmy Kelly for similarly making UNITE's premises available for the launch of *Eggs & Rashers*, Matt Merrigan's memoir.

Our titles are now being accessed by a wider audience with recent sales in the United States, and regular requests from Germany and the United Kingdom. Take-up from Irish booksellers is anaemic, though a few regulars oblige almost all the time. The staple back-bone for Umiskin has been the attendance and purchase of our titles at launches and subsequent political and trade union conferences in tandem with ILHS (Irish Labour History Society) publications. The last twelve months have seen extremely good sales in Belfast, Derry and Enniskillen. Many thanks are due to those who facilitated those launches especially NIC-ICTU, Fermanagh Council of Trade Unions, and NIC-ICTU affiliates who bulk bought copies of the Seán Byers & Francis Devine (eds), *William Walker, 1870-1918, Centenary Essays* and to Patricia Mc Keown (UNISON) and Alison Millar (NIPSA) for chairing the Walker Conference proceedings in the Mac Centre, Belfast, in October 2018.

This year 2019 promises to be Umiskin's most demanding year having already launched *Labouring Beside Lough Erne* (copies available from Jim Quinn at jim.quinn@btinternet.com), we now launch *Left Lives in Twentieth Century Ireland Volume 2*. Francis Devine has provided an introduction to what I regard as a very fine and varied production. In the autumn of 2019, Umiskin will bring to print Dr Mike Mecham's full biography of William Walker. Mike has already delivered seven of the eight chapters and the breadth of his scholarship is not only impressive but as a fledgling publisher daunting to have such a prestigious work on our hands. At this remove, I wish to thank Mike for his courtesy and work ethic and am looking forward to his visit to us before Easter in Dublin and Limerick for Centenary Soviet events. Mike has recently been offered the role of Research Fellow at St Mary's College, London, and has taken up the role of ILHS contact in England – Brexit, hard or soft.

In 2020, co-editors Francis Devine and Patrick Smylie will have drawn together *Left Lives in Twentieth Century Ireland Volume 3 – Communist Lives* which will examine the lives of Irish Communists from circa 1920 to the present. Chapters reveal the biographies of both well-known and obscure activists including trade union leaders, pioneering women, republican communists, writers, and communists active today. Some chapters detail lives lived beyond Ireland. Further essays will examine communist siblings and intergenerational communist families. The editors' introduction will explore the impact of communism in Ireland, and the importance of bibliography in establishing its appeal as well as its successes and limitations. The concise bibliographies will reflect the phases and strands of a century of communism in Ireland, and the broadly chronological essays will shed light on international influences, internal struggles, activity in the trade unions, republican/communist relations, migrant communities, communist critiques of Irish society, and whither Irish communism today. The book will appeal to all those with an interest in the Irish Left, communism and political biography.

Beyond that, Umiskin will just have to wait and see how sales in 2019/2020 replenish the funds and what new works flow into the Press. In this volume we welcome back contributors such as Francis Devine, Brian Kenny, Mike Mecham, Emmet O'Connor, Tony Brown, Brendan Halligan, pieces from colleagues with whom I have worked in other spheres in the past, Séamus Dooley (NUJ), Mags O'Brien (TCDSU/INOU/DAG/SIPTU), Des Derwin (SIPTU DDC/Dublin Region/DCTU), Niall Greene (LP), and most importantly encourage two young writers Dan O'Neill (SIPTU) and Luke Dineen (ILHS/UCC). A number of works failed to make the deadline, some for the second time. However in the future Umiskin hopes to find room for those works and encourage those authors to finish those pieces while broadening the search for new authors and topics.

Finally, I want to thank my wife Helen, for all things IT and for the support she gives me as well as space on the kitchen table for piles of work in progress; and to Francis Devine for more wonderful journeys and inspiration. His good company on many long journeys in the United Kingdom and Ireland broadens my labour history, trade union, and association football horizons. Many thanks too to Christy and the folk at CRM Design & Print Ltd., who do a splendid job of work without fuss, and are trade unionists to boot; to Artery Publications, London for use of the Bickerstaffe cartoon from *hung, drawn and quartered*, the caricatures of Ken Gill and the Ken Gill Memorial Trust; to Watchword Ltd for matter from *Dear Comrade;* to Kevin Murphy, Ed Penrose, Fionnuala Richardsonand John Feeley at the ILHS, particularly in relation to the Derry and Enniskillen events.

I hope you enjoy Umiskin's latest offering, and if you are new to Umiskin Press, you can email us on kmcginly@tcd.ie, or look us up online at www.umiskinpress.wordpress.com. For vendors looking for trade discount and/or enquiries re back issues or trade outside of Ireland the above contacts endure.

Thanking you in solidarity
Kieran Jack Mc Ginley, *Principal, Umiskin Press*

Introduction

This second volume of *Left Lives in Twentieth Century Ireland* builds on the first, published by Umiskin in October 2017 and containing the following essays: Séamus Cody, 'True to the cause: P.T. Daly, 1870-1943'; Emmet O'Connor, 'A Connolly for Unionists? William Walker, 1870-1918'; Bill McCamley, 'The third James – an unsung hero of our struggle: James Fearon, 1874-1924'; D.R. O'Connor Lysaght, 'The Irish Soviet man: Seán Dowling, 1885-1948'; John P. Swift, 'A solitary voice that echoes still: John Swift, 1896-1990'; Charles Callan, "Don't demean yourself': painter and trade unionist John Mulhall, 1911-1981'; Connal Parr, 'Two pokers: Sam Thompson, 1916-1965, and James Ellis, 1931-2014'; Francis Devine, "From the abstract to the reality': Jim McFall, 1926-1992, and Belfast boilermakers'; Michael Halpenny, 'The patriot game – Dominic Behan, 1928-1989'; Kieran Jack McGinley, 'Frank Cluskey, 1930-1989 – a man of principle'; Sheila Simmons & Francis Devine, 'Evelyn Owens, 1931-2010: equal rights campaigner and Labour Court Chair'; and Francis Devine, 'Changing everything: Inez McCormack, 1943-2013'.[1]

In 2018, Umiskin published *William Walker, 1870-1918, Belfast Labour Unionist Centenary Essays*, edited by Seán Byers and Francis Devine. In addition to biographical pieces on Walker himself, there were essays on pioneer Belfast socialist John Bruce Wallace; early women socialists, trade unionists and co-operators like Margaret McCoubrey and Ida Boyd, among others; boilermaker, Northern Ireland Labour Party MP and Irish Transport & General Workers' Union General (ITGWU) Officer William McMullen; little-known Fermanagh labour activists John Jones and William Kelly; the poet John Hewitt; and UNISON's Anna McGonigle from Omagh.[2]

This series of studies in labour biography adds to a growing corpus of similar work. It was not always thus. When the Irish Labour History Society (ILHS) was formed in 1973, few biographical publications existed, although C. Desmond Greaves, *The Life & Times of James Connolly* (1961), and Emmet Larkin, *James Larkin: Irish Labour Leader* (1965), came to be regarded as classics and have been re-published.[3] Little preceded them. R.M. Fox had contributed a number of biographies of labour movement figures, a tradition maintained by his fellow-journalist Michael McInerney in 1974.[4] Their works may now be neglected but they should not be diminished when set against their frantic lives and the limited resources available to them. In addition, they were personally acquainted with their subjects which could be regarded as advantage or handicap, something their readers can decide. They were both socialist and trade union activists.

J.W. Boyle – whose life is the subject of an essay below – broke new ground by bringing the RTÉ Radio Thomas Davis Lecture series to print with *Leaders & Workers* (1965) and expanded the subjects chosen beyond Connolly and Larkin to then relatively unknown figures – together with the times and circumstances in which they operated – of Michael Davitt, John Doherty, James Fintan Lalor, Bronterre O'Brien, Feargus O'Connor and WilliamWalker. Those writing were – in the absence of an alternative chronology of Irish labour – strongly influenced by the then well-known turning points of British labour history – Combination Acts and their repeal, Chartism, New Model unions, formation of the Trades Union Congress, New Unionism and the birth of the Labour Party. As a consequence, they searched for evidence of such phenomenon in Ireland – something arguably reflected by Andrew Boyd – another figure whose life is discussed below – in his *The Rise of the Irish Trade Unions* (1972), a widely read and influential book – rather than seeking to discover Irish workers' own history.

Biography was, nonetheless, a compelling form of investigation. Published from 1979, the ILHS journal *Saothar* carried biographical studies and obituaries of significant figures.[5] By 2000, in addition to Emmet O'Connor's sweeping *A Labour History of Ireland* which suggested new frameworks, full biographies were available for Louie Bennett, Alexander Bowman, Harry Midgley and Thomas Johnson, with many more figures covered in pamphlets and articles.[6] The biographical net widened further with works on, among others, characters as diverse as Walter Carpenter, Seán Dunne, James Everett, Rosie Hackett, Helena Molony and Michael O'Riordan.[7] From *Saothar 24*, 1999, an important feature has been 'Labour Lives' providing succinct entries on a broad range of figures: Tadhg Barry, Louie Bennett, Miriam Daly, Michael Enright, Thomas Foran, Eva Gore-Booth, Rosie Hackett, Marie Johnson, Thomas Kain, Peadar Macken, Edward McHugh, R.J.P. Mortished, Seán Murray, Cathal O'Shannon, James M. Pringle, Margaret Skinnider, May (Abraham) Tennant, William Upton and Jack White.[8]

In addition, although never with the intention that the series would necessarily be biographical, twelve of the fifteen pamphlets in the ILHS Studies in Irish Labour History (SILH) series have featured people's lives: Paddy Cardiff, Winifred Carney, Dermot Doolan, Peter Ennis, James Fearon, Desmond Greaves, Ellen Grimley (Gordon), Young Jim Larkin, Gilbert Lynch, Stephen McGonagle, Michael Moynihan and Peader O'Donnell.[9] As with those in both volumes of *Left Lives*, some figures were brought into the public gaze for the first time. Perhaps surprisingly the use of oral history remained an under-utilised tool for biographers, although *Saothar* published the reminiscences of Andy Barr, Paddy Bergin, Billy Blease, John Freeman, Malachy Gray, Jack Macgougan, Stephen McGonagle, Matt Merrigan, Eilís Ryan and Betty Sinclair, as well as the collective memories of secondary teachers, women domestic farm servants, Guinness staff and printers[10] – and the SILH series drew on the oral testimony of Paddy Cardiff, Joe Deasy, Dermot Doolan, and Michael Moynihan.

Beyond the ILHS and its publications, labour figures feature in the *Dictionary of Irish Biography*, first published in 2009, a trawl of its content revealing many beyond the 'only to be expected' Connolly, Davitt, Johnson, Larkin, and O'Brien. Similarly, the *Oxford Dictionary of National Biography* (2004) contains many Irish labour-related entries, particularly for those born or active in Britain, like Jack Macgougan. Published in Britain since 1972, the *Dictionary of Labour Biography* contains many entries of Irish interest including Jim Connell (volume X); Walter Hampson, 'Casey' (VI); Larkin (XIII); Richard McGhee (VII); Edward McHugh (VII); and William Walker (XII). For Labour Party and Northern Ireland Labour Party personalities, Charles Callan and Barry Desmond's excellent *Irish Labour Lives* (2010) presents a comprehensive gallery of elected Labour representatives.[11] In addition, Emmet O'Connor and John Cunningham's *Lives on the Left (2016)*, provides an examination of nineteen lives under themes such as 'primitive rebels', 'early labour radicals' and 'pioneering trade unionists', 'communists', 'mavericks', 'artists as socialists' and parliamentary figures.[12] Alongside this, the pamphleteering tradition has been maintained with studies of Tadhg Barry, Madge Davison, Joe Deasy, Seán Dunne, James Everett, Jimmy Gralton, Sam Nolan, and Mick O'Riordan, among others, appearing recently.[13] The opening of Rosie Hackett Bridge in Dublin produced a collection of essays in her honour.[14] Finally, there have been substantial new full studies of Connolly and Larkin, together with important, previously neglected figures like Seán McLoughlin and William Partridge.[15]

Left Lives 2 began to form even as the first volume was going to press. Some contributors could not meet the deadline and required more time while others, seeing *Left Lives* in print, contacted Umiskin to offer possible contributions for any future volume. The original idea was that contributors would reflect on those that they considered significant, expressing their reasoning for such an assessment. Although, as with perhaps all biography, though the authors began by suggesting individuals they admired or respected, had always been fascinated by or whom they felt had received insufficient recognition for their contribution to the cause, it became clear that such an approach risked hagiography. No subjects were suggested to contributors, however, and their approaches have, as can be seen, been very different in terms of their methodology, assessment and conclusions. Studies that encompassed craft, gender, industrial and political labour, the world of work beyond Belfast and Dublin were encouraged however. The result is a collection of apparently unconnected personalities, yet all are threaded together by their commitment to the cause of socialism, a socialism expressed very differently by, say, Brendan Corish or Sam Nolan, Bob Day or Sylvia Meehan. In addition, all those examined here demonstrated unceasing effort and commitment to the working class. Their lives reflect craft, general and administrative workers, public and private sector, north and south, east and west, equality and human rights, politics, culture and, above all, class. Their lives raise many questions and their study will hopefully generate further research in pursuit of those ideas raised.

The most disappointing element of *Left Lives 2* has been the difficulty in obtaining studies of women or persuading women to contribute material. It has not been for want of trying. Two commissioned contributors were unable to meet the deadline or were overtaken by other events in their lives. Umiskin wanted to publish studies of the contributions of significant women and remains committed to that ambition. Mags O'Brien's study of Sylvia Meehan therefore assumes particular importance within this collection. Meehan was a remarkable woman. Widowed at a young age, she raised a family who continuously acknowledged her loving support, and was a respected teacher and activist in the Association of Secondary Teachers, Ireland, occasionally appearing as a strong critic of the union's apparent reluctance to fight on equality issues. Through the ICTU Women's Committee, she was a leading figure among a cohort of women who campaigned on equal pay and broader equality issues, recognising that workplace discrimination could not be defeated without its sources in wider society being identified and eliminated.

Appointed as first Chair of the Employment Equality Agency in 1977 – its successor agency the Equality Authority becoming part of the Irish Human Rights & Equality Commission in 2014 – Meehan demonstrated imagination, courage, tenacity and leadership skills, defining her and the new Agency's brief although confronted by opposition from employers, reluctance by Government, even ambivalence from some trade union quarters. She maintained broad interests in equality and human rights matters, in Ireland and beyond, throughout her life, her legacy a significant one.

Luke Dineen's study of Robert 'Bob' Day sheds light on a man whose star shot across the Cork firmament in the heady days of the War of Independence. He was a central figure in the Cork Harbour Soviet, an impacting member of Cork Corporation and a Labour TD. While Dineen has examined Day's brief political and trade union career, much of his life remains obscure as he suffered a debilitating condition that forced his retreat from public activity while still a young man. What is revealed is a man of ability, firm socialist commitment and a diligent, hard-working representative for his class, whether in Dáil, City Hall or trade union arena. The tensions between Labour and Republican activists features strongly in the examination of Day's life raising interesting questions about how that inter-relationship played in other towns and cities.

In Wexford, Richard Corish was first elected to Dáil Éireann as a Republican before representing Labour and being succeeded by his son, Brendan. On 24 November 2018 in Wexford Town Library, the ILHS, in association with Wexford County Council and the Corish family, held a one-day seminar commemorating the Centenary of his birth, 'Remembering Brendan Corish (1918-1990)'. Three of the papers read that day – by Tony Brown, Niall Greene and Brendan Halligan – are reproduced here with a short biographical sketch of Corish providing introduction and context. These papers differ from all the other entries in that they are based on personal reminiscence – albeit with substantial documentation from their privately held papers, most of the material being the formal, contemporary record of the events described. All three contributors could be accused of being Corish admirers – indeed, together with Young James Larkin, all three cite Corish as being among the main influences on their own political formation – and the tone of their papers reflecting the excitement and pace of the times when, it was hoped, the seventies would be socialist! Corish's *New Republic* speech – in which Halligan in particular had a hand, although he insists all the ideas were ultimately those of Corish himself – was ground-breaking, creating an atmosphere of hope that attracted many young people of ability into the Labour Party. Corish's opposition to Coalition was broken by events from 1970 that persuaded him that Labour had to be in Government, not least to keep Fianna Fáil out. That Government of 1973-1977 is much maligned in commentaries on Labour's history and among socialist activists ever since. Brown, Greene and Halligan defend Labour's achievements, arguing that most are not acknowledged in the damning criticisms. Certainly, the house-building record would be one that a contemporary Government might aspire to.

The modernisation of Labour – and by extension politics generally – was facilitated or only made possible by – depending on your perspective – internal reforms that Greene outlines from his vantage point of having been central to the Administrative Committee and its proposals for change. The *New Republic* was painted with broad brush strokes which then demanded detailed proposals for each policy target such as the social policy detailed by Brown, again from the perspective of someone very closely involved in its construction and execution. Together, the three essays – whilst not biographical as such – inform us about Corish's essential character and charisma, his political courage and foresight.

In Northern Ireland, Paddy Devlin journeyed from physical force Republicanism to social democratic politics, even though the SDLP ultimately fell short of his vision for change and inclusivity. The recent arguments in Belfast City Council about whether the city should acknowledge Devlin's contribution in statue form have demonstrated that enemies, once made, remain unforgiving. That said, why it has to be a choice between, for instance, Winifred Carney or Paddy Devlin for a City Hall statue is nonsensical. In writing about Devlin, Connal Parr is uniquely enlightened or handicapped – again as the reader may chose to interpret it – by being his grandson. Like Brown, Greene and Halligan on Corish, there is obvious respect and affection for his subject but Parr's work is scholarly and, particularly when looking at Devlin's political formation through his choice of reading, informative. Devlin was an extremely controversial appointment among existing ITGWU Officials – and some vociferous members in Belfast – and not seen as having anything to contribute. Under his stewardship, however, the union's northern membership – long moribund and sequestered to the margins of the rapidly disappearing sectors of deep sea dockers and clothing workers – grew and he fought fiercely for low paid, women and public service workers. Devlin's leadership of the Antrim Crystal occupation indicated his imagination and preparedness to fight hard for his members. It is an aspect of Devlin's contribution that merits further investigation.

The typographical printer Samuel Monro was a founding figure in Belfast's labour movement closely associated with its Trades Council and, when the British Trades Union Congress (BTUC) assembled in the city, its President. His labour always had a small 'l', his unwillingness to embrace Labour with a big 'L' part of a wider reluctance, particularly among the crafts, to embrace an emerging socialist vision. Monro was also unionist – most probably with a small 'u' – another factor in his resistance to capitalising his 'L'. He was, despite what would be regarded by many as these stifling limitations, a tremendous campaigner for improved pay and conditions, not just for print workers but those in textiles and other trades, skilled and unskilled. He supported the organisation of women and wanted an extension of protective legislation to better the lives of children and factory hands. His late daughter Mavis presented the gong her father used to chair the BTUC to the ICTU and it is on display in the John Hewitt Bar.

Although now almost forgotten, Monro was familiar to two pioneer figures of labour history in the late twentieth century, John W. Boyle and Andrew Boyd, and here Mike Mecham and Emmet O'Connor paint finely-crafted portraits of both. Boyle and Boyd both experienced Belfast's sectarian divisions and discrimination. Boyle resolved matters by migrating to Canada where he and his wife Elizabeth contributed, as they had at home, to socialist politics in their new homeland. Mecham reflects on the Boyles, an indispensable partnership, each giving strength to the other. Boyle's major work – harshly dismissed by one reviewer as antique – lay unpublished for decades, an indication of how marginalised labour history and its historians could be. Yet, he persevered and now his study of the labour movement's emergence in the nineteenth and early twentieth centuries stands as solid reference point. Most interestingly, Boyle – through his command of French literature and language – had an outlook not confined to Ireland or Britain. His linguistic ability enabled his access to elements of Canada, its culture and life-style, frequently ignored or unnoticed by monoglot English speakers. In conversations or correspondence with Boyle – always a rewarding exercise – his view was from an eagle's height, providing perspective and comparative examples. Mecham, who never had opportunity to meet his subject, draws extremely accurate conclusions about Boyle's life, his personality and achievements, including the pain of an exile never-quite-contented in his new home.

Boyd became a sharp critic of the Northern Ireland régime, the ambivalence of the British and Irish Governments, and, not least, the response or – as he would see it – the lack of a meaningful response from the trade union movement on both islands. It did not endear him to many but he did not care, content that his criticisms were valid and required meaningful policy responses. His belief in Independent Working Class Education (IWCE) was betrayed not just by the British Trades Union Congress when they emasculated the work of Boyd's beloved National Council of Labour Colleges (NCLC) but by the inability or unwillingness, or both, of the Irish Congress to recognise the significance and potential of IWCE for all. Unlike Mecham and Boyle, O'Connor knew Boyd and the two frequently corresponded, their exchange featuring in the piece below. The ILHS once made a presentation to John W. and Elizabeth Boyle in recognition of their role in 'the making and recording' of labour history. This could have applied equally to Boyd, his shipyard Shop Steward days rarely being considered. Boyd and Boyle's works remain cornerstones for the development of Irish labour history even if, enabled by their pioneering introductions, those corners have been well turned since. Their lives and contributions raise questions as to the role of labour history and its historians in developing that history's future pages. While Boyle was an ILHS enthusiast, Boyd was not, dismissing the Society as 'academic', a criticism that was not valid. It might be reflected that Society and historian were each other's miss.

Boyd and Boyle both brought new figures to broad public attention. In Boyd's case, the recovery of the life of Jim Connell, author of 'The Red Flag' was one of his great contributions, acknowledged by a plaque at the Connell Monument in Crossakiel, County Meath. Each May Day, bands and banners parade through the village in homage to Connell and, for most unwittingly, Boyd. At least some of the banners are those of the actor, banner artist and activist Jer O'Leary whose death on St Stephen's Day 2018 was greeted with such widespread dismay. A much-loved 'Dublin character', O'Leary's wake and funeral attracted huge crowds gathered from his interwoven worlds of trade unionism, theatre and film, art, socialist, communist and Republican politics, as well as hundreds who simply knew him as great company. For many, the most public manifestation of his legacy will be in his colourful and politically overt banners that created a new vision for trade union art. O'Leary, while arriving at his own style in conjunction with the needlework skills and practical views of his wife Eithne, was very conscious of those that had produced banners before him. Admiring W.L. Reynolds's Boyne Fishermen and other banners in Drogheda Millmount Museum, O'Leary was as impressed as any by their magnificent, primitive imagery that, as art historian John Gorman claimed, would grace 'any art gallery anywhere in the world'. O'Leary was also aware of Thomas Kain whose early ITGWU banners broke the existing mould of banners that predominantly reflected craft and Nationalist [or Unionist] imagery in the style of their British counterparts. Kain's active involvement in the Irish Citizen Army gave his portraits of James Connolly particular poignancy and brought the socialist hero anew to the street. The lives of these three banner artists – Reynolds, Kain and O'Leary – while unconnected in time or location, form a linear view of trade union iconography that is rich, informative and reflective of the movement's changing values and aspirations. All three created a lasting legacy for which the movement is indebted.

Des Derwin, Séamus Dooley and Brian Kenny all write about people they knew well, personally, politically or both. In Derwin's study of the Amalgamated Transport & General Workers' Union's Mattie Merrigan, he draws on the recollections of Des Bonass, Rayner Lysaght and Mick O'Reilly, in an overtly political critique of the man they all felt, to varying degrees, left a 'marvellous legacy'. Of the lives here, Merrigan's was one of those which most interacted with or reflected socialist theory. Derwin offers constructive criticism, suggesting that Merrigan ultimately failed to maximise opportunities for decisive advance, the Socialist Labour Party being abandoned too quickly perhaps. He goes on to chide contemporary activists, within and without the Dáil, in the various recent Left alliances, fragile or not. These reflections from his old comrades provide interesting context for Merrigan's own memoir *Eggs & Rashers* published by Umiskin in 2014.

Kenny distils his picture of the remarkable Sam Nolan from a longer pamphlet he completed in 2013 and now available as a kindle.[16] It appears that Nolan's every breath had been political from his childhood days skipping out of his home below the portrait of Stalin defiantly hung in the hallway by his father, through the angst of his Communist years to the disappointments of watching Labour diminish itself. Through much of this, Nolan, active in the Amalgamated Society of Woodworkers, fought courageously for the unemployed, homeless, women and the internationally oppressed. His remarkable service as Dublin Trades Council's Correspondence Secretary is an historic achievement by any standard but it is not the longevity of his tenure but the breadth and depth of his contribution to struggle that is noteworthy. Like Merrigan, albeit from different shades of scarlet, Nolan was guided by theoretical debate and discussion, always prepared to amend his position, even to his personal cost or the loss of comrades. Neither Merrigan nor Nolan ever had opportunity to exercise real power and both operated through British-based unions.

Dooley writes of his predecessor as Irish Secretary of the National Union of Journalists, a union that, appropriately, sees itself as International. Jim Eadie is shown to be quietly effective, an informed and encouraging leader of a membership well-equipped to express itself through some trying times as the nature and production of the media experienced rapid change. Eadie, from a 'small union', arguably enabled the NUJ to punch above its weight and won important advances for women, for members' pay and conditions, and in training, press controls and freedom of speech. It is a compelling illustration of a hard-working union Official, blessed with integrity and the courage to retain that whether confronted by State, employer or member.

Dan O'Neill writes of another figure for whom the term 'integrity' seems synonymous, the National Union of Public Employees/UNISON leader, the late Rodney Bickerstaffe. Although born in South Yorkshire and never resident here, Bickerstaffe had a long interest in and involvement with Ireland, his influence reflected in the essays on Inez McCormack in *Left Lives* and on Anna McGonigle in the *William Walker Centenary Essays*. Beyond that, Bickerstaffe's remarkable mother who raised him single-handedly, always let him know that his absent father was Irish. When, in later life, Bickerstaffe sought to trace him, he discovered a Dublin family of like-minded kinsfolk – like SIPTU and Trades Council activist Tommy Simpson – who embraced him into their fold. For O'Neill, *Left Lives 2's* youngest contributor, a single meeting with Bickerstaffe sparked a continuing interest in his career.

Left Lives 2 does not seek to offer any conclusions. The lives presented here were – in almost all cases – not in any way inter-connected, although Boyd and Boyle certainly knew each other personally and through their writings, Boyd and Devlin met in written and verbal argument, Merrigan marched with O'Leary, Nolan jousted with Corish and those remembering him here, Meehan chided them all on gender equality and social exclusion, and Eadie probably wrote about them all before sharing rostrums and conference agendas. Reynolds, Monro, Kain and Day's lives were unconnected and it is possible that none had ever heard of the others. Bickerstaffe is the 'odd man out' despite his father being Irish, yet his political and organisational achievements were/are admired by many contemporary Irish workers, not just O'Neill. What unites all the lives discussed here is their dedication to work on behalf of their class – through their various chosen paths of industrial, political or cultural activity – in order to change society for the better and the common good. Appreciating that, surely all the lives concerned should serve as inspiration to young workers today to challenge, to organise for change, to lead *Left Lives* of their own?

As with any project, *Left Lives* has been generated through collective effort. The editors acknowledge the authors who willingly met tight deadlines despite many other pressing activities in their committed, active lives. The combination of professional and worker historians – a feature of the ILHS since its inception and much of labour history published since – characterised the *Left Lives* project. Editors Jack McGinley served on the SIPTU National Executive until very recently and is a member of both the SIPTU and ICTU Standing Orders Committees, and Francis Devine currently serves on the Musicians' Union of Ireland (MUI) Executive. Among the contributors, Tony Brown, Niall Greene and Brendan Halligan were significant figures in the Labour Party, particularly in the period they discuss; Séamus Dooley holds high office in the NUJ; Brian

Kenny is a political activist; Des Derwin is active in Left politics, SIPTU and Dublin Trades Council; and Dan O'Neill works in SIPTU College from which Mags O'Brien recently retired, although she remains active in equality and global solidarity campaigns. As the fuller notes on contributors indicate, all have published extensively on labour history in parallel to their other activities. Emmet O'Connor teaches history at the University of Ulster, Derry; Connal Parr at the University of Northumbria at Newcastle; Mike Mecham has recently completed a doctoral study of William Walker at the University of Westminster; and Luke Dineen, having just completed a doctorate on the labour movement in Cork and Derry at University College Cork, is embarking on a history of Connect. They are distinguished historians who simultaneously contribute to contemporary debates on issues confronting workers. Sadly, work pressures precluded intended pieces on Cathal Goulding, Tomás Mac Giolla and Proinsias de Rossa; Kathleen Lynn, Madeline ffrench Mullen and Maeve Cavanagh. Umiskin Press hopes to see these studies in print in the future. Images were provided courtesy of the Drogheda Millmount Museum; East Wall History Group; Irish Labour History Society Archives; National Union of Journalists; Elizabeth 'Liz' Boyle, Guelph, Canada; Helena Claringbold and Nuala Gilsenan; the Devlin family; Barbara Graham and Joan Boyd; and Clare, Margaret and Norah O'Leary. Others who contributed to *Left Lives 2* were Helen McGinley (Trinity College Dublin Library, Early Printed Books) for assistance with sources; Ann Riordan for proofing; and, outstandingly, Mark Daniel, Richie Kelly and, especially, Christy Hammond of CRM Design & Print who, as they always do, delivered design and production of the highest order.

Left Lives 2 is part of a considerable recent output from the ILHS and Umiskin Press. *Saothair 40-44,* 2015-2019, were very positively received. Indeed, the bumper and colourful *Saothar 41, Special 1916 Issue*, was highly acclaimed. Two SILH pamphlets, numbers 14 and 15, maintained the 1916 focus with Paul Ennis's examination of the life of Peter Ennis, Caretaker of Liberty Hall in 1916, and Rayner Lysaght's discussion of the 1916 Rising and the 1917 October Revolution in Russia. Finally, and in association with the Working Class Movement Library, Salford, the ILHS published the 588-page *Historical Directory of Trade Unions in Ireland*, already a sought-after collector's item and valuable reference tool. Readers can access these publications and keep up-to-date with ILHS news at www,irishlabour historysociety.com, where they can also join the Society. Details of all Umiskin Press publications can be accessed at https://umiskin press. wordpress.com.

Left Lives 2 sheds light on lives well lived, lives – in echo of Connolly – that were 'full'. In their lifetimes, few of those featured here received – or sought – significant public acclaim or reward. All merit further study, their achievements (and failures) worthy of reflection and – as all would undoubtedly concur – inspiration to live contemporary lives in their image, on the Left.

Notes

1   Francis Devine & Kieran Jack McGinley, *Left Lives in Twentieth Century Ireland*, (Umiskin Press, Dublin, 2017).

2   See Patrick Smylie, 'A cautionary antecedent: the Belfast career of John Bruce Wallace', pp. 15-26; Myrtle Hill, 'Voices from the margins: women and Belfast's early labour movement', pp. 51-62; Francis Devine, 'William McMullen's account of the Newry Dock

Strike, 1907', pp. 137-156; Jim Quinn, "No homes for people or books': labour's housing struggle in Ennisklillen, 1915-1932', pp. 157-168; Francis Devine, 'Mistress of her own history: UNISON's Anna McGonigle of Omagh', pp. 185-196; and Connal Parr, 'John Hewitt: ever hopeful', pp. 197-216.

3   The ILHS journal *Saothar* has begun to re-examine 'Labour classics', see Adrian Grant, 'C. Desmond Greaves, *The Life & Times of James Connolly'*, *Saothar 41*, 2016, pp. 139-144; and Conor McCabe. 'Labour Classic Re-visited: Dunsmore Clarkson, *Labour & Nationalism* (1925)', *Saothar 42*, 2017, pp. 117-120.

4   R.M. Fox, *Rebel Irishwomen*, (Talbot Press, Dublin, 1935); *James Larkin: The Rise of the Underman*, (Kerryman, Tralee, 1946); *James Connolly: The Forerunner*, (Lawrence & Wishart, London, 1957); and *Louie Bennett*, (Talbot Press, Dublin, 1958); and Michael McInerney, *Peadar O'Donnell: Irish Social Rebel*, (O'Brien Press, Dublin, 1974).

5   Francis Devine, *An Index to Saothar, Journal of the Irish Labour History Society & Other ILHS Publications, 1973-2000*, (Saothar Studies 1, ILHS/MSF, Dublin, 2000) and available online, *www.irishlabourhistorysociety.com/pdf/Saothar%20Index.pdf)* together with 'An index to *Saothar*, Journal of the Irish Labour History Society & other ILHS publications, 2001-2016', *www.irishlabourhistorysociety.com/pdf/Saothar%20Index%202012%20to%202017.pdf* [retrieved 14 February 2019].

6   Rosemary Cullen Owens, *Louie Bennett*, (Cork University Press, Cork, 2001); Terence Bowman, *Peoples' Champion: The Life of Alexander Bowman, Pioneer of Labour Politics in Ireland*, (Ulster Historical Foundation, Belfast, 1997); Graham Walker, *Harry Midgley:; The Politics of Frustration: Harry Midgley and the Failure of the Labour Party in Northern Ireland*, (Manchester University Press, Manchester, 1986); and J. Anthony Gaughan, *Thomas Johnson, 1872-1963, First Leader of the Labour Party in Dáil Éireann*, (Kingdom Books, Dublin, 1980).

7   Ellen Galvin, *Walter Carpenter: A Revolutionary Life*, (East Wall History Group, Dublin, 2016 and available at https://cedarlounge.files.wordpress.com/2006/07/jm-pamphlet-doc-apr-2016-latest-version.pdf); Henry Cairns & Owen Gallagher, *Seán Dunne, Bray, 1918-1969: The Story of Seán Dunne's Journey From Militant Socialist Republican to Labour TD*, (The Authors, Bray, 2007); John Kenna, *James Everett: From Trade Unionist to Government Minister*, (Wicklow, 2011); Mary McAuliffe (ed), *Rosie: Essays in Honour of Rosanna 'Rosie' Hackett (1893-1976): Revolutionary and Trade Unionist*, (Arlen House, Galway, 2016); Nell Regan, *Helena Molony: A Radical Life, 1883-1967*, (Arlen House, Baldoyle, 2017); and Michael Quinn, *The Making of an Irish Communist Leader: The Life & Times of Michael O'Riordan, 1938-1947*, (Communist Party of Ireland, Dublin, 2011).

8   Emmet O'Connor, '1. Cathal O'Shannon', *S24*, 89-90; Ellen Hazelkorn, '2, Louie Bennett, 1870-1956', *S25*, pp. 98-100; Fintan Lane, '3, William Upton, 1845-1925', *S26*, pp. 89-90; Fintan Lane, '4, Mary Daly', *S27*, pp. 101-102; Emmet O'Connor, '5, Seán Murray', *S28*, pp. 121-122; Deirdre Clancy, '6, Eva Gore-Booth, 1870-1926', *S29*, pp. 79-81; D.R. O'Connor Lysaght, '7, Thomas Foran', *S30*, pp. 99-100; Charles Callan, '8, Peadar Macken, 1878-1916', *S31*, pp. 121-123; Charles Callan, '9: R.J.P. Mortished, 1891-1957', *S32*, pp. 49-50; Dónal Ó Drisceoil, '10. Tadhg Barry, 1880-1921', *S33*, pp. 89-92; Charles Callan, '11: Marie Johnson, 1874-1974', *S34*, pp. 113-115; John Cunningham, '12, James M. Pringle, 1883-1949', *S35*, pp. 87-90; Theresa Moriarty, '13: May (Abraham) Tennant, 1869-1946', *S36*, pp. 99-101; Brendan Byrne, '14, Thomas Kain, 1886-1948', *S37*, pp. 99-101; Leo Keohane, '15: Captain James Robert (Jack) White, DSO, 1879-1946', *S38*, pp. 159-162; James Curry, '16. Rosie Hackett, 1893-1976', *S39*, pp. 77-80; Mary Muldowney, '17: Michael Enright (1952-1997), *S40*, pp. 89-92; Kirsty Lusk, '18: Margaret Skinnider (1892-1971)', *S41*, 199-201; Andrew G. Newby, '19. Edward McHugh (1853-1915), *S42*, pp. 99-102; and Tony Brown, '20: Brendan Corish: ambition to serve', *S43*, pp. 113-116 [although this entry is not numbered 20].

9   The full SILH series is: 1, Anthony Coughlan, *C. Desmond Greaves, 1913-1988: An Obituary Essay*, (1990, reprinted 1991); 2, Manus O'Riordan, *The Voice of a Thinking, Intelligent Movement: James Larkin Junior & the Ideological Modernisation of Irish Trade Unionism*, (1995, reprinted in updated edition, 2001); 3, Francis Devine, *Acting for the Actors: Dermot Doolan & the Organisation of Irish Actors & Performing Artists, 1947-1985*, (1997); 4, Bill McCamley, *The Third James: James Fearon, 1874-1924: an Unsung Hero of Our Struggle*, (2000); 5, Anton

McCabe, '*Stormy Petrel of the Transport Workers': Peadar O'Donnell, Trade Unionist, 1917-1920* and Francis Devine, *Navigating a Lone Channel: Stephen McGonagle, Trade Unionism & Labour Politics In Derry*, (2000); 6, Helga Woggon, *Silent Radical – Winifred Carney, 1887-1943: a Reconstruction of Her Biography*, (2000); 7, Helga Woggon, *Ellen Grimley (Nellie Gordon) – Reminiscences of Her Work With James Connolly in Belfast*, (2000); 8, Francis Devine, *Understanding Social Justice: Paddy Cardiff & the Discipline of Trade Unionism* (2002); 9, Joseph Deasy, *Fiery Cross: the Story of Jim Larkin* (2004); 10, Francis Devine, *An Eccentric Chemistry: Michael Moynihan & Labour in Kerry, 1917-2001*, (2004); 11, Francis Devine & Manus O'Riordan, James Connolly, *Liberty Hall & the 1916 Rising*, (2006); 12, Norman Croke & Francis Devine, '*More Permanent Than Bronze, More Enduring Than Stone': the James Connolly Labour College, 1919-1921 & Workers' Educational Institute, 1925-1927*, (2007); 13, Aindrias Ó Cathasaigh (ed), *The Life & Times of Gilbert Lynch*, (2011); 14, Paul Ennis, *Peter Ennis: The Man Who Kept Liberty Hall*, (2016); and 15, D.R. O'Connor Lysaght, *From the GPO to the Winter Palace: How a Workers' Revolution Was Lost & How a Workers' Revolution was Won*, (2016).

10 Peter Collins, 'John Freeman: a life on the left', *S24*, pp. 129-135; Terry Cradden, 'Billy Blease: from McClure Street to the House of Lords', *S19*, pp. 145-158; Francis Devine, 'Letting Labour lead: Jack Macgougan and the pursuit of unity, 1913-1958', *S14*, pp. 113-124; Francis Devine, 'An undiminished dream: Andy Barr, communist trade unionist', *S16*, pp. 95-111; Francis Devine & John Horne, 'A labour consciousness in Carlow: the young Paddy Bergin. 1916-1950', *S6*, pp. 109-117; Evanne Kilmurray, 'Joe Deasy: the evolution of an Irish Marxist, 1941-1950', *S13*, pp. 112-119; Hazel Morrissey, 'Betty Sinclair: a woman's fight for socialism, 1910-1981', *S9*, pp. 121-132; and Aodh Ó Canáinn, 'Éilís Ryan in her own words', *S21*, pp. 129-147. In addition, oral history was used in wider contexts: John Cunningham, "She nearly dropped dead at the idea that someone would join voluntarily': memories of ASTI activists, c1960-1990', *S34*, pp. 98-111; Marian Elders, Elizabeth Kiely, Máire Leane, & Clodagh O'Driscoll, ' 'A union in those days was husband and wife': women's narratives on trade unions in Munster, 1936-1960', *S27*, pp. 121-129; Elizabeth Kiely & Máire Leane, 'Female domestic servants and farm workers in Munster, 1936-1960: some insights from oral history', *S29*, pp. 57-65; Ida Milne, 'Gender, hierarchies and change: an oral history of Independent Newspapers since the 1960s', *S39*, pp. 55-61; and Mary Muldowney, "A world of its own: recollections of women workers in Guinness's Brewery in the 1940s', *S23*, pp. 103-117.

11 Charles Callan & Barry Desmond, *Irish Labour Lives: A Biographical Dictionary of Irish Labour Party Deputies, Senators, MPS & MEPs*, (Watchword, Dublin, 2010).

12 Emmet O'Connor & John Cunningham, *Studies in Irish Radical Leadership: Lives on the Left*, (Manchester University Press, Manchester, 2016).

13 Henry Cairns & Owen Gallagher, *Seán Dunne, Bray 1918-1969; The Story of Seán Dunne's Journey From Militant Socialist Republican to Labour TD*, (Authors, Bray, 2007); Dónal Ó Drisceoil, *Tadhg Barry (1880-1921): The Story of an Irish Revolutionary*, (Author, Cork, 2010); Des Guckian, *Jimmy Gralton, An Undesirable Alien: The Life of a Leitrim Socialist, 1886-1945*, (Communist Party of Ireland, Dublin, 2012); Brian Kenny, *Joe Deasy: A Life on the Left*, (Hugh Geraghty-Crumlin, Drimnagh. Walkinstown Branch, Labour Party, Dublin, 2010); John Kenna, *James Everett: Trade Unionist to Government Minister, 1917-1951*, (Wicklow, 2010); Brian Kenny, *Sam Nolan: A Long March on the Left*, (Kenny/Personal History Publishing, Dublin, 2010); Michael Quinn, *The Making of an Irish Communist Leader: Michael O'Riordan, 1938-1947*, (CPI, Dublin, 2011); and Lynda Walker, *Madge Davison: Revolutionary Firebrand: Recollections*, (Shanway Press, Belfast, 2011).

14 McAuliffe, *Rosie, op. cit.*

15 Donal Nevin, *James Larkin: Lion of the Fold*, (Gill & Macmillan, Dublin, 1998) and *James Connolly: 'A Full Life'*, (Gill & Macmillan, Dublin, 2006); Emmet O'Connor, *James Larkin*, (Cork University Press, 2008) and *Big Jim Larkin: Hero or Wrecker?* (UCD Press, Dublin, 2015); Charlie McGuire, *Seán McLoughlin: Ireland's Forgotten Revolutionary*, (Merlin Press, Pontypool, 2011); and Hugh Geraghty, *William Patrick Partridge & His Times (1974-1917)*, (Curlew Books, Drimnagh, 2003).

16 *www.amazon.com/Sam-Nolan-Long-March-Left-ebook/dp/B00C895RLS* [retrieved 6 March 2019].

Umiskin Press, Ireland

Umiskin Press is a not-for-profit publishing house, publishing commissioned and non-commissioned works mainly, though not exclusively, works of labour history, Labour interest, trade union issues, poetry and cultural matters. Umiskin is a townland in Kilcar, County Donegal, birthplace of the McGinleys.

Dr. Kieran Jack McGinley is the principal behind Umiskin Press, whose recent publications were: *Left Lives in 20th Century Ireland*, Francis Devine & Kieran Jack McGinley, (October 2017); *Stephen McGonagle, Ombudsman, Trade Unionist, Senator,* Owen McGonagle (April 2018); *William Walker Centenary Essays* (October 2018) and *Labouring Beside Lough Erne,* (February 2019).

Umiskin Press is mainly interested in publishing limited runs of between 150 and 500 copies in hardback and paperback limited editions which might otherwise not merit commercial publication and sale elsewhere.

Dedication to Francis Devine

Dear Reader, this being the tenth title from Umiskin Press, I thought as Principal of the Press it was a fitting occasion to pay tribute to my colleague, comrade and mentor, Francis Devine, for the work he has done since his retirement for Umiskin Press, the Irish Labour History Society and labour history in general.

I do not intend this to be a full bibliography of his work in that time but believe the breadth of his work deserves a fitting mention. His two centenary year titles *Organising the Union*, SIPTU, May 2009 & *Organising History - A Centenary of SIPTU*, Gill & Macmillan, Dublin 2009, began a decade of a continuum of publications and were followed by *Communicating the Union – A History of the Communications Workers Union*, CWU, Dublin 2015 and *A Historical Directory of Trade Unions in Ireland* compiled with the late John B. Smethurst, Irish Labour History Society & Working Class Movement Library, Mayday 2017.

For the Watchword title *Dear Comrade, SIPTU 1990-2010*, which I edited, Francis wrote pieces on Red Flag Rhyme, The Red Hand Badge, Commemorating the Lockout, Poem: Mick McGahey, Pat McKiernan: A Cedar of Lebanon, SIPTU Organising Change Changing Organisation and Tony Ayton.

In terms of ILHS publications he gave help and support in the research and writing as well as the editing process of *Saothar 41* as joint guest editor, along with Brian Hanley and Sarah-Anne Buckley and similarly aided Paul Ennis and Rayner Lysaght on *Studies in Labour History 14 & 15* on *Peter Ennis -The man who kept Liberty Hall* and *From the GPO to the Winter Palace* respectively.

Francis's scholarship in *Saothar* can be recognised from 2009 to 2014 with the following:

Editorials: With Brian Hanley & Sarah-Anne Buckley: Labour, Class, the 1916 Rising and Beyond; Daichead Bliain ag Fas: *Saothar 1-40, Saothar 41*, 2016

Essays: 'Second class citizens who are being subsidised by the men...' Women in the ITGWU & WUI 1945-1960, *Saothar 36*, 2011;

'Hearing the Children Weeping': Samuel Monro, 1846-1925, President Belfast Trades Council & British TUC, *Saothar 39*, 2014;

The Catholic Workers' College: Some Data from 1951-1961, Volume 40, 2015;

Labour Movement Reactions to the 1916 Rising: Post Office Workers and the Rising, *Saothar 41*, 2016;

'His Memory Still Lives With Us' - Two Bray Girls and Others Remember James Connolly, *Saothar 41*, 2016;

'A Great and Trusted Custodian of Confidences' Betrayed', Winifred Carney's Military Pension Application', *Saothar 41*, 2016;

'If that is not murder, then what is murder? A Note on Irish Labour and the *Titanic, Saothar 43, 2018*

'The sinking of *RMS Leinster* and the Association of Irish Post Office Clerks '*Saothar 44*, 2019

Obituaries: Evelyn Owens, with Sheila Simmons, Vol 36, 2011; Andrew Boyd, *Saothar 37*, 2012; Donal Nevin; Sean Redmond, (with Tom Redmond), *Saothar, 39*, 2014; Bob Purdie, *Saothar 40*, 2015; John Carroll (former President of ITGWU/SIPTU), Seamus Pattison (former Labour Party TD & trade union official); Jimmy Kelly (WUI/SIPTU); Sylvia Meehan; (All *Saothar 44*, 2019.)

Reviews: Philip O'Connor, *Road to Independence: Howth, Sutton and Baldoyle Play Their Part*, Howth Free Press, Howth, 2016;

Anthony McIntyre (Ed.) *Reflections on the 1916 Rising*, Old Drogheda Society, Drogheda 2016;

Robert Byrne, Commemorative Booklet, (Meelick-Parteen & Cratloe War of Independence Commemorative Committee);

Gerard Dooley, *Nenagh, 1914 – 21 Years of Crisis*, (Maynooth Studies in Local History 117), Four Courts Press, Dublin, 2015;

Emmet O'Connor, *Derry Labour in the Age of Agitation, 1889-1923, volume 2: Larkinism & Syndicalism, 1907-1923*. (Maynooth Studies in Local History 126), Four Courts Press, Dublin, 2015;

(All *Saothar* 42, 2017)

Stephen Coyle & Máirtín Ó Catháin (eds), *'We Will Rise Again': Ireland, Scotland & the Easter Rising*, (1916 Rising Centenary Committee (Scotland), Glasgow, 2018) *Saothar* 44, 2019

Sources:

Papers of the ITGWU in the National Library of Ireland (NLI) Vol 35, 2010;

Irish Sources in The Women's Library @ LSE London; *Saothar 38*, 2013

Some additions to the Historical Directory of Trade Unions in Ireland. *Saothar 44*, 2019

Labour History in Local History Journals, *Saothar 44*, 2019

Francis contributed on the Umiskin Press Title, *Cluskey: The Conscience of Labour*, June 2015, which he followed up with the next press title - *Outside Left, Poems 2007-2016*, which was his third book of verse following on from *May Dancer, Poems 1998-2007*, Watchword, Dublin, October 2007 & *Red Star, Blue Moon*, Elo Publications, Dublin, 1997.

In *Left Lives in Twentieth Century Ireland*, Francis jointly edited the title as well as contributing essays on *Jim McFall & The Belfast Boilermakers 1926-1992*; *Changing Everything, Inez McCormack 1943-2013*; and along with Sheila Simmons - *Evelyn Owens: Equal Rights Campaigner, Labour Court Chair, 1931-2010*.

On the musical side Francis is a member of the Howth Singing Circle, whose premium event for many years has been the Burns Night in The Abbey Tavern, Howth, with associated musical events over the weekend. Francis has also held two music-related themed events in recent years on Joe Hill and Jim Connell, Kilskyre, of 'Red Flag' fame, at the Clé Club in Liberty Hall (held on the third Wednesday of the month) in memory of the late ILHS President, Hugh Geraghty. Francis has been involved in a few Dublin City walking tours of labour history significance on which the odd song/poem or two is recited and/or sung. This year's Mayfest, the third of its kind, features a *Bring Out the Banners Walking Tour* commencing at 10.30 from Liberty Hall Lobby on Saturday May 4th. Francis's first CD, with Steve Byrne and Friends, *My Father Told Me*, can be accessed at **www.francydevine.bandcamp.com**

In 2018 Umiskin Press published two titles *Stephen McGonagle Ombudsman, Trade Unionist, Senator* by his son Owen, with assistance from Francis and *William Walker 1870-1918 Belfast Labour Unionist Centenary Essays* jointly edited by Francis and Sean Byers from Trademark N.I.

A few weeks ago, Jim Quinn and The Fermanagh Council of Trade Unions published *Labouring Beside Lough Erne - A Study of the Fermanagh Labour Movement 1826-1932*, Umiskin Press's ninth title, with which Francis gave Jim sage advice over a long time and brought forward an extremely polished publication.

Francis is currently assisting myself and Dr Mike Mecham with his full biography of *William Walker (1870-1918)* due in the Fall of 2019 and has begun work with Patrick Smylie on *Left Lives in 20th Century Ireland, Volume 3* on people who were associated with Communism in Ireland.

Finally, can I leave the last word on the subject to an earlier teacher, man of learning and early mentor, Tom Morrisey, S.J. in relation to *Organising History* in *Saothar* 36, 2011: "Francis Devine's major work has kept the pride for the past and has managed magnificently to ensure the continuation of the tradition of Connolly and Larkin in the new united union."

Kieran Jack McGinley
Principal
Umiskin Press

www.umiskinpress.wordpress.com   kmcginly@tcd.ie

Notes On Contributors

The Editors

Francis Devine, retired from SIPTU College since 2009, is a member, Musicians' Union of Ireland (MUI) Executive. He is author of *Organising History: A Centenary of SIPTU* (2009); *A Unique Association: A History of the Medical Laboratory Scientists' Association* (2012); *Communicating the Union: A History of the Communications Workers' Union From 1900* (2015); and, with John B. Smethurst, *Historical Directory of Trade Unions in Ireland* (2017). With Steve Byrne and Friends, he issued the CD, *My Father Told Me* (2014) and his second recording will be released in 2019.

Jack McGinley was educated at CBS Westland Row; graduated with a BA from NCIR (NCEA); and was awarded a PhD and Postgraduate Diploma in Conflict & Dispute Resolution at Trinity College Dublin. He is employed in the Library TCD and has served on the TCD Board 1989-1997/2005-2012. A FWUI/SIPTU member, he served on its National Executive Council, 2005-2010, 2010-2016 nominated by the Public Administrative & Community Division. He is Vice-Chair, SIPTU Education Sector and Chair, Dublin District Council & Cuban Solidarity Forum; Chair ICTU/SIPTU Standing Orders Committees; Chair, Citywide Drugs Crisis Campaign; President Irish Labour History Society; and Principal, Umiskin Press – not for profit private press.

The Contributors

Tony Brown was Special Advisor to Tánaiste Brendan Corish in the Department of Social Welfare working on EEC Social Policy with Junior Minister Frank Cluskey, 1973-1977; and Labour Party Honorary International Secretary, 1979-1997. Among many positions, he was a member, Commission on Social Welfare, 1983-1986; Vice Chair, Combat Poverty Agency 1986-1989; member. National Committee for the Study of International Affairs, Royal Irish Academy, 1979-1985, 1992-1997; and founder member, Institute of International & European Affairs, 1989 to date.

Helena Claringbold is an Irish-born living in Australia where she is a member of the Administrative Appeals Tribunal and an avid genealogist.

Des Derwin, born in Dublin 1952, worked in Unidare, 1973-1999; Munekata, 2000-2005; and Dublin Community Television, 2007-2013, where he was ITGWU-SIPTU Shop Steward. Involved with the *New Liberty* group within the ITGWU (1970s), he was President, SIPTU Electronics & Engineering Branch, and member, SIPTU Private Sector and Dublin Regional Committees. He is Vice-Chair, SIPTU Dublin District Council and was President, Dublin Council of Trade Unions, 2007-2009. He was active in the Young Socialists, 1968; Socialist Workers' Movement, 1972-1982; SWM tendency in the Socialist Labour Party, 1977-1980, acting as Trade Union Co-ordinator; Socialist Alliance, 2000; Campaign for an Independent Left until 2005; People Before Profit Alliance, 2007; United Left Alliance, 2010-2013, latterly as a nonaligned ULA member; and Left Forum, 2013. Now an independent socialist, he served the editorial boards of *Gralton*, 1982-1983; *Z Magazine*, 1989; *SIPTU Fightback*, 1997-2000; and *Red Banner*, 1998-2007. He wrote 'Trouble at t'mill: the Clondalkin sit-in 1982-83', *Red Banner* 4 & 5, May & November 1999; *Solidarity Not Social Partnership: Why SIPTU Should Say No To Another Partnership Deal*' (2005); and 'ULA! 'No one would have believed it …!", *Irish Left Review*, 13 December 2010.

Luke Dineen is a PhD candidate from the School of History at University College Cork. He has written and spoken about Irish, and specifically Cork, labour history, his article on the 1921 Cork Harbour Soviet appearing in *Saothar 42*, 2017. He is currently researching and writing a history of the Connect trade union,

Séamus Dooley served in various positions at Chapel, Branch and Executive level before his appointment as Irish Organiser, then Irish Secretary and now Assistant General Secretary/Irish Secretary of the National Union of Journalists, UK & Ireland. He is member of the Executive Council of the ICTU. A graduate of the Dublin Institute of Technology, he worked as a reporter with the *Tullamore Tribune* and later as Editor of the *Roscommon Champion* prior to his appointment as a Sub Editor with the *Irish Independent*. He is a founding member of the Clé Club, Chairman of the Larkin Hedge School and an occasional contributor to RTÉ Radio 1's *Sunday Miscellany*.

Niall Greene had an extensive career in the state, private and multinational sectors mainly in aviation-related activities. A Labour Party member since 1964, he was elected to the Administrative Council in 1965 and served as Financial Secretary, Vice Chairman and International Secretary. He was an adviser to the Minister for Labour, Michael O'Leary, 1973-1974.

Brendan Halligan, an economist, politician, public affairs consultant and academic, was Labour Party General Secretary, 1967-1980; Senator, 1973-1976; TD for Dublin South West, 1976-1977; and MEP for Dublin, 1983-1984. In 1991, he was formative to the creation of Institute of European Affairs, serving as Chair, 1985-1995, and lectured on European integration at the University of Limerick. From 2007-2014, he was Chair, Sustainable Energy Authority of Ireland.

Brian Kenny is a member of the Labour Party in Dublin South Central. His previous publications are *Joe Deasy: A Life on the Left; Sam Nolan: A Long March on the Left; Tony Heffernan: From Merrion Square to Merrion Street; The People's Republic: Labour and the Left in Dublin South Central;* and *When Ireland Went Red: The Soviet Experiment 1918-1923.* In January 2019, to mark the centenary of the Monaghan Asylum Soviet, his play, '*And a Red Flag Flying ...*', written with Aidan McQuillan, was performed in Monaghan.

Mike Mecham is an Irish labour historian and former visiting lecturer at St. Mary's University, London. He was awarded a doctorate in early 2018 by the University of Surrey for a thesis on William Walker and the Belfast labour movement. His subsequent article on Walker was published in *Saothar 43*. He was previously Director of the Latin America programme at the International Relations think-tank Chatham House.

Mags O'Brien is a retired trade union tutor, specialising in researching the Gender Pay Gap. She advocated for the Irish National Organisation of the Unemployed; was Chair, Divorce Action Group, 1990-1995; Board member, National Women's Council of Ireland; and Chair, ICTU Global Solidarity to 2016 remaining involved in GS campaigns, particularly on Palestine. A Gaza Action Ireland activist, she was a crew member of *MV Saoirse* illegally detained at sea and jailed by Israeli Defence Forces for attempting to break the siege of Gaza. She was an Official in SIPTU's Manufacturing, Services and Health Divisions and served on European Works Councils. Her keen interest in labour history was reflected in *Invisible Hands*, a play she wrote and acted in for the 2017 Mayfest about the lives of women cleaners.

Emmet O'Connor lectures in History in Ulster University. Between 1983-2001 he co-edited *Saothar* and is an Honorary President of the Irish Labour History Society. He has published widely on labour history, including *Big Jim Larkin: Hero or Wrecker?* (UCD Press, 2015). At present he is working on a study of the Irish in the International Brigades.

Dan O'Neill worked for Amnesty International before becoming a Learning Co-ordinator in SIPTU College. He graduated in English and History from UCD and has a MA in Public Affairs & Political Communication from Dublin Institute of Technology. Deputy President, Union of Students in Ireland, 2009-2010, he worked for organisations like Spunout.ie in the Houses of the Oireachtas.

Connal Parr studied Modern History at Oxford University and obtained his doctorate at Queen's University Belfast in 2014, before returning to Oxford as a postdoc at Hertford College. His first book *Inventing the Myth: Political Passions and the Ulster Protestant Imagination* was published by Oxford University Press in 2017 and was shortlisted for the Ewart-Biggs Literary Prize and the Royal Historical Society's Whitfield Prize. As well as being widely-reviewed, it was named as one of the books of the year in the *Irish Times*. In September 2018 he was made Lecturer in History at Northumbria University.

W.L. Reynolds's banner for the Boyne Fishermen.
(image courtesy of Drogheda Millmount Museum)

Jer O'Leary, as Jim Larkin, before his banner for the
Dublin Council of Trade Unions, May Day 2003
(Image courtesy of SIPTU)

Jer O'Leary at the 2018 Mayday Rally, Dublin
(Image courtesy of SIPTU)

Jer O'Leary's iconic banner of Big Jim Larkin for the Federated Union of Ireland
(image courtesy of the O'Leary family)

Jer O'Leary's banner for ITGWU Cork No 4 Branch featuring Tadgh Barry, shot dead in
Balkykinlar Internment Camp, County Down, on 21 November 1920
(image courtesy of the O'Leary family)

A WONDERFUL PICTURE OF EMPIRE—(See Pages 8 & 9.)

DAILY SKETCH.

GUARANTEED DAILY NETT SALE MORE THAN 1,000,000 COPIES.

No. 1,880.   LONDON, FRIDAY, MARCH 19, 1915.   [Registered as a Newspaper.]   ONE HALFPENNY.

Drummer Kenny's Mother Was The Proudest Of Them All.

The Mayor of Drogheda handing to Drummer Kenny the certificate of the freedom of his native town.

Kenny's father and mother.   The civic heads were proud of him.   The hero rode in the carriage with the Mayor.

Drogheda fêted its V.C. hero by conferring the freedom of the borough on Drummer Kenny, of the Gordon Highlanders, whose old father—himself the bearer of many medals and a veteran of the same famous regiment—and mother were present to look with glistening eyes on the honours rendered to their gallant son. The Mayor and Corporation accompanied the drummer to High Mass in civic state, and afterwards ceremonially presented the freedom, which the hero modestly accepted with a salute to the whole assemblage.

*Drogheda banners in Georges Square in March 1915 when Drummer Kenny
was being welcomed home after being awarded a Victoria Cross in WW1.*

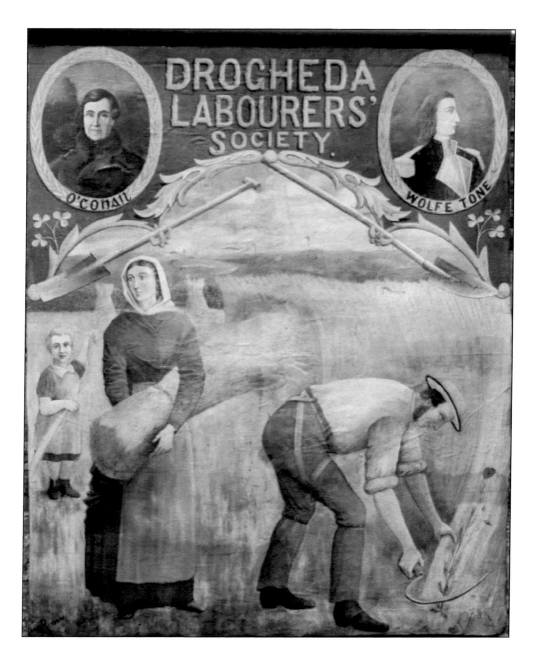

W.L. Reynolds's Drogheda Labourers' Society banner
(photograph courtesy of Drogheda Millmount Museum)

Kain's banner for ITGWU Band with portrait of James Connolly, c1920.
(Photograph courtesy of ILHS Archives)

FRANCIS DEVINE

With a Small 'l':
Samuel Monro, 1846-1925:
President, Belfast Trades Council
& British Trades Union Congress

Samuel Monro was born in Lurgan, County Armagh in 1846.[1] In 1901, a widower, he lived with his son-in-law and daughter James C. and Annie S. Hill, aged 25 and 24 respectively, at 43 Melrose Street, Windsor, Belfast. Monro and Hill were described as printer-compositors. Monro was Church of Ireland and his daughter and son-in-law Methodist.[2] In the 1907 *Street Directory*, Monro was listed as a General Printer operating from 4½ Donegall Street with a residence at 41 Victoria Avenue, Sydenham.[3] By 1911, Monro had re-married in 1905 to Sarah Irvine, born in County Down, a forty-three year-old Presbyterian. They resided at 8 Oakland Avenue, Victoria, with Monro's stepson George Welsh Lamont, aged sixteen, a school student and Presbyterian. Monro and Sara had a five year old son, Samuel, Church of Ireland.[4] The *Belfast Telephone Directory* for 1913 showed Monro operating as a General Printer at 4A Donegall Street, Belfast.[5] By 1918, Monro still resided at Oakland Avenue and his business, Monro & Company, ran from 3 Commercial Court.[6] Monro died in 1925. In 1943, a George Monroe was listed at 8 Oakland Avenue but it is not known if there was any connection with Samuel.[7]

Formation of Belfast Trades Council

Monro served as an apprentice typographer with the *Northern Whig* and became active in the Belfast Typographical Society (BTS), a body affiliated to the Manchester-based Typographical Society. After the disintegration of the Irish Typographical Association in 1845, some Irish printers applied to join the Provincial Typographical Association in the late 1840s, the National Typographical Association's (NTA) successor. The NTA's Sheffield Executive decided organisation in Ireland was too expensive and recommended formation of an Irish association and promised co-operation. After abortive attempts from 1861-1863, Irish printers joined the Relief Association formed in 1863 with the 'sole purpose of rationalising assistance to 'those on the tramp''. Nine Irish Societies outside Dublin – where the Dublin Typographical Provident Society remained aloof – joined the Relief Association. In 1877, the Typographical Association (TA) absorbed the Irish branches of the Relief Association. It made slow progress until 1894 when Hugh McManus, a 'Liverpool-born Irishman' became Irish Organiser, stationed in Belfast. He was successful in eradicating 'rat shops' and, at his death, left a solid and sustaining organisation which exists to this day outside Dublin. The Belfast Typographical Society was probably established in 1829 as reference is made to a Belfast Branch of the Irish Typographical Union which collapsed in 1841. In 1964, the TA merged with the London Typographical Society to create the National Graphical Association (NGA). The NGA merged with the Society of Graphical & Allied Trades in 1990 to form the Graphical, Paper & Media Union (GPMU). In 2005, the GPMU amalgamated with Amicus which, in 2007, was a founding element of Unite the Union.[8]

Monro was elected President of the BTS in 1878, the year after they merged with the TA. He was described as cautious and insisted that 'union meetings be dignified', ending the custom that they be held in public houses.[9] In May,1881, during a lengthy strike by members of the Belfast & North of Ireland Power Loom Tenters' Trade Union, Monro chaired a meeting of trades in the Painters' Hall to consider how they could offer support and/or solution. Among the trades represented were bookbinders, brassfounders, carpenters and joiners, flax dressers, painters, printers, shoemakers and yarndressers. That Monro chaired the meeting suggests he already enjoyed a reputation for leadership within the city. Although unsuccessful in assisting the Tenters, events led to the formation of Belfast Trades Council (BTC) on 29 October. Monro was elected President, Joseph Mitchell, Ironmoulders, Vice President, and Alexander Bowman, Flaxdressers' Trade & Benevolent Union, Secretary.

In May 1882, Monro and Bowman were vociferous in seeking rate-funded support for public library development. They met with the Town Council to request they apply the provisions of the Library Act as quickly as possible. Bowman made the address. The two men supervised the BTC's affiliation that year to the British Trades Union Congress (BTUC).[10] Monro showed an interest in industrial development and attended International Trades Fairs in Paris, 1881; Cork, 1883; and Glasgow, 1888. Founded in 1868, Irish representation at the BTUC had been irregular although Congress had been held in Dublin in 1880. Co-operation and co-ordination between workers within Ireland was limited and with cross-Channel unions almost non-existent across trades. Between 1884-1890, BTC was the only Irish affiliate to submit motions to the BTUC.

Monro at the BTUC
From 1887, Samuel Monro attended the BTUC as a delegate from BTC and as a member of the BTS or TA. Monro's address was 19 Gloucester Street, Belfast. When Standing Orders were suspended to allow condemnation of

the suppression of a meeting in Ennis, County Clare, on the grounds that free speech was being denied, Monro rose in opposition. The movers were Thomas Smyth and Frean (London Trades Council) and supportive speeches came from Parnell (London), Drummond (Glasgow) and Harvey (Durham). J. Holmes (Leicester) agreed that the motion was self-evidently worthy of support and that 'Conservatives, as well as Radicals, would stand up for the right of free speech'. They had a 'perfect right' to look upon 'the proposition from an industrial and not a political standpoint'. Veteran and much-respected agricultural labourers leader Joseph Arch added his weight in support: 'they would fail in their duty unless they were allowed to express their opinion about the tyranny of the present Government in Ireland (hear, hear)'. He rhetorically asked how would 'Englishmen feel if they were similarly treated?'

Undeterred Monro rose to express his 'surprise' that Standing Orders had been suspended to allow discussion of a clearly 'political' motion. He 'did not care whether he got a seconder or not' to an amendment: 'That Congress recognises the necessity of law and order being established in Ireland, and obedience to the law being enforced, as preliminary to the remedy of their grievances'. The motion was greeted with laughter and when he observed that 'he knew which way the vote would go' there was 'renewed laughter'. The Coercion Act, 'if that is what delegates wanted to call it', had been passed merely to seek 'obedience to the law'. Kershaw (Oldham) seconded Monro, re-stating the desire to see law and order maintained. Monro's amendment was defeated 7-85 and the substantive motion adopted 85-1, Monro presumably the dissenter.[11]

Belfast Trades Union Congress, 1893

At the Glasgow BTUC in 1892, Monro proposed that Congress be held in Belfast the following year. They could match Glasgow 'in the matter of regal entertainment' and, adding an organisational note, suggested that 'for the sake of female workers, the invitation should be accepted'. He was supported by fellow TA delegate, H. Slatter (Manchester) who suggested that 'trade unionism was the hope of that country'. When the vote was taken, Belfast won convincingly with 231 votes, defeating Norwich, 108; Manchester, 10; Cardiff, 7; and Barrow-in-Furness, 7.[12]

On 4 September 1893, the BTUC convened in the Ulster Hall, Belfast, the second occasion it had done so in Ireland after its formation in 1868, having been held in Dublin in 1880. Thirty-four of the 380 delegates were Irish: twenty-seven were from Belfast, six from Dublin and one, Newry. Monro was proposed as Chair by Richard Sheldon, Cabinetmaker and BTC Secretary, and seconded by Joseph Mitchell, Council Vice President. Monro was elected 'by acclamation'. He welcomed delegates 'in our native language' with a 'cead mile fáilte'. He proved an effective Chair, despite starting the week with an 'unfortunate physical difficulty' – he had nearly lost his voice! He proved popular, however, and narrowly missed election to the Parliamentary Committee. Had he been elected – and he polled a very creditable 101 votes – not only would he have been the first and still only Irish delegate to serve as Congress Chair but he would also have been the first Irishman ever elected to the Parliamentary Committee. That honour went to Richard Sheldon (Amalgamated Union of Cabinet Makers, Belfast) at the Norwich BTUC in 1894. Hugh McManus, Belfast TA Organiser, had successfully moved a change to Standing Orders in Belfast that the Parliamentary Committee be enlarged by two with one seat reserved for a 'duly qualified member of a trade union in Ireland'.[13]

Monro's Presidential Address

In his lengthy and closely argued Presidential Address to the BTUC, Monro reveals much of his character and politics. He took understandable pride in welcoming delegates to Belfast. Not all visitors received a warm welcome. On the Saturday following Congress, a demonstration was held with both Catholic and Protestant bands in attendance. Labour MPs John Burns and Keir Hardie, who had supported the Second Home Rule Bill rejected by the Lords on the previous Friday, were heckled. Some members of the Thomas Sexton Flute Band – Sexton was nationalist MP for West Belfast, 1886-1912 – were hospitalised and speakers suspected of socialist and pro-Home Rule, views were heckled. It was 'only the driver's rapid whipping-up of the horses' that saved Burns 'from a mauling when his brake was attacked by five to six hundred men armed with sticks'.[14]

Ironically, Monro began his Address by stating that he had 'unlimited faith in the good intentions of the British people and in their sincere wish to do justice in Ireland'. Perhaps with the Unionist majority view in BTC in mind, he added that trade unionism could 'help lead them to a right conclusion'. He had a clear love of poetry and cited Thomas Moore's 'Erin! The Tear and the Smile in Thine Eyes' to underline his view:

> Erin, thy silent tear shall never cease.
> Erin, thy languid smile ne'er shall increase
> Till, like the rainbow's light,
>
> Thy various tints unite,
> And form in heaven's sight
> One arch of peace.[15]

He recognised that 'I may be a dreamer' but believed that trade unionism was the 'honoured instrument by which the beautiful sentiments [could] be realised'. Trade unionism was the 'ism amongst all others, whose mission' was to 'free our unhappy land from all the terrible incubus of religious bigotry and political intolerance'. Such factors 'separated into hostile camps those who should be brethren and who should dwell together in unity and peace'. This was not a dream but a 'truth which may be realised'. He cited the great demonstration of 8 March 1892 when 'orange and green were blended in a true union'.

After welcoming delegates to Belfast, Monro hailed the emergence of the Board of Trade's *Labour Gazette* and newspapers published by various Trades Councils. He called for consideration of a national publication. He then 'departed from the beaten track' and examined the relationship between the State and Labour'. He asked, 'where did the legitimate concern' of the State in the relations between Capital and Labour 'end'? He thought that Parliament had 'always been and is likely to be, permeated by a thoroughly capitalist spirit'. He wanted greater labour representation – and he always used a small 'l' for labour – but cautioned that a 'purely labour Parliament' would view matters 'through an atmosphere coloured by its own prejudices'. Nevertheless, he hoped that future parliamentary 'labour representatives' would leave 'party ties a long way afterwards' when considering labour's needs. These comments raised cheers. He welcomed the fact that the laissez faire theories of James Mill and McCullough had been 'placed in the museum of political curiosities'.[16] He provided an economic history of the industrial revolution, summing up its full horrors for working people by citing 'the pathetic poem', 'The Weeping of the Child'. It was, in fact, an extract from Elizabeth Barrett Browning's 'The Cry of the Children'.

Do you hear the children weeping –
  oh, my brothers!
Before their sorrow comes with years;
They are leaning their young heads
  against their mothers,
But that cannot stop their tears.

The young lambs are skipping
  in the meadows,
The young birds are chirping
  in their nests;

The young fawns are playing
  with the shadows.
The young flowers are blowing
  towards the west.

But the weeping of the children –
  oh, my brothers
Weeping so bitterly;
Weeping in the playtime
  of the others,
Is this country of the free?

Fortunately, for Monro, political thinking was now 'advanced' and State interference to prevent excessive exploitation of workers was unquestioned. Interestingly, he cited factory legislation as a worthy example of the efficacy of State intervention as 'experience teaches us that the safety of workmen cannot be left to the sole guardianship even of the men themselves – that carelessness, indifference, necessity or fear may, and often does, induce men to incur avoidable dangers'. These dangers could 'only be reduced by vigorous measures, which make a breach of certain regulations an offence at law (Applause)'. He outlined the history of statutory wage fixing, the limitation of hours and guarding of dangerous machinery.

Monro praised Congress for the impact it had had on effecting protective legislation but wondered at the impact of the extension of the franchise and the apparent inability of 'labour representatives' to express independent positions beyond their party ties. Yet, Monro was not apparently convinced of the obvious solution to this dilemma – a Labour Party. He cited Sir John Gorst who thought there could never be a

Labour Party as workers were themselves not united and there was insufficient 'zeal' to break the mould of the Tory and Liberal parties. Monro cited divisions but did not call for unity. He did, however, outline broad plans for legislative reform, including the abolition of pauperism and State provision for Old Age Pensions, very radical demands in their day that again drew applause.[17]

Women Workers

Monro then turned his attention to women's organisational needs, praising the Women's Trade Union Provident League (WTUPL). Lady Dilke and, particularly, her 'able lieutenants, Miss Florence Routledge and Miss M.E. Abraham' who were well known in Belfast and had organised three societies three years previously, although none were still in existence, despite BTC's best efforts. In September 1890, organisers from the London-based WTUPL had begun organising in linen districts. BTC offered assistance by arranging public meetings, printing handbills and set up a special committee with its own fund. The special fund received £10 4s 9d compared to the £149 18s for municipal elections and £198 towards a sailors and firemen's strike in Cardiff, indication perhaps of the shallow depth of concern among the male delegates for the women's plight. The 1893, BTC's TUC fund raised £447, including donations from businessmen.[18]

Monro attributed the collapse to the 'want of a committee of disinterested ladies, who could have done the work the members of the Trades Council tried to do in a much more suitable and acceptable manner than men, however earnest, could possibly do'. He also blamed the 'persistent and malignant representation' of BTC's work by 'paid emissaries' and the 'impatience' of the new trade union members who 'wanted to see direct results ... long before it was possible anything tangible could be accomplished'. He 'earnestly trusted' that the BTUC's visit would 'sweep away at once and forever some of the abuses which exist in connection with the employment of women in our town'. He asked, was it too much to hope that those 'who luxuriated in their drawing rooms' on the product of female labour could be persuaded to pay a living wage and that wages 'when earned' would be paid 'without vexatious deductions in fines for every imaginable or unimaginable offence'? He demanded abolition of the 'unique system' in 'our warehouses' of 'compelling the workers to pay for the thread(for the material which, by the process of their labour, actually became part and parcels of the employers' goods, and is, therefore, claimed by him as his property)'.Was it

'too much to expect that our dress-making establishments (who, by the way, seem always in want of apprentices and improvers for they are always advertising for them) should, when they accept a fee from a workman on behalf of his daughter in order that she may learn the art and trade of dressmaking, make some attempt to keep their part of the contract, and endeavour to teach her at least the elementary portion of her business?'

Monro acknowledged that 'it may said that these statements are overdrawn' but 'they were not'. He was direct witness to such things. He asked how long was it since Thomas Hood wrote 'The Song of the Shirt'?

'With fingers weary and worn,   A woman sits in unwomanly rags
With eyelids heavy and red,   Plying her needle and thread.'

Many women had to take work home to make ends meet. Monro cited the expression 'working life out to keep it in'. He nonetheless, did not think Belfast employers worse than others – indeed, they compared favourably with any. He thought it 'extremely unfair and calculated to do harm to industry rather than good, that, for political purposes, employers as a class should be characterised as sweaters' without 'distinguishing good from bad'. He concluded, 'while blood-curdling pictures, existing only in the imagination of the versatile newspaper proprietor, are drawn of the scenes of wretchedness and misery which the houses of workers present', Belfast workers were 'more comfortably housed than are those of the majority of the large centres of industry'. Largely through the efforts of BTC's William Walker, Amalgamated Society of Carpenters & Joiners, the Textile Operatives Society of Ireland was formed in 1893 with Mary Galway as Secretary.[19]

On Strikes

On strikes, Monro believed it was 'criminal folly to hint at or recommend' strike until 'all the forces of civilisation have been exhausted'. Lockouts were more common among Belfast trade unions where the motto 'Defence Not Defiance' was 'very generally acted upon'. He hoped that the Royal Commission on Labour would formulate a system of conciliation and arbitration that would make 'industrial warfare' a rarity. He cited recent examples of State-sponsored arbitration in the United States. Monro had given evidence to the Royal Commission and strongly believed in arbitrated settlements.

Monro concluded his TUC Address by asking whether the world's wealthiest country – the United Kingdom – had truly progressed? He measured progress by the happiness and wellbeing of citizens. In this regard he strongly condemned the 'calamity and plague of drunkenness'. Finally, he asked members to be brief and constrained in their contributions.[20] It had been an engaging, well thought out speech that revealed Monro as a deep and progressive thinker on many matters. His attitude to a labour press and political representation were delivered very much in a British context. He does not appear to have addressed either issue with particular vigour in Belfast. Indeed, he seemed to consider politics anathema to BTC but then the politics of Belfast were very different to those of Britain. They readily and too easily divided on sectarian lines and perhaps Monro's contribution at the 1892 Congress was a more accurate reflection of his politics that his 1893 speech.

In Congress tradition, Monro was presented with the bell used during the proceedings by two very eminent figures. John Burns, MP, firstly thanked Monro for the 'admirable way he had discharged his duties ... with firmness, good temper and strict impartiality'. BTC had proved itself the equal of any other. Burns regretted that Monro had not secured election to the Parliamentary Committee, a sentiment echoed in cries of 'hear, hear' from the hall. Bailey (Nottingham) seconded and Monro accepted their kind comments with due modesty. James Keir Hardie, MP, made the presentation, observing how little it had been called into use during the week, further testimony to Monro's skills of chairmanship.[21]

New Unionism & Belfast Trades Council
In 1892, when Secretary, BTCouncil, Monro thought that while strikes were a 'barbarous method of settling disputes', they were nevertheless 'bound to admit (for it is impossible to close our eyes to the fact) that under the present conditions of society they are a necessity and have also their good side, and often display to us in various forms the true nobility and manhood of the great mass of workers'. Unskilled workers were beginning to organise in Belfast and the arrival of their delegates at BTC meetings was a culture shock to the staid, conservative – with a small 'c' – craft trade unionists that had hitherto had the monopoly. Monro asserted that Council were 'proud of having recognised the rights of the unskilled labourer to share in our work and advantages'. The National Amalgamated Union of Labour (NAUL) arrived in Belfast in 1890 and by 1895 had nine branches and 2,000 members in the city, mainly in shipyards. The National Union of Gasworkers & General Labourers (NUGGL) had established eight branches between 1889-1891.Unskilled workers soon suffered setbacks. Tobacco workers were defeated after a lockout and by December 1892, BTC were 'sorry to find that the unskilled labourers have, with one exception, not only failed to maintain their position, but have lost a great number of members'.

The resignations were somewhat ironic as, in 1892, BTC had supported the striking Linen Lappers. Some thirty Protestant and Catholic bands marched together in protest. So impacting was this demonstration of unity, that Monro began his 1893 BTUC Address by expressing his pride – and by extension – hope for future unity.

'Saturday's great labour demonstration in Belfast will go down to posterity as not the least important episode in the history of the labour movement of these countries, and certainly not as the least important event in the religious and political history of Ulster ... In the monster procession ... orange and green rosettes decked the breast of the District Master of the Orange Lodge, in common with that of the Vice President of the Irish National Federation. A Nationalist band cut out the route for an Orange Society, and many a stalwart body of Nationalist toilers beat tramp to the music of a Protestant fife and drum. Peace, order, harmony and the best of feeling characterised the proceedings from start to finish.'

Another paper had said 'a few years ago' it would have been 'utterly impossible'. Monro saw the event as a 'turning point' but, while clearly pleased by events, Monro would quickly react differently as the growing presence of unskilled workers upset the hegemony of the old craft unions within the BTC.[22]

Irish Trades Union Congress

On 4 May 1889, Monro attended the first conference of the Irish Federated Trade and Labour Union at the Angel Hotel, Dublin. Monro, BTUC President, was complimented by T.J. O'Reilly, Dublin Typoghraphical Provident Society and Treasurer, Dublin Trades Council (DTC), who thanked 'our Northern Brethren' who 'by their alacrity' were the 'first to infuse fresh vigour into us'. Monro replied 'somewhat hyperbolically' that there were 'only an imaginary difference between the men of Belfast and those of the rest of Ireland'.[23] The promise for the new Federation quickly collapsed, however, when, in August, DTC asked for contributions towards a Sunday sports meeting. Belfast recorded a 'solemn protest' and their interest dwindled.

Moves towards unity continued, however. In 1894, BTC sent six delegates to a new Irish Trades Union Congress (ITUC). A decision at the 1893 BTUC to exclude Trades Councils propelled BTC towards the ITUC perhaps rather more fully than might have been the case. In Belfast in 1893, nine Irish unions were direct BTUC affiliates and many British-based unions had Irish representation among their delegations. By 1900, when convening in Huddersfield, only one Irish union was in BTUC affiliation – the Belfast-based Flax Dressers' Trade Union – and only two Irishmen among British delegations – S.H. Nelson from Belfast, Boilermakers, Iron & Steel Shipbuilders, and Dubliner J. Clarke, Amalgamated Society of Carpenters & Joiners. By 1911, in Newcastle-on-Tyne, there were neither Irish affiliates nor Irish delegates. In short, organic links between the Irish and British movements had diminished considerably contributing to a sense of two distinctly separate movements and trade union jurisdictions.[24]

Monro clearly supported the ITUC although he had effectively severed his BTC the same year it was formed. Monro and Mitchell – two of its founders – resigned from the BTC as they objected to the way that delegates for the Norwich TUC had been selected and the growing and in their view over-representation of the emerging labourers' unions, primarily the NAUL and NUGGL. A heated discussion at Council only accepted their resignations by 28-27. Despite this close vote, one historian did not consider the resignations as 'particularly significant' as their particular viewpoint – non-Socialist Unionism – continued to be the majority one.[25]

Monro appeared at the first ITUC gatherings, however. In Cork, 1895, he seconded the toast to 'The Labour Cause' saying that their one purpose was 'to improve their conditions and that of those dependent on them, and with the view that they gladly accepted the help of influential men like the Mayor and the MPs'.[26] Monro attended the 1897 ITUC in Waterford contributing to a debate on the Childers Commission that concluded that Ireland had been overtaxed by Britain. Congress added its voice to those seeking a financial readjustment. Monro led the opposition within the hall, suggesting that the 'whole matter needed further investigation'. James McCarron (Amalgamated Society of Tailors, Londonderry), said this was a 'tactical move that would suit Monro and those who were opposed to giving justice to Ireland'.[27]

In Sligo in 1901, TA Organiser Hugh McManus condemned the 'present antiquated and inequitable system' that obliged 'contractors for Irish Stationery Office contracts ... to take all paper, cardboard, vellum, leather, cloth, and other unworked material from the Department'. This was 'penalising and handicapping fair employers in the printing business in Belfast, Cork, and other parts of Ireland by the heavy railway charges for freight and carriage to and from Dublin'. The TA wanted 'material sent direct from the mill or the Stationery Office warehouse, carriage free, to the contractor's works'. Monro 'strongly supported the motion and said one centre should not have an advantage over another'. This was typical of the many ITUC motions dealing with trade terms within Ireland, particularly for State or local authority contracts.[28]

While Monro was given the honour of proposing the vote of thanks to the visiting Scottish TUC delegates, he was clearly second fiddle to the TA's main figure McManus. McManus moved motions supporting members then in dispute with the *Leinster Leader* and calling for 'Technical Education and Irish Industries', both carried unanimously. Monro's only other brief contribution was to second the BTC's William Walker's attempt to have a motion opposing the practice of two year terms for Lord Mayors put back.[29] In Cork in 1902, Monro looked for the enforcement of Fair Contracts for all printing by Irish Public Boards, opposing any sub-letting or exporting of work 'while many willing and competent Irish workmen and Ratepayers are compelled to remain unemployed through such reprehensible and unpatriotic practices'.[30]

Monro's last appearance at Congress was in Newry in 1903. He seconded a motion from H. Rochford (Dublin Hairdressers' Trade Union) urging support for Sir Charles Dilke's Shops Bill which sought to reduce shop opening hours and thereby the extensive hours worked by shop assistants. With William Walker, Monro opposed a motion from T. Sheehan (Electrical Trades Union) calling for a fixed scale of charges for electricity users in Dublin. Monro thought 'the matter surely was one for the Dublin ratepayers, and not for' Congress and 'it would be a piece of impudence to interfere in the matter'. Walker considered 'it would be absurd to pass the resolution' but it was adopted anyway.[31]

Labour Politics

Monro's politics have been described as Conservative Unionist. This may have been so, but he did stand as a 'labour representative' to grant him his small 'l' for Labour. In general, Monro supported BTC's strict non-political line, although this might be viewed as non-political in an Ulster context. In May 1886, Monro, supported by Vice President Thomas Johnston, demanded that BTC discuss the actions of their Secretary, Alexander Bowman, who had written to the Liberal MP, Henry Broadhurst, then Under Secretary at the Home Office, supplying 'misleading information' regarding the situation in Belfast and Ireland generally. The Amalgamated Society of Carpenters & Joiners threatened to disaffiliate unless Bowman was removed from office. Monro's motion produced a Special Meeting which was reminded of BTC's commitment to the 'avoidance of political questions of a party or contentious nature'. Bowman, now active in the Irish Protestant Home Rule Association, forestalled any action by offering his resignation voluntarily. It was accepted unanimously and Monro explained that he acted 'simply for the good of the Council'.[32]

In 1891, BTC selected Monro to contest the local elections in Cromac. Had he been successful, he would have been required by his employer to resign his job. That said, boosted by a £100 surplus in the hospitality fund from the 1893 British TUC, the Council promised to subsidise Monro, if elected, £50 a year for his three years of office. Monro may well have succeeded had the polls not been illegally closed between 7pm and 8pm. The outcome was: Ritchie, 2,465 and Bell, 2,419, elected, with Monro narrowly missing out with 2,106.[33] Monro declined another invitation to stand in 1893 and Murray Davis (Belfast Bakers' Society) stood instead. Davis was opposed by Unionist elements within the BTC and was publicly denounced by them at several meetings in support of his Conservative rivals McCammond and McCorry. Davis vainly produced testimonies from two clergymen that he was neither a socialist nor a nationalist but it did not prevent him being outvoted two to one. He was accused of being a socialist, an atheist, an anarchist, and a Home Ruler. Four days later, the victor, William McCammond, was congratulated by BTC on his proposed election as Lord Mayor, calling him the 'workers' best friend'.[34]

Although invited to stand on a Labour platform by BTC, Monro, was known 'in his private capacity' to have been 'of considerable service to the conservative cause'. He was 'opposed to socialism on the grounds of its impracticality'. Although BTC was officially neutral on politics, Unionist sympathies prevailed among the majority which included Monro. When the Belfast Independent Labour Party was formed in September 1892, Monro was not among its number.[35]

Monro's Last Years

By the late 1890s, Monro had set himself up in business as a 'general printer'. He did job-printing for BTC in 1907 and 1909 but appears to have played no further part in trade unionism or labour politics.[36] He died in 1925. His fellow BTC pioneer Joseph Mitchell had been appointed Superintendent, Falls Road Baths when it opened in 1896. A United Irish League activist, he died in 1901.[37]

Samuel Monro holds the largely forgotten distinction of being the only Irish-based trade unionist to act as Chair of the BTUC.[38] He had moved that the BTUC be held in Belfast in 1893. A founder and officer of the Typographical Society and BTC, he also attended the foundation meetings of the ITUC His was an influential voice, one that provided stability and respectability to an emerging movement. He was conservative – small 'c' - and cautious by character and perhaps Conservative – big 'C' – by political inclination, in both Ulster and wider contexts. His 1893 BTUC address is illuminating and demonstrates a radical foresight with demands for the organisation of women, factory reform and protective legislation, temperance and 'labour representation' – this time very definitely with a small 'l' – very advanced for their time.

His idea of 'labour' representation appeared to be within existing political parties which he quite definitely saw as Conservative or Liberal and certainly not Nationalist. He represented the old and soon to be overtaken craft trade unionism that was deferential – 'defence not defiance' – and sectional, wary of the 'New Unionism' and the rise of the unskilled and their socialist visions. Monro's resignation from the BTC – if not his union – possibly forestalled his replacement by younger men. He was by 1894, nearly fifty years of age. When the TA did appoint a Belfast official it was Hugh McManus. Monro went back to his trade.

Monro was, however, a true pioneer and deserves to be remembered as such. His organisational and leadership skills were very evident from 1878-1897, a period of almost twenty years, and undoubtedly left their mark on an emerging movement that began, quite gingerly in Belfast and concluded proudly on a national stage. Monro might have argued – two national stages.

Notes

This is an amended version of my article "Hearing the children weeping': Samuel Monro, 1846-1925, President, Belfast Trades Council & British Trades Union Congress' which appeared in Saothar 39, 2014 pp. 5-20. I am grateful for assistance from Peter Bunting and Clare Moore (ICTU) and John Gray in compiling this article.

1   Anne McKee, *Belfast Trades Council: The First Hundred Years, 1881-1981*, (Belfast, 1981), p. 5; *Peter Collins, 'The Belfast Labour Movement, 1881-1921'* in Jürgen Elvert (ed), *Nordirland in Geschichte und Gegenwart*, (Framz Steiner Verlag, Stuttgart, 1994), *pp.82-98*; Peter Collins,

'William Walker and Belfast Trades Council' in Seán Byers & Francis Devine (eds), *William Walker 1870-1918: Belfast Labour Unionist: Centenary Essays*, (Umiskin Press, Dublin, 2018), pp. 39-50.

2   1901 Census, *www.census.nationalarchives.ie/reels/nai000324757/* The *Street Directory* lists a Samuel Monroe, compositor at 78 Melrose Street, *www.lennonwylie.co.uk/alphanames 1901M.htm* [retrieved 30 August 2018].

3   *www.lennonwylie.co.uk/alphanames1907M.htm* [retrieved 30 August 2018].

4   1911 Census, *www.census.nationalarchives.ie/reels/nai002207621/* [retrieved 30 August 2018].

5   *www.lennonwylie.co.uk/1913PhoneList5.htm* [retrieved 30 August 2018].

6   *www.lennonwylie.co.uk/alphanames1918M.htm* [retrieved 30 August 2018].

7   *www.lennonwylie.co.uk/nopcomplete1943.htm* [retrieved 30 August 2018].

8   Francis Devine & John B. Smethurst, *Historical Directory of Trade Unions in Ireland*, (Irish Labour History Society/Working Class Movement Library, Dublin & Salford, 2017), 'Print workers and journalists', pp. 275-287, 531-532.

9   McKee, *op. cit.*, pp. 5-7. Indeed, BTC was 'often accused of being a stronghold of the Temperance Movement'.

10 Terence Bowman, *People's Champion: The Life of Alexander Bowman, Pioneer of Labour Politics in Ireland*, (Ulster Historical Foundation, Belfast, 1997), pp. 16-22.

11 TUC, *Report of the 20ᵗʰ Annual TUC, Swansea, 5-10, September 1887*, pp. 17-18.

12 TUC, *Report of the 24ᵗʰ Annual TUC, Glasgow, 5-10, September 1892*, p. 76.

13 TUC, *Report of the 26ᵗʰ Annual TUC, Norwich, 3-8 September 1894*, pp. 74, 81.

14 John W. Boyle, *The Irish Labour Movement in the Nineteenth Century*, (Catholic University of America, Washington, DC, 1988), p. 142.

15 The first and missing verse from Moore's 1808 poem, to be sung to 'Aileen Aroon', was 'Erin! the tear and the smile in thine eyes / Blend like the rainbow that hangs in thy skies / Shining through sorrow's stream / Saddening through pleasure's beam / Thy suns with doubtful gleam / Weep while they rise'.

16 Mill, 6 April, 1773 -23 June, 1836, was a Scottish historian, economist, political theorist, and philosopher. He is regarded as the founder of classical economics with David Ricardo. Mill was the father of influential philosopher of liberalism, John Stuart Mill. John Ramsey McCulloch,1 March, 1789-11 November, 1864, was a Scottish economist, author and editor, and widely regarded as the leader of the Ricardian school of economists after Ricardo's death in 1823. McCullough was the first Professor of Political Economy, University College London, 1828. He was a pioneer in the collection, statistical analysis and publication of economic data. McCulloch was a co-founder and editor of *The Scotsman*, worked on the Edinburgh Review, and edited the 1828 edition of The Wealth of Nations

17 Sir John Eldon Gorst PC, QC, FRS, 24 May 1835-4 April 1916, was a British lawyer and politician, serving as Solicitor General for England and Wales, 1885-1886 and Vice-President, Committee on Education, 1895-1902.

18 Emilia, Lady Dilke, 2 September 1840-23 October 1904, born Emily Francis Strong, was an author, art historian, feminist and trade unionist. She married the English Liberal MP, Sir Charles Dilke. May Tennant,1869-1946, née Abraham, born in Rathgar, County Dublin, was a Civil Servant, trade unionist, Factory Inspector, and tireless campaigner who worked to improve conditions for industrial workers and women's health and education. Florence Routledge was closely associated with Dilke and wrote *Trade Unionism Among Women*. The WTUL was founded by Emma Paterson in 1875 and briefly known as the Women's Protective and Provident League, represented dressmakers, upholsterers, bookbinders, artificial-flower makers, feather dressers, tobacco, jam and pickle workers, shop assistants and typists. In 1903, it became the WTUL with Mary Macarthur as Secretary. Other important figures in the WTUL included Margaret Bondfield, Dorothy Jewson and Susan Lawrence. In 1906, this became the National Federation of Women Workers. In 1921, in decline, it quietly merged with the National Union of General & Municipal Workers, today's GMB.

19 John Gray, *City in Revolt: Jim Larkin & the Belfast Dock Strike of 1907*, (SIPTU/Linen Hall Library, Belfast & Dublin, 2007), p. 28. TOSI were finally dissolved in 1980 and had begun as the Textile Operatives' Association.

20 TUC, *Report of the 25th Annual TUC, Belfast, 4-9 September 1893*, pp. 27-33.

21 TUC, *Report of the 25th Annual TUC, Belfast, 4-9 September 1893*, pp. 89-91.

22 Patterson, *Class Conflict & Sectarianism: The Protestant Working Class & the Belfast Labour Movement, 1868-1920*, (Blackstaff Press, Belfast, 1992), p. 38.

23 Boyle, *op. cit.*, pp. 130-133.

24 Francis Devine, 'The Irish Transport & General Workers' Union and labour unrest in Ireland, 1911', *Historical Studies in Industrial Relations*, issue 33, September 2012, pp. 169-188.

25 Patterson, *Class Conflict, op. cit.*, p. 38.

26 Boyle, *op. cit.*, p. 224.

27 Boyle, *op. cit.*, p. 154.

28 ITUC, *Eighth ITUC Report, Sligo, 27-29 May 1901*, pp. 13-16, *http://centenaries-ituc.nationalarchives.ie/wp-content/uploads/2014/10/8th-annual-report-1901.pdf* [retrieved 30 August 2018].

29 ITUC, *Eighth ITUC Report, Sligo, 27-29 May 1901*, pp. 40, 46-48, 52-53.

30 ITUC, *Ninth ITUC Report, Cork, 18-21 May 1902*, pp. 15-16, *http://centenaries-ituc.nationalarchives.ie/wp-content/uploads/2014/10/9th-annual-report-1902.pdf* [retrieved 30 August 2018].

31 ITUC, *Tenth ITUC Report, Newry, 1-3 June 1903*, pp. 14-15, 20, *http://centenaries-ituc.nationalarchives.ie/wp-content/uploads/2014/10/10th-annual-report-1903.pdf* [retrieved 30 August 2018].

32 Bowman, op. cit., p. 65.

33 Boyle, *op. cit.*, pp. 160, 168.

34 Boyle, *op. cit.*, p, 161.

35 I Boyle, *op. cit.*, p. 183,

36 Boyle, *op. cit.*, p. 278.

37 Bowman, *op. cit.*, p. 205. William McCammond was born near Carnmoney on 8 September 1831. A master shipbuilder, he started a building firm in Duncairn Street and built the Grand Restaurant between Castle Lane and Cornmarket and Agnes Street Methodist Church. He was Lord Mayor, 1894-1896; was knighted in 1895; and died in 1898.

38 A.E. Musson, *The Typographical Association, Origins & History Up to 1949*, (Oxford University Press, Oxford, 1949) makes no reference to Munro. Sadly, perhaps Musson was unaware that Monro was a TA member.

'I Have Got Every Worker in the City of Cork Behind Me': Robert Day, 1885-1949

Robert 'Bob' Day was born in 1885 to a working-class family in Cork city. The 1901 Census records them at 269 Old Youghal Road. His Kerry-born father, John, 1835-c1905, an Army Pensioner and Church of Ireland member, spoke Irish and English. In c1872, he married Mary, 1852-c1905, a Cork Catholic. An army career made for an itinerant lifestyle from 1873-1885. While Robert, then sixteen, was like his younger brothers – Leslie Joseph, 12, and Patrick, 9 – Cork born, his elder brothers – James, 28, John, 26, and Richard, 24 - were born in England, Scotland and Waterford respectively. No occupation is listed for the older sons suggesting they were unemployed.[1] By 1911, the family were in the same house  but both parents were deceased and Richard, 34, a laundry van man, was married to Hannah, 24, with three children. Robert, now 26, also a laundry van man, lived in the house with brothers James, 38, a labourer in an engineering works; Leslie, 23, and Patrick, 19, both unemployed labourers.[2] As their father lacked a trade, the Day brothers had no inroad to the 'labour aristocracy' of the crafts. Times were hard for the Day family, even for those in employment. Between 1905-1912, James's wage remained static at 18s. even though rents and retail prices increased by 13% over the same period. His pay was half of what engineers earned, typical of the vast wage gulf that existed between tradesmen and labourers at this time.[3]

The Day family travails reflected the hardships experienced by Cork's working class in the early twentieth century. The previous century had transformed working life. The advent of factory-based machinery seriously undermined the city's traditional crafts, many then still operating in pre-industrial workshops. This milieu was compounded by the collapse of manufacturing caused by the integration of the Irish and British economies. The removal of tariffs devastated local industry as it was unable to compete with British products that were often cheaper and/or of superior quality, sending many trades into terminal decline. By 1914, as with other Irish cities outside of Ulster, Cork had reached an economic nadir.[4] De-industrialisation contributed to abject levels of poverty, afflicting a quarter of Corkonians in 1914.[5] Public health problems were widespread. In 1915, infant mortality was 132 per 1,000 births, while tuberculosis deaths totalled 2.88 per 1,000.[6] In 1913, Cork Corporation estimated that 8,765, almost one-ninth of the population, resided in tenements.[7]

Labour in Cork, 1889-1920

In the late 1880s, labourers across Ireland, including Cork, began to organise on a mass scale for the first time. Lasting until the early 1890s, this 'New Unionism' was led by British unions who brought an organisational methodology born of the simultaneous labourers' revolt in Britain. Aggressive strikebreaking by employers did much to smash the movement, but there was another reason for its demise: the hostility of the tradesmen. At this time, craft unionism was exclusive, insular and conservative.[8] As his livelihood depended upon strict control over the available labour force, the tradesman was motivated by a suspicion of the labourer rooted in craft rather than class consciousness.[9] New Unionism accelerated Irish labour's assimilation into the British movement, the latter's contribution to the anglicisation of Ireland, most obvious in the adoption of the English language. Despite vast economic differences between the two countries, Irish labour adopted British trade-union methodology, the epitome of what Emmet O'Connor describes as 'mental colonisation'.[10]

After New Unionism's collapse, organised labour drifted back to its conservative ways, once more dominated by craft unions. In 1900, only 30% of labourers were unionised compared to 70% of tradesmen.[11] It was not until Big Jim Larkin founded the Irish Transport & General Workers' Union (ITGWU) in January 1909 that mental de-colonisation began, allowing labourers to organise into a potent force. Day embodied those whom Larkin sought to empower. His impulses were radical, as subsequently shown by his republican and syndicalist sympathies. Larkin envisaged workers like Day forming a vital weapon in the union's armoury. Indeed, his sector of work (transportation) was of such importance that it was explicitly recognised in the new union's name.[12] A Cork branch was among the first established but collapsed after a disastrous lockout that summer, leaving labourers like Day with nothing to counter the employers' deep intransigence. The ITGWU's re-establishment in Cork in 1913 presaged a major revival in working-class fortunes, in part inadvertently brought about by the First World War. From 1917, syndicalism became trade unionism's beating heart.

Having spent so long on the margins, labourers were now in a position of unprecedented influence – and Day would seize the moment like few others.

The outbreak of war in July 1914 brought adversities to the working class that were novel in nature and unprecedented in scale. Chief among them was the mass inflation and food shortages caused by Germany's devastating U-boat campaign against merchant shipping in the Atlantic.[13] By the war's end, the cost of living was 203% higher than July 1914; at its 1920 peak, it was 249% higher.[14] Throughout 1915 and 1916, Irish employers largely resisted demands for increases and instead offered temporary 'war bonuses'. From 1917, however, labour's renaissance compelled employers to give permanent wage increases and a shorter working week. This culminated in labour's two *anni mirabiles* – 1919 and 1920 – when the class war swung decidedly in favour of the workers. A boom fuelled by the re-emergence of products unavailable in wartime ensured that inflation continued. However, it was now superseded by wage increases.

Syndicalism provided the basis for success. It encouraged proletarian solidarity and the organisation of new sectors like non-manual workers and women. Originating in France in the early 1890s, syndicalism was born out of the perceived failure of existing socialist politics and reformist trade unionism.[15] Syndicalists maintained that political parties created an unaccountable elite that would inevitably betray the membership. Besides, political power simply reflected economic power. They wanted to transform trade unionism – the most authentic expression of proletarian struggle – from remedying industrial grievances to instilling revolutionary class consciousness. Organisation of all workers into 'One Big Union' was the means to do this. The working class could then utilise its most effective weapon, the general strike, to seize power at the point of production.[16] A truly democratic society and economy governed by the unions could then be implemented. Ideologically, syndicalism was a synthesis of Marxism, anarchism and, predominantly, revolutionary trade unionism.[17]

From 1917, a confluence of internal and external factors – war, mass inflation and revolution at home and abroad – converged to produce Irish syndicalism. Syndicalism influenced all unions to some extent but was embodied *par excellence* in the ITGWU, which strove to become Ireland's OBU. Labourers like Day were plentiful in number and therefore indispensable to this goal. There were grounds for optimism. At its 1920 peak, the ITGWU had 120,000-130,000 members.[18]

Bob Day – Town Councillor & Harbour Commissioner, 1920-1922
When the 1920 Municipal Elections were held on 15 January, Irish Labour was in an unofficial but open alliance with Republicans. The 1916 Rising began a realignment in Irish politics, and the two movements had grown immeasurably closer since. This alliance was perhaps stronger in Cork than

anywhere else – and workers benefited. By subverting British institutional authority in Ireland and establishing rival institutions of state, Republicans undermined the legitimacy of the heretofore recognised authority. Additionally, the IRA's armed campaign crippled state agencies' power, especially the military and police. The revolutionary nature of the independence struggle, as well as its popular support, further radicalised labour, even if Republicans were slow to reciprocate.[19]

The elections were a highpoint for the republicanisation of Cork labour. It was the first time that proportional representation, which the British Government hoped would undermine Republican success, was used in Ireland. In Cork, as elsewhere, Day and his ITGWU comrades publicly nailed their Republican colours to the mast by running on a joint ticket with Sinn Féin. The coalition contested all wards and won thirty out of a possible fifty-six seats – securing 47% of the first preference vote – giving them a four-seat majority.[20] Day, still a vanman for Metropole Laundry and now resident in 9 Nicholas Street, was elected in Cork's North-eastern Ward. Cork Trades Council (CTC) ran twelve candidates in five wards for the Labour Party, three being elected.[21] Liam de Róiste, Sinn Féin MP for Cork City since December 1918 and a Corporation Councillor, believed that 'Labour, official or otherwise, has done very badly. These elections clearly show that the appeal to a war between classes is not a very moving one in Ireland'.[22] The results contradict this assertion. Nationally, Labour had its best Municipal Election, returning 324 candidates and securing a quarter of the first preference vote. Sinn Féin obtained a third of the vote and returned 422, compared to 213 Nationalists and 297 Unionists.[23]

The new Councillors took office with widespread working-class support. Sinn Féin were eager to prove their ability as administrators and root out the jobbery and corruption which, they believed, characterised the old Nationalist Corporation. The new Corporation was a disparate mix, none more so than the Sinn Féin-ITGWU coalition itself. Day was preoccupied with advancing workers' interests, while Sinn Féiner and UCC Professor Alfred O'Rahilly was keen to promote Catholic Social Teaching. The early signs were positive for the working class, as demonstrated by new Lord Mayor Tomás Mac Curtain, elected with Day's support on 30 January. Mac Curtain opposed a Nationalist Party motion to increase the annual mayoral salary to £1,000, a £400 rise. This amount was significantly above local wage levels. Mac Curtain argued that a reduction would set an example because many workers were at subsistence level. Accordingly, a motion set the salary at £500.[24] But it took just one month for tensions between Sinn Féin and ITGWU to become evident, something that was unavoidable given the coalition's cross-class composition. In March, ITGWU Councillors opposed Richard Beamish's election as Vice-Chair of the powerful Public Works Committee.[25] The appointment took place amidst a labourers' strike for a wage increase at the city's breweries, proving to the ITGWU men that Beamish was an archetypal capitalist who cared more about profits than his workers' welfare.

Despite the tensions, proletarian influence over the Corporation, long-dominated by Cork's bourgeoisie, was never stronger. Day was joined by nine trade unionists (six ITGWU) and their influence ensured that this Corporation was more favourable to workers than its predecessors.[26] Day was nominated to the Public Works, Tolls & Markets, Hackney Carriages and Waterworks Committees. These positions helped him steer through a major wage increase for Corporation employees in May 1920. Labourers now earned a weekly wage of 62s. 6d, an increase of 12s 6d.[27] While it must be seen in the context of an ongoing inflationary spiral, the wage was among the highest paid for general labour in Ireland. By late 1920, the rate was the local standardised minimum, with only a few establishments paying above it. Day also helped to ensure that a motion mandating that all Corporation vacancies be filled only by trade union labour was passed.[28]

It was an extraordinary time to be a Cork Corporation Councillor. On 19 March, Mac Curtain was murdered by members of the RIC at his home in front of his family in reprisal for the assassination of a RIC constable. Two days later, CTC took its commitment to the Republic to new heights. It passed its strongest ever denunciation of British rule and called a one-day general strike for 22 March.[29] It had acted on its own initiative, not in response to a call from the Irish Trades Union Congress (ITUC). Although Cork labour had long supported nationalist causes, the strike was its first independent act of direct solidarity with the republicans.[30] Violence escalated throughout the summer of 1920. In July, as permitted under the Restoration of Order in Ireland Act 1920, a curfew was imposed on Cork. Citizens were mandated to be indoors between 10pm and 3am every night. Municipal workers suffered the consequences of repression. On 17 July, the night of the IRA's assassination of RIC Divisional Commissioner Gerald Smyth, lamplighters were held up by the military when carrying out their work. Previously, a lamplighter was attacked by three men while doing his job, putting him out of work for some time. The work was demanding because the city's lamps were in constant need of repair. By the summer, just under half of them had been deliberately broken. The Black and Tans, who often used lamps as target practice during curfew hours, were responsible for much of this damage. Republicans recognised the lamplighters' courage under such circumstances. The testimony of one working on the night of Mac Curtain's murder was vital to the establishment of the RIC as the culprits.[31]

Day was keen to reward the lamplighters. In July, his Public Works Committee granted them an 83s. 3d. wage (a 16s 6d advance), the best non-craft rate outside of Ford's. Lamplighters were not the only workers to benefit from the efforts of Day and the other ITGWU Councillors. In early June, the Waterworks Committee was among the first employers to grant their engineers the 25s advance for which they had downed tools. The stoppage ended in July with the men obtaining their full demands. Their wage was now fixed at 105s, the highest in Britain and Ireland. The

Corporation fixed its plumbers' pay at 100s in tandem with an increase in the local rate.[32] The following month, however, Cork Corporation became the centre of a crisis that gained international attention. Day's goal of bettering Cork workers' lot was inevitably relegated in importance.

In a rare instance of British intelligence in Cork, City Hall was raided on 12 August and Lord Mayor Terence McSwiney, Mac Curtain's successor, arrested. He was incarcerated at Brixton Prison and immediately went on hunger strike. Deputy Lord Mayor Dónal O'Callaghan took over from him. The chaos meant that the Corporation barely functioned between August and October. Meetings were routinely suspended to protest MacSwiney's detention. Day's attendance during this period was poor, even when the Corporation did meet. MacSwiney died in Brixton Prison on 25 October after seventy-four days on hunger strike. His death made global headlines, bringing attention to the national struggle and condemnation of the British Government. The next day, CTC held a special meeting and unanimously condemned 'the tyranny which has caused his untimely end in a foreign dungeon'. The Corporation also held a special meeting to pass resolutions of sympathy and condemnation which Day did not attend.[33]

McSwiney's death intensified Republican resolve to end British rule, leading to an escalation of violence. In November, some of the most significant incidents of the war took place, culminating in the declaration of Martial Law in Cork and surrounding counties. On 21 November, the RIC and its reviled Auxiliary Division unleashed an indiscriminate massacre in Dublin's Croke Park, 'Bloody Sunday'. A week later, the IRA's West Cork Brigade ambushed an Auxiliary patrol at Kilmichael in a stunning victory. British reprisals on the civilian population became more common. On 11 December – after an ambush at Dillon's Cross and a day after the proclamation of Martial Law – the Auxiliaries and Black and Tans set fire to Cork city centre leaving much of it, including City Hall, a smouldered ruin.[34] The Corporation held an emergency meeting at the Corn Exchange and estimated the damage at £3,000,000. A Relief Committee was set up to deal with the 2,000 people made unemployed. Once again, Day did not attend.[35] Ill-health may explain his absence from these crucial meetings. He suffered from arthritis, which would incapacitate him later in life.

Cork's destruction accelerated and intensified the concurrent economic slump condemning many workers to unemployment. The demands of the War had led to a massive increase in output, which in turn produced a capitalist crisis of overproduction in the summer of 1920. By December, the boom was over, and a deep recession began. Across Ireland, pay advances virtually ended and it would be many years before workers experienced them again. Employers sought to cut wages and shed surplus labour as prices and demand plunged. Defending hard earned gains became the workers' imperative.[36] The slump quickly made Cork an unemployment blackspot. Accordingly, in 1921 Day immersed himself more deeply into civic life. That February, he was appointed to the same Committees he had served the previous year, and to the Working-Class Dwellings and influential Law & Finance Committees. He often chaired their proceedings and sometimes the Corporation itself.[37] In June, he was reappointed to the Harbour Board, serving on its Pilotage, Law & Finance and Dredge & Works Committees until 1923.[38]

In his capacity as a Councillor, Day worked tirelessly to address the unemployment question. He and the other ITGWU Councillors regularly urged the Corporation to expedite the re-building of Patrick's Street to provide jobs in the building trade. In February, the Corporation established the Cork Reconstruction Committee, on which Day and other trade unionists sat, to do this. As with other relief schemes, however, progress was slow.[39] At a Public Works Committee meeting, Day clashed with Beamish on when the brewer claimed that high rates and wages were the reasons for the absence of reconstruction work. Day was lauded by CTC for the 'manly' stand he took in repudiating Beamish's remarks.[40] Day had an unenviable task in an extraordinarily difficult time and achieved little in his efforts to tackle unemployment.

The War of Independence continued and intensified throughout the first half of 1921. The methods of counterinsurgency remained the same, creating a symbiotic relationship between State atrocities and the growing national desire for independence. Like most of the populace, Day's Republicanism became more visible and explicit. In March 1921, he was one of Cork Corporation's representatives to the funerals of George Clancy, Mayor of Limerick, his predecessor Michael O'Callaghan and City Clerk Joseph O'Donoghue, who had been murdered by the Auxiliaries.[41] From the July 1921 Truce, the Corporation reflected the conflict between Labourites and Republicans emerging across Ireland. Sinn Féin had sought benign neutrality from Labour in the hope that militant trade unionism would not undermine the independence fight. Labour gave it just that. But the conflicting class composition between Labour movement and the petit-bourgeois Sinn Féin ensured conflict between them when peace was declared. Day was at the heart of an event that crystallised these irreconcilable differences.

The 1921 Cork Harbour Soviet

Instituted in 1814, the Cork Harbour Board (CHB) was composed of five ex-officio members, five Corporation representatives and twenty-five mercantile representatives, all appointed by the Corporation. Though the CHB had long been a home for Cork's commercial elite like railway directors, shipping agents and large merchants, the presence of Sinn Féin-ITGWU members like Day from 1920 gave it a more democratic veneer.[42] CHB wages mirrored those at the Corporation.

On 9 March 1920, CHB convened to discuss potential remedies to the city's constant labour disputes. At Mac Curtain's behest, the meeting established a twenty-man Cost of Living Commission to determine a proper living wage for Cork.[43] In August, the Cost of Living Commission reported that this was 70s a week, a significant increase on a labourers' rate.[44] On 16 February 1921, CHB received a letter from the ITGWU asking that the 70s rate be put into effect. The CHB deferred the matter.[45] Since February 1920, Day had been a Corporation nominee to the CHB. He had helped to secure the labourers' 62. 6d wage via his membership of its Law & Finance and Dredge & Works Committees.[46]

In June 1921, the expected rejection of the claim finally came when CHB maintained that it could not afford to implement it. Nevertheless, the ITGWU persisted. On 10 August, CHB again refused the claim. Five days later, the ITGWU served strike notice for 26 August. On 24 August, Day proposed arbitration at a CHB meeting. His motion collapsed as it did not have a seconder. The next day, CTC also called for arbitration and passed a motion to discuss the situation with the CHB.[47] When delegates met CHB Chairman Frank Daly, he agreed to arbitration and the strike was deferred for a week.[48] However, on 31 August CHB rejected its Chairman's idea. At the same meeting, arbitration under Dáil Éireann's Department of Labour was also dismissed.[49] The latter vote provoked a heated exchange between Day and Captain Collins, the eccentric Sinn Féiner and sea captain. When Collins told CHB that men from outside would be provided in the event of a strike, Day 'thanked' him for his offer to provide scabs. Collins's response was characteristic: 'How dare you insult me by associating me with blacklegs. If you have anything to say to me come out there and I'll knock the stuffing out of you. I'll not be insulted by you'.[50]

Collins's grandiose threats did not deter the men, who struck work on 2 September. In total, 180 were affected, of which 150 began the strike by marching behind a Red Flag before raising another one over the CHB offices at the Custom House. They then blockaded the port.[51] Next day, the ITGWU declared its willingness to issue permits for the pilotage of the seven ships stranded in or outside Cork and Cóbh.[52] Day proposed a motion to take over the harbour which was carried with great enthusiasm. He was then elected the new Harbour Master.[53] The conservative Cork press expressed typical hostility to the strike. The Redmondite *Cork Examiner* feared that the Shipping Federation would boycott the harbour and the *Cork Constitution* – the reactionary, Unionist mouthpiece of the employers – warned that the city's merchant class would do the same.[54]

At a special CHB meeting on 5 September, de Róiste proposed arbitration under Dáil Éireann's Department of Labour. Day was one of only three to vote against it. CHB Secretary, Sir James Long, was mandated to write to the ITGWU. The letter stated that CHB now accepted arbitration and had nominated its Chairman as its representative; and asked the union if it accepted arbitration and, if so, to give the name of its representative. But in an extraordinary outburst, Day made it clear that the time for arbitration had passed as far as he was concerned:

'If this Board are willing to eat its own words and give the men a 70s minimum from the day the application was sent in, the men will go back under the control of this Board and present officials. If not, the men are going back, but not under the control of the Board ... We are going to take action. If you say you cannot run the port and pay these men a living wage, then the men are going to run the board themselves. If they have got to do it they are going to do it, and if the full demand is not conceded we will take control ... I have got every worker in the City of Cork behind me. It is true that I am Day, the ex-driver of a one-horse van, but now I am a Harbour Commissioner and Town Councillor. True, I never hired a man in my life, but I am going to hire men to-morrow if you are going to turn down the men. I will send them into the yard to work under my control, and we are going, if allowed, to make the port pay ... The position, Mr. Chairman, is that we are prepared to take the action and we are prepared to abide by the consequences ... If the Irish Republican Government put me out of the office tomorrow they can do it, but they have to count the cost.'[55]

Day warned CHB that the Red Flag was 'not coming down until the workers get every penny they are looking for. If anyone else wanted to take that flag down they will do so against my life, and 10, 20, aye 100 lives'.[56] The meeting adjourned to give the ITGWU sufficient time to respond to the letter. Upon resuming, Daly read the reply: 'No'. The union had effectively announced its full support for Day and Long locked away the CHB's documentation in preparation for the takeover. Reflecting Sinn Féin policy, de Róiste added: 'the Irish Government recognises the right to strike, and also to protect property'.[57] The next day, the *Constitution* declared that 'the material interests of the Port of Cork are seriously menaced by the strike of harbour employees'. It also described Day's warning as an 'amazing statement' and denounced the offer of arbitration as an 'abdication' of the Board's responsibility.[58] It was right to be worried, as events the following day would prove.

Early on 7 September, 135 of the strikers gathered outside the Custom House. At 10.30am, Day, accompanied by his ITGWU comrades William Kenneally and Thomas Coyle, entered Long's office. They informed him of their intentions to take over the running of the port and enquired if he was prepared to continue as Secretary under the new régime. He refused and was duly replaced by Day, who announced that ships could only enter and leave the port with his permission. The three men collected dues from ships to pay the 70s wage and issued the following permit to captains and their agents: 'Customs House' Cork, 6th Sept. 1921. Permit SS ... Captain ... to proceed to Port immediately (signed) Robt. Day – Chief Commissioner'.[59]

Nobody was coerced into the Soviet and any worker could leave if he so wished. The engineers, telephonists and caretakers agreed to partake, but clerks were less favourable with most in the Accountant's and Collector's Department voting to leave. One man there proclaimed that he pledged his allegiance to Dáil Éireann only. Nevertheless, the takeover was successful, and Day was elected 'Chief Commissioner of the Port of Cork'.[60] He announced that 'no man is to go inside that building unless he gets an order from me. I am Chief Commissioner now. You are members of the workers' army, and as workers go and do your duty'.[61] Day ordered Coyle and Thomas Murphy to proceed to Cóbh and seize the harbour offices.[62]

Shortly afterwards, Daly arrived. He was soon joined by Seán French, Secretary to the Minister for Labour, and Mercier, Higgins, Dowdall and de Róiste. Together with Day and Keneally, they reached an agreement. Day and Kenneally now proposed to surrender to what had previously been rejected. Work would be resumed at the old rate, pending Dáil-sponsored arbitration on 10 September which would decide the wage claim retrospective to February. At a mass meeting, Day sold the agreement on a spurious claim that the talks did not constitute arbitration but a conference. He also promised to renew the Soviet if the claim was not won.[63] His frivolous speech was aimed at the antagonistic local press and was reported in the *Examiner*:

> 'Friends, comrades and Bolsheviks (laughter) ... He did not think that there was any better title for them than Bolsheviks, for the word meant to him an anxiety that the bottom dog should go up and the top dog should come down (cheers) ... When they raised their Red Flag people laughed at them and said they were a pack of sillies. They had proved that whatever flag the people had faith in, the workers had faith in the Red Flag, and the Red Flag only (loud cheers). Whatever the terms of settlement of the fight for the nation, it should be remembered that they were all patriots and Irishmen. And we, the workers, will have to fight the Republicans harder than we ever fought the bosses for a just share of the government of the country. We have shown them we can govern ... To-day, we have given the employers of Cork and Ireland a lesson ... We are not afraid of the IRA ... for there are a good many of the IRA here around me ... But if the IRA are going to make blacklegs or strike-breakers, there is trouble in store for them.'[64]

The Red Flag had flown over a workers' soviet for approximately five hours before it was replaced with a tricolour. Watchmen resumed work that night and the remaining staff the following morning.[65] The conference held on 10 September gave the workers what they demanded: 7s 6d backdated to 14 February in a lump sum until another Cost of Living Commission report.[66] CHB ratified the agreement on 14 September. However, the next day CTC passed a motion refusing to work with the allegedly capitalistic Commission. One delegate condemned the Soviet, but he was alone in this.[67] Although the Cork Employers' Federation was willing to work with the Commission, the ITGWU agreed with CTC. Consequently, the Commission was never established and the 70s wage never instituted.[68] The rate would have given harbour workers higher wages in real terms than those paid in 1914 and possibly 1904.[69]

The political aftermath of the Cork Harbour Soviet led to a breach in the Sinn Féin-ITGWU coalition.[70] The breakdown was perhaps inevitable given Sinn Féin's predominately lower-middle-class composition.[71] Hart shows that 'artisans and trades provided a solid core of support for' Republicanism 'throughout the revolution' with 'another key group of Volunteers' coming from the 'white-collar world of shops and offices'. These men's employers 'rarely joined the movement, but their sons (who often worked as apprentices or assistants for their fathers) frequently did'. The 'chronically underemployed general labourers ... may have voiced support for' the IRA but 'remained outsiders to the movement'.[72] Most 'professionals' in the IRA were lower middle class: teachers and assistant or part-time teachers. Nearly all skilled workers in the movement were apprentices or journeymen.[73]

The raising of the Red Flag angered Republicans who felt that the tricolour had been dishonoured. The IRA was willing to expel the workers and reinstate the old CHB.[74] The Cork Sinn Féin Executive charged Day with defying Dáil authority, prompting the ITGWU to respond by endorsing its Secretary's actions as being 'in accordance with trade-union principles'.[75] Day was tried at Cork Courthouse and expelled from the Republican movement, ending an involvement that began in 1913 when he joined the Cork Corps, Irish Volunteers.[76] He had worked for the Republican Court system.[77] Significantly, Day's actions revealed the social outlook of those leading the Irish revolution, which de Róiste made explicit in his diary:

> 'Republicans and Conservatives are united in their opposition to the Red Flag ... It must be a surprise to the Conservatives [Unionists] that Republicans are so strenuously in opposition to the Red Flag and what it signifies ... In fact, it is of intense interest to me to see how this struggle of what I may term Red Flag versus Irish tricolour has come about so soon ... It is one of the things I anticipated but did not expect would come so soon in Cork.'[78]

These 'conservatives' were hysterical in their denunciation of Day, who sent tremors through the bourgeois press, Nationalist and Unionist alike. The *Constitution* praised the Dáil for the first time for dismantling the Soviet, ludicrously blaming its creation on the influence of communists.[79] It attacked Day as a man 'of autocratic disposition' who had illegally 'constituted himself Commissioner-in-Chief, and for a day or two dispensed with the co-operation of his colleagues'.[80] The Unionist *Irish Times* had a similar opinion of Day, 'the leader of the enterprise' who had 'dictated his terms with more than Cromwellian arrogance'. This was indicative of how 'to-day Irish Labour is permeated with a spirit of revolt against all the principles and conventions of ordered society ... the wild teachings of the Russian Revolution have fallen on willing ears'.[81] The *Examiner* published letters from 'An Old Trade Unionist' and 'A Country Worker' that expressed deep hostility to socialism and the Soviet rooted in nationalism and Catholic dogma. The *Irish Independent* – voice of the conservative, Catholic middle class – condemned Day's 'indefensible ... unjustifiable ... experiment in Sovietism'.[82]

But neither Republicans nor Unionists need have worried. Despite Day's flamboyant rhetoric, there was little revolutionary potential in the Soviet. Its lavish pageantry masked its true nature as a newly-acquired strike tactic carried out by a confident proletariat and ended by a pragmatic leadership.[83] Relations between Labour and the Republican movement were irreparably damaged. The RIC noted: 'The Labour Party are not so much interested in Sinn Féin as heretofore; their attitude towards it has changed considerably'.[84] Day's increasingly fraught relationship with Sinn Féin is emblematic of this broader split. In October, O'Callaghan (now Lord Mayor), who was not as sympathetic to labour as his two predecessors, clashed with Day when he suspended two clerks for disobeying a timekeeping order. The Mayor provoked anger when he requested other clerks to scab on their suspended comrades.[85] Another break in the Republican-Labour link was the murder of Cork ITGWU Organiser Tadgh Barry by Crown forces on 15 November 1921 in Ballykinler internment camp, County Down. His death, mourned by trade unionists and Republicans, removed a major personality who straddled both camps. Barry had been ITGWU Secretary, Day taking over as Acting Secretary when elected in 1922.[86]

The Treaty Split and 1922 General Election

The signing of the Anglo-Irish Treaty on 5 December 1921 presented an awkward dilemma for Labour. In Cork, in contrast to the commercial classes, Labour largely abstained from the Treaty debate, remaining neutral. A call for a plebiscite was all that ITUC officials could muster.[87] Even the famously militant and republican ITGWU urged neutrality from its members.[88] On 7 January 1922, amid much dissent, the Dáil ratified the Treaty. For over a year, Irish employers had felt hamstrung by the lack of effective policing and were anxious for a return to political stability. While the Treaty split was not strictly a socio-economic one, elements of class-based divisions can be detected. The Irish bourgeoisie overwhelmingly supported the Treaty, a major reason being an eagerness to launch their counterattack on wages.[89] The support it received from the 'men of property' gave the new State much needed legitimacy and created a solid nexus of interests between employers and Treatyites.[90]

By spring, the political situation was spiralling out of control. The ITUC had tried in vain to stop the slide into fratricidal violence. Whereas Labour had, on four occasions since 1918, brought out workers to aid the Republic, it now did so in opposition to nationalism.[91] On 24 April, the ITUC conducted a one-day general strike against 'the spirit of militarism'. In Cork, thousands of workers gathered in what was possibility the city's biggest labour gathering and listened to anti-war speeches condemning both sides. Day spoke to second a resolution supporting the ITUC's call, reflecting the scale of the breakdown of working-class support for the Republican struggle:

> 'For the past four of five years they had taken their part in the fight for the nation's independence, and in the present crisis it was up to them to fight for their employment and their bread and butter, and say they would allow no party of Irishmen to come between them and divide their workers' platform ... They were out to see that every man in Ireland who was able to work should get it, and the men who were not able to work would have to be supported by the state. They wanted no more militarism in Ireland ... nobody suffered more from that than the workers ... the present trouble in Ireland must stop immediately, and the rights of workers must be respected.'[92]

The strike was totally ineffective and signalled of the return of Labour ambiguity and ambivalence to the National Question. Whereas Labour's attitude to Sinn Féin during the War of Independence can be summarised as 'first the Republic, then the Workers' Republic', it now felt that the Treaty split was a 'plague on both your houses'.[93]

Day was as popular with workers as he had ever been. Later in April, he was chosen to contest the General Election, to be held on 16 June 1922, 'in the interests of the Transport Workers' Union'. A few days later, 'amid scenes of enthusiasm', he was unanimously selected by CTC to stand for the Labour Party in Cork Borough.[94] He was the first Labour candidate to stand for Parliamentary election in Cork. As Secretary, Cork Electoral Committee, Richard Cody (Typographical Association) oversaw Day's campaign. Charles K. Murray, solicitor, South Mall, was his Agent.

Little distinguished Day's campaign from that of other Labour candidates.[95] Reflecting the party's confidence, Day's appeals to voters were extravagant, urging workers to 'arise' and to 'rally to the standard of Labour!'.[96] On 4 June, he addressed a large meeting at Whitechurch about Labour's platform and the primacy of national self-determination. His speech was peppered with radical pronouncements:

> 'We workers demand the right to work ... the system wherein the land, factories and all the implements of wealth production are the property of private individuals ... cannot guarantee continuous employment to the workers ... we say it is the duty of the State to provide work to ensure that every man ... shall receive a living wage ... We claim that as long as the present system of land ownership lasts the Government should compel a certain amount of tillage ... If the farmer tilled on a British Government order in the interests of the British ruling class ... surely it is not too much to ask the farmers to till in the interests of a large section of the Irish nation – the landless rural workers.'[97]

At another mass meeting on 13 June, Day further demonstrated how estranged Labour had become from Republicans.

> 'They were told Labour was represented in the present Dáil. Which of the present Cork members represented the workers of Cork? Was it the member who stated, 'The more I see of official Labour, the less I am inclined to have anything to do with it'? Take the Harbour Board, where a fight was put up from February 1921 to September for the minimum wage laid down by Republican Commission ... it was only by taking control, and letting these people see we meant what we said, that we succeeded in getting them to see the justice of our claim.'[98]

His rhetoric tapped into widespread working-class discontent. Day topped the poll with 6,836 votes in a stunning victory, defeating pro- and anti-Treaty Sinn Féiners as well as two candidates fielded by the commercial class.[99] Even the *Examiner* was impressed.[100] Nationally, Labour surpassed all expectations as it benefited from anti-Treatyite losses: non-Republican parties gained over 78% the vote. Labour won seventeen out of the eighteen seats it contested.[101] Day received messages of congratulations from all over Ireland, including from Sam Kyle and the Belfast Labour Party.[102] Day was at the peak of his influence. He was put forward for the Chairmanship,

Committee of Management, Cork District Mental Hospital, but refused as not having the time to devote to it.[103] Any celebrations were short-lived.

On 27 June, Free State troops shelled Dublin's Four Courts to dislodge occupying IRA units. The Civil War had begun. Much of Munster, including Cork, remained beyond the Provisional Government's reach. Republicans quickly cut off the city and established military rule. Trade unionists initially accommodated the new régime with some success. But the irreconcilable conflict between class politics and nationalism meant rapport soon broke down. The working class suffered terribly under the Republicans. Isolation caused the economy to drop into depression. Unemployment approached 8,000, over 30% of the male workforce, with many homeless. The Cork Reconstruction Committee tried to expediate the re-building of Patrick's Street but progress again moved at snail's pace.[104] Unemployment was so acute that a Cork Unemployed Central Committee was established with the aid of Day and ITGWU. On Monday 8 August, posters appeared advertising an unemployed meeting for the following Sunday which Day helped organise. However, once again events moved too quickly. That same Monday, National Army troops sailed into Cork Harbour to oust the Anti-Treatyites. The ensuing Battle for Cork was a decisive victory for the Free State.[105]

Given the economic context, it is unsurprising that Labour lost faith in the 'Cork Republic' so quickly. On 17 July, Day helped to initiate the local peace movement at a special conference at the Custom House attended by public and commercial bodies. Here, Day rubbed shoulders with the business elite and established the People's Rights Association, which demanded an end to hostilities and a reconvening of the Dáil.[106] In August, he joined with employers again to defeat the anti-Treatyites. With Free State blessing, the employers spearheaded the establishment of an unarmed municipal police force, the Cork Civic Patrol. Advertisements called for recruits with good education only, a move designed to exclude working men. The force was overseen by the Cork Civic Committee, which included Day, and operated until November.[107]

Day in the Dáil, 1922-1923

By then, Day was, like his fellow Labour TDs, trying to be an effectual opposition in the Dáil to the increasingly reactionary Government. By September 1922, the IRA was largely defeated, forcing it to resort to a guerrilla campaign until the Civil War's conclusion in May 1923. The Government was becoming aggressively authoritarian in its efforts to defeat them. From November 1922, Military Courts with the power to inflict the death penalty for subversive activity were active.[108] Such repression became an attack on workers. From September to October, Government successfully broke a strike provoked by its decision to cut the bonus given to postal workers. With its perception of the strike skewed by Civil War, ministers were ruthless. Scabs were utilised, pickets were broken up, strikers harassed, and workers victimised.[109] In the Dáil, Day raised the case of Cork telegraphic workers suspended for alleged co-operation with Anti-Treatyites, as well as others arrested for 'subversive' activity.[110] In August 1923, after four months of campaigning, he successfully secured the release of two ITGWU Bishopstown men sentenced to three years' penal servitude for a bomb-related offence during a labour dispute.[111]

Day increasingly focussed his energies on agitating in the Dáil. He campaigned indefatigably for greater State intervention in the economy with some significant success given Government conservatism. In late 1922, £332,000 was granted for relief work to reduce unemployment. Though welcome, it fell far short of what was needed. Day pushed for additional grants but Government refused to budge.[112] He fought for State contracts to be awarded to Cork companies like printing firms and Hauwbowline Dockyard. His efforts were frustrated by a Government becoming more free-market fundamentalist.[113] In early 1923, Day obtained a £15,000 Government contract to produce 20,000 pairs of army leggings in Cork.[114] Reconstruction remained his abiding parliamentary concern and he worked tirelessly to bring it about.[115] He urged Government to compel firms who had been financially compensated to start re-building Cork immediately as they persistently refused to do so. Government refused.[116] He spoke in favour of tariffs for industries struggling against cheaper imports.[117] His formidable ability earned him a grudging respect from those who had previously attacked him – like the *Examiner*:

> 'It will be conceded by all classes that Mr. Robert Day, TD, has shown a very marked interest in the industrial welfare of the city ... his constant attending to his parliamentary duties prove that he is admirably performing duties which the citizens of Cork elected him to fulfil.'[118]

But Parliamentary effort could do little to protect Cork's working class against what was coming. By springtime 1923, with the IRA's campaign all but defeated, stability was restored. Irish employers breathed a collective sigh of relief. Government could finally effectively police matters and guarantee to protect employer property. Thus, the Cork Employers' Federation announced their long-awaited, all-out assault against wages and conditions. Employers across the Free State sought massive wage cuts, provoking intense class conflict that became physically violent at times.[119] The crisis climaxed that autumn. Cork was crippled by a general lockout from August to October, the most all-encompassing labour dispute since the 1913 Dublin Lockout. The ITGWU was at the heart of the struggle. However, though still Cork Secretary, Day was largely absent from the dispute and had no role in bringing it to an end.[120]

Amidst the chaos, Day and the Labour Party prepared for the General Election held on 27 August. Labour nominated Day, William Kenneally and Richard Anthony (Typographical Association), going into the election with unprecedented confidence that workers' discontent with Government would translate into seats.[121] This enthusiasm was seriously misguided. The election was a disaster for Labour. It lost all but one seat. In Cork, four of the five seats were taken by conservatives. Day lost his seat and Kenneally his deposit. Labour totalled only 5,300 votes in Cork. Some blamed Labour's terrible performance on the industrial disputes, but the reality was more complex. Workers may have abandoned Day because he had distanced himself from industrial struggle. But Civil War had ended only four months before and workers voted along Civil War lines. Class politics was swamped by the National Question. Furthermore, Labour's 1922 success had been artificially high, inflated by the anti-Republican protest vote it received.[122]

Bob Day – Resignation & Demise

Deflated by defeat, Day retreated from civic life. His influence over the Corporation had diminished since February 1922 when he was voted off the Law & Finance and Public Works Committees having, as he put it himself, 'united again, against Labour'. He did, however, retain his place on the Tolls & Markets Committee. In 1923, he was nominated to the Public Health, Water and Working-Class Dwellings Committees.[123] But this was the year when his rheumatoid arthritis became serious, causing him to frequently miss Corporation meetings. By then, he worked as a ledger clerk in the Corporation's Accounts Department. Illness forced his resignation from the Corporation and the Mental Hospital Board in June 1924, a sad end to a colourful tenure.[124] In August, Day was a Cork Branch delegate to the ITGWU Annual Conference, his last known public involvement with the union.[125] On 31 October, Cork Corporation was formally dissolved by the Minister for Local Government & Public Health under the Local Government (Temporary Provisions) Act 1923. From 11 November, the city was administrated by Philip Monahan, Government-appointed Commissioner, who immediately cut the wages that Day had done so much to implement and protect. Monahan's appointment was warmly welcomed by the city's bourgeoisie.[126] Day's last position of influence was on the Cork Workers' and Hospitals' Committee which he held until 1924.[127] By 1925, he had left the ITGWU and was confined to bed as an invalid. On 1 May 1949, after twenty-five years of illness and obscurity, he died at his Nicholas Street home. He was survived by his widow C. Day and their sons John, Robert, James, Leslie and Richard, and daughters Elizabeth and T. Lynch. Tributes came from several sectors of Cork society and his funeral was attended by many prominent public officials and trade unionists. He is buried at Rathcooney cemetery.[128]

Robert Day's rise and demise reflects that of his union, his party and the labour movement to which he devoted so much of his life. Between 1916-1923, the zeitgeist in Ireland travelled from revolutionary upheaval to a conservative consensus that included the Irish left. Across Europe, the First World War had destabilised or obliterated conservative politics, leading to national and proletarian uprisings across the continent. The milieu allowed Day to display his considerable intellect and ability on a local and national scale. He blossomed in the flush of domestic and international radicalism of 1919-1921, making international headlines in September 1921 for his Bolshevik sympathies. But the working-class politics he championed was the chief casualty of the Treaty settlement and capitalist counterattack of 1921-1923. By 1924, the Irish revolution had swung firmly to the right, heralding the return of a conservative consensus that would dominate the Irish State for decades. By then, Day, his politics and his union had all been marginalised.

Notes

1   www.census.nationalarchives.ie/reels/nai000512544/ [retrieved 29 January 2018]. In Charles Callan & Barry Desmond, 'Robert Day (1879-1949)', *Irish Labour Lives: A Biographical Dictionary of Irish Labour Party Deputies, Senators, MPs and MEPs*, (Watchword, Dublin, 2010), pp. 72, 271, notes that some contended that he was born in 1879 either in Cork City or Kilgarvan, County Kerry.

2   The children were Mary, 4; Hannah, 3; and Ellen, 2. Richard's sister-in-law Ellen Bradley, 13, was also resident, *www.census.nationalarchives.ie/reels/nai001855915/* [retrieved 29 January 2018].

3   *Report of an Enquiry by the Board of Trade into Working-class Rents & Retail Prices, Together With the Rates of Wages in Certain Occupations in Industrial Towns of the United Kingdom in 1912*, 1913, Cd. 6955, LXVI, United Kingdom Parliamentary Papers, p. 288

4   Andy Bielenberg, *Cork's Industrial Revolution, 1780-1880: Development or Decline?*, (Cork University Press, Cork, 1991), p. 116; Cormac Ó Gráda, *A New Economic History, 1780-1939*, (Clarendon Press, Oxford, 1995), pp. 306-313.

5   Paddy McCarthy, *Cork During the Years of the Great War, 1914-1918: Years that Shaped the Future*, (Paddy McCarthy, Cork, 2009), p. 35.

6   J.C. Saunders, *Annual Report of the Medical Officer of Health for 1935*, (Guy & Co. Ltd, Cork, 1936).

7   Colman O'Mahony, *In the Shadows: Life in Cork, 1750-1930*, (Tower Books, Cork, 1997), p. 316.

8   Maura Cronin, 'Place, Class and Politics' in J.S. Crowley, R.J.N. Devoy, D. Linehan and P. O'Flanagan (eds.) *Atlas of Cork City*, (Cork University Press, Cork, 2005), p. 208.

9   Maura Cronin, *Country, Class or Craft?: The Politicisation of the Skilled Artisan in Nineteenth-Century Cork*, (Cork University Press, Cork, 1994), p. 192.

10 Emmet O'Connor, 'Labour and Politics, 1830-1945: Colonisation and Mental Colonisation', in Fintan Lane & Donal Ó Drisceoil (eds.), *Politics and the Irish Working Class, 1830-1945*, (Palgrave Macmillan, Basingstoke, 2005), p. 31.

11 Maura Cronin, 'Work and workers in Cork City and County, 1800-1900' in Patrick O'Flanagan & Cornelius G. Buttimer (eds.), *Cork: History and Society: Interdisciplinary Essays on the History of an Irish County*, (Geography Publications, Dublin, 1993), p. 745.

12 The Taff Vale case was the result of a law suit taken against the ASRS by the Taff Vale Railway Company in South Wales. Its judgment meant that trade unions were liable for the loss of profits to employers that were caused by strikes. It had a devastating impact on labour militancy across the UK.

13 Kennedy has cited Government suspension of the Gold Standard, huge deficit spending and the belated implementation of price control as the reasons for wartime inflation, see Liam Kennedy, 'The Cost of Living in Ireland, 1698-1998' in David Dickson & Cormac Ó Gráda (eds.), *Refiguring Ireland: Essays in Honour of L.M. Cullen*, (Lilliput Press, Dublin, 2003), p. 262. See also A.L. Bowley, *Prices and Wages in United Kingdom, 1914-1920*, (Oxford University Press, Oxford. 1921), pp. 35-36.

14 B.R. Mitchell, *British Historical Statistics*, (Cambridge University Press, Cambridge, 1988), p. 739.

15 Marcel van der Linden, 'The Rise and Fall of Revolutionary Syndicalism (1890-1940)' in Marcel van der Linden, *Transnational Labour History: Explorations*, (Ashgate Publishing, Aldershot, 2003), p. 49.

16 *ibid*, pp. 25-27; Emmet O'Connor, *Syndicalism in Ireland, 1917-23*, (Cork University Press, Cork, 1988) pp. 1-18

17 Ralph Darlington, *Radical Unionism: The Rise and Fall of Revolutionary Syndicalism*, (Haymarket Books, Chicago, 2008), pp. 21, 74-77.

18 Francis Devine, *Organising History: A Centenary of SIPTU, 1909-2009*, (Gill & Macmillan, Dublin, 2009), p. 93.

19 O'Connor, *Syndicalism, op. cit.*, pp. 87-88.

20 Kevin O'Brien, *Cork Corporation and Republican Administration 1920-1921*, (MA: UCC, 2013), p. 12.

21 *Cork Examiner*, 6, 12, 22 January 1920; Conor McCabe, 'The Irish Labour Party and the 1920 Local Elections', *Saothar 34*, 2010, pp. 7, 12-13, 16-17; Diarmaid Ferriter, *A Nation and Not a Rabble: The Irish Revolution, 1913-1923*, (Profile Books, London, 2015), p. 218

22 Liam de Róiste diaries, 18 January 1920, U271/A/26, CCCA.

23 Arthur Mitchell, *Labour in Irish Politics, 1890-1930: The Irish Labour Movement in an Age of Revolution*, (Irish University Press, Dublin, 1974), pp. 126-127.

24 O'Brien, 'Cork Corporation', *op. cit.*, p. 18.

25 *Cork Examiner*, 10 March 1920.

26 The six ITGWU councillors were Day, William Kennally, Thomas Daly, Patrick Higgins, James Allen and Tadgh Barry.

27 *Cork Examiner*, 4 March, 21 April, 10, 19, 28 May 1920. Day also served on the toothless and ineffectual Cork Profiteering Committee, established under the Profiteering Act 1919 to monitor local prices. See *Cork Examiner*, 3 March, 20 October 1920.

28 *Cork Examiner*, 10 April, 15 May 1920. The original motion, which was moved by Tadgh Barry, proposed that all vacancies other than those of clerks and tradesmen be filled by ITGWU members. It was amended to include all trade unionists after objection from Barry's fellow Labour-republican and NUR man John Good. Alderman Beamish dissented. Barry had previously put forward the motion in April.

29 *Cork Examiner*, 22 March 1920.

30 Edward Lahiff, *Industry and Labour in Cork, 1890-1921*, (MA: UCC, 1988), p. 208.

31 O'Brien, 'Cork Corporation', *op. cit.*, pp. 37-40.

32 *Cork Examiner*, 2 June, 14 July 1920.

33 *Cork Examiner*, 26 October 1920

34 John Borgonovo, *Spies, Informers, and the 'Anti-Sinn Féin Society': The Intelligence War in Cork City, 1920-1921*, (Irish Academic Press, Dublin, 2007), pp. 37-38; Gerry White & Brendan O'Shea, *The Burning of Cork*, (Mercier Press, Cork, 2006).

35 O'Brien, 'Cork Corporation and Republican Administration', pp. 60-61; *CE*, 13, 14 Dec. 1920.

36 Lahiff, 'Industry and Labour', *op. cit.*, p. 211.

37 *Cork Examiner*, 2, 18 February, 6, 20 April, 4, 18 May, 2 June 1921

38 *ibid*, 25 June 1921.

39 *Cork Examiner*, 1 February, 6, 18 June, 16 July, 30 August, 26, 27, 30 September, 18 October 1921.

40 *Cork Examiner*, 7, 9 April 1921.

41 *Cork Examiner*, 11 March 1921.

42 John Borgonovo, *The Dynamics of War & Revolution: Cork City, 1916-1918*, (Cork University Press, 2013), p. 1.

43 Cork Corporation Minutes, 9, 14 March, 9 April 1920, CP/CO/M/13, CCCA; D.R. O'Connor Lysaght, 'September 1921, Month of Soviets', *The Plough*, no. 1 (1972). The Commission was comprised of six representatives from the Corporation; six from Cork Employers' Federation; six from CTC, with three of them coming from the ITGWU; and two from the Cork Industrial Development Association.

44 *Watchword of Labour*, 2 October 1920.

45 Cork Harbour Board minutes, 16 February 1921, CCCA; *Freeman's Journal*, 3 September 1921.

46   *Cork Examiner*, 31 January, 10 February 1920; ITGWU Cork branch minutes, 3 April. 1921, TU-IT, CCCA; Devine, *Organising History, op. cit.*, p. 119.

47   CHB minutes, 8 June, 20 July, 10, 17, 24 August 1921, PC/1/51, CCCA; ITGWU Cork branch minutes, 30 June 1921, TU-IT, CCCA; *CE*, 26 August1921.

48   Liam Beecher, 'The Cork Harbour strike of 1921, part I', *Liberty*, September 1976.

49   *Cork Examiner*, 1 September 1921.

50   Cork Harbour Commission minutes, 31 August 1921, PC/001/053, CCCA.

51   *Freeman's Journal*, 3 September 1921; *Cork Examiner*, 3, 5 September 1921; *Cork Constitution*, 5 September 1921.

52   *Cork Examiner*, 5 September 1921.

53   Liam Beecher, 'The Cork Harbour strike of 1921, part II', *Liberty*, October 1976.

54   *Cork Examiner*, 3 September 1921; O'Connor-Lysaght, 'September 1921'.

55   CHB minutes, 5 September 1921, PC/1/51, CCCA; *Cork Examiner*, 6 September1921; *Freeman's Journal*, 6 September 1921.

56   *Cork Examiner* 6 September 1921.

57   CHB minutes, 5 September 1921, PC/1/51, CCCA.

58   *ibid; Cork Constitution*, 6 September 1921.

59   Beecher, 'Part II', *op. cit.; Cork Constitution*, 7 Sept. 1921; *CE*, 7 Sept. 1921.

60   O'Connor Lysaght, 'September 1921, Month of Soviets'; Conor Kostick, *Revolution in Ireland: Popular Militancy, 1917-1923*, (Cork University Press, Cork, 2009), p. 176.

61   *Cork Examiner*, 7 September 1921.

62   William Keneally, 'Rebel Song, part II', *Irish Democrat*, Nov. 1956.

63   *ibid*; de Róiste diaries, 6 Sept. 1921, U271/A/39, CCCA.

64   Kostick, *Revolution in Ireland, op. cit.*, p. 176., *Cork Examiner*, 7 September 1921.

65   *Cork Examiner.*, 7, 8 September 1921.

66   *Cork Examiner* 12 September 1921; O'Connor-Lysaght, 'September 1921, Month of Soviets'.

67   CHB minutes, 14 September 1921, PC/1/51, CCCA; Cork Corporation minutes, 14 September 1921, CP/CO/M/14, CCCA; *CE*, 16 September 1921.

68   Cork Corporation minutes, 14 September, 12 October, 9 November 1921, 11 January 1922, CP/CO/M/14, CCCA; CHB, 7, 14 December 1921, PC/1/51, CCCA.

69   O'Connor-Lysaght, *Class Struggle During the Irish War of Independence and Civil War, 1916-1924*, (MA, UCD, 1982), p. 138.

70   In the 1920 local elections CTC was not part of the Sinn Féin-ITGWU pact and fielded twelve candidates in five districts. Three of these candidates were successful. Thirty Sinn Féin-ITGWU candidates were elected in Cork. See McCabe, 'The Irish Labour Party', *op. cit.*, pp. 12, 17.

71   Edward Norman, *A History of Modern Ireland*, (Fletcher & Son, London, 1971), p. 269; Joost Augusteijn, *From Public Defiance to Guerrilla Warfare: The Experience of Ordinary Volunteers in the Irish War of Independence, 1916-1921*, (Irish Academic Press, Dublin, 1996), p. 175; Tom Garvin, *The Evolution of Irish Nationalist Politics*, (Gill & Macmillan, Dublin, 1981), pp. 123-125; F.S.L. Lyons, *Ireland Since the Famine*, (Weidenfeld & Nicolson, London, 1971), p. 403.

72   Peter Hart, *The IRA and its Enemies: Violence and Community in Cork, 1916-1923*, (Clarendon Press, Oxford, 1998), pp. 155-157.

73   *ibid*, p. 157.

74   *New York Times*, 7 September 1921.

75   ITGWU Cork branch minutes, 26 September 1921, TU-IT, CCCA; Beecher, 'Part I', *op. cit.*.

76   William Keneally, 'Rebel Song, part II', *Irish Democrat*, November 1956; Liam Beecher, 'The ITGWU in Cork', *Liberty*, June 1977; 'Irish Volunteers, Cork Corps, Membership 1913-1914, (Alphabetical List)', *Corkarchives.ie, http://www.corkarchives.ie/media/Irish%20Volunteers%20Cork%20List-by%20name.pdf* (retrieved, 15 Jan. 2019).

77   This is according to an obituary published in the *Irish Press*, 2 May 1949. The Republican Courts were formally established by Dáil decree in July 1920, having been operational since June 1919. Their chief goal was to undermine the authority and operation of the British judicial system in Ireland. Republicans saw class conflict as a threat to the pan-

class unity on which the national struggle was based. Thus, the courts regularly arbitrated industrial disputes. See Michael Laffan, *The Resurrection of Ireland: The Sinn Féin Party, 1916-1923,* (Cambridge: Cambridge University Press, 1999), pp. 252-259; Charles Desmond Greaves, *The Irish Transport and General Workers' Union: The Formative Years, 1909-23,* (Gill & Macmillan, Dublin, 1982), p. 285; and Dorothy Macardle, *The Irish Republic: a documented chronicle of the Anglo-Irish conflict and the partitioning of Ireland, with a detailed account of the period 1916-1923,* (Victor Gallancz, London, 1937), pp. 347-351.

78 De Róste Diaries, 6 September, U271/A/39, CCCA.
79 *Cork Constitution,* 8, 10 September 1921.
80 *Cork Constitution,* 26 November 1921.
81 *Irish Times,* 7 September1921.
82 *Cork Examiner,* 13, 16 September 1921; *Irish Independent,* 7 Sept. 1921.
83 Michael Laffan, "Labour must wait': Ireland's conservative revolution' in P.J. Corish (ed.), *Radicals, Rebels and Establishments,* (Appletree Press, Belfast, 1985), p. 210; O'Connor Lysaght, 'September 1921, Month of Soviets'.
84 Cited in O'Connor, *Syndicalism, op. cit.,* pp. 72-3.
85 *Cork Examiner,* 6, 7, 15 October 1921.
86 *Cork Examiner,* 16-30 November 1921, 25 January 1922.
87 John Borgonovo, *The Battle for Cork, July-August 1922,* (Mercier Press, Cork, 2011), pp. 26, 30.
88 On 8 December 1921, Cathal O'Shannon announced his support for the Treaty at a meeting at Charleville. On 1 January 1922, the Bandon ITGWU branch unanimously voted to support the treaty. See *Cork Examiner,* 14 December 1921, 2 January 1922.
89 Borgonovo, *The Battle for Cork, op. cit.,* pp. 24-26.
90 John M. Regan, *The Irish Counter-Revolution, 1921-1936: Treatyite Politics & Settlement in Independent Ireland,* (Gill & Macmillan, Dublin,1999), pp. 82-84; Tom Garvin, 'The Anatomy of a Nationalist Revolution: Ireland, 1858-1928', *Comparative Studies in Society & History,* vol. 28, no. 3, July 1986, pp. 484-491.
91 Specifically, the four occasions were the April 1918 strike against conscription; the strike against the Motor Permits Order from November 1919 to February 1920; the strike for the release of republican hunger strikers in April 1920; and the munitions embargo from May to December 1920. See Townshend, Charles, 'The Irish railway strike of 1920: Industrial action and civil resistance in the struggle for independence', *Irish Historical Studies,* vol. 21, 1978, pp. 265-282.
92 *Cork Examiner* 25 April 1922.
93 Niamh Purséil, *The Irish Labour Party, 1922-73,* (UCD Press, Dublin, 2007), p. 11.
94 *Cork Examiner,* 29 Apr., 2 May 1922.
95 *Cork Examiner,* 22, 30 May, 7 June 1922.
96 *Cork Examiner,* 3 June 1922.
97 *Cork Examiner,* 5 June 1922.
98 *Cork Examiner,* 14 June 1922.
99 Borgonovo, *The Battle for Cork, op. cit.,* pp. 43-44. The full result was Day, 6,836; J.J. Walsh (Coalition Treaty), 5,731; de Roiste (CT), 5,657; and Mary MacSwiney (Coalition Republic), 4,016. Not elected: R.H. Beamish (Ind), 3,485; Francis J. Daly (Ind), 2,826; Dónal O'Callaghan (CR), 1,796, Brian M. Walker, *Parliamentary Election Results in Ireland, 1918-1992,* (RIA/IIS, Queen's University Belfast; Dublin/Belfast, 1992), p. 104.
100 Purséil, *Irish Labour Party op. cit; Cork Examiner,* 19 June 1922.
101 Purséil, *Irish Labour Party, op. cit.,* , p. 11.
102 *Cork Examiner,* 19-23 June 1922. Kyle, 1884-1962, a Belfast Protestant, was active in the Independent Labour Party and Organiser, (British) Workers' Union. In 1918, he unsuccessfully contested Belfast Shankill for the Belfast Labour Representation Committee but was elected to Belfast City Council, 1920. He represented Belfast North at Stormont for the NILP, 1925-1929, and was unsuccessful in Belfast Oldpark, 192i. He was Irish Secretary, Amalgamated TGWU, 1932-1949-; President, ITUC, 1943 and 1950; and Irish Labour Party in Seanad Éireann, 1943-1948.
103 *Cork Examiner,* 20 June 1922.

104 Borgonovo, *Battle for Cork*, p. 56; *Cork Examine*, 12, 15 June, 1, 5, 8, 12, 19, 21, 26, 29 July 1922.
105 Borgonovo, *Battle for Cork*, p. 60; *Cork Examiner*, 15 August 1922.
106 Borgonovo, *Battle for Cork*, pp. 57-59; *Cork Examiner*, 13-18, 24, 25 July 1922; Bill Kissane, *The Politics of the Irish Civil War*, (Oxford University Press, Oxford, 2005), p. 132. See *Cork Examiner*, 18 July 1922 for the full texts of the resolutions passed on 17 July.
107 *Cork Examiner*, 14-24 August, 1, 6, 7, 12, 14, 15, 19, 20, 25, 26 September, 2, 7, 10, 12, 28 October, 2, 9 November 1922, 6 February 1923; Borgonovo, *The Battle for Cork, op. cit.*, pp. 125-126. The Cork Civic Patrol was the successor of another employer-controlled, ad-hoc police force established the previous April. See *Cork Examiner*, 22 April 1922; Cork Incorporated Chamber of Commerce and Shipping, *Annual Report*, 1922, MP 507, Boole Library, UCC; Cork Incorporated Chamber of Commerce and Shipping minutes, 28 Apr. 1922, B619/B/1/5, CCCA; 'City of Cork Police Force', TSCH/1/S1705, Department of An Taoiseach records, National Archives of Ireland.
108 Eunan O'Halpin, *Defending Ireland: The Irish State and its Enemies since 1922*, (Oxford University Press, Oxford, 1999), pp. 30-31.
109 For a comprehensive account of the strike, see Cathal Brennan, 'The Postal Strike of 1922', *The Irish Story*, (retrieved 23 January 2019); Francis Devine, *Communicating the Union: A History of the Communications Workers' Union*, (CWU, Dublin, 2015), pp.97-128; Francis Devine, *Connecting Communities: A Pictorial History of the Communications Workers' Union*, (CWU, Dublin,2013), pp.23-26.
110 Robert Day, 'Cork Telegraphic Staff', 14 September 1922, Dáil Éireann Debates, vol. 1, no. 5; Robert Day, 'Cobh Junction Arrest', Dáil Éireann Debates, 3rd Dáil, vol. 1, no. 28; Robert Day, 'Detention of William Cahill', Dáil Éireann Debates, 27 February 1923, 3rd Dáil, vol. 2, no. 33
111 Robert Day, 'Workers' Arrest', 20 April 1923, Dáil Éireann Debates, 3rd Dáil, vol. 3, no. 6; Robert Day, 'Prisoners and their Sentence', 4 May 1923, Dáil Éireann Debates, 3rd Dáil, vol. 3, vo. 10; *Cork Examiner*, 14 Aug. 1923.
112 *Cork Examiner*, 13 October, 23 December 1922, 3, 6, 9, 11, 13, 15, 17 Jan. 1923.
113 Robert Day, 'Printing Trade in Cork', 29 November 1929, Dáil Éireann Debates, 3rd Dáil, vol. 1, no. 32; Robert Day, 'Committee on Finance – Haulbowline Dockyard', 26 July 1923, 3rd Dáil, vol. 4, no. 18.
114 *Cork Examiner*, 3, 6, 23 March, 28 April 1923.
115 In March, his efforts helped to ensure that the Department of Finance resolved a delay in payment for reconstruction work. In April, he extracted from the government that over £50,000 had been paid to firms and people in Cork to compensate their destroyed property. See *Cork Examiner*, 9 March, 19 April 1923; and Robert Day, 'Pre-Truce Burnings and Destruction', 9 February 1923, Dáil Éireann Debates, 3rd Dáil, vol. 2, no. 28.
116 Robert Day, 'Rebuilding of Cork', 25 October 1922, Dáil Éireann Debates, 3rd Dáil, vol. 1, no. 26.
117 Robert Day, 'Irish Flour Mills (Importation of Foreign Flour)', Dáil Éireann Debates, 3rd Dáil, 19 September 1922, no. 1, vol. 7; Robert Day, 'Importation of Cardboard Boxes, 17 November 1922, Dáil Éireann Debates, 3rd Dáil, vol. 1, no. 30.
118 *Cork Examiner*, 28 April 1923.
119 For example, a 1923 strike of farm labourers against a wage cut became violent. See Emmet O'Connor, 'Agrarian unrest and the labour movement in County Waterford, 1917-1923', *Saothar 6*, 1980, pp. 40-58. See also Foster, *The Irish Civil War & Society, op. cit.*, pp. 138-141. For the 1923 counterattack in a national context, see Devine, *Organising History, op. cit.*, pp. 130-142.
120 *Cork Examiner*, 1 August-10 November 1923.
121 Regan, *The Irish Counter-Revolution, op. cit*, p. 238; de Róiste diaries, 10 June 1923, U271/A/49, CCCA.
122 Mitchell, *Labour in Irish Politic, op. cit.*, pp. 186-191; Puirséil, *Irish Labour Party, op. cit*, pp.16-18; O'Connor, Big *James Larkin: Hero or Wrecker?* (UCD Press, Dublin, 2015) p. 76. See press commentary on Labour's electoral performance, see *Manchester Guardian*, 1 September 1923; and *Irish Times*, 31 August 1923. The *Irish Times* alleged that an incident at a funeral – where drivers of hearses were ordered off their cars – contributed to the

Labour Party's poor result in Cork. See *CE*, 20 Aug. 1923. Those elected were J.J. Walsh (Cumann na Gaedheal), 17,151 [Postmaster General during the infamous Postal Strike of 1922]; Mary MacSwiney (Republican), 6,109; R.H. Beamish (Progressive Association), 5,822; Alfred O'Rahilly (CnG), 2,506; and Andrew O'Shaughnessy (PA), 766. Not elected were Richard Anthony (Labour), 2,492; Con Lacey (Republican), 1,870; Timothy Corcoran (Famers' Union), 1,616; Day (Lab), 1,431; William Kenneally (Lab), 1,358; Sir John Harley Scott (Ind), 786; Frederick Murray (Republican), 461; and Capt Jeremiah Collins (Ind), 243, Walker, *op. cit.*, p. 109.

123 *Cork Examiner,* 27 February 1922, 21 February 1923.
124 *Cork Examiner*, 31 October 1923, 16 June; Callan & Desmond, 'Robert Day', *op. cit.*
125 ITGWU *Report of Special Delegate Conference,* Connolly Hall, Cork, 8-9 August 1924, p. 1.
126 For the dissolution of Cork Corporation, see Aodh Quinlivan, *Dissolved: The remarkable story of how Cork lost its Corporation in 1924,* (Cork City Library, 2017).
127 *Cork Examiner* 19 June, 16 July 1924.
128 *Cork Examiner,* 2, 3, 4, 7 May 1949; *Irish Press,* 2 May 1949. One of his sons worked in the Process Engraving Department of the *Irish Press* while another (Richard) worked at the Cork GPO.

MIKE MECHAM

'For Quality of Life and Brotherhood': John W. Boyle, 1914-1998

'In all you say or do the wiser part
is but your impulse working in the blood,
for quality of life and brotherhood.'[1]

These lines come from a short poem written by the great Ulster poet John Hewitt (1907-1987), another notable Irish 'Left life', about the influence of his father on the development of his social consciousness. They might also apply to John W. Boyle (1914-1998) who inspired countless students and was 'seldom to be seen without a circle of enthusiastic students, seeking his opinion and advice or asking questions merely to savour the erudition of the reply'.[2] But the association with Hewitt goes further. With only a small age difference, both men were near contemporaries in Belfast, shared similar democratic socialist convictions and suffered personally in a society that would not tolerate an 'anti-Union, Fenian Protestant',[3] or in Hewitt's case a 'communist and pro-Catholic'.[4] Such denigration was well established in Belfast and in the 1920s both would have been lumped together with other 'rotten Prods' and victimised as Fenian fellow-travellers.[5] Both eventually left Ireland because of the discrimination they encountered, particularly in their careers: Boyle went to Canada in 1966, where he would live out his life returning to Ireland only for periodic visits; and Hewitt to Coventry, England, in 1957, though he returned to live in Belfast in 1972 after his retirement. As McCormack observes of Hewitt and which could equally apply to Boyle, 'he had an active social conscience. And that, in his own view, doomed him an outsider in his home town'.[6] While both men inevitably had their regrets in leaving

Ireland they each made a success of their new ventures. Nevertheless, despite their years in Canada the Boyles remained essentially Irish and 'very European'.[7] Similarly, Hewitt was always an Ulsterman, reflecting a sense of belonging in many of his poems. In 'An Ulsterman' he seeks to cling 'to the inflexions of my origin'; and his poem of return as the Troubles were intensifying, '1957-1972', calls on 'some translated poet' to reflect on '*this betraying, violent city/irremediably home*'.[8]

While both men might also have admired the work of W.B. Yeats, Boyle especially the drama, and appeared to be natural comrades, there is no record of them ever meeting. But it would have been surprising if their paths had not crossed. Each was involved in various ways with the Northern Ireland labour movement including the Northern Ireland Labour Party (NILP).[9] Moreover, when Boyle was teaching at Queen's University, Belfast, Hewitt was along the road at the Ulster Museum (formerly the Belfast Museum and Art Gallery) eventually becoming Deputy Director and Keeper of Art. Both men also had long marriages – to Elizabeth Boyle (1908-1995)[10] and Roberta Hewitt (1905-1975);[11] and both men suffered in the loss of those wives.[12] But as Boyle reflected, after more than fifty years with Elizabeth he had both a sense of great loss 'but also a sense of pride that I was able to share with her in all the splendid work that she did'.[13]

While this essay will focus on Boyle, and from time-to-time Hewitt will make his presence felt, any account of Boyle's life and social activism must recognise Elizabeth's essential place in it and how in many ways she was his inspiration, and more. As an academic, he recalls Elizabeth urging him on to his PhD.[14] In every respect, therefore, and like so many 'Left lives', the Boyles had shared and mutually supporting lives. This essay would therefore fall short if both their lives were not reflected in it. As Francis Devine rightly observed, simply to refer to Elizabeth as John W. Boyle's wife 'would be to offend her memory and to seriously misunderstand the integral and interdependent nature of their creative and supportive relationship'.[15] However, for many readers of this essay, Boyle will be known and remembered primarily for his principal work on the Irish labour movement in the nineteenth century.[16] It is central to his academic reputation and standing, although this essay aims to show that it was but one aspect of a fuller life. Many people, of course, would have known him as a teacher, supporter of the Irish Labour History Society (ILHS) and of various political and social causes. It is this full life that is the subject of the essay. However, the centrality of his principal research project must be addressed though principally in terms of its harmony with other aspects of his life. Like his relationship with Elizabeth they cannot be separated. A key question will be how relevant his major work remains for today's students and researchers. Finally, this essay, authored by someone who never met Boyle, relies on the testimony of friends, colleagues and family. Most importantly it is indebted to the generosity of his daughter, Elizabeth ('Liz') Boyle, who lovingly went through all of her father's private papers (hereinafter the *Boyle Papers*), sending key family and research documents over from Canada.[17] It is hoped, therefore, that in combination all of these aspects will provide an account of a notable life on the Left that graces this collection of 'Left lives.' It is also written with tinge of regret that Boyle was not here to question nor to challenge the questioner. As one of his friends and colleagues put it: he was 'a man of decided opinion as well as broad learning … [who] … derived great enjoyment in seeing wrongs set right through the thoughts he expressed …'[18] One wonders what he would have made of this essay?

'The Inflexions of My Origin': The Irish Years [9]

John Hewitt's great poem affirming his origins as an Ulsterman ends with a declaration that 'My heritage is not their violence'.[20] For John William ('J.W.') Boyle, who was born into a Dublin Protestant (Church of Ireland) working class family on Sunday 4 October 1914, conflict was indeed part of his heritage.[21] It was a world on the brink of violence and change, globally as well as in Ireland. Weeks earlier saw the outbreak of the First World War just after the British Parliament had enacted Irish Home Rule which was immediately suspended for the war's duration. On the day he was born large meetings were taking place in Ireland addressing the country's role in the conflict. One in Wexford by Irish Party Leader John Redmond and another in Belfast by his Parliamentary colleague Joe Devlin, the Home Rule MP for Belfast West.[22] The war, and Redmond's call for Irishmen to support it, divided nationalists; and the Unionist leaning *Belfast News-Letter* was still arguing the same day that Home Rule was still not a done deal for the whole of Ireland and could still be thwarted by determined Unionist and Conservative political forces.[23] It was in such a febrile atmosphere of suspicion that eighteen months later the Easter Rising took place in 1916. Although Boyle would have been oblivious to these developments, his family certainly would not have been. His father, Edmond Boyle, was working as a bottler in Dublin's Guinness factory which was one of the focal points in the 1916 Rising. The company was strongly supportive of the British Government, while having many Catholic workers who would have been in sympathy with the insurgents. Not only did Guinness donate £100,000 in 1913 to the Loyalist Ulster Volunteer Force (UVF), but during the 1916 Rising company trucks were converted into military vehicles and used against the insurgents.[24] On the other hand, Guinness Chief Medical Officer, Dr John Lumsden, founded the St John's Ambulance in Dublin which distinguished itself in 1916 by acting with considerable courage treating both insurgents and British soldiers during the conflict.[25]

Although Boyle's schooling opportunities were severely limited, like so many others from his class, during his primary school years Ireland was changing around him. With the end of the war in 1918, and a vastly increased franchise, Ireland saw the end of Redmond's Irish Home Rule Party and the growing domination of Sinn Féin. Ireland became largely independent, but partitioned, when he was eight; and, once again, the streets of Dublin rang with the sounds of conflict as civil war erupted across what became the new Saorstát Éireann [Irish Free State] in December 1922. But through the strength of his own intellect and a determination that would never leave him, Boyle eventually won a scholarship to Trinity College, Dublin, in 1935, though he still needed the support of his two sisters, Margaret and Frances. And it was these early life experiences that were to drive Boyle's social consciousness and a feminist perspective born out of the struggles of his sisters through sacrifices that were characteristic of so many women in Ireland.[26] The measure and depth of such sacrifices stayed with him for the rest of his life.[27]

But these formative years were also set within a political environment that James Connolly most feared with the partition of the island, a 'carnival of reaction both North and South' where socialism and conciliation were suspect, if not seen as offensive.[28] While denying any discrimination against the Catholic community, as Boyle entered Trinity College, the *Belfast News-Letter* was also proclaiming that the Government of Northern Ireland 'is a loyal Government ... and a Protestant Government in that its personnel reflect the religious standpoint of the majority'.[29] Delaney has also described the worsening environment that Protestants in the Irish Free State increasingly experienced during the 1930s and which led to a gradual decline in their numbers through migration until the 1990s, though a good deal of that would also have been economically driven.[30] As Boyle revealed in a letter in 1972, in 1937 he had voted against the new Irish Constitution 'because I regarded it as enforcing Catholic morality on all'.[31] This fear was given substance in 1957 with the economic boycott of Protestants in Fethard-on-Sea, County Wexford, over Catholic education for children of mixed families.[32] This would have offended Boyle's sectarian sensibilities, whose studies reflected his broader and more generous outlook, and in his internationalism. His degree was in Modern Languages and Economic and Political Science, and his intellectual abilities were fully realised when he graduated with First-Class Honours from Trinity in 1937. For this he was awarded the prestigious Gold Medal and Graduate Research Prize 'in recognition of his outstanding scholarship'.[33] The high quality of Boyle's research methods would continue and be fully expressed in his doctoral thesis also awarded by Trinity College in 1961 which will be discussed below. In the meantime, at the age of twenty-five, he was awarded an MA in Old French and an MLitt in Anglo-Norman Poetry in 1939.[34] A considerable achievement but yet another demonstration of his intellectual capacity and drive.

With the outbreak of the Second World War, Boyle moved from the relative safety of neutral Ireland into the war zone of Belfast where he began a long tenure as a Senior Assistant in the Department of English and History at the Royal Belfast Academical Institute (locally referred to as 'Inst'), where Hewitt had dropped out of as a pupil in 1920. From 1946 until 1955 he also became a part-time Lecturer in the Department of Economic and Social History at Queen's University, Belfast, where Hewitt had also received an MA, with a thesis on the Ulster poets, in 1951 while working in the Belfast Museum. As Devine observes:

> 'Extra-mural work was particularly gratifying for Boyle, as he met worker-students who, like himself in the 1930s, were struggling to access third-level education, realise their potential and simply enjoy the thrill of learning and self-exploration that he so valued.'[35]

Boyle would take the 'thrill of learning' further when he embarked on the research that would not only lead to the award of a PhD by Trinity College, but would also establish him as one of the founding fathers of the modern Irish labour history movement.

But it was during the war years that he had the great good fortune to meet in 1941, and to marry in 1942, Elizabeth Morwood.[36] She was born in India to an Irish father and American mother.[37] Although Elizabeth left India when she was eight-years-old, the country left an indelible impression on her, most notably its poverty. For the rest of her life she would have an abiding commitment to Third World development and as an adult she would strongly argue for aid and debt relief.[38] After spending most of the war years with her mother in America, the whole family were finally reunited in Belfast in 1919 when her father retired. The family were to occupy Air Lawn, 4 Malone Park for over forty years and it was where John and Elizabeth first lived after they were married.[39] Elizabeth was now eleven-years-old and until the age of sixteen went to the renowned Victoria College for Girls, Belfast, which had been founded by the formidable Margaret Byers, a campaigner for women's education.[40] The school has always been renowned for its academic excellence and Elizabeth thrived. Then in 1926 she accepted a place at Girton Women's College, Cambridge. There she came under the influence of the controversial literary critic F.R. 'Frank' Leavis who testified to her 'lively intelligence'.[41] It was at Cambridge where her lifelong political leanings developed – she was 'always Left' she said. She became a member of the Labour Club and would later be active in the Independent Labour Party (ILP).[42] In 1933, John and Roberta Hewitt had also attended an ILP summer school in England. Meanwhile, Boyle had joined the Irish Labour Party through the newly formed Fabian Society.[43]

Elizabeth's instinctively open outlook took her off to America to study for an MA, returning first to Belfast and then on to London where she taught in London County Council institutions from 1934-1939.[44] She also acted as an instructor (general studies teacher) for ballet students at the Sadler's Wells Company. During the 1930s, Elizabeth had been an active campaigner for the Republican cause in Spain. She joined protests in London and persuaded her father to take in refugee Basque children. Her deep concern for the treatment of political prisoners also inspired her later involvement with Amnesty International in Canada. As Devine observes, behind

Elizabeth 'there was an informed concern born of avid reading, intellectual and political curiosity, but, above all else, a fundamental human interest'.[45] The coming together of John and Elizabeth in 1941 was therefore an ideal match in every sense. 'Our shared interests in politics was very important', Boyle later recalled.[46] They became members of the South Belfast NILP despite hearing 'a diatribe against the Communist Party' by NILP leader Harry Midgley.[47] They were intellectual equals, inclined to the political left with a passion for human rights and opponents of authoritarianism in all its guises; they were both internationalists with particular concerns for the Third World. As the Second World War continued they also joined the Ulster Union Club which brought together 'Protestants interested in Irish Culture and in favour of a united Ireland'.[48] As a result, both John and Elizabeth were separately raided by Royal Ulster Constabulary (RUC) Officers.[49] Such raids would not be the last as they were to find out in the early 1960s.

In the early 1960s, a number of initiatives challenging discrimination and inequality were already emerging in Northern Ireland. They were partly inspired by the Civil Rights Movement in the US and also by local social initiatives in British cities such as Glasgow. An early important example was the Campaign for Social Justice set up by Conn and Patricia McCluskey from Dungannon.[50] As concerned political activists, the Boyles would undoubtedly have been aware of these developments and supportive of them. Indeed, John Boyle had been elected onto the Executive Committee of the NILP and Elizabeth headed its Women's Council.[51] But as Devine records: 'frustration at the lack of progress within the NILP on the developing issue of civil rights led to the Boyle's resignation'.[52] In hindsight, this move may have been a prescient one. For some, the advent of the Northern Ireland civil rights movement confronted the NILP with what became a terminal difficulty. While it might have been sympathetic to the movement's demands, and had pushed for reforms before 1967 and the advent of the Northern Ireland Civil Rights Association (NICRA),[53] organisationally it was not up to leading street protest; nor the likelihood that it would alienate its working-class support base in Belfast by seeming to involve itself in protests from one side of a fragile community.[54] Yet, the NILP continued to attract a large vote although it would not last. From a peak of nearly 100,000 votes in the 1970 General Election it went into protracted electoral decline as the Northern Ireland 'Troubles' intensified.[55] By the 1980s its core support dispersed to an array of new liberal-left leaning parties, including the Social Democratic & Labour Party (SDLP).[56] By 1987 it was no longer a separate political party.

But away from the political arena, Boyle's reputation as a labour historian had been growing even as he began his doctoral research. In 1956, the *Belfast News-Letter* carried a report of a BBC broadcast on 28 December by John W. Boyle. He was speaking in a series entitled 'Ulster Since 1800'. After describing the poor living standards of the working class in the nineteenth century, particularly in the agricultural and linen industries, he argued that the great change since 1939 'had been the improvement in the pay of the general worker' which he attributed to the 'organising success of the general trade unions'.[57] Two years later he was delivering one of the prestigious Thomas Davis lectures (TDL) on Radio Éireann on rural labourers;[58] and in 1961 he helped to co-ordinate the series on Irish labour leaders, which included a lecture by him on Belfast labour leader William Walker, which he subsequently edited for publication.[59]

Nevertheless, the Boyles were increasingly being confronted with an array of pressures and barriers. But there was unimaginable pain for them in 1958 with the sudden death of their twelve-year-old son Conor. Joy came later in the year when on Christmas Eve they adopted a young girl from birth, their daughter Elizabeth Frances, who through her own political and social activism became a true Boyle of the finest lineage.[60] In 1965, Boyle was appointed as a Special Lecturer in the Department of Economic and Social History of Queen's University, but on a part-time basis. Academic advancement, however, appeared to be limited for someone of his political views and reputation. As Devine notes: 'John's involvement in the NILP saw various applications for promotion rejected ...'[61] They also suffered police searches of their home and threats to their personal security. Like so many of their Irish compatriots, both before and since, the Boyles escaped through emigration to Canada, and this will be discussed more fully below. In 1966, Boyle accepted a position as an Associate Professor in the Department of History, Mount Allison University, New Brunswick. It was a difficult decision but perhaps just as inevitable as Hewitt's departure for England nine years earlier in 1957.

On the Margins: Irish Labour History
As well as his family, his hopes and ambitions, Boyle was also accompanied to Canada by a masterly, but as yet unpublished, doctoral thesis. It would rest, however, in Trinity College, Dublin, for a further twenty years before being made available to a wider public by the Catholic University of America in 1988. It is surely of considerable regret that it did not appear earlier, especially as many of the key chapters vary little from the thesis. One can only imagine however that the move from Ireland to Canada, the need to set down both new roots and build a new career, were more than enough to cope with. But stepping back to 1955 we might also ask why Boyle chose Irish labour history to devote five years to when many considered the subject area marginal at best. It had always struggled to find its place in the story of twentieth century Ireland. At times it almost seemed that the working class did not exist; as if they had been 'locked out' of Irish history.[62] Were the few labour historians in the 1950s therefore participating in an act of liberation as it was later said of the journal *Saothar*:

'Rather than being 'trapped by class history ... *Saothar* has clearly been a force of liberation. Many 'hidden from history' have been revealed through its pages. Many 'denied by history' have been given access and encouragement through its pages.'[63]

Both Joe Lee and Emmet O'Connor have provided valuable reflections on the place of labour history in Ireland. In an essay on the founding of the ILHS in 1973, and then its journal *Saothar*, Lee notes that while there was clearly some labour history interest before then it was mostly biographically driven; the most important examples being C. Desmond Greaves on James Connolly (1961) and Emmet Larkin on Jim Larkin (1965).[64] 'But', he adds, 'there was little systematic study of the labour movement'.[65] Both Greaves and Larkin were published after Boyle had completed his thesis although he received help from Larkin.[66] Nevertheless, a decade or more after Boyle's research Donal Nevin was still arguing that Irish labour history remained grossly under-researched,[67] although Lee argued that this was also the case for other areas of Irish history.[68] What labour history there was, later argued O'Connor, was greatly influence by Connolly's writings and included: radical pamphleteering and people's histories; a handful of biographies and official trade union histories; and some general studies produced outside of Ireland.[69] It was notable that until the 1970s, with publications by Arthur Mitchell and Charles McCarthy,[70] the best general survey dated from 1925 and was written by the American Jesse Dunsmore Clarkson and published in the United States but not Ireland.[71] There had been no substantive book on labour by an Irish academic since O'Brien's history of Irish trade unions in 1921.[72] Boyle's work could therefore be portrayed as an important Irish link between the 1920s and 1970s.

But the marginalisation of labour and the working class in Irish history, and other subaltern groups such as women could also be included, did reflect 'an ingrained conservatism' within the 'historical establishment'.[73] Fintan Lane, for example, has highlighted the early hostility of eminent academic historians such as W.E.H. Lecky (1838-1903). He was hostile to contemporary socialist developments and 'acted to legitimise the State'. He defended both the status quo and political Unionism. Elsewhere 'the new ideas' were nationalist rather than socialist.[74] Nevertheless, Lee insisted that while there was not a 'pervasive animus' against labour history, or social and economic history within which labour studies were generally encompassed, few resources were made available. Not only was research across the discipline grossly underfunded but more broadly Irish history in a post-colonial country, where the struggle for independence continued to dominate the public mind, could be expected to focus 'on history as national history'.[75] Added to which the 'historical establishment' was proclaiming that their discipline had to be value free to retain its credibility and thus 'the identification of labour history with the Connolly school led it to be regarded as ideological and subversive'.[76]

So, what drew Boyle to a subject area that was not only marginalised but to some off bounds? One where resources and expertise were limited, and was viewed with suspicion by academia? Part of the answer could have been his chosen supervisor at Trinity College, Professor T.W. Moody, criticised by some as a revisionist.[77] Nevertheless, he led a more questioning approach to Irish history and what he, and others, perceived as its array of 'myths'.

He sought greater diversity in historical approaches and a broader agenda. Moody was the son of a poor Belfast family who would later take a PhD in London. He was an admirer of both Connolly and Larkin but particularly of Land Leaguer Michael Davitt.[78] From early experiences in Belfast and throughout his life, Moody, like Boyle, abhorred sectarianism of all kinds. It was also Moody who created the Thomas Davis Lecture series on RTÉ to which Boyle would contribute to as well as a organise.[79] Moody's 1954 lecture series on BBC Northern Ireland Home Service presented a political and economic survey of Ulster. A second series, a 'social survey', in 1957 included, amongst twenty-lectures, one by Boyle which was later published.[80]

Moody therefore offered a sympathetic and receptive environment for Boyle. Yet it might still be asked what the impulses were that drove him to Irish labour history in the first place? Were they political impulses? The answer may well lie in his inclusion in this volume of essays. Indeed, the reader might ask more generally what constitutes a 'Left life' and in what ways it manifests itself? One response might be that it involves a broadly socialist worldview, perhaps within the labour movement, and involves a determined search for greater equality and justice in society, primarily, but not exclusively, for the working or labouring classes. It would also embrace a conviction that the dissemination of knowledge through lifelong opportunities to education are key elements in the process, and a recognition that in writing history the lives of the working class must also be studied and elevated. Consequently, someone leading a left life could range from a trade union and political activist to teacher, or in combination. In terms of Irish labour history Devine and O'Connor suggest for example:

> 'Without making a necessary connection between labour historians and socialism, it is a fact that socialism has made positive contributions to our approach to history. The discipline draws some of its relevance from an ethical impulse to portray the lives of the 'ordinary people' and remind society of the conditions which trade unionism in particular was formed to eradicate.'[81]

To underline this, it is clear that the strength of Irish labour history today has been the result of a longstanding collaboration between academics and the labour movement. This is exemplified by the ILHS and particularly its journal *Saothar*.[82] Yet despite these developments O'Connor laments that although much research material has been undertaken it appears to have had 'limited impact on public history - the view of the past generated by museums, libraries, the media, local societies and so on - which remains inordinately engrossed in nationalism'.[83]

'Neither an Elegy Nor a Manifesto': The Boyle Thesis [84]

In his private papers covering the period when he was undertaking further research in preparation for the publication of his thesis, Boyle was fretting over events taking place in Ireland as The Troubles were taking hold. As he wrote in a letter in February 1972, 'I have been heart-sickened by recent events in N. Ireland'.[85] It was written just after the events of 'Bloody Sunday' in Derry (30 January 1972). Shortly after Boyle's letter was written, Hewitt published his powerful poem of The Troubles and historic violence in Ireland, 'Neither An Elegy Nor A Manifesto', in which he pleaded to the reader to 'bear in mind these dead' and dedicated it to 'the people of my province and the rest of Ireland'.[86] In October he returned to live for the rest of his life in Belfast while in December Loyalist bombs exploded in Dublin. When Boyle began his doctoral research in 1955, the Republic of Ireland was politically flat, despite the IRA launching its 'Border Campaign' in 1956, and it was also economically stagnant. Joe Lee characterised the decade 1945-1958 as the 'malaise', one of conservative resistance to change.[87] In 1951, the country's Finance Minister, Seán MacEntee, had described its financial position as 'difficult to the verge of desperation'.[88] By the time of the fortieth anniversary of the Easter Rising in 1956, an editorial in the *Irish Times* was stark: 'If the present trend disclosed continues unchecked ... Ireland will die - not in the remote unpredictable future, but quite soon'.[89] But in the 1960s, under the stewardship of Seán Lemass, Ireland experienced a 'new wave of industrialisation, a big growth in union membership' and greater harmony amongst the trade unions.[90] By 1972, it was described as experiencing 'extraordinarily rapid' growth, although a world recession would soon follow.[91] Even by 1955, trade union membership had already reached 46% of the workforce.[92]

In 1972 Boyle was finalising his thesis for publication. His move to Canada had made the task more difficult in a pre-internet age with costly travel although he did receive some funding from the Canadian Council for occasional visits.[93] He had therefore come to rely on Fred Carson from Belfast as a research assistant. Carson had already been helpful to Boyle during his doctoral research. He described Carson as someone 'who spent a lifetime in the engineering industry and was acquainted with leading members of labour and socialist organisations in Belfast ...'[94] The *Boyle Papers* contain a raft of correspondence between the two men as well as research notes prepared by Carson in Belfast. By the summer of 1969 Boyle indicated that he had completed his additional research and was finalising a manuscript for submission to Clarendon Press, Oxford.[95] He was hoping that Clarendon would publish it in two volumes, covering the period 1823-1923.[96] In the event the plan came to nothing and it was to be another sixteen years before it would see the light of day and then only in one volume, possibly the first of the originally planned two. Was it just pressure of work or the reluctance of Clarendon to publish two volumes, or events in Ireland in 1972? If he had published then would it had been an elegy for what seemed to be lost hopes in Ireland for the working class or a manifesto for the future? Like Hewitt's poem it seemed to be neither. But with the formation of the ILHS the following year there were grounds for optimism.

In many ways it was a missed opportunity that Boyle's thesis was not published in 1972 as it may well have been more influential and secured a more central place in the annals of Irish labour history. After all, that would have been before Mitchell (1974), McCarthy (1977) and Patterson (1981)[97] were published, and two decades before O'Connor's majestic and sweeping labour history of Ireland.[98] It might also have avoided one criticism in 1990 that it was an 'antique'.[99] A finished text was clearly close to submission in 1972 and when it did eventually appear in 1988 there were great similarities between thesis and book.[100] In essence, Boyle's work explores the development of the Irish labour movement from the repeal of the Combination Acts in 1824-1825, which severely restricted the ability of labour to organise, until just before Jim Larkin's arrival in Ireland in 1907. It also provides a valuable summary of the historical antecedents from the eighteenth century. It was essentially an institutional and urban study concentrating on Dublin and Belfast. Due in large part to the paucity of sources available to him, Boyle's study covered little of the living standards or the social and cultural experiences of the working class. Indeed, in a *Saothar* editorial in 2000, Lane and O'Connor were still asking where the writing was on the everyday lives of the workers.[101] Boyle's study of the development of the Dublin United Trades Council was, however, ground breaking as little had been previously published.[102] Similarly, the two chapters devoted to the Belfast labour movement and its influential trades council remain essential reading.[103] In fact, for Boyle, the establishment of trades councils more widely in Ireland was an important development creating fora for expressing and pressing trade grievances.[104] But as Cronin notes: 'Professor Boyle's study shows the Belfast and Dublin labour experiences as both similar and diverse' with their different approaches 'shaped by their contrasting political backgrounds'.[105] Of particular concern to Boyle was the intense social conservatism of the labour movements in both cities.

However, of considerable importance are Boyle's reflections on the relationship between the British and Irish labour movements, the role of the British unions and the attempt, essentially by the Belfast labour movement under the leadership of William Walker, to incorporate the Irish trade unions into the British Labour Representation Committee (later re-named the Labour Party). It was at the suggestion of the leading British labour historian Henry Pelling that Boyle traced the early growth of British general unions in Ireland.[106] This was seen by some as a particularly valuable aspect of Boyle's study and, as one reviewer noted, his 'treatment of the New Unionism in Ireland from the late 1890s is unquestionably the best treatment of the subject to be found anywhere'.[107] Furthermore, another useful addition in the book was Boyle's examination of the relationship between Ireland and the First International. It was the first 'to establish the thin but real links between the International and Ireland in the 1870s on the one hand and the emergence of socialists in Dublin in the 1880s on the other'.[108] In contrast, a rural dimension is largely absent in both thesis and book, although the thesis briefly looked at Irish agriculture. Boyle argued in fact that 'the agricultural population was a poor source of recruitment

... [for organised labour] ... composed as it was of tenant proprietors, and a steadily diminishing number of labourers'.[109] Elsewhere, he describes the Irish rural labourer as a 'marginal figure'.[110] Comparison of book with thesis also shows that in the book's conclusions Boyle expanded his argument that there were huge divisions between developments in Scotland and Ireland which Foster saw as offering a particularly 'illuminating' dimension.[111]

Boyle's study was inevitably going to have its limitations, partly due to both time constraints and the dearth of secondary materials. Consequently, he had to establish its scope and parameters and generally stick to them. He would therefore have had to go where the available primary sources were and, to the benefit of his study, where he had to create them. For example, tracking down labour activists from the early decades of the twentieth century and drawing out their recollections, however imperfect. This was amongst its greatest achievements and one of its legacies. But, like all research, it remained work in progress. When it was published in 1988 it was well received by Irish and British reviewers. It was variously described as an 'excellent study of labour activity'[112] offering 'extensive research which will ... make this an indisputable reference text';[113] 'a pathbreaking history of the Irish labour movement', 'a major contribution to further exploration' and a 'long needed replacement ... [for Clarkson] ... based on an impressive range of primary sources'.[114] In the most substantive and penetrating review, Foster suggests what surely was, and to a great extent remains, the book's place in Irish labour history (with my emphasis): 'the book's significant contribution is that it *provides the basis* for a comprehensive understanding of how ... the labour movement developed'.[115] But admirers and critics also identified what they saw as some of its flaws. These included: its exclusion of urban centres such as Cork, Limerick and Derry;[116] its urban focus and exclusion of a substantive rural dimension;[117] its adoption of an 'anglicised' construct;[118] its lack of theorising;[119] its exclusion of more recent research, such as Patterson's;[120] and its 'old school' approach.[121] One went even so far as to describe it as 'an amazing antique' providing 'useful background material'.[122] Here is not the place to consider each of these points. However, a general response might be made in terms of the context in which the research was conducted, as was discussed earlier. It was undertaken at a time when Irish labour history was in the doldrums. So it is not surprising therefore that it might have reflected prevailing approaches which might now be thought of as 'old school'. Nor that it reflected British labour history approaches which were more developed at that time.

The reviewers of the book were also largely seasoned historians operating in a more positive era for Irish labour history. A key question therefore is what value and relevance Boyle's research has thirty years on, especially for today's students and researchers entering a field which in many ways is still developing? And in an era when trade union activities and membership have been under great pressure. Labour historians may diverge in how they approach the subject. This may be the cause of debate and disagreement, of criticism and sometimes hostility. But like any movement there is invariably a shared common purpose. In Irish labour history this was perhaps summed up in the founding principles of the ILHS:

'to promote the knowledge of Irish labour history ... which in its broadest sense refers to the economic, social and political formation of the Irish working class; the labour movement and working-class culture; and the experiences of Irish people working at home and abroad.'[123]

I would argue, therefore, that Boyle's legacy is that his work remains an important reference text that contributes to the ongoing quest to understand how the working class was crucial to the development of social democracy. In many respects it remains a virtual archive in itself, covering not just the major organisations but also long forgotten figures and events as well as obscure working-class groups. Often these have to be teased out of the text and pieced together from different parts of the book, but the result is always rewarding. Equally important was Boyle's referencing of hundreds of reports and items from the Belfast and other Irish newspapers, hugely beneficial as a signposting for research. As Paul Bew has argued, local newspapers may sometimes be partial and very unmediated, but they were important in conveying 'the mood of popular politics'.[124]

From a researcher's perspective, Boyle's private papers also offer a masterclass in research methodology and commitment. It was an era without the internet and libraries were only beginning to expand their investment in microfilm, largely for fragile newspaper archives. Not only did Boyle have to scrutinise primary sources first hand, sometimes for the first time, but also had to meticulously record and catalogue the findings. Virtually everything was typed up and cross referenced. He was also able to interview many in the early labour movement towards the end of their lives. A legacy to be cherished in itself. The papers also reveal information that did not find its way into publication and, in some cases, offers a different perspective on some event or person. The research for the doctorate was impressive not because it drew, as Foster suggested, on 'a lifetime's work together ... with perceptions, balance and realism'[125] but because it did so at such an early stage, between 1955 and 1961. Indeed, for Austen Morgan, the founding of the ILHS and *Saothar* 'probably owes most to the inspiration of John W. Boyle, whose well-known doctoral thesis of 1961 has only recently been published'.[126]

To 'A Further Shore', Canada

Boyle was renowned for his ability to quote poetry in conversation. He would therefore have warmed to Séamus Heaney's lines from *The Cure of Troy* when the Chorus calls:

'Believe that a further shore   Believe in miracles
Is reachable from here.   And cures and healing wells.'[127]

The Boyles's continued frustration with life in Belfast led them to seek the escape route of so many of their fellow Irish men and women before them, emigration to another country. It was Elizabeth who suggested Canada and when they left for this potentially alien shore in 1966 they found both a welcome and a place where they would have freedom to express their ideas fully and forcefully.[128] From there, Boyle was able to record a Connolly century lecture for BBC Radio.[129] As Associate Professor in the Department of History at Mount Allison University, it was not all plain sailing, although as always it was the students that were his life blood. As early as 1968, he was 'groaning under bureaucracy'.[130] But he was also 'heavily engaged in work for the Canadian Association of University Teachers (CAUT)'.[131] However, it was the administration of the university that so incensed him. In his own words, 'it was authoritarian to an incredible degree ... [with] ... an absence of procedures to determine who should stay and who should go'.[132] It was victimising some lecturers with dismissals and suspensions, and by refusing to commit to tenures. As usual Boyle stepped up to the plate. The university was being challenged by the CAUT and Boyle acted as adviser to one of the victims when it came to a head in 1970. He was joined by the student body and between them they forced the university to give way. Although he admits that it took up a considerable amount of his time he took solace in the fact 'that for the first time they made the administration realise that they will not get away with arbitrary conduct'.[133] But he admitted that while all the effort had brought 'some degree of elementary justice into the administration ... I am so thoroughly fed up that I am moving to the University of Guelph'.[134] The move gave him a full Professorship with the Boyles at last achieving the sort of stability they had been seeking.

Since arriving in Canada the Boyles had wasted little time immersing themselves into Canadian society. In a country that was divided on ethnic and language grounds, Boyle's fluent French and his understanding of French culture was a distinct asset. Politically, it was perhaps no surprise that they became active in the New Democratic Party (NDP) which had been formed in 1961 out of the Co-operative Commonwealth Federation (CCF) and the Canadian Labour Congress (CLC). Then, as now, the Party's constitution affirmed that it worked 'within the social democratic and democratic socialist traditions'.[135] In a sense this was a new lease of life as the Boyles commenced on a 'mission' of socialist agitation in Canada. But it was by no means their only form of activism and, as Devine notes, they 'engaged in many progressive causes and activities'.[136] This was particularly so in Elizabeth's case as John Boyle concentrated on the immense work of his new academic responsibilities. Devine lists a catalogue of causes that Elizabeth supported in Canada.[137] Particularly important to her – and reflecting her lifelong concern with civil liberties and human rights – was the establishment of a Canadian Section of Amnesty International in 1973.[138] Elizabeth set about founding branches in Sackville and Guelph and would remain a lifelong activist. Building on earlier research from 1966, she also found time to publish in 1971 a book on lace-making and embroidery through the women who supplemented their small-farmer husbands' incomes. *The Irish Flowerers* has become the standard work on the subject and is much sought-after through booksellers.[139]

Meanwhile, Boyle was making his mark as an academic in Guelph. He remained both a researcher and a teacher, always seeking but also always sharing and giving. He embraced his new home and it embraced both himself and Elizabeth, relishing learning about its history and complexities, particularly the place of the Irish migrant in Canada.[140] In a sense his scholarship was an integral part of his social being. His research into the labour movement in Ireland and across continents caused him never to forget the struggles of countless numbers of his fellow citizens. But teaching was his true vocation. He brought an empathy to it which was reflected, said one of his former colleagues, in 'his humility and dedication'.[141] This was best summed up when he was asked to sign some NDP nomination papers, describing himself simply and modestly as 'John Boyle, teacher'.[142] With students he was seen as unfailingly kind and natural. But despite the distance in between, the Boyles never forgot Ireland, or indeed Europe. Although the ILHS was established in 1973 when they were in Canada, Boyle was possibly one of the inspirations for it and both Boyles remained ardent supporters for the rest of their lives. Boyle also became a member of the *Saothar* Editorial Advisory Board as well as addressing numerous conferences.[143] Indeed, he was seen by the labour movement as 'Our Man in Canada'.[144] This support of the Boyles was marked in 1990 by the presentation of a crafted plaque inscribed, 'To John and Elizabeth Boyle for their contribution to the making and recording of Irish labour history'.[145] Words that aptly summed up why the Boyles are in this volume.

Elizabeth Boyle died on 16 November 1995 and three years later to the day John Boyle also died. By 1995, Hewitt had been a widower for two decades. His own homage to his wife Roberta in a poem published several years after her death might also have spoken to the grieving Boyle. In writing of a time when Roberta was at her happiest, Hewitt wrote that 'to life's bright process you belong'.[146] Like so many other partnerships in the labour movement, some more prominent than others, the Boyles were greater together than just their own single lives. What his friends, family and colleagues celebrated at Boyle's funeral in 1998 was surely equally applicable to Elizabeth, and indeed to Hewitt, as well:

> 'The strength we derived from John Boyle stemmed from his ability to see his own life as a whole. John never played parts or assumed roles. To him all the world was not simply a stage, but a place for purposeful action.'[147]

John W. Boyle's life was a whole one and all he did was interwoven with a purposeful action 'for quality of life and brotherhood'.

Notes

1 John Hewitt, 'To Robert Telford Hewitt', in Frank Ormsby (ed), *The Collected Poems of John Hewitt*, (Blackstaff Press, Belfast, 1991), p. 13.

2 Francis Devine, 'A gentle flowering: Elizabeth and John W. Boyle, Historians and labour activists' in Francis Devine, Fintan Lane & Niamh Puirséil, *Essays in Irish Labour History: A Festschrift for Elizabeth and John W. Boyle*, (Irish Academic Press, Dublin, 2008), p. 6.

3 Francis Devine, 'J. W. Boyle', *Saothar 24*, 1999, pp. 7-10.

4 Introduction to Michael Longley & Frank Ormsby (eds), *John Hewitt: Selected Poems*, (Blackstaff Press, Belfast, 2007), p. xiii.

5 See Austen Morgan, *Labour and Partition: The Belfast Working Class, 1905-1923*, (Pluto Press, London, 1991), p. 270; and Alan F. Parkinson, *Belfast's Unholy War: The Troubles of the 1920s*, (Four Courts Press, Dublin, 2004), pp. 36-37. Parkinson notes that Belfast Labour Councillor James Baird described the plight of socialists to a 1921 TUC conference that included the burning down of the Independent Labour Party (ILP) hall in North Belfast.

6 W. J. Mc Cormack, *Northman - John Hewitt, 1907-87 - An Irish Writer, His World, and His Times*, (Oxford University Press, Oxford, 2015), p. xx.

7 Devine, 'A gentle flowering', *op. cit.*, p. 5.

8 Hewitt, 'An Ulsterman' and '1957-1972', in Ormsby (ed), *Collected Poems, op. cit.*, pp. 132 and 221-222.

9 McCormack notes Hewitt and his wife participated in the unsuccessful campaign to get Simon Napier of the NILP elected to one of the Queen's University's four seats - *Northman, op. cit.*, p. 148. See Connal Parr, 'John Hewitt: ever hopeful' in Seán Byers & Francis Devine (eds), *William Walker, 1870-1918: Belfast Labour Unionist Centenary Essays*, (Umiskin Press, Dublin, 2018), pp. 185-196.

10 Francis Devine, obituary, 'Elizabeth Boyle', *Saothar 21*, 1996, pp. 11-12

11 See McCormack, *Northman*. Roberta Hewitt's journals can be found at the Public Record Office of Northern Ireland (PRONI), D/3838/4/7.

12 The Boyles were married from 1942 to 1995; and the Hewitts from 1934 to 1975.

13 John W. Boyle, *A Biography of My Wife, Elizabeth Boyle, Neé Morwood (1908-1995)*, p. 10. This is an unpublished memoir circulated to family and friends and kindly provided by Liz Boyle.

14 *ibid.*

15 Devine, 'A gentle flowering', *op. cit.*, p. 3.

16 John W. Boyle, *The Rise of the Labour Movement, 1888-1907*, PhD thesis, Trinity College, Dublin, 1961 (hereinafter, PhD thesis) and John W. Boyle, *The Irish Labor Movement in the Nineteenth Century*, (The Catholic University of America Press, Washington, D.C., 1988) (hereinafter *Irish Labor Movement* or the book).

17 Most of the *Boyle papers* have been donated to the ILHS archive.

18 Terry Crowley, University of Guelph, *John Boyle (1914-1998)*, tribute read at the funeral of John W. Boyle. *Boyle Papers*.

19 John Hewitt, 'An Ulsterman', in Ormsby (ed), *Collected Poems, op. cit.*, p. 132.

20 *ibid.*

21 The 1911 census shows the family to consist of his father Edmond (born in County Kilkenny), mother Francis (born in County Carlow) and sister Margaret of just 11 months, and living in Malachi Road, Arran Quay, North Dublin. Available at www.census.nationalarchives.ie/pages/1911/Dublin/Arran_Quay/Malachi_Road/44084 / [retrieved 20 June 2018].

22 *Dublin Evening Telegraph*, 5 October 1914.

23 *Belfast News-Letter*, 5 October 1914, p. 6.

24 Mark Moloney, 'Guinness's - 'Steadfast in the loyalty to the British Crown", *Green Left Weekly*, Issue 983, 25 September 2013.

25 But see also Pádraig Allen, 'St John's Ambulance and the Easter Rising,' *Irish Times*, 27 March 2016. Available at www.irishtimes.com/life-and-style/health-family/st-john-ambulance-and-the-easter-rising-1.2583272 [retrieved 29 May 2018].

26 Devine, John Boyle obituary, *op. cit.*, p. 7 and 'Gentle Flowering', *op. cit.*, p. 6.

27 Email from Liz Boyle, 22 July 2018.

28 James Connolly, 'Labour and the Proposed Partition of Ireland', *Irish Worker*, 14 March 1914. Available at www.marxists.org/archive/connolly/1914/03/laborpar.htm [retrieved 22 June 2018].

29 *Belfast News-Letter*, 2 September 1935, p. 6.

30 Enda Delaney, *Demography, State and Society: Irish Migration to Britain, 1921-1971*, (Liverpool University Press, Liverpool, 2000), pp. 71-81.

31 Letter from Boyle to Fred Carson, 25 March 1972.

32 S. J. Connolly (ed), *Oxford Companion to Irish History*, (Oxford University Press, Oxford, 2ns edition, 2007), p. 199.

33 Devine, 'A gentle flowering', *op. cit.*, p. 1.

34 *ibid.*

35 *ibid.*, p. 2.

36 They married in the Malone Presbyterian Church, Lisburn Road, Belfast, on 6 April 1942. See Boyle, *Biography of My Wife, op. cit.*, p. 8.

37 Elizabeth's father was James Morwood, a doctor in the Indian medical service and her mother Mary Bell, an American from New Orleans and California. This account of Elizabeth Boyle's life relies heavily on John W. Boyle, *Biography of My Wife, op. cit.* and Francis Devine, 'Elizabeth Boyle', *Saothar 21, 1*996, pp. 11-12 and 'Gentle Flowering', *op. cit.*, pp. 3-7.

38 Devine, 'A gentle flowering', *op. cit.*, p. 3.

39 James Morwood was head of a large military hospital in India for the duration of the war. Boyle, *Biography of My Wife*, pp. 1-2

40 See Allison Jordan, *Margaret Byers: Pioneer of Victoria College, Belfast*, (Institute of Irish Studies, Belfast, 1990).

41 Boyle, *Biography of My Wife, op. cit.*, p. 4

42 John Boyle recalls a 1935 photograph showing Elizabeth as a member of the ILP. Boyle, *Biography of My Wife, op. cit.*, p. 11.

43 *ibid.*

44 Devine, 'A gentle flowering', *op. cit.*, p. 4.

45 *ibid.*

46 *ibid.*

47 Boyle, *Biography of My Wife, op. cit.*, p. 12.

48 *ibid.*

49 *ibid.*, pp. 12-13.

50 *Irish Times* obituaries: 'Social activist who blazed a trail in Northern Ireland' (Patricia), 15 June 2011; and 'Doctor and leading light of the North's early civil rights movement' (Conn), 28 December 2013.

51 Devine, 'A gentle flowering', *op. cit.*, p. 5.

52 *ibid.*

53 See Connal Parr, 'David Wylie Bleakley (1925-2017)', *Saothar 43*, 2018, pp. 144-146.

54 Jonathan Tonge, review of Aaron Edwards, *A History of the Northern Ireland Labour Party - Democratic Socialism & Sectarianism*, (Manchester University Press, Manchester, 2009). Available at http://blogs.lse.ac.uk/politicsandpolicy/book-review-a-history-of-the-northern-ireland-labour-party/ [retrieved 23 June 2018].

55 Edwards, *Northern Ireland Labour Party, op. cit.*, p. 229

56 *ibid.*, p.231.

57 'Reduction in the gap between craftsman and general worker,' *BN-L*, 29 December 1956, p. 6. The full text was later published as 'Industrial Conditions in the twentieth century', in T.W. Moody & J.C. Beckett (eds), *Ulster Since 1800: A Social Survey*, (BBC, London, 1957).

58 John W. Boyle, 'The Rural Labourer', *Threshold*, 3:1, Spring 1959.

59 J.W. Boyle, 'William Walker' (pp. 57-65) and 'The Sum of Things' (pp. 87-95), in Boyle (ed), *Leaders & Workers*, (Mercier Press, Cork, 1965).

60 John Boyle, *Biography of My Wife, op. cit.*, pp. 9-10.

61 Devine, 'A gentle flowering', *op. cit.*, p. 5. In a letter to Francis Devine in 1996, John Boyle said that 'in those days Queen's was sectarian.'

62   David Convery, 'Introduction', Convery (ed), *Locked Out: A Century of Irish Working-Class Life*, (Irish Academic Press, Dublin, 2013), pp. 1-7.

63   Francis Devine & Emmet O'Connor, 'Editorial: Saothar, Labour History And The Future', *Saothar 22*, 1997, p. 5.

64   C. Desmond Greaves, *The Life and Times of James Connolly*, (Lawrence & Wishart, London, 1961) and Emmet Larkin, *James Larkin, Irish Labour Leader, 1876-1947*, (Pluto Press edition, 1989). Larkin notes in a new introduction (p.xi) that 'When this biography was first published in 1965 very little scholarly work had been done on Irish labour history.'

65   J. J. Lee, '*Saothar* And Its Contribution to Irish Historical Studies' in Francis Devine (ed), *An Index to Saothar, Journal of the Irish Labour History Society and Other ILHS Publications, 1973-2000*, (ILHS, Dublin, September 2000), p. 8. Available at http://www.irishlabour historysociety.com/pdf/Saothar%20Index.pdf [retrieved 29 June 2018].

66   Emmet Larkin, *James Larkin and the Irish Labour Movement, 1876-1947*, PhD thesis, Columbia University, 1957.

67   Donal Nevin, 'The state of Irish labour history', symposium on Irish Labour History, Belfast, 1974. See Miriam Daly, 'Belfast symposium on Irish labour history,' *Saothar 2* (1976), pp. 1-2.

68   Lee, *Saothar, op. cit.*, p. 8.

69   Emmet O'Connor, 'Irish labour historiography: an overview'. Originally published in *Labour/La Travail 50 (2002)*, pp. 243-248, and subsequently posted in May 2009 at http://irishlabour.com/?p=12 [retrieved 12 May 2013]. See also Emmet O'Connor, 'Essay in historiography', *Labour History Review*, 60:1 (April 1995), pp. 21-34.

70   Arthur Mitchell, *Labour in Irish Politics, 1890-1930*, (Dublin University Press, Dublin, 1974) and Charles McCarthy, *Trade Unions in Ireland, 1894-1960*, (Institute of Public Administration, Dublin, 1977)

71   J. Dunsmore Clarkson, *Labour and Nationalism in Ireland*, (Columbia University Press, New York, 1925). A valuable re-evaluation of Clarkson and how it speaks to us today can be found in Conor McCabe, 'Labour Classic: J. Dunmore Clarkson, Labour and Nationalism in Ireland (1925)', *Saothar 42*, 2017, pp. 117-119.

72   George O'Brien, *Labour Organisation*, (Methuen, London, 1921) and Charles McCarthy, *Trade Unions in Ireland, op. cit.*

73   O'Connor, 'Irish Labour Historiography', *op. cit.*

74   Fintan Lane, 'Envisaging labour history: some reflections on Irish historiography and the working class' in Devine et al, *Essays in Irish Labour History, op. cit.*, p. 10.

75   Lee, '*Saothar*', *op. cit.*, p. 9.

76   O'Connor, 'Irish Labour Historiography', *op. cit.*

77   See Marnie Hughes-Warrington, 'Theodore William Moody' in *Fifty Key Thinkers on History*, (Routledge, Abingdon, 3rd edition, 2015), pp. 232-237. Another, but shorter, discussion of Moody's motivations and contribution to Irish history can be found in Alvin Jackson, 'Irish history in the twentieth and twenty-first centuries', in Jackson (ed), *The Oxford Handbook of Modern Irish History*, (Oxford University Press, Oxford, 2017), pp. 4-7.

78   See T. W. Moody, *Davitt and Irish Revolution*, (Clarendon, Oxford, 1981).

79   Boyle (ed), *Leaders & Workers, op. cit.*

80   John W. Boyle, 'Industrial conditions in the twentieth century', in T. W. Moody and J. C. Beckett, *Ulster Since 1800: A Social Survey* (BBC, London, 1957).

81   Francis Devine & Emmet O'Connor, 'Editorial: Marxism, modernisation and memory', *Saothar 15*, 1990, p. 3.

82   Francis Devine, '*Saothar*: the Irish Labour History Society and labour history, 1973-2000' in Francis Devine (ed), *An Index to Saothar, Journal of the Irish Labour History Society and Other ILHS Publications, 1973-2000*, (ILHS, Dublin, September 2000), p. 12. Available at www.irishlabourhistorysociety.com/pdf/Saothar%20Index.pdf [retrieved 29 June 2018]. See also Emmet O'Connor, 'The Irish Labour History Society: an outline history', *Labour History Review*, 75: supplement 1 (April 2010), pp. 147-159.

83   Emmet O'Connor, *A Labour History of Ireland 1824-2000*, (University College Dublin, Dublin, new edition, 2011), pp. xi-xii.

84   John Hewitt, 'Neither An Elegy Nor A Manifesto', in Ormsby (ed), *Collected Poems, op. cit.*, pp. 188-189.

85 Letter Boyle to Carson, 25 March 1972. *Boyle Papers*
86 The poem was first published in *Alliance*, June 1972 and then in the collection, *Out of My Time: Poems 1967-1974.*
87 J. J. Lee, *Ireland, 1912-1985: Politics and Society*, (Cambridge University Press, Cambridge, 1989), pp. 271-328.
88 *ibid.*, p. 323.
89 Cited in Paul Bew, *Ireland, The Politics of Enmity, 1789-2006*, (Oxford University Press, Oxford, 2007), p. 476.
90 O'Connor, *A Labour History*, p. xi.
91 Peter Bacon, Joe Durkan & Joe O'Leary, *The Irish Economy: Policy and Performance, 1972-1981*, (Economic and Social Research Institute, Dublin, 1982), p. 1.
92 *ibid.*
93 Letter Boyle to Carson, 2 February 1969. *Boyle papers.*
94 Boyle, PhD thesis, p. 481. A letter of 12 April 1973 from Mrs Carson to Boyle records that her husband had died on 12 February 1972 and bundles of research papers were waiting to be collected. *Boyle papers.*
95 'John W. Boyle, Curriculum Vitae' prepared for application for the position of Professor of History at the University of Guelph, Canada, 1972. *Boyle Papers.*
96 Letter Boyle to Carson, 25 March 1972. *Boyle papers.*
97 Mitchell, *Labour in Irish Politics, op. cit.*, McCarthy, *Trade Unions in Ireland, op. cit.*, and Henry Patterson, *Class Conflict and Sectarianism: The Protestant Working Class and the Belfast Labour Movement, 1868-1920*, (Blackstaff, Belfast, 1981).
98 O'Connor, *Labour History of Ireland, op. cit.*
99 Donald H. Akenson, 'Reviewed work: *The Irish Labour Movement in the Nineteenth Century* by John W. Boyle', *Labour/Le Travail*, 25 (Spring 1990), p. 288.
100 The first third of the book was a reworking of the early sections of the thesis with some new material introduced e.g. Ireland and the First International. The first section of the thesis, which was a profile of the country and people, was largely omitted. However, the second two-thirds of the book covering the formation and growth of the labour movement in large part reproduced material from the thesis.
101 Fintan Lane & Emmet O'Connor, 'Speed the Plough', *Saothar 26*, 2000, pp. 3-4.
102 See F. A. D'Arcy, 'Reviewed Work: *The Irish Labor Movement in the Nineteenth Century* by John W. Boyle', in *Irish Historical Studies*, 27: 106, November 1990, p. 176.
103 It coincided with the completion of Peter Collins's PhD thesis devoted to the Belfast Trades Council which has not been published in full - Peter Collins, *Belfast Trades Council, 1821-1921*, Ulster University, 1988.
104 Maura Cronin, 'Review: John W. Boyle, *The Irish Labor Movement in the Nineteenth Century*' in *The Irish Review*, No. 7 (Autumn, 1989), p. 138.
105 *ibid.*
106 Boyle, *Irish Labor Movement, op. cit.*, p. xii.
107 D'Arcy, 'Review', *op. cit.*, p. 176
108 *ibid.*
109 Boyle thesis, p. 379, where he uses the term 'peasant proprietors' rather than 'tenant proprietors' in the book, p. 330.
110 John W. Boyle, 'A marginal figure: the Irish rural labourer', in Samuel Clark & James S. Donnelly Jr. (eds), *Irish Peasants: Violence and Political Unrest, 1780-1914*, (University of Wisconsin Press, Madison, Wisconsin, new edition, 2003). The original edition was published in Dublin in 1983. Boyle also delivered one of the Thomas Davis Lectures on the Irish agricultural labourer, the text of which was published as 'The Rural Labourer, in *Threshold, 3:1*, (1959).
111 John Foster, 'Completing the first task: Irish labour in the nineteenth century,' *Saothar 15*, 1990, p. 68.
112 Cronin review, *op. cit.*, p. 139.
113 John Gray, 'The Irish Labour Movement in the Nineteenth Century by John W. Boyle,' *The Linen Hall Review*, 7:1/2 (Summer 1990), p. 39.
114 Foster review, *op. cit*, p. 65; O'Connor, 'Irish labour historiography', D'Arcy review, *op. cit.*, p. 175 with reference to Clarkson, *Labour and Nationalism op. cit.*
115 *ibid.*

116 D'Arcy, review, *op. cit.*, p. 176 and Cronin, review, *op. cit.*, p.139.
117 *ibid.*
118 O'Connor & Devine, 'Editorial: Marxism, modernisation and memory', *Saothar 15*, 1990, p. 4.
119 D'Arcy review, p. 176.
120 *ibid.*; Henry Patterson, *Class Conflict, op. cit.*
121 O'Connor, 'Irish Labour Historiography', *op. cit.*
122 Akenson, 'Review', *op. cit.*, pp. 288-289.
123 Irish Labour History Society. Available at www.irishlabourhsitorysociety.com [retrieved 8 July 2018].
124 Paul Bew, *Ireland, The Politics of Enmity 1789-2006*, (Oxford University Press, Oxford, 2007), p. ix
125 Foster review, *op. cit.*, p. 69.
126 Morgan, *Labour and Partition, op. cit.*, p. xix.
127 Séamus Heaney, *The Cure of Troy*, (Faber & Faber, London, 1990), p. 77.
128 Crowley, funeral tribute, *op. cit.*, p. 2.
129 It was later published as 'Connolly, the Citizen Army and the Rising' in K. B. Nowlan (ed), *The Making of 1916: Studies in the History of the Rising*, (Dublin, 1969).
130 Letter Boyle to Carson, 21 October 1968. *Boyle Papers.*
131 *ibid.*, 18 December 1968. In November 1949, the Association of Teaching Staff of the University of Alberta explored the idea of creating a national association to raise the issues of 'salaries and pensions, sabbatical leave and academic freedom'. When the Learned Societies, now Canadian Federation for the Humanities and Social Sciences held their annual session Kingston, Ontario, in 1950 a decision was taken to form CAUT. By 1957, CAUT represented 78% of university staff organised in twenty-six associations which were not actual trade unions. Full unionisation did not occur until 1971 when L'Association des Ingenieurs Professeurs en Science Appliques de l'Université de Sherbrooke in Quebec tool that step. CAUT encouraged member associations to certify and in 2019, 79% of academic staff are unionised as against an average of less than 50% for other occupations, see *www.caut.ca* [retrieved 7 February 2019].
132 *ibid.*, 18 April 1970.
133 *ibid.*
134 *ibid.*, 25 March 1972.
135 *Constitution of the New Democratic Party of Canada: Effective April 2016.* Available at http://xfer.ndp.ca/2016/documents/NDP-CONSTITUTION-EN.pdf [retrieved 2 August 2018].
136 Devine, 'A gentle flowering', *op. cit.*, p. 5.
137 These ranged from milling machinery supplied to women in developing countries, help for the elderly, to international women's rights. See Devine, 'A gentle flowering', *op. cit.*, p. 4.
138 Amnesty International timeline. Available at http://static.amnesty.org/ai50/ai50-amnesty-international-timeline.pdf [retrieved 2 August 2018].
139 Elizabeth Boyle, *The Irish Flowerers*, (Belfast, 1971). See also Elizabeth Boyle, 'Irish embroidery and lacemaking, 1600-1800', *Ulster Folk Life*, 12 (1966), pp. 52-65.
140 See for example, John W. Boyle, 'A Fenian Protestant in Canada: Robert Lindsay Crawford, 1910-1922,' *Canadian Historical Review*, 52:2 (June 1971).
141 Crowley, funeral tribute, *op. cit.*
142 Ruth Kaufman, 'Tribute to a teacher', *TAB – The Action Bulletin off Guelph-Welling New Democratic Party*, , January 1999.
143 Devine, 'A gentle flowering', *op. cit.*, p. 6.
144 *ibid.*, p. 7.
145 The plaque was hand-crafted by retired Inchicore Works coppersmith Dermot 'Derry' Barrett. It remains in the possession of their daughter Liz.
146 John Hewitt, 'For Roberta in the Garden,' in Ormsby (ed), *Collected Poems, op. cit.*, p. 357.
147 Crowley, funeral tribute, *op. cit.*

BRENDAN HALLIGAN, NIALL GREENE & TONY BROWNE

Three Reflections on
Brendan Corish, 1918-1990,
and the New Republic

On Saturday, 24 November 2018 in Wexford Town Library, the Irish Labour History Society (ILHS) in association with Wexford County Council held a seminar, 'Remembering Brendan Corish (1918-1990)'. At the event, papers reflected aspects of Corish's life and legacy.[1] Among them were those of Tony Brown, Niall Greene and Brendan Halligan which are produced here. The papers were on issues that their writers felt contributed to an understanding of Brendan Corish's legacy. The *New Republic* speech at the 1967 Labour Party Annual Conference remains, for many, the high watermark of his reform and modernisation of the party, an exhilarating time for many young people who joined the party in the hopes – even the expectation – that the 1970s would indeed be socialist. Halligan, a key Party Official for Corish, recalls the speech, its impact and its footprint in the political landscape. Greene provides an unusual and interesting insight into the structural changes that facilitated the party's modernisation and which Corish considered vital to the change of Labour's role and performance that he sought. Brown examines the detailed work that provided depth and substance to the broad brushstrokes of the *New Republic*, painstaking work that achieved genuine change that benefited tens of thousands and yet has been neglected in standard analyses of the 1973-1977 Government that condemn it for its failures to deal with global economic crises and violence in the North, and for the introduction of repressive legislation. Before presenting the papers, however, a brief biography of Corish.

Brendan Corish: A Brief Biography

Brendan Corish was born on 19 November 1918 in Wexford, fourth of the six children of Richard (1886-1945), a trade unionist and politician, and Catherine Bergin (1888-1987), daughter of Daniel Bergin, a baker. Richard, son of a carpenter, became an apprentice fitter in the Star Engineering Works and a founder member of the Irish Transport & General Workers; Union (ITGWU) in the factory. A bitter lockout ensued from July 1911 until 8 February 1912 when the employers finally conceded recognition of the Irish Foundry Workers' Union, in reality a branch of the ITGWU.[2] The event was a foundation stone for labour movement activity in the town and is commemorated by Peter Hodnett's wonderful memorial installation at The Faythe, unveiled by President Michael D. Higgins in 2012.[3] Richard Corish remained an ITGWU Official and served on the union's Executive and Wexford Trades Council, while supplementing his income with an insurance book. He served as Alderman on Wexford Corporation, 1913-1945; was Mayor, 1920-1945; and was returned to Wexford County Council, 1920-1945. In 1921, he was elected as a Sinn Féin TD, accepted the Treaty and represented Labour in the Dáil, 1922-1945. He died on 19 July 1945.[4]

Brendan Corish thus grew up in a political household, son of a father who was a huge presence in the town. Educated at the Christian Brothers' School, Corish became a Clerical Officer with Wexford County Council, 1937-1945, and played Gaelic football to inter-county level, although, as far as football was concerned, he liked 'all codes'.[5] Following his father's death, Corish in a bye-election on 4 December 1945, won the seat with 50.2% of the vote. He held Wexford for Labour until he retired from politics in February 1982. High office rapidly followed. He was Labour's Vice Chair, 1946; Chief Whip, Parliamentary Labour Party (PLP), 1947; Parliamentary Secretary to the Ministers for Local Government and Defence, 1948-1951; and Minister Social Welfare, 1954-1957. He admitted to not totally enjoying his time in office. The *Report of the Commission on Emigration* confirmed the dreadful state of unemployment and migration and Corish later confessed that 'I used to lie awake at night, worrying about the unemployed', indication of his sincerely held concerns and acceptance of political responsibility, significant factors in the ideas in *The New Republic*.[6] He was, by then, absolutely convinced that Labour needed to pursue an independent, socialist line.

When long-serving Labour Leader William Norton resigned in February 1960, Corish was unanimously elected in his place.[7] Corish was, like Norton, a Knight of Columbanus and once told the Dáil during the Mother & Child debate in 1953 that

> 'I am an Irishman second, I am a Catholic first. If the hierarchy give me any direction with regard to Catholic Social Teaching or Catholic moral teaching, I accept without qualification in all respects the teaching of the hierarchy and the church in which I belong.'

Party colleague John Horgan thought Corish was a 'late developer' and that this comment was 'thrown against him on more than one occasion afterwards when it had ceased to be relevant'.[8] Although Norton continued to occupy his desk in the Labour Leader's office until his death in 1963 – not making it straightforward for Corish – at heart a mannerly, unassuming man – to assert his leadership, for Emmet O'Connor, the 'long night of the 'Norton years' gave way to a pink-hued dawn'.[9] In fact, Corish immediately began recasting Labour's position starting with a declaration in Tullamore in 1961 that Labour would henceforth adopt an independent position in any election. In 1963, not always with Corish's approval, Noël Browne[10] and Jack McQuillan[11] were admitted to the party, disbanding their National Progressive Democrats in the process, and Seán Dunne followed.[12] Corish sought the assistance of advisers 'from the outside', most notably Proinsias Mac Aonghusa, and Catherine McGuinness who was already a member.[13]

In 1964, Corish first described Labour policy as socialist, the word 'Christian' – a constant prefix in both Labour and trade union circles since the 1920s – being dropped. Corish began to mould the party into a genuine national party, improving organisation, discipline and morale. His intent was to present Labour to the electorate as the 'natural party of social justice, answering the needs of a rapidly urbanising society'.[14] By 1969, Labour came close to fielding 100 candidates and many long-sitting TDs had to stomach a running mate, breaking the established tradition that fiefdoms were unchallenged. In 1966, Fianna Fáil's Seán Lemass dismissed Labour TDs as 'the most conservative element in our community … a nice, respectable, docile, harmless body of men'.[15] Corish changed that.

The 1969 General Election was fought on the *New Republic* ideas, the period being regarded as that when Corish was 'at his most innovative and imaginative', although some damn the project with faint praise: 'whatever one may say about the quality of the policy papers, it cannot be denied that they were ambitious and aimed to be comprehensive'.[16] Corish was considered, 'in some ways' to have 'acted out of character, throwing caution to the wind in his attempt to forge a new tomorrow' as 'The Seventies Would Be Socialist'. Those contemporaries close to Corish would argue that it was 'completely in character' and that so many, particularly young, people joined the party precisely because it was in character and they recognised the 'scale of the ambition and were excited by it'.[17] New TDs included Conor Cruise O'Brien,[18] Justin Keating[19] and David Thornley, talented, high-profile figures.[20] Labour polled its highest-ever vote – 17.02% - yet lost seats – 18 compared to 22 in 1965, a huge disappointment, Corish's deflated angst for all to see on television as the results came in.

Corish was greatly affected and, in Halligan's words, 'brooded again' and began to wonder about his firm anti-Coalition stand.[21] Halligan added that 'it is critical to an understanding of his thinking that because of his experience in the 1954-1957 Government he would not have gone into Coalition with Fine Gael if Gerry Sweetman had remained as its Deputy

Leader'. Sweetman was killed in a fatal car accident near Monasterevin, County Kildare, on 28 January 1970.[22] The Arms Crisis of 1970 and escalating violence in Northern Ireland impacted on his thinking – and of those influential voices around him – as well as the fierce internal divisions on Northern matters between strongly Republican voices like Michael Mullen, Thornley and Kerry TD Dan Spring on one side and Cruise O'Brien on the other.[23] It was significant that Corish made Cruise O'Brien Labour's Spokesman in Government on Northern Ireland. By 1972, whilst leading Labour and broad trade union movement opposition to entry to the European Economic Community (EEC), Corish had been quietly negotiating with Fine Gael's Liam Cosgrave regarding the possibility of Coalition after the next election.[24] The Cosgrave/Corish discussions opened after the EEC Referendum on 10 May 1972 and Corish publicly spoke on the matter on 13 June, a speech discussed with the Front Bench and PLP.[25] At a PLP meeting after the General Election on 7 March 1973 – the week before a Government was appointed, Corish made it a pre-condition for accepting reappointment as Party Leader that the Leader would have sole power to nominate to Cabinet. The practice had been that any Deputy securing support from fellow Deputies could secure Cabinet placement, leaving the Leader no authority in the matter.[26]

After the 1973 election, Corish became Tánaiste and Minister for Health & Social Welfare. His choice of ministry spoke volumes about his ideas as to Labour's purpose in Government and it has been suggested that more strategic posts were left to Fine Gael. Cosgrave had offered Corish Finance, for example. In fact, Labour got five Cabinet seats, more than their mathematical entitlement, and felt their appointments reflected their policy priorities and personalities. They also secured the first 'super Junior Minister' in Cluskey and the post of Ceann Comhairle. The much-maligned Government grappled with Irish entry to the EEC, rising Loyalist and Republican violence, finely balanced negotiations leading to the ill-fated Sunningdale Agreement, and rising unemployment and inflation fuelled by the global oil crisis. The strengthening of the Offences Against the State Act was strongly criticised by the broad Left and human rights bodies. Corish and Cluskey's social welfare advances were, however, far-reaching and have received insufficient acknowledgement since. The qualifying age for Old Age pensions was reduced from 70 to 66; means tests for non-contributory pensions were modified; Deserted Wives Benefit, Unmarried Mothers' Allowances and new allowances for single women over 58 were introduced. In Labour, Michael O'Leary brought in new legislation for equal pay and employment equality, unfair dismissals and minimum notice; Justin Keating, Industry & Commerce, tackled mining licensing and kept the oil flowing; and records were set under Tully, Local Government, for the construction of local authority housing.[27]

Corish was said not to have enjoyed Government – nor indeed public life generally. Michael O'Leary offered an interesting summary

'He was an ordinary man in an extraordinary role. A true democrat, he was unambiguous in his opposition to violence. He was devoid of personal ambition and had the ability to listen and to bring divided strands and diverse personalities to the Cabinet table for the sake of the national good. He brought stability and coherence into Government in the wake of exceptional political tensions nationally and a rising ecoconomic crisis internationally.'[28]

Corish's capacity to lead the party through so many changes – of policy, practice and administration – drew appreciative comments from John Horgan who felt that his

'contribution in holding the party together during an exceptionally difficult period, and in taking a number of historic policy initiatives, is all too easily underrated. It is difficult to think of any other leader who could have survived the spectacular reversal of party policy on Coalition in 1970, or who could have taken office in a Coalition Government after having promised to support Coalition only from the back benches. In Corish's Labour Party this produces grumbles and indeed opposition. In the same party led by anyone else, it would have provoked outright rebellion, and probably a split.'[29]

It was not that Corish was immune from challenge from disgruntled colleagues or those opposing his policies, his apparent freedom to Cruise O'Brien in his handling of Northern Ireland generating opposition.[30]

Corish resigned as Party Leader in 1977 to be succeeded by the man he would most likely have chosen himself, Cluskey. Re-elected in Wexford in June 1981, Corish declined to stand in February 1982. On 13 May 1984, he was made a Freeman of Wexford, an honour previously bestowed on his father Richard in January 1945. On 4 January 1949, Corish had married Dubliner Phyllis Donohoe and they had three sons. He died on 17 February 1990.

Memories of Corish

The three recollections of Corish that follow are all written by figures who worked closely with him, who admired him and who continue to hold him in the highest regard. For Greene, Corish and Young Jim Larkin were the two most inspirational figures in his life. His insight into the reformation of Labour Party governance is fascinating. When a Party Whip in 1950, Corish had threatened to resign over difficulties in enforcing Party discipline or, indeed, getting Labour members even to attend or vote in the Dáil. Fine Gael Leader James Dillon styled the PLP 'the Quiet Mice' so inconspicuous were they.[31] Changing matters would not prove straightforward and, in 1955, Corish was strongly criticised for writing, in a report on the state of the Party, that it was 'functioning as a virile entity'. Labour veteran Mícheál Ó Maoláin, feeling 'patronised by an aloof leadership', told Young Jim Larkin,

'I rather think that Brendan Corish is a young man who imagines that everybody looks up to him, but they *don't* even look *down* on him … I think the great fault of the Labour Party (like all other parties) is they don't give 'the *great unwashed* … credit for having any *brains* at all.'[32]

Such criticism was not untypical from left-wing voices as Labour struggled to make headway. By 1961, Corish was raising the party's collective self confidence but, in practical terms, 'little had changed for the better'. With an election pending, Labour's 'central organisation' remained 'pitifully weak, particularly on the financial side'. Generating candidates largely depended on those capable and willing to garner their own financial backing or on trade union support – often more in kind than in coin – postage and postering, providing door knockers and envelopes.[33] Corish had a vision of a truly national organisation. The 1965 General Election was encouraging, the party returning twenty-two TDs, its best performance since 1927. It would prove deceptive but, in the short-term, gave strength to Corish's drive and the number of branches rose from 248 in 1964 – many arguably paper branches often funded by the sitting Deputy – to 501 in 1969. In Dublin, 'which usually contained a higher proportion of ideologically committed activists', branches increased from 29 to 83.[35] A new energy and youthful vigour was filling the party sails and Brown, Greene and Halligan were among the many young, university-educated members supportive of change, a time remembered as 'the point at which the party took off in the giddy excitement of believing that anything was possible'. For all three, it remains a 'gloriously thrilling experience'.[36]

The *New Republic*, when it came, 'did not seem unnatural, unusual or unique at the time. It just seemed inevitable'.[37] Halligan insists that Corish was more central to the document's conception and construction that has been assumed.

> 'These were *his* ideas not anyone else's. Others, myself particularly, wrote down the words which he then read. But the sweep of ideas, the inner feeling and the most telling phrases were his alone. Later representations of him as a compliant frontman were as cruel as they were inaccurate.'[38]

The 'sting in the tail' was that policy positions had to be written to flesh out the broad brush-strokes but this resulted in 'an explosion of creative endeavour', a flavour of which can be gleaned from Brown's reflections on the development of social policy, its implementation being regarded as Corish's 'most enduring contribution to Irish life'.[39]

Despite Corish's outwardly imposing leadership and 'despite the subsequent re-writing of history', Halligan makes it clear as the General Secretary that

> 'His strategy did not have universal support in the party. In fact, during the 1969 Annual Conference he very nearly lost the vote on a motion reaffirming the no Coalition stance. It was saved only by a powerful impromptu intervention in which he uttered the prophetic warning that Coalition would assuredly give the 'kiss of life' to Fine Gael.'[40]

Equally, Corish took personal responsibility to move the reversal of strategy on Coalition at the Conference on 13 December 1970, a proposal 'delivered from the floor – not the stage', seen as a 'psychological masterpiece' but one that could have finished his career. It was the commencement of the third stage of Corish's career, as understood by Halligan: 1960-1966, preparing the ground; 1967-1969, trying for the impossible; 1970-1972, accommodating to the Arms Crisis; and 1973-1977, ruling in the eye of the storm.[40]

Given Labour's recent decline – a decline some view as terminal – embracing the poisoned chalice of Coalition can, of course, be viewed less favourably than by those making the decision in 1970, including Brown, Greene and Halligan. They could be accused of wearing rose-tinted glasses and Halligan openly talks of the 'man I loved and for whom I worked for ten glorious years' was

> 'honest, kind, modest, decent, witty, humane, committed, selfless and without guile or ambition, above all, authentic, especially loyal to his roots as a Labour man and a Wexfordman. He was all of these things. They are personality traits with which he was born and which he never distorted or betrayed.'[41]

Halligan added that Corish was 'a consummate parliamentarian, a skilled debater, an inspiring orator, the industrious committee man, a great talker a good listener, a loyal comrade, and a great companion'. Yet, it would be difficult to deny that much of this was true and it was those qualities that underpinned Corish's leadership and the continued esteem in which he is held. Halligan argued that

> 'his legacy is clear enough. He was pivotal in transforming Irish politics; during a decade of social change Ireland kept pace with change elsewhere; he re-wrote the grammar and vocabulary of Irish politics; he created space in public life for the accomplished and he set social reform on a path that could not be reversed.'

More controversially for some, not least many in contemporary politics, but critical to those central to national politics at the time, Corish 'ensured' that Labour and the trade unions 'became a bulwark against political terrorism and that, with Fine Gael, the democratic institutions of the State were protected from subversion'.

In contrast to today, Corish talked socialism, a vision for an inclusive new society, something that would not be amiss today as Brexit looms and new dispensations on the island and between the islands are both possible and desirable. From whatever perspective Corish's career is judged, it cannot be doubted that he attempted to 'leave Ireland a better country than he found it'.

Browne, Greene & Halligan

So, who were and are Brown, Greene and Halligan? Tony Brown, born in Dublin on 21 January 1940, was educated at Blackrock College and University College Dublin, graduating in 1961 with a MSc. From 1962, he was employed as economist by the Irish Sugar Company in a new division charged with preparation for EEC entry. He met Brendan Halligan who recruited him to the Labour Party, where Brown worked on party social policy. In 1973, he was Special Advisor to Tánaiste Corish in the Department of Social Welfare where he worked on EEC Social Policy with Cluskey and first Irish Commissioner, Patrick Hillery. In 1977, Brown returned to the Sugar Company and worked on European food and consumer policies, became President, European Food Industry Confederation, 1982-1985; and from 1988 worked as an independent European Affairs consultant. He was Labour Party Honorary International Secretary, 1979-1997; member, Commission on Social Welfare, 1983-1986; Vice Chair, Combat Poverty Agency,1986-1989; Special Advisor to Minister of State for Tourism and Trade, 1995-1997; and Advisor to Oireachtas Delegation to European Convention, 2002-2003, working with MEP Proinsias de Rossa. He has been a member, National Committee for the Study of International Affairs, Royal Irish Academy, 1979-1985, 1992-1997, and founder member, Institute of International & European Affairs from 1989.

Niall Greene was born in Bradford, Yorkshire, 17 April 1943 and reared in Donegal. He has had an extensive career in the state, private and multinational sectors mainly in aviation-related activities. He joined the Labour Party in 1964 and has been in continuous membership since then. He was elected to the Administrative Council in 1965 and served as Financial Secretary, 1968-1970; Vice Chairman, 1970-19730; and was the Party's first International Secretary, 1975-1978. He was an adviser to the Minister for Labour, Michael O'Leary, 1973-1974. In 1985-1986, he chaired the Party's Commission on Electoral Strategy which brought an end to a long period of internal strife about participation in Coalition.

Brendan Halligan was born in Dublin on 5 July 1936 and was educated at St James's Christian Brothers School, Dublin Institute of Technology and University College Dublin, gaining a Masters in economics in 1964.[42] An economist with Comhlucht Siúcre Éireann (Irish Sugar Company), in 1967 he was appointed Political Director and then General Secretary of the Labour Party. Party Leader Corish relied heavily on Halligan's intellectual and political skills and the party, as is evident in the essays below, underwent an energetic re-organisation. Halligan strongly supported the leftward policy shift and acute anti-Coalition stance, but was instrumental in securing Labour's eventual, somewhat unwilling, reversal of its anti-Coalition stance after the disappointing outcome of the 1969 General Election.

After the formation of the Fine Gael-Labour Coalition in 1973, Halligan was appointed to Seanad Éireann. On 1973, he won a bye-election in Dublin South West. He stood again, unsuccessfully, in the newly-drawn Dublin Finglas in 1977, suffering similar disappointments in Dublin North West in 1981 and November 1982. Halligan was appointed as an MEP, 1983-1984, replacing Frank Cluskey. After ceasing to be Party Secretary in 1980, Halligan set up CIPA, a public affairs company, lectured in economics and in European integration at the University of Limerick, and founded the Institute of European Affairs (IEA), later Institute of International & European Affairs (IIEA), of which he is Chair.[43] From 1985-1995, he was

Chair, Bord na Móna; from 2007-2014, Chair, Sustainable Energy Authority of Ireland; and currently serves on the Board of Mainstream Renewable Energy.

What follows are their recollections of their roles in the heady years of the *New Republic*.

Brendan Corish after his election to the Dáil in 1949.

'A Noble Adventure':
The New Republic Speech in Retrospect

Brendan Halligan

The Context

When he rose in Liberty Hall to address the 1967 Labour Party Annual Conference, Brendan Corish was about to deliver what was later described both as a manifesto and as a sermon. But whether sermon or manifesto, it was about to shock the assembled delegates. It is true that they were anticipating something special. So, too the media. But what they got went beyond all expectations and has since been included in an anthology of the fifty 'Greatest Irish Speeches', and rightly so.[44]

The address opened like a thunderclap with five words that reverberated around Liberty Hall and have since gone into political folklore: 'The Seventies will be Socialist'. Before that could be absorbed, Corish went even further: 'What I offer now is the outline of a new society, A New Republic'. Nothing like this had been done since the Democratic Programme of the First Dáil.[45] What is more, he said, this New Republic would be forged by Labour, the half party in a two-and-a-half party system.

And Labour really was a half party. With the exception of County Meath, half the country north of a line from Dublin to Galway was without a Labour TD.[46] Within Dublin itself, where it should have been at its strongest, it was at its weakest. With only 15% of the national vote, and little more than a loose collection of rural independents, Labour seemed a most improbable candidate for leading a political revolution. Yet that was to be the thrust of the New Republic speech.

But Corish had become Leader at the right moment. Change was the spirit of the age, the *Zeitgeist*. The generation that had won independence had quit the stage. De Valera was already gone; and just ten months earlier, so too his successor, Seán Lemass. 1967 was one of those moments when a profound generational shift takes place and fortunately for Labour, Corish was part of that change. Fortunate too that he was highly conscious of this transition and of the opportunity to discard the old and fashion the new. Since becoming Leader in 1961, he had doubled the number of Labour seats in Dáil Éireann.[47] In short, he took the rostrum in Liberty Hall with the aura of a successful general.

The occasion was significant in its own right. In the Labour tradition, Annual Conference is the supreme policy-making body of the party with the Leader's Address as its centrepiece. Read from a prepared script, and lasting about fifty minutes, it normally dealt with contemporary politics and current party affairs. But this, by his own choice, was to be something completely different. It was intended as the next logical step in a series of advances accomplished over the previous six years: an independent electoral strategy, a new political ideology, the professionalisation of the organisation and expansion of its membership, the reaffiliation of the Workers' Union of Ireland (WUI) and Irish Transport & General Workers' Union (ITGWU),[48] plus electoral successes. Twelve months earlier, Corish had electrified the Annual Conference by stating socialism was the only alternative to capitalism. The mere use of the hitherto banned word 'Socialist' had been intoxicating and, for those who experienced it, the 1966 Conference had been heady stuff. No wonder the delegates were expectant. That is the context in which he delivered his speech.

Corish prepared meticulously for weeks and set a pattern for all subsequent speeches. We would first talk privately and in 1967 we initially met in Hoynes Hotel in Arklow, a convenient half-way house between Wexford and Dublin, supplemented by meetings in our homes. In these opening conversations, he would settle on the theme he wanted to develop, go on to outline his thoughts, which would be transcribed and typed up. He would also consult with his intimates and sometimes with outside experts. The speech would go through many drafts, seldom less than ten.

For the New Republic speech, the theme emerged from an irrefutable fact. The old Republic had failed in every one of the national objectives. The population was still falling, the work-force declining, economic growth stagnating, the standard of living one of the lowest in Europe and no sign of an economic breakthrough. Private enterprise had failed as the engine of growth. Hence, the State had to step in and plan the economy. Communal and social objectives would take precedence over private profit and the fruits of growth would be devoted to increased welfare and the elimination of poverty.

Socialism would replace capitalism as the basis of society. In short, a New Republic was needed and would be created by a Labour Government. In the Ireland of the day these were heretical proposals. This line of reasoning demanded a philosophic underpinning and so the speech set out a moral basis for socialism and then systematically applied it to the problems of economic stagnation and social inequality. This, of course, is what Corish had always intended to do – to give practical meaning to socialism – but instead of putting political and philosophical principles first he positioned them at the heart of the speech, justifying them on grounds of practicality as well as morality, and then letting them serve as the inspiration for the political transformation with which he intended to conclude.

This structure of the speech was continuously reviewed and revised and finally fixed at the last working session. The structure chosen gave great coherence to the speech, starting as it did with an examination of the present and finishing with a vision of the future, with the two joined together by moral principles that no person of good will could reject. It ranged from history to economics, from ethics to philosophy, from politics to public administration, from the abstract to the concrete. It was full of common sense and an uncommon passion for ending injustice.

It was all of these things because it was the culmination of a long process of reflection on his life experience and he had reached quite startling conclusions which a lesser man might have kept to himself for fear of ridicule. Instead, Corish put them before the party and the public in terms as simple as they were dramatic: he intended to change the world of politics. The speech was broken into eight separate sections and here is a summary of what he said. But it is only a summary.

The Introduction

The opening section of the speech is the shortest but the most memorable – and is also the most illuminating. It opened with the by now famous forecast that the Seventies would be Socialist, but immediately acknowledged that for this to happen Labour would have to make a breakthrough in seats and votes in the upcoming election, then expected to be two years away. The present position was merely a transition to power.

Corish then revealed the purpose of the speech; 'What I offer now is the outline of a new society, a New Republic'. That word, outline, was not a device to dodge detailed policies because he was to initiate an unprecedented policy-making exercise over the following months which produced policy statements adopted by the subsequent Annual Conference and which formed the basis of the 1969 election manifesto.

Crisis of Decision

Corish began his speech proper by arguing that the Irish people had never decided on the type of society they wanted. Because of our history, it had been impossible to debate political alternatives but there was now an urgency to make a choice because of a widespread belief that the Irish were unable to solve any of the major problems confronting them. The result was disquiet, apathy, cynicism and indifference.

As a judgement on contemporary society this was hardly contestable. The previous decade had been an economic and social disaster. For that reason, Corish framed the crisis of decision like this:

> 'Do we want to export another million people by the end of the century and fall so far behind the rest of Europe that we will never catch up, or do we want to put an end to national failure and construct a New Republic?'

In order to frame the choice, Labour would provide a socialist solution. That would leave the decision as one between the status quo and a new beginning.

Others were of similar mind but did not reach the revolutionary conclusions he was about to unveil. The 'Grey Book', published by Whitaker and his colleagues a decade earlier, had been predicated on the imperative of making a fresh economic start.[49] In fact, there was more than a hint of desperation about their initiative. The Fianna Fáil Government had responded with a faltering commitment to what it called 'economic expansion' with a target of doubling the annual growth rate to 2%, that seems ridiculous now but was almost revolutionary then.

At least, the Grey Book had the great merit of being honest, it was an admission of failure and the subsequent *Programme for Economic Expansion* had been a welcome departure from the inertia of the previous decade, but for Corish it was not enough. Faced with monumental failure on a grand scale, he began by putting responsibility on the individual citizen to examine the real issues facing society and to decide on the future. This was bringing everything back to the crisis of decision.

For its part, Labour would put forward a vision of the future and if the electorate were to reject it then, for the first time, a genuine political choice would have been made. And that is what he wanted. Corish wanted people to think about political choices and he was convinced that if they did that they would agree with his proposals. That would be the value of the process – a thinking and socially responsible citizenry - and he was prepared to risk electoral failure if only he could get that process started.

Analysis of the Old Republic

To stimulate that sort of thinking, Corish devoted the next section to a rigorous analysis of the old Republic and why it had failed. This was a logical preclude to the solution he was about to unveil. The diagnosis was almost entirely economic and dealt with the decade of Fianna Fáil rule from 1957, whose economic record he dismissed as the poorest in Europe. Far from catching up with other economies, Ireland had fallen further behind, coming second last among OECD countries in terms of growth. In a graphic passage, he clinically dissected the Ireland of his day:

> 'We have failed in every national objective, whether cultural, such as restoring the language; political, such as ending partition; social, such as halting rural depopulation; or economic, such as providing full employment.'

The key question was, what had gone wrong? His answer was surprising, and it led to some surprising conclusions. We went wrong, he said, in underestimating the magnitude of the national problems facing us on achieving independence. More than that, and arguably this is the core of the speech, independent Ireland had entered on a period of nation-building with an imperfect social philosophy and an almost pathetic belief in the ability of the private enterprise system to provide employment and secure equality. It is hard to find any comparable analysis of the failings of independent Ireland.

Furthermore, the capitalists, and that's the word he used, had 'fought every attempt to use the State as a real instrument of economic growth'. The interest of the private investor was safeguarded, he alleged, 'even if it meant that a million emigrants would be discarded as surplus labour in a land starved of employment'. Ordinary people suffered while the gombeen man flourished. Self-evidently, this was the language of outrage; a devastating attack on individualism and served as the moral basis for what came next, an economic solution.

Economic Planning

In the printed version of the speech, published some months later in the form of a booklet, that section is broken into two parts, the first being dubbed 'Economic Planning' and the second 'The Structure of Government'. The rationale for planning was utilitarian. The profit motive had failed as the engine of growth, consequently, the State must plan the economy by controlling the use of capital and investing it in those sectors that were of most benefit to the community. Whereas private individuals and companies operated only on the profit motive, the State must expand the range of investment to include social objectives. Profit could not be used as the sole determinant of investment. It followed that the banks, insurance companies and other financial institutions could not be left as the preserve of private enterprise. This was established Labour Party policy but it had been quietly buried over the years – yet here it was being resurrected in a thunderous reappearance.

This part of the speech broke several taboos. It pitted socialism against capitalism, it placed social objectives above private profit, it made planning superior to free market forces and called for finance to be subject to the state as the guardian of the people. Up to this point economic planning had no place in the political vocabulary of official Ireland because of its association with Soviet communism, yet Corish was openly talking about the need for a planned economy.

The concept, and indeed the practice, of economic planning was, however, an integral part of the French approach to post-war reconstruction and there had been a UCD seminar on the subject a few years earlier which had excited some economists, such as Professor Paddy Lynch, one of the team assembled by Whitaker to draft the Grey Book.[50] But *planification*, as the French called it, was a step too far for conservative Ireland because it rejected the allocative law guiding investment decisions and so struck at the heart of the *laissez faire* system.

Corish anticipated the conventional criticism that planning was totalitarian by saying 'we are democrats, not bureaucrats' and hence the planning process would be open and participative. We Irish, he went on, would have to use 'our collective intelligence by deciding together on what was most important and by giving it priority'. That, of course, was anathema to conventional economic theory and had clearly drawn a line between Labour and the two conservative parties.

Corish's advocacy of a planned economy must have caused tremors in Merrion Street but surely nothing to the reaction in Dame Street, the heart of the financial sector.

The Structure of Government

Corish then turned to the structure of government because if the Government is to be involved in planning as a continuous activity then it must be geared for dealing with a huge range of problems efficiently. Speaking from his twenty-six years' experience as a member of Dáil Éireann, he questioned its suitability for the task of running the economy.

The existing system made no allowance for recruiting the best brains available either for specific periods or specific tasks. There should be more interchange between the public and private sectors. Indeed, it was worth examining the advisability of drawing Government members from the Oireachtas alone, which would mean recasting the Westminster model we had inherited. He advocated the reorganisation of Departmental responsibilities and the consolidation of responsibility for semi-state bodies. The public service must itself be efficient.

In a telling passage Corish warned that unless the role of Government was seen as that of stimulating growth then 'every attempt at innovation will be resisted'. For its part, the Labour Party committed itself to using the State as the instrument for growth, drawing up a national plan, extending state activities, guiding and controlling investment and offering a different motive for enterprise to that of the present system. This section was to prove prophetic because on entering Government in the 1970s, the resistance to change was palpable and, in many cases, proved insuperable. That was a tragedy given the scale of our economic failure.

The Welfare Society

Having diagnosed the problem, and having offered a solution to economic failure, Corish next turned to the fundamental question of what sort of society we wanted: an individualist one which reluctantly and inadequately discharged its social responsibilities, or a society based on welfare and equality. He turned his fire on a social system in which, he asserted, there was no equality of opportunity or of rights, no cherishing of all the children of the nation equally. In language that might be familiar now he blasted a society which proclaimed paper equality but did little to offset the consequences of unequal wealth and opportunity.

The choice he emphasised yet again, was between individualism and socialism, between welfare and want, between a society that set out to achieve equality, as well as freedom, or one that begrudgingly accepted a small portion of social responsibility and closed its eyes to great areas of distress. Again, he returned to the question of whether individuals were to fend for themselves in a spirit of competitive hostility or to work together to provide a high level of welfare?

Socialism

There was much more in that vein leading to the meat of the speech, an open exploration, for the first time in democratic Ireland, of what was meant by socialism. In a piece of home-spun wisdom, Corish said socialism was not 'a magic word that will dispel all evil simply by being uttered'. This section of the speech was the most carefully researched and was the product of conversations with leading thinkers, the most prominent of whom was the Dominican friar, Father Fergal O'Connor.[51]

In fact, O'Connor wrote him a long treatise on socialism after one of their conversations and many of its ideas were incorporated into the speech, particularly the basic beliefs of socialism, such as freedom, including economic freedom; equality; the equitable distribution of wealth; co-operation, rather than competition, which only bred cruelty and diminished social responsibility; efficiency, because private enterprise was inherently inefficient in meeting social goals. The result was a comprehensive and accessible mini-treatise on the meaning of socialism which still stands the test to time. It was, of course, music to the ears of the delegates.

The Party

The last section dealt with the Party, which is the way Corish structured all his Leader's Addresses to Annual Conference. In fact, this section is a speech within a speech and is devoted entirely to politics. Here again, he took an unexpected approach and began by openly admitting that the prospect of a Labour Government lacked credibility but that the Local Election successes a few months earlier meant that Labour had emerged as a balanced party, geographically and socially, and could no longer be ignored as a national force, as it had been to date.[52] By dint of its successes it was now the party of the future.

Ireland, Corish said, had been a country ruled by tired old men, bitter and frustrated by their failures, who had sunk into an apathy which had infected public life, business, commerce, agriculture and the arts. Now they were gone. A new era was at hand and people had different aspirations and new attitudes, the primitive belief in the infallibility of one party had died out. His personal credo was that when people asked 'what is politics all about' then Labour's future would be assured. But by way of preparation it had to initiate what he called 'the great debate on the future of the Labour movement and it objectives'.

That is what the New Republic speech was all about. It was the first step in the intellectual renewal of the Labour movement. Quite properly, Corish returned to the past in order to plan the future. 'We are heirs to a tradition of brave struggle' which he categorised defiantly as 'the defence of working class rights'. He invoked the Defenders of the eighteenth century, the '98 Rising, Tone, the Fenians, 1913 and, of course, 1916.

Corish called on all to rally to this call, castigating those who had held back, such as the trade unions, who had failed Connolly and Larkin, rural supporters who were satisfied with partial success, young urban radicals who criticised from the outside and the party at large which had fallen victim of cynicism. He finished on a high note, as he always did.

> 'I am convinced that the people will accept this alternative of the New Republic. We have embarked on a noble adventure ... Comrades, let us go forward together.'

At which point the delegates arose and gave him a prolonged standing ovation. The conference was euphoric, said one report, and the atmosphere ecstatic. We know what happened afterwards, but it was enough to have dreamed. The core task of a Leader is to inspire with a noble vision. That he had done.

We who worked with Brendan Corish were privileged to have shared in the noble adventure he launched in Liberty Hall with his speech on 'The New Republic'.

Corish addressing 1969 Election rally
(image courtesy of the Labour Party)

The Administrative Committee of the Labour Party in the 1960s

Niall Greene

I have been asked to address myself to a little known but seminal development in the Labour Party of the 1960s – the role of the Administrative Committee (not to be confused with the Administrative Council or Party Executive of which the Administrative Committee was a sub-committee). It was seminal in the evolution of Brendan Corish's own thinking about how the party should be managed and the dynamic which it gave to the political and organisational evolution of the party.

I joined the Labour Party through the Seán Connolly Branch in Dublin South East on 1 October 1964.[53] Our local TD was Noël Browne who, with Jack Mc Quillan of Roscommon, had joined the Labour Party the previous year. Browne was one of only three Labour TDs in the Dublin area, the others being Mickey Mullen,[54] Dublin North West and ITGWU General Secretary, and the great Seán Dunne in County Dublin.[55] At national level, Labour was, of course, led by Brendan Corish since 1960 when he succeeded William Norton, Chair of the Administrative Council was Jimmy Tully, TD for Meath; Vice chair was Proinsias Mac Aonghusa;[56] and Financial Secretary [Treasurer], Barry Desmond. Senator Molly Davidson was Secretary of the Administrative Council and of the Parliamentary Party (not General Secretary of the Party) and she and her Assistant, Dympna Tannam, were the only occupants of Head Office at 20 Earlsfort Terrace.[57] The only others employed by the Party were Brendan Corish's Secretary, Mrs King, and the Parliamentary Officer, Catherine Mc Guinness, both with offices in the Dáil.

In 1964 there were eighteen Labour TDs, sixteen elected in the 1961 General Election with the later addition of Browne and Jack Mc Quillan. This was to rise to twenty-two in the 1965 General Election, with a much larger Dublin component of six seats. Our number of Senators dropped from seven in 1961 to five in 1965. There were no changes in the Officer Board at the Party's 1965 Annual Conference. I was elected to the Administrative Council as was a young Tom Powell of Carlow/Kilkenny – we were probably less than half the average age of the rest!

The 1965 election was a watershed for the Party and not just because of the breakthrough in Dublin. Corish's elevation to the Leadership in 1960 had not, perhaps, yet brought much of a shift in policy, other than in respect of participation in Government, but:

- the rhetoric was changing - 'socialism' and 'social democracy' were no longer forbidden terms;
- the scope of the issues with which the party concerned itself widened,
- there were vibrant university branches in UCD and Trinity;

- young people were joining the party in fairly large numbers;
- and there were early efforts to expand into parts of the country which were not traditional Labour areas;
- trades unions, led by the action of the WUI in 1965, were beginning to reaffiliate;
- a comprehensive education policy document published in 1963, *Challenge & Change in Education*, driven largely by Catherine Mc Guinness and Barry Desmond, had attracted considerable media and public attention;
- and, in his 'Tullamore speech' in 1961 Corish had set a road of parliamentary independence for the Party by ruling out Coalition.[58]

But Corish was conscious of the fact that the Party was not well set up to exploit the potential for growth and influence that was facing it both internally and externally.

One of the great and enduring legacies of the Party's origins in the trades union movement was its robust governance system. Who had authority to do what was well documented and understood in the organisation – Annual Conference was at the pinnacle as the last word on policy matters, the Administrative Council ran things between conferences and the constituencies and branches had their tasks and authority defined. The relationship with the Parliamentary Labour Party (PLP) was one area that was poorly defined and, of course, it was nonetheless the case that the PLP had more influence on the party's public tone than any other organ and in the 1960s that was largely a conservative and, in some respects, a reactionary influence. At the first meeting of the Administrative Committee on 14 April 1966, Jimmy Tully is recorded as remarking that 'We have a party of independents in the House'.

The Labour Party was ideally structured to ensure that it made few mistakes, but it was essentially reactive and not at all suited to exploiting the potential for creating a large and dynamic party that lay all around us. Corish could see that a more active, outward looking party was needed.

What was to be done? [59]

At its meeting on 31 March 1966, the Administrative Council unanimously adopted a resolution

'That a Committee, consisting of not more than 5 persons, or which at least two should be members of the Parliamentary Party, be set up to examine the administration of the Labour Party and to report its findings and any recommendations it might wish to make to the next meeting of the Administrative Council.'

It was proposed by Mac Aonghusa and seconded by Corish and clearly was an initiative about which the two of them, who were at that time very close, had given some considerable thought. It was very carefully pitched at the 'administration' of the Party about which there was widespread disquiet as the Head Office struggled to deal cope with a much expanded and continuously growing organisation. For instance, the number of delegates to Annual Conference had expanded from about 100 in 1960 to 350 in 1965.

But it became very clear when the Administrative Committee met that Corish had a much wider political objective in mind for the exercise. Notwithstanding the 'not more than five persons' rule in the resolution there were, in fact, six persons appointed: TDs Corish, Tully and Michael O'Leary, Joe Connolly,[60] Mac Aonghusa and me. Mac Aonghusa was appointed Chair. We had our first meeting on 14 April (at which Frances McGuinness was appointed minutes secretary), met nine times in all, completed our report on 21 June and submitted it to the Administrative Council on 28 June and 13 July – not bad for the days before word processing and mobile phones.

A little side show is illustrative of the tensions surrounding the renewing of the party. The only party Officer not appointed to the Committee was Financial Secretary, Barry Desmond. This reflected the very strained relations which he had with Tully and Mac Aonghusa. In my view, Desmond could have made a considerable contribution to the work of the Committee as evidenced by the content of the lengthy written submission which he distributed to its members before the first meeting. The minutes of that meeting record that 'it was agreed to take note of the memorandum from Mr Barth. Desmond about administration'. But by the next meeting on 21 April, when the submission had obviously come up for discussion again, the record is that 'There was a brief discussion on the activities of the Financial Secretary in circulating a document, marked for the attention of the Administrative Committee. It was agreed that Mr Tully would raise this matter with the Financial Secretary'. No more was heard of it although on my own copy I made extensive notes and its contents found some reflection in the final report of the Committee.

The Committee worked largely on the basis of papers written and submitted by its members. These were discussed and amended, and the conclusions incorporated in a final draft report by Mac Aonghusa. The main papers were by:

- Mac Aonghusa – an undated paper setting out the scope of the Committee's work prior to its first meeting and a second document, dated 20 April 1966, setting out a range of specific proposals for change;
- O'Leary - a memo, 21 April, on process of policy formation and specific areas for priority attention; and Connolly, an organogram and commentary, undated, on the 'Labour Party Machine' - the existing party structure and suggestions for its development;
- Joe Connolly submitted (undated) a schematic of the organization and decision-making structure of the Party.

I submitted a memo, 26 April, setting out the role of the then Secretary and outlining what the role of an 'Executive Secretary' might be; a 'Five-year costing for post of Organising Secretary of the Labour Party', 23 May; proposals, 28 May, for a committee structure for the Administrative Council; 'Draft proposals regarding Head Office to be included in final report of the Administrative Committee' (undated);and a handwritten and undated note on pension provision for the then Secretary.

On 24 May, the Committee considered a detailed note prepared at the request of the Party Leader which set out an exhaustive list of the issues that had been covered up to that point and the preliminary determinations that had been made on them. This was a timely intervention by Corish as it enabled him to put his own stamp on a large and rapidly moving agenda. One of the proposals that the Committee had considered, at Tully's suggestion, but which the document deferred and, in effect buried, was that the posts of Party Leader and Chair of the Administrative Council be combined.

The Final Report of the first Administrative Committee was approved by it on 21 June and adopted without amendment by the Administrative Council (AC) at 28 June and 13 July. The 13 July meeting appears to have been called specially to consider the report as it is out of sequence with the general schedule for the AC. The key points covered in the report were:

- the 'long-term objective of the Labour Party is to win a majority of seats in both Irish Parliaments and to set up a Democratic Republic, the constitution of which will be based on the social principles and aims of James Connolly';
- the immediate aim is to win as many seats as possible in Dail Eireann, in Seanad Eireann and on all local bodies, to win control of those bodies and to seek at all times to use them to forward Labour policies';
- Party Head Office 'must be a proper centre on which will depend, to a great extent, the future success of the Labour Party';
- the 'most important Officer of the Party should be the General Secretary [who must be] a person of considerable ability, enthusiasm and energy';
- the realignment of the work of the AC around five Standing Committees (Finance, Organisation, Policy Co-ordination, Publicity and Public Relations, Staff and Premises);
- detailed proposals on public relations – a simple weekly newsletter, regular press conferences, leaflets and pamphlets;
- 'harnessing the intellectual power within the Party and among its supporters for policy formation noting that 'Labour in Britain is a combination of trade unionists and intellectuals [and that] neither could gain power without the other. Traditionally ours has been an anti-intellectual party without being altogether a Trade Union Party. We have suffered as a result';
- the need for updating existing policies ranging from Workmen's Compensation to the Irish language – but it was interesting that job creation which was to figure so prominently in Corish's 'New Republic' speech to the Party Conference in October 1967 got no specific mention;
- improving relations with the trades unions;
- bringing the salaries, pension arrangements and working conditions of existing staff up to best practice of the time;
- and the re-equipping of head office (its typewriters dated from 1934!) and the expansion of the space devoted to the Party.

Predictably, there were, of course, leaks to the media! In its Final Report the Committee had noted that during its work ('done in secret') 'no memorandum fell into unauthorised hands and no unauthorised statements appeared in the newspapers'. But on 15 July the Irish Independent ran an extensive story based on the report and the *Irish Times* carried a similar piece on 20 June. On 19 June the *Sunday Independent* carried a briefing on the report by Corish himself to an unnamed Political Correspondent, presumably Chris Glennon.[61] The first two reports caused great hand flapping at the time but were probably not at all a bad thing as without them even Party members would have been unaware of the wide-ranging scope of the Committee's recommendations and the general public unaware of the Party's ambitions.

Despite the unanimous endorsement of the recommendations in the report progress on implementation was slow. At its meeting on 10 November, the AC reconstituted the Administrative Committee with a mandate to proceed to implement the report. The membership was changed to add Barry Desmond (now AC Vice Chair in succession to Mac Aonghusa) and Dan Browne.[62] For reasons that are not at all clear to me, I was appointed Chair.

In its report to the AC on 12 January 1967, the Committee dwelt at some length on the scope and membership of the policy committees which it had established from among party members and sympathisers (Finance, Local Government, Health, Education and Agriculture – but, again, not employment and job creation!) and then went on to deal with the question of a senior political appointment in the Party. The AC meeting, on the proposal of Frank Cluskey, seconded by Corish, adopted without amendment the proposals set out for the appointment of a 'Political Director' of the Party 'to develop those areas of activity which, because of lack of manpower, we have not been able to exploit fully in the past'. The report recommended that:

- the terms of reference for the appointment should be those adopted on 28 June/13 July;
- arrangements for the appointment should proceed 'so that the person appointed may be enabled to take up office well before the local elections' (due in June);
- the Committee should be responsible for the selection process and the submission of a 'final name' to the AC;
- the post be advertised in the national press and to branches and councils of the Party.

The report dealt at some length with the financing of the post and noted that all of the Party's available cash would only sustain the cost for eight or nine months and that 'it would be unreasonable to expect anyone to take the position in the current circumstances of the Party'. It went on to say that 'We believe that sympathetic consideration would be given, particularly by affiliated Trade Unions, to an appeal for assistance over, say, the next three years, in financing the position'. In fact, Corish had already put in place a financial package with the trades unions covering two years. It had been discussed as a financing mechanism by the original Committee but, at Corish's suggestion, dropped at the 24 May meeting – no doubt to give him more flexibility.

The Administrative Committee put together a high-powered Selection Committee for the appointment in the selection of which Corish was the dominant player. It comprised Jim Larkin, WUI General Secretary; John

Carroll, ITGWU Vice President; and Paddy Murphy, Federation of Rural Workers General Secretary.[63] It was given a detailed mandate on 3 March. The Selection Committee reported back on 14 March that 'From the applicants interviewed, the Committee unanimously recommend Mr Brendan Halligan … for appointment to the position of Political Director'. No time wasting there!

What was the significance of the work of the Administrative Committee of 1966/1967? The first and most obvious was the appointment of Brendan Halligan, first as Political Director in 1967 and then as General Secretary. There was much political work to be done as the Party had not had a senior official thinking strategically about the development of the Party since the resignation of Luke Duffy as General Secretary in 1951.[64] Corish's 'New Republic' speech to the 1967 Party Conference was a direct outcome of the Committee's work, not just because of Halligan's critical role in its construction, but because of the meeting of the need, identified by the Administrative Committee, to start stating clearly what Labour stood for. That speech together with the Outline Policy Document exercise (in which large numbers of Party members participated) was to set the ideology and tone of the Party, notwithstanding deep and often bitter disputes about Northern Ireland and Coalition, for some twenty years.

And some results came quickly. The Party rans its first branded campaign in Dublin in the 1967 Local Elections under the slogan 'Win Dublin with Labour' and almost doubled its membership on the City Council. The 1969 General Election may not have been the thundering success for which everyone in the Party had hoped but we should never ignore the fact that the popular vote did go up by 16% to 17% of the national electorate and that every constituency in the country was contested – the kind of ambition that the Party needed. We were, of course, hammered by Jack Lynch's 'Cuban communism' tour of the country's convents and by our own very poor vote management, particularly in Dublin.

Directionally, this was the sort of outcome that Corish had wanted when he set out on the Administrative Committee project. He knew very well that the PLP was by and large well able to handle the day-to-day but essentially short-term parliamentary manoeuvrings but there had to be some function in the Party that thought long-term and strategically. For all his great parliamentary record, Corish recognised that the energy of the Party came from the organisation as a whole and he set out to create the conditions under which that energy could be released and channeled into building the Party, organisationally and politically. By and large it worked and, while counterfactual speculation is rarely all that productive, it is interesting to consider how the Party might have developed if we had not been dragged into Coalition Government in 1973 by the Northern crisis and the fall-out from the Arms Trials.

But that is for another day.

Brendan Corish on Social Welfare, Combatting Poverty and Social Inclusion

'His selfless dedication to the welfare of the weakest sections of the people has left a legacy of goodwill and appreciation. He was totally devoid of self-interest and motivated only by the public interest and a desire to serve the public good', Liam Cosgrave

Tony Brown

My memories of Brendan Corish are mainly of the decade 1967-1977 during which I joined the Labour Party, participated in some of the seminal years of his leadership and had the privilege of working with him in the National Coalition Government of 1973-1977 as Special Advisor to him and to Frank Cluskey in the Department of Social Welfare. Thus, I am writing of a relatively short period in a remarkable political life which spanned five decades from his election to Dáil Éireann in December 1945, succeeding his father Richard Corish, to his retirement from the Dáil in December 1982, having served in three Coalition Governments (1948-1951; 1954-1957 and 1973-1977). But these were years in which Corish played a part in events and developments of great historic significance and displayed leadership of a truly remarkable kind.

Joining the Labour Party

I became involved in the Labour Party in the mid-1960s through the influence of my friend and erstwhile colleague in the Irish Sugar Company, Brendan Halligan, who had become Labour's General Secretary and who was working with Corish to set the political agenda. I had a professional background in economics, public enterprise and a specific interest in the European Economic Community (EEC). Ireland's application to join the EEC had stalled but I was involved in the European dimension of the sugar and food industries and was an active member of the Irish Council of the European Movement. Outside my career interests, I was involved in the fields of adult education and social policy through bodies such as the Commission for Justice and Peace, of which I became Chairman in the 1970s.

Halligan involved me in some very active Labour Party policy committees and, at an early moment, introduced me to Party Leader Corish. At once, I was impressed by his warmth and his openness – he was a listener and someone who sought answers to serious questions. He encouraged the policy process and he devoted a lot of time to making contact with party members and hearing their concerns. As an Advisor in later years I became familiar with the local concerns to be taken fully into account in drafting speeches for Corish's visits to party branches around the country. Belief in Labour's values and aspirations and in the importance of developing appropriate policy prescriptions was the driving force for so much of his activity. His honesty, commitment and, importantly, his realism were deeply attractive and inspirational and quickly led me to an involvement of more than forty years, including twenty years as International Secretary. From the mid-1960s a policy development process was driven by the Party Leader and the new General Secretary who was part of the intake of new, young members seeking to play a positive role in a new phase of development in Irish politics, with a more radical outlook. It was recognised that there was a need to produce policies to match aspirations and slogans.

Kevin Rafter, in *Making the Difference*, wrote that

'throughout 1968 a raft of policy papers were published. This new socialist agenda was eventually aggregated into a 150-page booklet and later distilled into the party's election manifesto *The New Republic* in May 1969. The process was described as involving 'a complete critique of Irish society'.'[65]

I joined policy working groups on Health and Social Welfare and Workers' Democracy. A Special Consultative Conference was held in July 1968 at Liberty Hall where four hundred delegates debated ten policy papers which were then circulated to Party branches for consultation in advance of the Annual Conference in January 1969 where they were formally adopted. I was asked to introduce the policy paper on Social Welfare, my first effort at conference speaking!

Labour Party Outline Policy, January 1969 – Health and Social Welfare

On Health, the policy was based on the principle that

'the community has the responsibility of providing a free medical health service for all citizens without distinction. Its aim is to provide a health service which permits no discrimination between patients and which encourages the maximum involvement of the doctor with his patient. A socialist policy on health is based on the acceptance of equality and of the right of every citizen to medical treatment without cost.'

The paper covered ten detailed areas: Community Health Care; The Hospital Service; Medicines and Appliances; Geriatrics; Mental Health; Alcoholism and Drug Addiction; The Medical Profession; Research; Administration; and Finance. On Social Welfare the paper stated that

'It will be the primary concern of a Labour Government to shape the Social Services so that they intelligently relate to the immediate and long-term needs of the community. Social welfare must be based on a coherent political ideology which recognises the inherent dignity of each individual and the responsibility of society to preserve it.'

The objective of Social Welfare policy was 'to secure for each person a basic standard of living in terms of income and services, thereby eliminating poverty from society. The paper set out Labour's proposals under six headings: Basic Standard of Living; The Social Fund; Social Fund Incomes (Pensions; Unemployment; Illness); Incomes from General Taxation (Children's Allowances; the Incapacitated; Maternal; Marriage; Unmarried Mothers; Abandoned Wives); Administration; and Transition Phase.

Particular reference was made to the need for a policy on Poverty.

'Based on figures supplied in response to Dáil questions, Brendan Corish TD estimated that there were a half-million men, women and children in this country living on or below the poverty line. Many of the Irish poor do not appear simply because our present social welfare system chooses to ignore them. A good example is the case of unmarried mothers and their children.'

'Statistics of Shame': Labour Party Policy on Poverty

The Party's growing interest in policy on poverty was given impetus by a pioneering action of the Council of Social Welfare, an advisory body to the Irish Catholic hierarchy. In November 1971, the Council held a conference in Kilkenny which featured a number of position papers, one of which was to become the inspiration for major policy initiatives on the central social challenge of poverty. Séamus Ó Cinnéide's paper on 'The Extent of Poverty in Ireland' proved quite explosive in its conclusions on the facts and figures of poverty and disadvantage in the Ireland of the early 1970s, concluding that 24% of the whole population including 21% of all children aged under 14 years had a personal income below the poverty line. The paper provoked an intensive debate with contributions from notable individuals like Dr Garret FitzGerald, Professor Martin O'Donoghue, Denis Larkin, Bishop Peter Birch, Father James McDyer and Sister Stanislaus Kennedy.[66] I attended the conference, representing the Commission for Justice and Peace.

Much academic and political discussion followed the Kilkenny conference. In the Labour Party, a Policy Group on Poverty was established in 1972, with Niall Greene as Chair, Barry Desmond and Michael D. Higgins among the members and myself as Secretary. We produced a report which opened with the firm statement that 'the facts of poverty in Ireland are statistics of shame'. The report was developed as a draft party policy document which I took to the Party HQ for printing on the afternoon of 5 February 1973 only to learn that the Dáil had just been dissolved by Taoiseach Jack Lynch and that a General Election had been called for 28 February. The policy paper was shelved but resurfaced after the election, with Labour now in Government. The detailed paper was formally adopted as party policy in October 1973 and informed the intensive work on poverty which was initiated by the National Coalition Government in the context of EEC Social Policy development led by Ireland's first nominee to the European Commission, and future President, Dr Patrick Hillery.

The New Republic 1967

As the policy development programme continued, at the Labour Party Annual Conference at Liberty Hall in October 1967, Brendan Corish delivered a major address under the title 'The New Republic'. The speech was the product of at least three months' work, from early handwritten notes on Corish's Dáil Éireann notepaper to later drafts reviewed and argued over by his close collaborators. As those who worked with him on this, and on other speeches, have confirmed these were his ideas, not those of advisors or scriptwriters. Often in a clear written brief, he set out the themes, the spirit and the key expressions of what was then worked through by colleagues to produce a text for the Dáil or for a major conference or party occasion

Becoming Leader of the Labour Party in 1960, Corish was deeply conscious of the party's experience over the previous two decades when it had taken part in the short lived Coalition administrations in 1948-1951 and 1954-1957 – in which he held ministerial office in the Department of Social Welfare – with outcomes for Labour that were, to say the least, frustrating and that pointed to an urgent need to achieve both internal party unity and a communicable identity. The 'New Republic' speech delivered to the Labour Party Annual Conference was a milestone in the history of the Party and in the political life of the country. Its subsequently derided opening statement that 'The Seventies will be Socialist' left its hearers in no doubt that this was no conventional Party Leader's Address but a statement of intent and purpose – a call to action for those within the party and a challenge to those without to look to Labour as the party of the future. He spoke of a Party initiating a debate on the future of the Labour Movement, working on new statements of policy and strategy and attracting new members 'from areas which ten years ago would not have considered voting Labour, let alone joining us'.

A key element of the speech dealt with Welfare:

'The crisis of decision which is facing us as a people goes further than the problem of economic growth. Growth is not an end in itself but must be used to raise the welfare of the whole community. The fundamental decision we have yet to make relates to the type of society we want – an individualist one which reluctantly and inadequately discharges its social responsibility, or a society which is based in the concept of welfare. What are we to do with increased wealth? How are we to share it within society? Are we to leave things as they are or are we going to root out social injustice wherever it appears?

There is an uneasy truce at present in our society because equality is not really accepted as a social objective. We may have political equality but this is not enough, since real equality can only be achieved by ensuring social and economic equality as well, In many ways this is the central problem of democracy ... In a competitive society which glorifies the pursuit of profit, our social needs come a very bad second to those of the individual. As a result our rulers see nothing wrong in giving a widow with two children 81/- per week, a disabled man 92/6 per week to look after himself and his wife, an unemployed man £5.12.6 per week to care for a wife and four children and a youth just out of school with no job, nothing at all ...

Irish society today does not appear to believe in equality. The Democratic Programme of the First Dáil, which was largely socialist inspired, has been ignored for fear of upsetting the status quo. If we want to rectify the grave defects in our community, we must change our inherited attitudes. We must not be afraid of making fundamental changes, otherwise we shall merely continue with the national hypocrisy of the last forty-five years. The philosophy of our social services is based on the nineteenth century notion that it is a crime to be poor ...

It is the principle that is important here, not the detailed policies. Any politician knows that policies apply principles and that if you start from the wrong beliefs then no matter what you do your policies will be defective. In this area of social services, including education, housing, health, and social security, it has yet to be made a general principle of Government policy that the State accepts responsibility for providing these services to every citizen without exception.'

General Election 1969 & Cork City Hall, December 1970

The 1969 General Election saw the promise of the New Republic and the aspirations of the Outline Policy exercise, as reflected in the party manifesto, dashed as Labour increased its vote but not its Dáil representation and as Fianna Fáil won yet another victory in a series which saw them in power for sixteen years. Corish determined to continue his campaign for a Labour future but, within a year, was confronted by a national crisis – arising from the Arms Trial of May 1970 and all it represented – that demanded a response which he was to provide with honesty and vigour. That response, asserting Labour's determination to act decisively in the national interest, would show the way to future Labour Leaders – O'Leary, Spring and Gilmore – who in their day were to accept the challenge, responsibility, and the cost, of government.

In Cork City Hall, on 13 December 1970, Corish proposed a dramatic change of Labour Party strategy – reversing his own words about retiring to the back benches if Labour ever decided to go into Coalition. In what was subsequently described as a psychological masterpiece he delivered his speech from the delegate's podium on the floor of conference, not from the platform, and he carried the day decisively, setting the stage for the emergence of the National Coalition of 1973. That change of course arose directly from the Arms Crisis. Halligan has written that the crisis 'changed everything utterly, and Brendan concluded, almost immediately it seemed to me, that providing an alternative government to Fianna Fáil in the national interest, that much derided phrase, took precedence over his political strategy'.[67]

The City Hall speech and the crucial change of direction led directly to the decision to offer, with Fine Gael, a clear electoral alternative to Fianna Fáil in the 1973 General Election. Corish directed the Labour Party team which negotiated the remarkable 'Statement of Intent' with its fourteen specific policy points, offering the prospect of 'an entirely new government committed to democratic processes, economic development and social reform'.

EEC Referendum 1972

The 1972 Referendum on EEC accession saw the Labour Party opposing entry and advocating a form of associate membership designed to protect vulnerable sectors of the Irish economy. Corish strongly advanced the party line which he saw as a reflection of the views of much of the trade union movement.[68] That line resulted in Labour campaigning against Fianna Fáil and Fine Gael, but on the same side as Sinn Féin, leading Conor Cruise O'Brien to comment that 'I disliked our allies more than I disliked either set of our adversaries'.[69]

On 10 May 1972 the Irish electorate dealt with the EEC issue in a most decisive manner – voting 'Yes' by a margin of five to one, thus putting many party members 'out of their misery'. Corish immediately accepted the decision and demonstrated his intention to work positively in the new situation by nominating two outstanding members – Cruise O'Brien and Justin Keating - to the pre-direct election European Parliament. They were to return after just three months to enter the National Coalition cabinet. In that administration, Corish was most supportive of the efforts of colleagues, including myself in my work with Cluskey on the European Social Action Programme, as we became familiar with the new realities of EEC Councils and Committees and of the charms of Brussels and Strasbourg. Corish played a positive role in Ireland's first Presidency of the EEC Council of Ministers in 1975 which saw this country firmly established at the heart of the European project of peace and progress.

Statement of Intent 1973

With a General Election seeming imminent talks began in late 1972 between the Labour Party and Fine Gael with a view to agreeing a Joint Statement of Intent as an Election Manifesto. Corish led those talks for Labour with Liam Cosgrave leading for Fine Gael. The text, as endorsed by the party's AC, contained fourteen policy points including a crucial commitment to uphold the democratic institutions of the State in the face of the Northern Ireland crisis and the activity of the IRA and a clear statement on ending 'all forms of existing discrimination against women'.

The Statement contained a lengthy section on Social Reform which was inserted at Corish's insistence, with the strong support of Fine Gael's Declan Costello, author of *Towards A Just Society*.[70] Under 'Social Reform', the Statement read

'The elimination of poverty and the ending of social injustice will be a major priority in the next Government's programme. It is conservatively estimated that under Fianna Fáil a quarter of our people live in poverty. The social policy of the new Government will bring immediate assistance to those in need and lay the foundations of long-term policy that will root out the causes of low incomes, and bad housing and poor educational facilities. Special legislation will be passed to deal with the plight of the aged, deprived children, the widowed, orphaned and deserted and the physically and mentally handicapped.

The money saved as a result of EEC membership will be applied by the new Government to a radical improvement of pensions and social benefits such as payment of old age pensions at an earlier age without a means test to both men and women.

A central feature of this social policy will be a complete reform of the system of financing social services through the introduction of a comprehensive social security system covering all citizens.'

National Coalition Government, 1973-1977

The National Coalition Government was in office from 1973-1977 ... and it is relevant to recall the contribution of Corish – and with him Cluskey as his Junior Minister – in the Department of Social Welfare. At that time, total spending on Social Welfare increased more than three times – from £150 million to £490 million; from 6.5% of GDP to 10.5%. In 2018 spending exceeded €20 billion! The scope and scale of Social Welfare coverage was greatly extended:

- by reducing the pension age in four successive budgets to 66 years, with the intention of reaching 65 denied by the 1977 election;
- by extending entitlement to welfare to single mothers, deserted wives and prisoners' dependents
- by providing pensions for women at the age of 58 where they were the principal carers of parents or relatives
- by making Children's Allowances payable directly to mothers whereas previously they were payable to fathers
- by easing means tests and removing income limits in many schemes.

Corish told the ITGWU Annual Conference in 1975 that the Government's commitment to reform extended across a broad front: social welfare, health, housing, the law and industrial relations emphasising:

'I believe the Social Welfare system has been given a new national status by this Government and this represents one of the greatest achievements of Labour in Government. The importance of developing a welfare system which will provide a comprehensive income maintenance service for all citizens, with full recognition of the rights and dignity of those in receipt of benefits and allowances, has always been basic Labour policy and is now accepted by the Government.'

Becoming an Advisor

I served as Special Advisor to Corish during his term of office as Tánaiste and Minister for Health and Social Welfare from 1973-1977. My main duties related to the Social Welfare brief and led to me devoting much of my time and attention to working closely with the remarkable Frank Cluskey, who was Parliamentary Secretary to the Minister for Social Welfare (Ministers of State were a later innovation). With my colleague and friend, Flor O'Mahony, who worked mainly on the Health brief we provided support and advice to Corish as Tánaiste and Minister but also as Leader of the Labour Party in a Coalition administration. This led to a great deal of work – in close and detailed dialogue with the Tánaiste on content – on speeches and speaking notes for the many engagements which crowded his diary.

In particular, I became involved in the significant EEC dimension of the Social Welfare Department as Ireland became part of the enlarged European Community's policy programme, following the path outlined by, among others, the German Chancellor Willy Brandt who had argued that

'Social justice must not remain an abstract concept nor must social progress be misconstrued as a mere appendage of economic growth. If we develop a European view of social policy, many of our countries' citizens will more readily identify themselves with the community.'

A central aspect of that experience was the reality of the Northern Ireland crisis which reached appalling levels of violence in the early 1970s. There was a direct IRA threat to the security of the State, with atrocities such as the murder of the British Ambassador Christopher Ewart Biggs and a series of kidnappings and bank robberies. Corish, like all members of the Government, was protected at all times by a heavy Special Branch presence – including that of armed officers in the ministerial corridor of the Social Welfare HQ, Aras Mhic Dhiarmada.

Social Inclusion

Re-reading Corish's speeches and recalling many conversations the concept of Social Inclusion was central to his vision and thinking. Going back to the New Republic speech we read that

> 'The fundamental decision we have yet to make relates to the type of society we want – an individualist one which reluctantly and inadequately discharges its social responsibility, or a society which is based in the concept of welfare. What are we to do with increased wealth? How are we to share it within society? Are we to leave things as they are or are we going to root out social injustice wherever it appears?'

A number of examples of actions to follow up on those ideas may be cited.

National Economic and Social Council (NESC)

NESC was established in 1973 and advises the Taoiseach on strategic policy issues relating to sustainable economic, social and environmental development in Ireland. Its members are representatives of business and employers' associations, trade unions, agricultural and farming bodies, community and voluntary groups, and environmental organisations, as well as heads of Government Departments and independent experts. NESC's composition means that it plays an important and unique role in bringing different perspectives from civil society together with Government. This helps NESC to analyse the challenges facing Irish society and to develop a shared understanding among its members of how to tackle these challenges. The Council also works at international level with the national economic and social councils of other EU member states. It is a member of AICESIS (International Association of Economic and Social Councils and Similar Institutions).[71]

Cabinet Sub-Committee on Social Affairs

In 1974, Government established ac Sub-Committee on Social Affairs with a broad agenda covering areas requiring innovative thinking and prioritisation. Corish nominated Flor O'Mahony and myself to represent him in a group which included Labour and Fine Gael Ministers and the Attorney General. The Committee addressed issues including the need for citizens' advice bureaux (established as Community Information Centres under the National Social Services Council); services for itinerant families (with the remarkable input of Victor Bewley who had pioneered new approaches and promoted new attitudes to the issue);[72] identification of specific poverty categories, budget priorities, social work services; and family planning legislation (where a Bill, introduced on the initiative of the Labour Party permitting the sale of contraceptives was defeated in the Dáil with the Taoiseach voting against the measure).

A Seminar on Family Problems and Homosexuality
A memorable occasion was Cluskey's attendance at a Seminar organised by the Church of Ireland Board for Social Responsibility on 6 February 1976, devoted to consideration of 'Family Problems and Homosexuality'. This took place as much as seventeen years before the 1993 legalisation legislation. Church of Ireland Archbishop of Dublin Alan Buchanan asked Cluskey to join a gathering of clergy, social researchers, social workers and members of groups within the gay community. Cluskey who, as Lord Mayor, had granted the Freedom of Dublin City to Micheál MacLiammóir and Hilton Edwards, accepted the invitation following a discussion with Corish who fully supported his intention to participate. They asked me to draft, with Cluskey, an appropriate speaking note on the importance of open and honest discussion about public attitudes and public prejudices. He quoted the Scottish poet, Edwin Muir, 'it is easy for the false imagination to hate a whole class but it is hard for the true imagination to hate a single human being'.[73]

General Election, June 1977
By mid-1977, I had worked for four years on the agenda set by Corish and Cluskey in particular in respect of the EEC and Irish programmes to combat poverty. We had contributed to the poverty element of the EEC Social Action Programme in which the Programme of Pilot Schemes to Combat Poverty became a cross-community endeavours and had created the National Committee on Pilot Schemes to Combat Poverty, with the remarkable Sister Stanislaus Kennedy in the Chair, and then the Combat Poverty Agency. The 1977 General Election saw the defeat of the National Coalition and the return of Lynch as Taoiseach.

Brendan Corish the Communicator
As Leader of the Labour Party, Corish devoted a great deal of effort to communicating with the party membership. He was firm in his conviction that Labour's policies and priorities were in the long-term interest of the country but he never tired of telling party colleagues that it was necessary to be realists:

> 'The attainment of our socialist objectives depends upon our ability to persuade the Irish electorate to support our policies and our candidates. It is not just a matter of believing we are right and telling ourselves that we are right – we must be able to convince the people that our policies are right and that we are capable of implementing those policies in government.'

Many of Corish's speeches dealt with the major issues of a period of national and international challenges. A strong and often passionate parliamentary debater, he was also aware of the need to speak at some length to audiences which he knew were unlikely to be satisfied with 'one liners' or glib generalisations. He respected his audiences and, very often, gained their respect in turn.

Corish was deeply proud of his connection with the trade union movement and of his membership of the ITGWU. His speeches to ITGWU Annual Conferences were invariably long and wide-ranging, touching on the main issues on the agenda which reflected opinion and concerns within the wider union movement. His speech to the 1974 conference in Bundoran contained a characteristic underlining of his sincere commitment to the National Coalition Government and to its programme which he described as a 'progressive course of action in areas of social and economic policy'. He concluded with a reference to one of his deepest political convictions, arguing that 'social priorities particularly are the touchstone of political will in modern society'.

Looking at the range of his speeches the degree of Corish's social commitment becomes evident. This is not just a concern for local, Irish issues but a global concept. I travelled with him to a number of international meetings and conferences at which he always played a positive role. Several speeches deal with the need to tackle world poverty and hunger and to enhance Ireland's efforts in that direction. His address to the Annual Dinner of the Federated Union of Employers (forerunner of IBEC) in March 1974 is a case in point. Speaking to Irish employers only months after the Yom Kippur oil crisis had shaken the economies of Europe and the world, he told them that he wished to address three issues which he saw as crucial: inflation, which was certainly no surprise; the need to combat poverty, which caused a few raised eyebrows; and the importance of participation in the face of serious national problems, which may have been somewhat ahead of its time. I vividly recall the reaction of many of his audience that night in the Gresham Hotel who, while commenting that this was not the usual kind of speech at their annual get together, went on to say that it was a good thing to hear something that clearly came from the heart, but also the head, of the speaker and not from the Departmental speech recycling unit.

Legacy
Brendan Halligan has done this job for me:

> 'His legacy is clear enough. He was pivotal in transforming Irish politics: during a decade of global change Ireland kept pace with change elsewhere; he rewrote the grammar and vocabulary of politics; he created space in public life for the accomplished and he set social reform on a path that could not be reversed, for many his greatest achievement. He ensured that the Labour Party and Labour Movement became a bulwark against political terrorism and that, with Fine Gael, the democratic institutions of the state were protected from subversion. He left Ireland a better country than he found it.'[74]

To those, like me, who worked with him there is a personal legacy. On the morning I left the Department of Social Welfare for the last time following the defeat of the National Coalition Government, I assembled a compilation of the speeches I had helped to draft. I made a copy for him and inscribed this with the simple words 'Thanks for the opportunity of participating in writing these'. Looking back, that was a considerable understatement of my emotions. I had the privilege of working with someone who personified the values and achievements of the Labour Movement but whose strong political presence was, in Ruairí Quinn's words, 'combined with humility and a gentleness that comfortably accompanied his forceful personality and clearly held conviction'. Liam Cosgrave was right.

Brendan Corish retired from politics forty years ago. Forty years later we face many pressing social issues in Ireland – housing, health services, childhood poverty; and at a global level – the great challenges of inequality, the future demographics of Africa, the migration crisis. We are challenged by the UN Sustainable Development Goals and by the European Union Pillar of Social Rights. Recalling Corish's vision and achievements, we can recognise the necessity of finding political and civil society leadership dedicated to meeting the demands of development and social justice.

Notes

1   After welcoming addresses from Mayor Tony Dempsey, Deputy Mayor George Lawlor and Joe Thomas, Chair, Wexford Trades Council, papers were delivered by Helen Corish; Barry Desmond on the 1973-1977 Coalition; Brendan Halligan, 'Corish and the New Republic'; Tony Brown, 'Corish on Social Welfare'; and Niall Greene, 'Corish and Labour Party administrative reform'. Closing remarks were from Labour Leader Brendan Howlin. Time did not permit Francis Devine deliver his paper on 'The Corish family and the ITGWU', see *Irish Labour History News*, November 2018.

2   Francis Devine, *Organising History: A Centenary of SIPTU, 1909-2009*, (Gill & Macmillan, Dublin, 2009), pp. 35-38; Michael Enright, *Men of Iron: Wexford Foundry Disputes 1890 & 1911*, (Wexford Council of Trade Unions, Wexford, 1987). In the final agreement between the ITGWU and the employers, negotiated by Connolly, Corish was the only worker not taken back into employment which as Halligan recalls 'remained a sore point with the family', e-mail 20 February 2019.

3   Michael D. Higgins, 'Remarks at the unveiling of a Memorial Sculpture to commemorate the Wexford Lockout of 1912 Wexford, 12th May 2012', https://president.ie/en/media-library/speeches/wexford-lockout [retrieved 7 February 2019].

4   Kieran S. Roche, *Richard Corish: A Biography*, (Original Writing, Dublin, 2012)); Pauric J. Dempsey, 'Corish, Richard (1886-1945), trade unionist and politician', *Dictionary of Irish Biography (DIB), vol. 2*, (RIA/Cambridge University Press, Cambridge, 2009), pp. 853-854; 'Corish, Richard (1886-1945)' in Charles Callan & Barry Desmond, *Irish Labour Lives: A Biographical Dictionary of Irish Labour Party Deputies, Senators, MPs & MEPs*, (Watchword, Dublin, 2010), pp. 53-55, 268-269. Callan & Desmond record Richard's wife as Kathleen,

5   Michael O'Leary 'Corish, Brendan (1918-1990), politician', *DIB, vol 2, op. cit.*, pp. 851-853; 'Corish, Brendan (1918-1990) in Callan & Desmond, *Irish Labour Lives, op. cit.*, pp. 50-51, 268.

6   Niamh Puirséil, *The Irish Labour Party, 1922-1973*, (University College Press, Dublin, 2007), p. 189. In what some might consider a cheap shot, John O'Connell, on hearing of Corish's fretful insomnia, said, 'Brendan, the difference between you and me is that I would sleep at night – and I'd do something about them during the day', *Dr John: Crusading Doctor & Politician*, (Poolbeg Press, Swords, 1989), p. 87. O'Connell, 20 January 1927- 8 March 2013, qualified as a doctor in the Royal College of Surgeons and in 1960 founded *MIMS Ireland* and in 1967 the *Irish Medical Times*. He was Labour TD for Dublin South West, 1965-1981, but expelled for refusing to stand in Dublin West. He was returned as Independent in Dublin South Central, the split vote costing Cluskey his seat. A MEP for Dublin from 1979, O'Connell became Ceann Comhairle, 1981-1983, before joining Fianna Fáil. He lost his seat in 1987 but, after two years in Seanad Éireann, regained it in 1989 and was Minister for Health, 1992-1993, 'Dr John O'Connell: Colourful politician with strong commitment to the poor', *Irish Times*, 16 March 2013,www.irishtimes.com/life-and-style/people/obituary-dr-john-o-connell-1.1327690 [retrieved 13 February 2019].

7   Norton, 2 November 1900 -4 December 1963, was General Secretary, Post Office Workers' Union, 1924-1957, and Labour TD for Dublin County. 1926-1927, and for Kildare, 1932-1963. He was Labour Leader, 1932-1960, and Tánasite and Minister for Social Welfare, 1948-1951, and Tánaiste and Minister for Industry & Commerce, 1954-1957, Callan & Desmond, *Irish Labour Lives, op. cit.*, pp. 199-203, 295-296; and Francis Devine, *Communicating the Union: A History of the Communications Workers' Union From 1900*, (CWU, Dublin, 2015), pp. 763-765.

8   John Horgan, *The Price of Power*, (Gill & Macmillan, Dublin, 1986), pp. 33.

9   Emmet O'Connor, *A Labour History of Ireland, 1824-2000*, (UCD Press, Dublin, 2011), p. 187.

10 Corish, despite the announcement that Browne's admission had been unanimous, actually voted against his and McQuillan's admission, Puirséil, *The Labour Party, op. cit.*, p. 227. Browne, 20 December 1915-21 May 1997, was born in Waterford and educated in England and Trinity College where he qualified as a doctor. He suffered from TB and lost both his parents and some siblings to the disease. He became Minister for Health, 1948-1951, on his first day in the Dáil as a Clann na Poblachta TD, resigning over the Mother & Child Scheme debacle. After a brief time in Fianna Fáil, he led the National Progressive Democrats, 1958-1963, before joining Labour, 1963-1973, and the Socialist Labour Party,. 1977-1982. He served in Seanad Éireann for the University of Dublin, 1973-1977. See his *Against the Tide*, (Gill & Macmillan, Dublin, 1986, 2007) and John Horgan, *Noël Browne: Passionate Outsider*, (Gill & Macmillan, Dublin, 2000).

11 McQuillan, 1920-1998, from Ballyforan, won All-Ireland Championships with Roscommon in 1943-1944. He was TD for Roscommon, 1948-1965, being returned for Clann na Poblachta, 1948; Independent Republican, 1951; National Progressive Democratic Party, 1958. He served as Labour Senator, 1965-1968, and was expelled in 1969; and was a founder, with Browne, of the SLP, 1977. In 1966, he was appointed General Secretary, Irish Post Office Officials' Association, a breakaway, non-ICTU affiliated body from the Post Office Workers' Union. See Lawrence William White, 'McQuillan, John ('Jack') (1920-1998), Gaelic footballer and politician', *DIB, vol. 6*, pp. 179-181; 'John McQuillan (1920-1998)' in Callan & Desmond, *Irish Labour Lives, op. cit.*, pp. 182, 292.

12 Dunne, 18 December 1918-25 June 1969, was Labour TD for Dublin County, 1948-1957; and Independent, 1961-1965; and Labour again, 1965-1969. An active Republican, he was imprisoned and interned in the 1930s and 1940s. He became WUI Official in Bray in the late 1930s and an Organiser in the WUI Head Office from 1942 until appointed as the first Organising Secretary, Federation of Rural Workers, 1946-1954, having served on the ITUC Executive, Callan & Desmond, *Irish Labour Lives, op. cit.* pp. 91-94, 275-276; Henry Cairns & Owen Gallagher, *Seán Dunne, Bray, 1918-1969: The Story of Seán Dunne's Journey From Militant Socialist Republican to Labour TD*, (The Authors, Bray, 2007).

13 Mac Aonghusa, 23 June 1933-28 September 2003, broadcast for Radio Éireann from 1952, and for RTÉ, UTV and BBC from the 1960s. He served as Labour Party Vice Chairman and ran unsuccessfully in Louth, 1965, and inspired the formation of the Young Labour League. He was expelled from the Labour Party on 12 January 1967 because of his refusal

to engage with an internal party investigation into the origins of *Labour News*, a stenciled news sheet that criticised the Party leadership - especially the Party chairman, James Tully. Mac Aonghusa contested Dún Laoghaire-Rathdown in 1969 as Independent and thence campaigned for the Irish language and nationalist politics. Catherine McGuinness (née Ellis), was born in Belfast on 14 November 1934 and educated at Alexandra College, Trinity College and the King's Inns. She was a Parliamentary Assistant to Corish, 1961-1967, and active in the Party as Secretary of the Seán Connolly Branch in Dublin South East. She resigned from the Party in 1967 when the appeal of her husband, Proinsias Mac Aonghusa, against his expulsion from the Party was rejected by the 1967 Annual Conference. She was called to the bar in 1977 and was the first woman to be appointed a Circuit Court Judge in 1994, moving to the High Court, 1996, and Supreme Court, 2000-2006. An Independent to Seanad Éireann for Dublin University, 1979-1987, she twice served on the Council of State, 1988-1990 and 2012-. She was President, Law Reform Commission, 2007-2011, among many similar roles on expert groups and commissions.

14 O'Leary, 'Corish, Brendan', *op. cit.*, p. 851.
15 Lemass, Dáil Debates, vol. 223, cols. 2,550-2,551, 8 July 1966,
16 O'Leary, 'Corish, Brendan', *op. cit.*, p. 851.
17 E-mail from Halligan, 20 February 2019.
18 O'Brien, 3 November 1917-18 December 2008 was born in Dublin to journalist Francis Cruise O'Brien and Kathleen Sheehy, an Irish teacher and sister of Hanna Sheehy Skeffington, was educated at Sandford Park and Trinity College, and joined the Department of External [Foreign] Affairs, being seconded in 1961 as a Special Representative to Dag Hammarskjöld, Secretary General, United Nations in Katanga, Congo. He was Labour TD, Dublin North East, 1969-1977, serving as Minister for Posts & Telegraphs, 1973-1977. He served the TCD constituency in Seanad Éireann, 1977-1979, resigning to become Editor-in-Chief of the *Observer* in London, 1978-1981. In 1985, he supported Unionist opposition to the Anglo-Irish Agreement, in 1996 joined Robert McCartney's UK Unionist Party and was elected to the Northern Ireland Forum; and in 1998 opposed the Good Friday Agreement. He re-joined Labour in 2005, Callan & Desmond, *Irish Labour Lives, op. cit.*, pp. 60-61, 269.
19 Keating, born in Ballymore Eustace. son of the noted painter Seán Keating and Mary Walsh, was educated at Sandford Park, UCD and London University, becoming a Lecturer in Anatomy in UCD's Veterinary School, 1955-1960, then Senior Lecturer at TCD, 1960-1965 and 1967-1990, in between presenting RTÉ's *Telefís Feirme*. A member of the Irish Workers' Party in the 1950s/1960s, he was elected Labour TD in Dublin North County, 1969-1977, serving as Minister for Industry & Commerce, 1973-1977. He was twice briefly a MEP in 1973 and 1984 and sat in Seanad Éireann, 1977-1981 and subsequently an MEP Feb-June 1984, 'Justin Keating (1930-2009)' in Callan & Desmond, *Irish Labour Lives, op. cit.*, pp. 130-131, 283.
20 Thornley, 31 July 1935-18 June 1978, was born in Surrey and educated at Trinity College, gaining a doctorate in history in 1959. He was a member of Trinity staff from 1958 becoming a Fellow in 1965 and Associate Professor of Political Science, 1968. He was Labour TD, Dublin North West, 1969-1977, before joining the SLP, Callan & Desmond, *Irish Labour Lives, op. cit.*, 247-249, 304; Yseult Thornley, *Unquiet Spirit – Essays in Memory of David Thornley*, (Liberties Press, Dublin, 2008).
21 Brendan Halligan, 'On Brendan Corish: the man who transformed Labour', *Irish Independent*, 19 February 1990, and reprinted in Brendan Halligan (ed), *The Brendan Corish Seminar Proceedings, 11 March 2006*, (Scáthán Publications, Dublin, 2006), pp. 52-54.
22 E-mail from Halligan, 20 February 2019. Sweetman, 10 June 1908-1970, was educated in Britain and Trinity College Dublin, becoming a barrister in 1930. Active in the Blueshirts, he was elected for FG in Kildare, 1948-1970. He served as Minister for Finance, 1954-1957, and Tom Garvin has styled him as a moderniser, responsible, in part, for changes in economic policy and elevation of T.K. Whitaker. He was, however, deeply conservative and opposed FG's 'Just Society' manifesto in 1965.
23 Seán Treacy was the most public pro-Republican voice while O'Leary, Cluskey, Denis Larkin, Roddy Connolly and Barry Desmond took the opposite view, e-mail from Halligan, 20 February 2019.

24 Halligan argued that the Coalition was not 'hastily arranged' confirming a two-year period of contact, *The Brendan Corish Seminar Proceedings*, pp. 19-20,

25 Recollections of Halligan by e-mail, 20 February 2019. Corish received endorsement from the PLP for further meetings which then included Deputy Leaders.

26 Corish was not in fact at the meeting as he was in London that day along with Cosgrave for a meeting with the British Prime Minister and Foreign Secretary. Halligan recalls, 'in effect the PLP gave him carte blanche to do as he wished with government appointments', e-mail 20 February 2019.

27 For fuller discussion and exploration see Tony Brown, 'Europe and beyond' and Sister Stanislas Kennedy, 'Frank Cluskey and Combat Poverty' in Kieran Jack McGinley (ed), *Cluskey: The Conscience of Labour*, (Umiskin Press, Dublin, 2015), pp.54-75, 76-96.

28 O'Leary, 'Corish, Brendan', *op. cit.*, p. 852.

29 Horgan, *The Price of Power*, *op. cit.*, pp. 31-32. Horgan, born 26 October 1940, was a journalist with the *Evening Press*, *Catholic Herald* and *Irish Times*. He was elected to Seanad Éireann in 1972-1977 for the National University of Ireland and from 1977-1981 as Labour TD for Dublin South County. He replaced John O'Connell as MEP for Dublin, 1981-1983. From 1983-2007, he lectured in journalism at NIHE/Dublin City University, becoming Professor, 1989-2006, after which he served as Ireland's first Press Ombudsman until 2014

30 Horgan, *The Price of Power*, *op. cit.*, pp. 36-40. Halligan observes that at Labour Party and ITGWU conferences, on Northern Ireland, Corish and Cruise O'Brien said the same things, e-mail 20 February 2019.

31 Puirséil, *The Labour Party*, *op. cit.*, p. 142, citing Molly Davidson. Corish's frustration was shared by Waterford's Tom Kyne.

32 Ó Maoláin to Larkin, 25 October 1955, ILHS Archives JLJ/3, emphasis in original, cited in Puirséil, *The Labour Party*, *op. cit.*, p. 185, fn. 38. Ó Maoláin was born on Inis Meáin and was active in Conradh na Gaeilge, moving to Dublin and work as a shop assistant, for Dublin Corporation and in teaching. Imprisoned for his ITGWU activities in 1911 and 1913, he was a founder member of the Irish Citizen Army and fought in 1916. A friend of Seán Ó Casey and P.T. Daly, he was an ardent Larkinite. He unsuccessfully contested Galway West for Labour in 1943 but was elected Dublin Corporation, 1943-1944, Angela Murphy, 'Ó Maoláin, Micheál (Michael Mullins) (1881-1956), trade union and Gaelic League activist', *DIB, vol.* 7, pp. 683-684; Ó Maoláin, Micheál (1881-1956)', www.ainm.ie/Bio.aspx?ID=531 [retrieved 13 February 2019].

33 Puirséil, *The Labour Party*, *op. cit.*, pp. 219-220.

34 O'Connor, *op. cit.*, p. 227.

35 Halligan, *Corish Seminar*, *op. cit.*, p. 20.

36 Halligan, *Corish Seminar*, *op. cit.*, p. 21.

37 Halligan, 'On Brendan Corish', *op. cit.*, reproduced in *Corish Seminar*, *op. cit.*, pp. 52-54.

38 *Corish Seminar*, *op. cit.*, pp. 52-54.

39 *Corish Seminar*, *op. cit.*, p. 53; Puirséil, *Labour Party*, *op. cit.*, 260-262.

40 *Corish Seminar*, *op. cit.*, p. 22.

41 *Corish Seminar*, *op. cit.*, p. 19.

42 http://brendanhalligan.com/

43 https://www.iiea.com/iiea-about-us/

44 Richard Aldous, *Great Irish Speeches*, (Trafalgar Square, London, 2008).

45 Brendan Halligan, 'The Democratic Programme & the First Dáil', http://brendanhalligan.com/the-democratic-programme-and-the-first-dail [retrieved 7 February 2019].

46 Labour returned 21 TDs in the 1965 General Election: Carlow-Kilkenny, Séamus Pattison; Cork Borough, Seán Casey; Cork Mid, Eileen Desmond; Cork North East, Patrick McAuliffe; Cork South West, Michael Murphy; Dublin County, Seán Dunne; Dublin North Central, Michael O'Leary; Dublin North East, Denis Larkin, Dublin North West, Michael Mullen; Dublin South Central, Frank Cluskey; Dublin South West, John O'Connell; Kerry North, Dan Spring; Kildare, Patrick Norton; Laois-Offaly, Henry Byrne; Limerick East, Stephen Coughlan; Meath, Jimmy Tully; Tipperary North, Patrick Tierney; Tipperary South, Sean Treacy; Waterford, Thomas Kyne; Wexford, Corish; and Wicklow, James Everett. Norton resigned from Labour in November 1967.

47 Labour had won 12 seats in 1957 and 16 in 1961.
48 The WUI affiliated on 1 January 1965 for 25,000 members and ITGWU from 1 January 1968 for 100,000, Devine, *Organising History: A Centenary of SIPTU, 1909-2009*, (Gill & Macmillan, Dublin, 2009), pp. 548-550, 582-584.
49 Thomas Kenneth 'T.K.' Whitaker, 8 December 1916- 9 January 2017, was born in Rostrevor, County Down, and reared in Drogheda. His mother Jane O'Connor came from Ballyguirey East, Labasheeda, County Clare, and his father Edward, an Assistant Manager in a linen mill, from Westmeath. In 1956, Whitaker was appointed Secretary of the Department of Finance and in November 1958 the *First Programme for Economic Expansion*, known as the 'Grey Book', crystallised his ideas for economic reform into policy by encouraging foreign investment.
50 Patrick Lynch, 5 May 1917-16 November 2001, worked in Finance, 1941-1948, and became Private Secretary to Taoiseach John A. Costello. Assistant Secretary to the Inter-Party Government in 1950, he was retained by Fianna Fáil until 1952. Teaching economics in UCD from 1952, he was Associate Professor, Political Economy, 1966-1975, and Professor of Economics, 1975-1984. He was Senator for the National University, 1973-1977.
51 Thomas O'Connor, born in Causeway, County Kerry, 6 December 1926, joined the Dominicans in 1944 and took the name Fergal. He taught political philosphy at UCD, 1962-1991, and was a controversial contributor to *The Late Late Show* in the 1960s/1970s. He set up a hostel for homeless women in Sherrard Street, Dublin, and Ally, an organisation for unmarried mothers. He died in Dublin on 29 September 2005, see 'Beloved freethinker and mentor', *Irish Times*, 8 October 2005, www.irishtimes.com/news/beloved-freethinker-and-mentor-1.503232 [retrieved 7 February 2019]; Joseph Dunne, Attracta Ingram & Frank Litton (eds), *Questioning Ireland: Debates in Political Philosophy & Public Policy*, (Institute of Public Administration, 2000, Dublin).
52 Labour won 80 seats.
53 Greene still has 'my first party card signed by the then secretary of the branch, Catherine Mc Guinness'.
54 Mullen, 1919-3 November 1982, became an ITGWU Shop Steward in Ever Ready Batteries and active in Dublin No 1 Branch. He graduated from Fianna Éireann to IRA but joined Labour in 1945. He was Dublin No 1 Branch Assistant, 1949-1950; Secretary, Dublin No 4 Branch (Hotel & Catering), 1950-1964; National Group Secretary, 1964-1966; Senior Adviser to the NEC, 1966; and General Secretary from 1969. He left politics on his election as General Secretary having served on Dublin Corporation, 1960-1969, and as TD Dublin North West, 1961-1969. He was a Taoiseach's nominee to Seanad Éireann, 1973-1977, Devine, *Organising History, op. cit.*, pp. 967-968.
55 Dunne, see fn. 12 above.
56 For Mac Aonghusa see fn. 13 above. Tully, 18 September 1915-20 May 1992, born Carlanstown, County Meath, son of an ITGWU Branch Secretary. He was TD for Meath, 1954-1957 and 1961-1982, serving as Minister for Local Government, 1973-1977 – his re-drawing of constituencies in the Electoral (Amendment) Act 1974 the disastrous 'Tullymander' – and Defence, 1981-1982. He was Federation of Rural Workers Meath County Secretary, 1947; Regional Organiser, 1951; and General Secretary, 1954-1973, serving on the ITUC and ICTU Executives at various times, Callan & Desmond, *Irish Labour Lives, op. cit.*, pp. 252-253, 304.
57 Earlsfort Terrace was a substantial building owned by the party but mainly leased out on a commercial basis as a source of income for the Party.
58 There is disagreement as to whether this speech was delivered in Tullamore or Killarney.
59 The account which follows is based on original papers about the work of the Administrative Committee held by Niall Greene. They are a substantially but not entirely complete record of the work of the Committee.
60 Joe Connolly was the founder of the Community Games and a long-time Labour Councillor in West Dublin. He was employed by CIÉ as an expert on work organisation.
61 Glennon was Political Editor, *Irish Independent*.
62 Dan Browne was an Amalgamated Transport & General Workers' Union Official; Labour Councillor and, in 1982-1983, Lord Mayor of Dublin. He died on 30 October 2010.

63 Larkin, 1904-1969, was WUI General Secretary, 1947-1969; TD, Dublin South, 1943-1948, and Dublin South Central, 1948-1957. A moderniser and thinking Official, he was highly respected. Carroll, 1925-2018, was an ITGWU Official from 1944 serving in the 'Movement's section of Head Office until becoming Chief Industrial Officer, 1964-1969; Vice President, 1969; and General President, 1981-1990. For a week in January 1990, he was Joint General President, SIPTU. Murphy, was a founding Official on the Federation of Rural Workers, becoming General Secretary in 1973. In 1979, the FRW merged with the WUI and he became Assistant General Secretary, FWUI, General Officer SIPTU until his death in 1991, see Manus O'Riordan, *The Voice of a Thinking, Intelligent Movement: James Larkin Junior & the Ideological Modernisation of Irish Trade Unionism*, (Studies in Irish Labour History 2, ILHS, Dublin, 1995, 2001); Devine, *Organising History, op. cit.*, pp. 981, 983-985.

64 Duffy, 1890-1961, was born in Coumty Sligo and became a draper's assistant in Galway and active in the Irish Drapers' Assistants' Association, later Irish Union of Distributivee Workers & Clerks, in Galway, acting as General Secretary, 1922-1934. Her served on the Irish Labour Party & TUC Executive, 1920-1933 and as President, 1923-1924 and 1929-1930. He was Labour Party Secretary, 1934-1949, serving on many Commissions. He served in Seanad Éireann, 1944-1949, see Callan & Desmond, *Irish Labour Lives, op. cit.*, pp. 85-86, 274.

65 Kevin Rafter, 'Labour and the media: the promise of socialism, negative campaigning and the *Irish Times*' in Paul Daly, Rónán O'Brien & Paul Rouse, *Making the Difference? The Irish Labour Party 1912-2012*, (Collins Press, Dublin, 2012).

66 The papers are reproduced in *Social Studies*, vol. 1, no. 4, August 1972.

67 Halligan, *Corish Seminar, op. cit.*, p. 21.

68 John Swift's Bakers' Union and the WUI were the only two main unions in favour of entry. The WUI arrived at their decision after a famous day-long debate in Dún Laoghaire, see Devine, *Organising History, op. cit.*, pp. 668-672 and for ITGWU 627-630; and Francis Devine, *Understanding Social Justice: Paddy Cardiff & the Discipline of Trade Unionism*, (Studied in Irish Labour History 8, ILHS, Dublin, 2002).

69 This was a personal comment to Brown from Cruise O'Brien.

70 http://historyhub.ie/towards-a-just-society A JUST SOCIETY FOR IRELAND? 1964-1987 (Palgrave Macmillan, 2013)

71 See www.aicesis.org/ [retrieved 16 February 2019].

72 Bewley, 1912-19 May 1999, Quaker and proprietor Bewley's cafés of the Dublin cafés, supported Irish Travellers, prisoners, and the Northern Peace Movement. He turned the family business into a trust for the staff, Fiona Murdoch, *Victor Bewley's Memoirs*, (Veritas, Dublin, 1989).

73 Micheál Mac Liammóir, 25 October 1899-6 March 1978, was born Alfred Willmore in Kensal Green, London, was a child actor. He came to Ireland to tour with his brother-in-law Anew McMaster and at the Athenaeum, Enniscorthy, met Londoner Hilton Edwards, 2 February 1903-18 November 1982. They formed the Gate Theatre in Dublin in 1928 and, while not living an openly gay life, were accepted as such and the President and Taoiseach attended Mac Liammóir's funeral.

74 Halligan, *Corish Seminar, op. cit.*, p. 22.

Above: Brendan and Phyllis Corish on their wedding day in 1948

*Below: Corish Centenary event, Wexford Library, November 2018:
l-r, Helen Corish Wylde, Richard Corish, Brendan Howlin, Joe Thomas (President,
Wexford Council of Trade Unions); Jack McGinley; Tony Brown,
Francis Devine, Barry Desmond and Phyllis Corish*

EMMET O'CONNOR

Persona Non Grata :
Andrew Boyd, 1921-2011

'I don't forget that what I am today was because of the NCLC'
Andrew Boyd, 3 October 1964[1]

Andrew Boyd was one of the great working-class autodidacts of twentieth century Ireland, and offered a unique perspective on Irish politics, one that was socialist republican in essence, but qualified by the knowledge of his own Protestant working class stock and peppered with his acerbic views on fellow Labour personalities. Boyd was born on 28 March 1921 to John Boyd and Annie, née Heaney, 38 Kingswood Street, in east Belfast. He was the second of four children, and the only boy. John (1881-1948) was raised in the Unitarian (Non-Subscribing Presbyterian) Church

and Annie (1894-1976) was Church of Ireland. John had joined the Royal Irish Rifles and fought in the Boer War. He left the army after several years, including service in India, but re-enlisted in the Royal Garrison Artillery for the entirety of World War 1.[2] On Andrew Boyd's birth, John gave his occupation as 'labourer'. One of Boyd's earliest memories, and a remarkable one, was of his father in the uniform of an A Special Constable guarding Larne Workhouse, which was being used as a prison for captured Irish Republican Army (IRA) volunteers. Recruited mainly from ex-soldiers and the Ulster Volunteer Force, the A Specials would go on to become the full-time Royal Ulster Constabulary (RUC) in June 1922. Though John was neither in the Ulster Volunteer Force or the RUC, Boyd leaves no doubt that his family was Unionist. One of his proudest achievements was getting his father to vote Labour before he died.[3]

Boyd attended his nearest school initially. A dislike of the master led him to switch to Elmgrove Elementary on Beersbridge Road after it opened in

1932. The master in Elmgrove, Walter Hamill, originally from Tipperary, would have a positive impact, and throughout his life he would credit Hamill for stimulating his interest in radicalism. For recreation he played the pipes with the Duke of York Pipe Band, and enjoyed body building and boxing as a teenager, and swimming into middle-age. Showing an early curiosity with current affairs, Boyd would don headphones to hear the BBC on the family's crystal set at a time when radio carried little other than news and 'serious' culture. His spirited independence is evident in his rejection of religion by the age of twelve.[4] On 24 March 1937, Boyd was indentured to serve his time as a machine turner in the marine engineering department of Harland & Wolff. The indenture provided that he would earn 6s per week in his first year, rising to 15s per week in his fifth year, and be entitled to holidays on Christmas Day, Easter Sunday, and three whole days between 1 March and 1 October each year.[5] The shipyard was an icon of Unionism, but would become a hotbed of radicalism during the war years. Boyd immersed himself in the work of the National Council of Labour Colleges (NCLC) and rose to prominence as a shop-steward. His zeal for what he called IWCE (Independent Working-Class Education) shaped his mission in life.[6] The true workers' organisation, he insisted, should be independent of employers or government, committed to the working class, and aspiring to the emancipation of that class. He applied that philosophy as Organiser for the NCLC, and the death of the NCLC at the hands of the British Trades Union Congress (BTUC) came as a bitter blow. His belief in IWCE also led him to develop as a journalist, and the demise of the NCLC encouraged him to shift his intellectual energies to history and political commentary. The skills of those trades were his weapons of choice, and he found them more to his taste than political parties. He was a perennial critic of union officialdom, cronyism, and willingness to collude with the State, best known for his hostility to the pieties and clichés of Northern Ireland Labour. In a divided society, where many felt that only the humbug held the movement together, he made enemies on all sides.

The AEU Communist

Boyd felt called on to respond to the poverty he saw about him and the rise of fascism in Europe. One of his first political acts was to attend a reception in Belfast to welcome home local members of the International Brigades. The Spanish Civil War marked the dawn of a purple patch for the far Left in Northern Ireland. With the Catholic clergy whipping-up a climate of intolerance on Spain in the Free State, the North became the more liberal part of Ireland, and its greater engagement with international events and the cross-channel Left sustained a vigorous radical sub-culture in Belfast. The particular turn of Boyd's politicisation was fairly typical of his cohort. He also recalled being at Belfast's Custom House steps to protest against the Munich Agreement, and buy a copy of John Strachey's pamphlet *Why You Ought to Be a Socialist*. Coincidentally, it was here he first saw Jack Dorricott, one of the speakers, whom he would succeed as NCLC Organiser.

Boyd also took to frequenting the bookshop run by Betty Sinclair for the Communist Party of Ireland (CP) in Skipper Street and Davy McClean's Progressive Bookshop in Union Street. McClean was Belfast agent for the Left Book Club, launched in May 1936 by Strachey, Stafford Cripps, and Victor Gollancz to educate British workers. The Club was broadly pro-Communist.[7]

On the outbreak of the Second World War, Boyd found himself in Belfast's key industry. It was a mixed blessing. He was rejected for military service by the Royal Navy, to his great regret, but had the consolation of becoming the youngest member of the Shipyard Committee for War Procurements. Joining Section Four of the Cregagh Branch, Amalgamated Engineering Union (AEU) on 11 June 1940, he became a Shop Steward for electrical repair, member of the AEU Labour Group, AEU delegate to the British Trades Union Congress (BTUC), and one of the youngest members ever to sit on the AEU's Belfast District Committee.[8] The AEU was then the most influential union in Belfast, and Boyd was conscious of how it had been controlled by the Ulster Unionist Labour Association until the mid-1920s, when the Unionists were displaced by socialists. It was not until 1939 that the AEU Labour Group had been established, and as late as 1959 Catholics made up just 12% of the AEU's Branch Secretaries in Northern Ireland.[9] Boyd was advised by his own Branch Secretary that if he wished to 'get on' in the AEU he should join the Freemasons. Boyd reckoned the masons were well placed throughout trade union officialdom in Northern Ireland.[10]

Weeks after the Molotov-Ribbentrop Non-Aggression pact on 23 August 1939, the Communist International – the controlling body of all Communist parties – instructed comrades to cease anti-fascist propaganda and oppose the world war as imperialist. The CP's official history makes no reference to the effect on Dublin but, in its only admission of internal dissention, it says of Belfast: 'As might be expected, there was some confusion among Party members in the North and it took much discussion to convince some members of the correctness of the party's political position'.[11] Boyd was unaffected. Arguably, his attitude was an early indication of how he could be perversely subjective. Searching for an alternative to capitalism, he decided he had found it in Marx's dialectical materialism. The CP's Belfast branch impressed him. Munich had led it recruit a significant number of Jews and intellectuals, and he recalled it as 'excellent on tactics and propaganda, and well versed in Marxist theory'.[12] He joined the Party in late 1940 or early 1941 and enrolled immediately for an eighteen-month course in Marxist economics taught by Bill McCullough, Party Secretary and a former NCLC student. 'There was I', Boyd recalled, 'an engineering apprentice, keeping company with university students and such like people of the professional classes as well as with the officials [of] trade unions'.[13] Months later, the German invasion of Russia in June 1941 and the Red Army's heroic resistance made all things Soviet phenomenally popular and the next two years unusually propitious.

From a few dozen in the 1930s, membership mushroomed to 1,000 in 1943. By the end of the war the Party had six full-time workers. Boyd was appalled at the party's welcome for 'lumpen proletarians' who were neither revolutionary or bothered about Marxism.[14] Moreover, progress came despite the CP's priority for the war effort over action to improve what Malachy Gray, of the CP's Industrial Committee, described years later as 'dangerous and primitive working conditions'. Workers in Northern Ireland generally tried to exploit their wartime value to close the gap with cross-channel pay rates. Though strikes were illegal under wartime regulations, Boyd was prominent in an apprentices' strike in 1941, and directed oblique criticism at the Party for its opposition to rank-and-file militancy. Privately, he regarded the CP leadership as being too supportive of the wartime Unionist Government, and suspected it enjoyed 'friendly relations' with the RUC Special Branch in return for information on Trotskyists.[15]

Though the Cold War brought cold times, and the muster had shrivelled to 172 by 1949, the CP would retain positions of influence, in the engineering unions especially, and the Party became synonymous with what Dublin comrades would call, with a mixture of derision and envy, 'AEU communists'.[16] Boyd too grew sceptical.

> 'I came to the conclusion a long time ago that one did not need to be even interested in Marxism to be a member of the CPI. And that, I believe, is why the CPI (or the CPNI) was unable to face the challenge of politics in N. Ireland. I think the CP did better in the south, but there the Communists had a more revolutionary tradition upon which to build – Fenianism, Connolly, the early ITGWU [Irish Transport and General Workers' Union], Larkin. The North was not only isolated from but in every sense hostile to the revolutionary tradition of the south. And that is why the CPNI sought refuge in the trade union movement and had no impact politically.'[17]

Boyd also chafed under the discipline of following the Party line on all things. He left, saying that the Communists were 'as happy to get rid of me as I was to get away from them'. Boyd lived briefly in Manchester in 1948, and subsequently moved to London, where he became a friend and admirer of Wal Hannington, a founding member of the Communist Party of Great Britain, leader of the National Unemployed Workers' Movement in the inter-war years, and subsequently AEU National Organiser.[18]

In 1952, Boyd married Catherine Kelly in Ealing. Known to friends as Kathleen or Kitty, Boyd always called her Catherine. Her father was a docker from North Queen Street in Belfast. She shared her husband's passion for labour politics and introduced the family to Irish. They would have four daughters: Geraldine, Barbara, Catherine, and Joan, 'all of them very competent Irish speakers'. Their father's knowledge of the language never went beyond a 'bun cúrsa', to his repeated regret, but he loved to hear Catherine singing 'as Gaeilge'. The girls remember their father as keen on education for women and quite happy to be seen pushing a pram in the 1950s.[19] After the first was born, in London, Catherine's homesickness led him to take her back to Belfast in 1953. Boyd found a job with BVC Industries in Castlereagh, where he served as an AEU Shop Steward.[20]

Happy Days With the NCLC

On 1 September 1954, Boyd took up an appointment as Divisional Organiser for Ireland of the NCLC. It would be the role that would shape his public profile. Emerging from an older, Marxist tradition, the NCLC had been founded in 1921 to co-ordinate the various institutions and movements for working class education. It was essentially an education service for some thirty affiliated unions, party branches, co-operative societies, and Clarion Clubs. Intent on offering a politically directed education, it differed radically from the Workers' Educational Association and its emphasis on liberal arts courses, or the Workers' Education Trade Union Committee, founded in 1919 by the Workers' Educational Association and the Iron & Steel Trades Confederation to offer courses that would be more union and workshop related. The NCLC became operational in Ireland in 1925 from a base in Belfast directed by Albert Ellis, from Newton-le-Willows in Lancashire. Irish unions were engaged initially, and ITGWU General Secretary William O'Brien chaired a large conference on a Dublin College in 1924, but their enthusiasm for what was an anglicised project did not last long.[21] Some could not forget the NCLC's British provenance. In the *Ulster Herald*'s otherwise generous coverage of the Omagh Labour College, it was styled the 'National' Council of Labour Colleges.[22] Ellis retired in 1929 and was succeeded by Dorricott, an ex-miner from Durham.[23] Dorricott made the NCLC a significant factor in the politicisation of emerging activists and accepted as step towards advancement in the Labour movement.[24] Though a member of the Northern Ireland Labour Party (NILP), Dorricott made no secret of his Communist sympathies or pro-Soviet views, which were broadly in keeping with the NCLC's Marxist philosophy. It was a time when working class education was taken seriously. Over the summer of 1930, for example, when inter-war trade unionism in Northern Ireland was at its lowest ebb, Dorricott spoke to twenty-five union branches.[25]

The AEU was particularly supportive, and Boyd acquired an almost romantic love of the project. Getting involved with the NCLC on joining the AEU, he plunged into work on the Committee of the Belfast Labour College – the colleges were in effect the branches of the NCLC – taking classes or correspondence courses in economics, English, labour journalism, public speaking, mathematics, and statistics, and becoming a voluntary tutor and 'frequent speaker' at the NCLC's regular Sunday evening forums. Lecturing came naturally to him. Walter Ellis, later a journalist and novelist, recalled his style: 'I remember him being sharp and well-informed and clever, yet speaking like a shipyard foreman. He had good one-liners – he could be quite cutting too, but in an amusing, not condescending way'.[26] A chance meeting one Sunday morning with his 'long-time friend' Jack Mulvenna, a veteran Belfast socialist republican and Charlotte Despard's driver, alerted Boyd to Dorricott's transfer back to his native Durham. By lunchtime, Boyd had his application for the impending vacancy in the post to the NCLC head office at Tillicoultry in Scotland. After sitting a three-hour examination in English, economics, and British and international politics, followed by an interview before the NCLC Executive Committee at Transport House in London, Boyd was given the job.[27]

Boyd inherited a network of contacts with trade unions, trades councils, and branches of the NILP or the Irish Labour Party (IrLP), and a team of voluntary tutors, most of them in the NILP and 'varied in intellectual calibre'.[28] In his personal history of the NCLC in Ireland, *Fermenting Elements*, Boyd titles his chapter as NCLC Organiser 'Persona non grata'. Why is unclear, though it reflected his self-image as a fearless Socrates to the muddled, the puddled, the powerful, and the pretentious on all sides. A clue may be found in his introduction of two innovations. First, while he continued with the prescribed curriculum, as he was obliged to do, he shifted the focus in teaching from the materialist conception of history to practical economic issues of the day. It was a topic on which Unionists felt vulnerable, as Northern Ireland remained the only part of the United Kingdom with high unemployment, and its economy was patently drifting towards crisis in consequence of Stormont's failure to diversify beyond the traditional and ailing staples of shipbuilding, engineering, textiles and clothing. Boyd stirred a controversy in 1955 by criticising the Government's policy of attracting external investment with subsidies, and some of his tutors added fuel to the flame by contrasting Northern Ireland's public sector with the 'outstanding contribution' of semi-state industries in the Republic. Belfast's three Unionist papers, the *Northern Whig*, *Telegraph*, and *Newsletter*, all objected to what they portrayed as a hostile campaign. It was also embarrassing for the NILP, which was uncomfortable about appearing 'disloyal'.[29]

Boyd's second innovation was to address the Constitutional Question in so far as it affected Labour. It was a time when the Question threatened to take existing divisions and set them in stone. In 1945, fifteen Irish unions had left the Irish Trades Union Congress (ITUC) to form the Congress of Irish Unions (CIU), demanding that all unions in Éire be Irish-based. In 1949, the NILP had swapped its 'non-committal' policy for a pro-Union position on Northern Ireland's status, and anti-partitionists had departed to join the IrLP, which became an all-Ireland party for the next twenty-two years. Boyd himself rejected what passed for the 'Connolly line', which saw Partition as a device of British imperialism and its bourgeois retainers in the Six Counties to divide Irish workers. He blamed nationalists for splitting Congress and argued that they had fallen into a Unionist trap in provoking the split in the NILP.[30] At the same time he held that Partition was a disaster for Irish Labour. Being from a Protestant background, he was all the more angry that Unionists maintained power 'by exploiting the ignorance and fears of Protestants, thriving on recurring violence, the inflaming of hatreds and the continuance of divisions'.[31] His answer to the National Question was to deconstruct it from a Labour perspective and look at each aspect in terms of its economic impact on workers. His approach was pragmatic and flexible, scathing equally about the NILP's timorous Unionism and the plaintive arguments of anti-partitionists who took little account of the obstinate fact that Unionists were the majority in the North. Yet he did not believe in 'balance' between those seeking civil rights and those denying them, and clung to the fundamental convictions that Northern Ireland was a failed state economically and one all-Ireland movement was necessary to rid Northern Labour of sectarianism.[32] These opinions made him better known as a critic of Unionism than anything else.

Boyd made more enemies over the merger of the ITUC and CIU in 1959. He had no sympathy with the CIU's aspiration for an Irish-controlled movement, seeing it as xenophobic, and objected to two concessions to the CIU: officials of British-based unions were to be excluded from conferences of the new Irish Congress of Trade Unions (ICTU) unless domiciled in Ireland, and the nineteen strong ICTU Executive was always to have a minimum of ten members of Irish unions. Boyd was not alone in Belfast in his reservations. The AEU was notably critical. In timeworn fashion, officialdom scrambled to smother a divisive debate. Efforts were made to exclude the Belfast Labour College from union rooms and have Boyd barred from giving lectures on the ICTU constitution. It did not help that he was writing regularly for *Tribune*, fortnightly paper of the British Labour left, or that an article of his in *Tribune*, deploring the Orange Order, was circulated by the Unionist Party in the 1958 Stormont elections to blacken the NILP. The NILP went so far as to publish a notice in the *Belfast Telegraph* dissociating itself from Boyd.[33]

Under the BTUC

From the late 1950s, the rationalisation of worker education appeared on the agenda of every NCLC conference. As the NCLC drifted away from Marxism after 1945 its once intense differences with the Workers' Educational Association and the Workers' Educational Trade Union Committee yielded to a feeling that they were all wearily tilling the same field. Since 1946 there had been proposals in the BTUC for amalgamation. In the NCLC, Executive Council morale sagged under the financial burden of sustaining a duplication of services, and Divisional Organisers complained that their salaries would be better under the aegis of the BTUC. General Secretary J.P.M. Millar, of whom Boyd thought highly, was ageing and ready to retire.[34] Plans were devised on foot of a resolution at the 1957 BTUC, and lengthy negotiations led to the BTUC Education Committee taking over the NCLC, the Workers' Education Trade Union Committee, and Ruskin College's Correspondence Course Department in 1964. The utter disappearance of the NCLC came as a shock. As recently as 1962 it was known to be fighting for the retention of its colleges. Now, it would be swept away, and just a few of its staff, the Divisional Organisers, would be retained as BTUC Regional Education Officers. Boyd was bitterly disappointed by the liquidation of his cherished IWCE. The new dispensation would entail instruction that had little to do with politics and more to do with things like industrial relations, chairing a union branch, and time and motion. In the NCLC Boyd enjoyed 'almost complete autonomy [and] almost endless scope for innovation and experimentation in education, ample time to study, encouragement to write, and freedom to make all sorts of contacts that would further the work of the NCLC'. The BTUC Education Committee would operate on a more bureaucratic basis, and mean subordination to people who welcomed collaboration with employers and state agencies. Quite aside from that Boyd had developed a peculiar aversion to union officials as place hunters, trimmers, and manipulators. He agonised over his options. After part-time study, he had recently graduated with a BSc in Economics from Queen's University, Belfast and was qualified to seek a post in a College of Further Education. Universities were still the preserve of the elite, and he was the only NCLC tutor with a degree. Peadar O'Donnell told him to continue with the BTUC but 'treat it as a civil service job', in the manner of so many Dublin literary men with day jobs in the public service at that time.[35] Boyd took his advice.

Boyd suffered a miserable time over the next seven years. His cards were marked from the outset. Anxious for better relations with Stormont when Terence O'Neill replaced Brookeborough as Prime Minister, some members of the ICTU's Northern Ireland Committee informed the BTUC that Boyd would not be the best choice as Regional Education Officer for the North. In 1967 Ruaidhrí Roberts, ICTU General Secretary and former Secretary of the People's College in Dublin, initiated discussions with the BTUC for the transfer of its education service in Northern Ireland to the ICTU. Opposition from Northern trade unionists eventually scuppered the idea. Boyd believed the real intent of the project was to silence him, and that his criticism of Ulster Unionists, especially in *Tribune*, was more intolerable to Roberts and the ICTU than to the BTUC. It was one of many such anomalies that Northern Ireland fell within the remit of the former, but its worker education was run by the latter. London, Boyd reckoned, had little interest in the North, and never grumbled about his political writings. But working for the BTUC was another matter. Boyd found it restrictive and complained of constant fault-finding with former NCLC employees in a relentless campaign to get them out. By 1971, only seven of the original eighteen NCLC Divisional Organisers were still in situ. Further trouble arose when the BTUC refused to deal with Boyd's union, the Irish National Teachers' Organisation, in negotiations on pay and conditions. Though it refused to say why the Irish union was 'inappropriate', the only explanation could be that it was Irish. Boyd subsequently recruited his fellow education officers into the London-based Clerical & Administrative Workers' Union.[36]

Boyd's final dispute with the BTUC arose in 1969 after the ICTU's Northern Ireland Committee accepted a grant of £10,000 a year for a 'training programme'. In keeping with traditional NCLC principles, Boyd objected, arguing that the money was not necessary and could only have a corrosive effect on trade union independence. The controversy generated considerable publicity and demands from shop stewards and union branches that the grant be handed back. Vic Feather, BTUC General Secretary, told Boyd he was creating bad feeling between the British and Irish Congresses and he would have to go. By now exasperated, Boyd was happy to oblige. Coincidentally, in the autumn of 1971, a temporary vacancy for a teacher of English and Economics arose in the Belfast College of Business Studies. In June 1972 Boyd was awarded a permanent lectureship in the College. He bade farewell to 'people in both the TUC and the ICTU who, in my opinion, were a drag upon the Labour movement and utterly incapable of visualising anything like a socialist future for either Britain or Ireland'. Apart from his membership of the National Association of Teachers in Further & Higher Education, Boyd ceased to be connected with trade unionism. He now had the time and the freedom to criticise the 'abysmal record' of the BTUC and ICTU on Northern Ireland.[37]

Journalism and Writing

Boyd had shown a talent for commentary as early as the late 1940s, when he started to write regularly for Glasgow's famous socialist paper *Forward* when it was edited by Emrys Hughes. His personal and political inclinations became evident too in his association with comrades of a literary bent in the Communist, Labour, and socialist republican traditions. Close friends included writers and activists such as O'Donnell, Dominic Behan, Seán Murray, *Tribune* editor Dick Clements, folklorist Hamish Henderson, and John de Courcy Ireland. His independence of mind was evident in the range of outlets for his pen. While he wrote mainly for the *Daily Worker*, *New Statesman*, and *Tribune*, he was also published in the *Economist*, *Spectator*, *Contemporary Review*, *History Today*, *Irish News*, and all of the Dublin daily and Sunday papers. For a time, he was Ireland correspondent for the *Nation* magazine in New York and a contributor to New York's *Monthly Review*. With the outbreak of the Northern conflict, he did occasional interviews with the BBC, Ulster Television, RTÉ, and Italian television, having a good command of Italian. In August 1969, the Irish Embassy in London purchased all remaining copies of his Fabian pamphlet *The Two Irelands* (1966) for distribution internationally.[38]

Since the mid 1950s, Boyd had been raising the question of introducing Direct Rule in Northern Ireland to get Westminster to address civil rights issues. He called for a Commission of Enquiry into Stormont governance, mapped out a blueprint for North-South economic co-operation, and urged Brookeborough to meet Seán Lemass.[39] When the Civil Rights Movement gained traction in the mid-1960s, Boyd persuaded Richard Crossman and Michael Foot, editors of *New Statesman* and *Tribune*, that the abolition of Stormont was inevitable.[40] Boyd's response to the outbreak of the Troubles was literary. With remarkable timing, *Holy War in Belfast* appeared in August 1969. Based on research done for a PhD at Queen's University on the history of sectarian disturbances in the city, it was regarded as his most scholarly work. Its 'immense supply of facts' challenged the tendency of academic historians and the bien pensants to downplay Loyalist sectarianism, apportion blame to both sides, or believe that the bad old days had been banished by O'Neill and Lemass. '[It] did help shock many people, lulled by the soft soap of Terence O'Neill, into recognising the sordidity that had infected Belfast society in the nineteenth century', conceded D.R. O'Connor Lysaght in an otherwise waspish attack on Boyd's politics, or lack of politics. *Holy War* ran to three editions.[41] Boyd continued his assault on Unionism with *The Guilty Men of Ulster* and *Brian Faulkner (and the Crisis of Ulster Unionism)*. Faulkner, he thought, was a man 'who could hardly be regarded as fit to be Prime Minister even of so miserable a place as Northern Ireland'.[42] In 1984, a prolific year for him, Boyd published the bluntly titled *Northern Ireland: Who is to Blame?* and *The Informers: A Chilling Account of the Supergrasses in Northern Ireland*, both with Mercier Press, Cork.

Most of Boyd's later books were labour-related. One of his best known is *The Rise of the Irish Trade Unions*. Based on his NCLC lectures, it filled a void in the literature, notably on the eighteenth and early nineteenth centuries, and though it appears somewhat anglo-centric today, it was unusually Irish-focused for its time.[43] There followed *Have the Trade Unions Failed the North?* Boyd had wanted to call it '*No Politics Please, We're ICTU*'.[44] It was a rare and useful critique of Northern Labour and its compromises with the state and sectarianism, and disgracefully neglected. Indeed, the corruption spotlighted by Boyd got worse. The introduction of Direct Rule had led to a profusion of quangos to offset the 'democratic deficit'. By 2000, the ICTU Northern Ireland Committee (NIC) had representation on forty of Northern Ireland's 144 quangos.[45] A well-connected official of an important union could expect multiple appointments, lucrative additions to his salary, opportunities for travel, and the possibility of making contacts that would take his career into human resource management. Seats on quangos were much sought after and created a mutual interest between the Northern Ireland Office and the ICTU-NIC. Inevitably, the fattening sense of entitlement at the top generated resentment on the shop floor. *Fermenting Elements* was the closest Boyd came to an autobiography. It summed up his life's work and struggles and was his favourite book. It also allowed him to vent his spleen at those who adulterated the CP and destroyed IWCE, as he saw it. Displaying great stamina for his age, he continued into his ninth decade with two pamphlets on Captain Jack White and *Republicanism and Loyalty in Ireland* and two more for the (British) Socialist History Society, formerly the Communist Party Historians' Group, *Marx, Engels, and the Irish* and *Jim Connell*. The latter was the culmination of four decades of effort to recover Connell from relative obscurity, beginning with an article for *Plebs* in 1961 and a BBC radio broadcast in 1962. Boyd canvassed British trade unions about erecting a monument, and wrote the entry on Connell in the *Dictionary of Labour Biography*, which reached volume ten before including the author of 'The Red Flag'.[46] In May 2012, Boyd's daughters Barbara and Joan unveiled a plaque to their father at the Jim Connell memorial in Crossakiel, County Meath.[47] Boyd concluded his publishing career with a booklet on the Presbyterian firebrands Henry Cooke and Henry Montgomery.[48]

Boyd had grown steadily more estranged from the politics of Northern Ireland. His own political world began to disintegrate in the early 1970s. The NILP virtually collapsed and the IrLP pulled out of Northern Ireland – something he condemned at the inaugural meeting of the Irish Labour History Society in Dublin on 27 October 1973, and for which he blamed Conor Cruise O'Brien.[49] He had no time for the politics of identity, and was appalled at the IRA, which he declared had decided 'to kill thousands of decent, inoffensive people and innocent children, destroy commercial and private property to the value of billions of pounds and incite the bloodlust of the most brutal loyalists'.[50] He was cynical about the government and media hype surrounding the 'Peace Process'. The Belfast Agreement, he predicted, would institutionalise sectarianism and render more difficult the old radical dream of uniting Catholic, Protestant, and Dissenter. His jaundiced view of the endless choreography required to gentrify forces and values that belonged in a chamber of horrors was expressed in letters to the *Irish Times,* and several articles in the *Irish News* in 2002. That same year he penned a 'poem' modelled on Shakespeare's 'Fear no more the heat o' the sun'.

Fear no more the IRA
nor Mo Mowlam's moving deadlines.
Fear not Paisley, Adams, Blair,
nor the media's happy headlines.
All guns, agreements, Mitchell must
like David Trimble come to dust.

Fear no more the Orange Order
nor the Spirit of Drumcree.
Fear not Provos on the border;
they matter not to you and me.

The banners, Semtex, Lambegs must
all follow all and come to dust.

Let Stormont not alarm thee,
nor Assembly members charm thee.
Make spinning doctors fear thee;
let none of them come near thee.
Trimble, Blair and Adams have
laid peace, Good Friday, in the grave
and – there will be no Resurrection.[51]

Retirement

Boyd retired as a Senior Lecturer from the Belfast College of Business Studies in 1986, and lived his final years in leafy Ben Madigan Park, under Cave Hill, where the United Irish leaders met in 1795 to plan rebellion. He continued to give occasional public lectures into the 1990s and of course to write into the next century. Maintaining a lively correspondence with friends and historians, he also kept his mind active by realising a longstanding ambition to read French literature in the original, despite his limited command of the language.[52] With the aid of a dictionary he would plough through such as Flaubert, Zola and Maupassant. In time he was able to read three novels a week. Aside from literature and Latin grammar, he loved mathematics, and liked to amuse his grandchildren with puzzles and conundrums.[53] Having outlived all his close friends, the loss of his wife on 11 February 2007 came as an inordinately cruel blow. 'With her death', he wrote, 'I have lost three-quarters of my own life. I am not in the least interested in anything'. He grew doubtful about his life's work: 'Recalling the past and the years I wasted in the CPI I now see the futility of what Marx imagined to be 'scientific socialism'. There is no such thing'. In 2009, he began an autobiography. The project did not get far, but he said a lot in the title: 'Persona Non Grata: Recollections of a Socialist in Ulster'.[54] 'Individualism was his defining characteristic, absolutely and completely', according to his daughter Joan who followed him into journalism.[55] Of course there was a contradiction in subscribing to a collectivist ideology and being so discrete. With Boyd, individuality sometimes slipped into subjectivity. And in drilling a lonely furrow he sacrificed the opportunity to make a more substantial contribution by throwing his weight behind others pushing for change. But had he done so, his unique voice might have been lost. By playing to his strengths, he made a singular impression as one of the few to examine the National Question from a Labour perspective. Independent, critical, and sceptical to the last, he remained convinced of the stupidity of partition, and the need for trade unions to be unbeholden to the state, democratic, and politically engaged.

At 3.11pm on Tuesday 5 July 2011 the Press Association wired the news that the 'straight talking trade unionist' was dead. He had died in the Mater Hospital, Belfast of bronchopneumonia, after a short illness. There followed a non-religious service – he had requested 'no hymns and no lamentations' – at Roselawn crematorium on 8 July.[56] On history he wrote:

> 'Finally may I say this about the study of Irish Labour history. I think that the history of the trade unions should be studied not simply to satisfy academic curiosity but to stimulate ideas, to gain inspiration from the achievements of the pioneers, to learn from them, and so set Labour on a course that will make it a power to be respected and taken seriously in Ireland and in all democratic countries.'[57]

Notes

1 J.P.M. Millar, *The Labour College Movement*, (National Council of Labour Colleges, London, 1976), p.181.

2 General Register Office for Northern Ireland (GRONI), birth certificate; I am obliged to Andrew Boyd's daughters, Barbara and Joan, for information on his family background and home life.

3 *Belfast Telegraph*, 6 July 2011; 'Persona non grata (recollections of a socialist in Ulster)', typescript, with the author; e-mail from Barbara Graham, 30 June 2018. Established in October 1920 to supplement the demoralised Royal Irish Constabulary, the 'A Specials' were issued with armbands and peaked caps initially and uniforms in 1922. In memory, Andrew was either mistaken or precocious. Barbara believes John was an A Special but not in the Royal Irish Constabulary or the RUC, e-mail from Barbara Graham, 11 July 2018.

4 Letter to the author from Andrew Boyd, 17 June 2009; e-mail from Barbara Graham, 30 June 2018.

5 Public Record Office of Northern Ireland (PRONI), Belfast, Andrew Boyd mss, Indenture, D2389/1; letter to the author from Andrew Boyd, 17 June 2009.

6 IWCE was a term with origins in the NCLC as explained by Belfast socialist Hugh Gemmell, 'Tutor, Belfast Labour College' in 'IWCE Independent working class education', *Voice of Labour*, 28 February 1925, reproduced as Appendix 4 in Norman Croke & Francis Devine, *James Connolly Labour College, 1919-1921*, (ILHS/SIPTU, Studies in Irish Labour History 12, Dublin, 2007), pp. 90-93.

7   Andrew Boyd, *Fermenting Elements: The Labour Colleges in Ireland, 1924-1964*, (Donaldson Archives, Belfast, 1999), pp.79, 95. For similar experiences of politicisation see Malachy Gray, 'A shop steward remembers', *Saothar 11*, 1986, pp.110-11; [Francis Devine], 'Letting labour lead: Jack Macgougan and the pursuit of unity, 1913-1958', *Saothar 14*, 1989, pp.113-24; [Francis Devine], 'An undiminished dream: Andy Barr, communist trade unionist', *Saothar 16*, 1991, pp.95-111.

8   PRONI, Andrew Boyd mss, AEU card, D2389/3a, D2389/3c; Boyd, *Fermenting Elements*, pp.79-80, 86, 94, 142; 'Biographical details', no date, with the author; letter from Andrew Boyd to the author, 26 December 2002.

9   Denis P. Barritt & Charles F. Carter, *The Northern Ireland Problem: A Study in Group Relations*, (Oxford University Press, London, 1962), p.141.

10 Boyd, *Fermenting Elements*, p.60; letter from Andrew Boyd to the author, 17 June 2009.

11 Communist Party of Ireland, *Communist Party of Ireland: Outline History*, (CPI, Dublin, 1975), p.38.

12 Emmet O'Connor, *Reds and the Green: Ireland, Russia, and the Communist Internationals*, (UCD Press, Dublin, 2004), pp.230-233. The CP in Éire was dissolved in 1941 but continued in Northern Ireland, nominally as the CP of Ireland but often referred to simply as the CP or the CP, North Ireland. Boyd claims that the name CP of Ireland was replaced with CP of Northern Ireland in the late 1950s. In 1970 the parties in Northern Ireland and the Republic united as the (third) CP of Ireland. Boyd, *Fermenting Elements*, p.115.

13 Letter from Andrew Boyd to the author, 2 December 2003.

14 Letter from Andrew Boyd to Ruth Frow, 15 June 2000; letter from Andrew Boyd to the author, 25 March 2008.

15 Letters from Andrew Boyd to the author, 2 December 2003, 29 March 2009; *Unity*, 16 January, 23 December 1943; Seán Byers, *Seán Murray, the Irish Republican Left and international Communism, 1916-1962*, (PhD, Ulster University, 2012), p.198.

16 O'Connor, *Reds and the Green*, pp.230-3; Devine, 'An undiminished dream', p.99.

17 Letter from Andrew Boyd to the author, 8 March 1994. Joe Bowers believed that Boyd left the CP over what he regarded as its reluctance to address the National Question. Interview with Joe Bowers, Belfast, 18 July 2018.

18 Letter from Andrew Boyd to Ruth Frow, 15 June 2000; 'David McKittrick remembers Andrew Boyd', *http://www.bbc.co.uk/news/uk-northern-ireland-14033833* [retrieved 27 May 2018].

19 General Register Office, marriage certificate; Peta Steel, 'Andrew Boyd: writer and trade unionist who chronicled the history of sectarianism in Northern Ireland', *Independent*, 6 July 2011, *https://www.independent.co.uk/news/obituaries/andrew-boyd-writer-and-trade-unionist-who-chronicled-the-history-of-sectarianism-in-northern-ireland-2365479.html*, [retrieved 12 June 2018]; Francis Devine, 'Arrivederci Hamish, a chara': letters from Andrew Boyd to Hamish Henderson, c.1950-2000' in Steve Byrne (ed), *The Hamish Henderson Papers: A Commemorative Collection of Essays*, (Hamish Henderson Archive Trust, Edinburgh, 2013), pp.18, 28-29.

20 PRONI, Andrew Boyd mss, D2389/3a.

21 Millar, *The Labour College Movement*, pp.52-53.

22 See, for example, the *Ulster Herald*, 9 April 1955.

23 Boyd, *Fermenting Elements*, pp.33, 79, 110-111.

24 Gray, 'A shop steward remembers', p.111; [Francis Devine], 'Socialist trade unionist: Matt Merrigan's political formation', *Saothar 12*, 1987, p.103.

25 Boyd, *Fermenting Elements*, p.62

26 'David McKittrick remembers Andrew Boyd'..

27 Boyd, *Fermenting Elements*, Preface, pp.31-33, 94; Gray, 'A shop steward remembers', p.110.

28 Boyd, *Fermenting Elements*, pp.97-98.

29 Boyd, *Fermenting Elements*, pp.97-98.

30 Andrew Boyd, *The Guilty Men of Ulster*, (Everyman, Benburb, 1970).

31 *Belfast Telegraph*, 6 July 2011.

32 Boyd, *Fermenting Elements*, pp.100-104; letter from Andrew Boyd to the author, 12 March 2009.

33 Boyd, *Fermenting Elements*, pp.121, 125.

34 Millar, *The Labour College Movement*, p.181. I am obliged to John Halstead, whom Boyd cites in *Fermenting Elements*, for his recollections on the NCLC. He is not responsible for the interpretations offered here.

35 Boyd, *Fermenting Elements*, pp.138-142.

36 Boyd, *Fermenting Elements*, pp.144-146, 150-151; Ruaidhrí Roberts, *The Story of the People's College*, (O'Brien Press, Dublin, 1986).

37 Andrew Boyd, 'NCLC takeover by TUC 1964: a personal memoir', typescript in the author's possession; letter from Andrew Boyd to the author, 22 February 2001; Boyd, *Fermenting Elements*, pp.152-155.

38 'David McKittrick remembers Andrew Boyd'; Thomas Donaldson, 'Biographical details [blurb on Andrew Boyd]', with author; email from Barbara Graham, 30 June 2018.

39 *Ulster Herald*, 22 December 1962.

40 Thomas Donaldson, 'Biographical details [blurb on Andrew Boyd]', with author.

41 D.R. O'Connor Lysaght, 'Obituary: Andrew Boyd, 1921-2011', 6 August 2011, *http://www.socialistdemocracy.org/RecentArticles/RecentObituaryAndrewBoyd.html* [retrieved 16 June 2018]; Andrew Boyd, *Holy War in Belfast*, (Anvil Books, Tralee, 1969; Grove Press, New York, 1972; Pretani Press, Belfast, 1987).

42 Andrew Boyd, *Brian Faulkner (and the Crisis of Ulster Unionism)*, (Anvil Books, Tralee, 1972); BBC News, 5 July 2011, 'Author of *Holy War in Belfast* remembered', *https://www.bbc.co.uk/news/uk-northern-ireland-14033833* [retrieved 16 June 2018].

43 Andrew Boyd, *The Rise of the Irish Trade Unions*, (Anvil Books, Tralee, 1972, 1976, 1985).

44 Andrew Boyd, *Have the Trade Unions Failed the North?*, (Mercier Press, Cork, 1984); letter from Andrew Boyd to the author, 25 November 1994.

45 See Emmet O'Connor, *A Labour History of Ireland, 1824-2000*, (UCD Press, Dublin, 2011), p.276.

46 Andrew Boyd, *Jack White: First Commander of the Irish Citizen Army*, (Parchment, Oxford, Donaldson Archives, Belfast, 2001); *Republicanism and Loyalty in Ireland*, (Donaldson Archives, Belfast, 2001); *Jim Connell: Author* of *The Red Flag*, (Donaldson Archives, Belfast, Socialist History Society, 2001), Occasional Papers Series no.13; *Marx, Engels, and the Irish*, (Donaldson Archives, Belfast, Socialist History Society, 2004), Occasional Papers Series no.18; Andrew Boyd, Francis Devine & Tommy Grimes, 'Norah Walshe and the rescue of Jim Connell', *Saothar 24*, 1999, pp.91-4.

47 Devine, 'Arrivederci Hamish, a chara', p.18.

48 Andrew Boyd, *Montgomery and the Black Man: Religion and Politics in Nineteenth-century Ulster*, (Columba Press, Dublin, 2006).

49 'Meeting of Irish Labour History Society, Newman House, Dublin, 27 October 1973, lecture by Andrew Boyd', typescript with author.

50 David McKittrick remembers Andrew Boyd'.

51 Letter from Andrew Boyd to the author, 15 June 2004.

52 Boyd's private papers are scattered in various locations. Belfast Central Library holds an 'Andrew Boyd Archive', consisting of five radio typescripts 'Embassy in Ireland: journey to a sunny land'; 'Life and times of Doctor Madden'; 'Montgomery and the black man'; 'Within our province'; and 'Masters and men, how trade unionism began in Ireland'. The PRONI holds his apprenticeship indenture, union cards, and papers on the NCLC. His letters lie with various correspondents and his newspaper and journal articles have yet to be catalogued. Some of Boyd's tutor's notes and other papers are held in the ILHS Archives, Beggar's Bush, Dublin. All papers from Boyd to the author have been gifted to the PRONI.

53 'David McKittrick remembers Andrew Boyd'; email from Barbara Graham, 30 June 2018.

54 Letters from Andrew Boyd to the author, 23 April 2007, 10 June 2009.

55 *Belfast Telegraph*, 6 July 2011.

56 GRONI, death certificate; *http://passedaway.com/notice/andrew_boyd/5586/* [retrieved 19 June 2018]. The news was carried in the *Belfast Telegraph*, the *Irish News*, the *Irish Times*, the *Daily Mirror*, the London *Independent*, and by the BBC; email from Joan Boyd, 28 June 2018. See also obituary, Francis Devine, 'Andrew Boyd', *Saothar*, 37 (2012), pp.137-40.

57 Andrew Boyd, 'Trade unionism in nineteenth century Ireland', talk written and recorded for the Irish Labour History Society, Dublin, 6/7 October 1990, with author.

DES DERWIN

Memories of 'A Marvellous Legacy': Matt Merrigan, 1921-2000

Mattie Merrigan was a leader to many and a mentor to some. Do we have the same pattern of response to leaders as we do to parents: starting with wonder and trust in infallibility, continuing though adolescent distance and disavowal and finally marvelling at what they did and how they could do it under the circumstances? In the 1970s, my political circles regarded Merrigan as – albeit a great trade union leader – a left social democrat. D.R. O'Connor Lysaght expresses part of this stance below and regrets how Merrigan did not raise a clear revolutionary banner and build an organisation around it. There is something to this, or at least there seemed to be in the turbulent opportunities of the late 1960s and early 1970s. Merrigan sometimes referred to 'the micro groups' or, with varying fairness, 'the left sectarian groups'. What was – is – the balance between political and organisational principle, clear socialist statement, and relevance to a meaningful social force? Between sectarianism and opportunism? What were – are – the means of marrying alternative ideas to a mass movement and popular support? Did Merrigan find it? Or did he lean too much one way? Has the Left fumbled upon it today, a kind of 'Merrigan's Way', and if so when will it fully implement it?

Looking back now, to the lonely days before the late 1960s/early 1970s, and to the days of defeat and retreat since, the thought arises that, in the first phase, Merrigan wrought a minor miracle of survival and effectiveness, marooned as he was within the worldview of the country and even of the 'Left of the Left'. And in the second phase, not quite as isolated – although this only by degree – did Merrigan not operate, or pioneer, the United Front tactics and 'broad party' strategy that the far Left (internationally) are slowly and haltingly embracing (or rediscovering) in the new century? The revolutionary groups did indeed take a leaf from Merrigan's book for a while by joining the Socialist Labour Party (SLP) in the late 1970s. Perhaps parts of the 'Left of the Left', then and in other episodes, were not radical enough, or perhaps the revolutionary Left were not yet ready to reach out beyond their own analyses, beyond the 'circle politics' condemned in their own classics? Perhaps Merrigan and others were too close to the former and too cautious for the *elan* of the latter?

It could be said, if there is any truth in this view of Merrigan as a Robinson Crusoe making the most of what he had to hand, successfully or not, that he 'should be living at this hour', thus painting him as a tragic figure in his own time. But, the way it looks (though you never know!), all senior socialists must depart before more fruitful times for their politics and efforts. Considering what Merrigan *did do*, and *was*, the judgement cannot be tragedy but, in the words of Mick O'Reilly below, 'a marvellous legacy'. What follows are the memories of Merrigan from former Amalgamated Transport & General Workers' Union (ATGWU) colleagues O'Reilly and Des Bonass, with a short bibliography of his writings and my political assessment and that of O'Connor Lysaght. In the recollections, dots and square brackets indicate my edits.

Matt Merrigan: Brief Biography

Matthew 'Matt' Merrigan was born on 25 June 1921 in a two-room cottage at 5 Thomas's Place, Dolphin's Barn, Dublin, the eighth of Matthew and Anne 'Nanny' (née Clifford] Merrigan's nine children.[1] The family's poverty became significantly more acute when Matthew senior died of TB in 1927. Young Merrigan and all the children took jobs outside of school hours to augment their mother's income from char work. Despite their struggles, Merrigan recalled his childhood with pleasure and family became an essential part of his life.[2] Having attended Rialto National School, Merrigan left at age thirteen to become a van boy with a laundry. After a short spell as a porter in a textile factory, in 1936/1937 Merrigan became a general operative in the Rowntree-Mackintosh plant in Kilmainham and joined the ATGWU Dublin 11/19 Branch. He became an Assistant Shop Steward, c1942, and Senior Shop Steward and Branch Committee member in the late 1940s.[3]

Merrigan was appointed full-time ATGWU 11/19 Branch Secretary in 1957 and Republic of Ireland District Secretary in 1960, a position he held until retirement in 1986. He 'provided militant leadership, retaining wide popularity with his union's membership despite frequent conflict' with more moderate trade union leaders.[4] Regarding corporate profits as the 'unpaid wages of the workers', Merrigan opposed National Wage Agreements for minimising workers' share of national wealth and for incorporating the trade unions in compliant partnership with Government.[5] He argued that the more socialist stance of British-based unions like the ATGWU explained the Irish Government's discrimination against them in favour of less militant Irish-based unions – like the Irish Transport & General Workers' Union (ITGWU) – in accommodating the anti-union culture of foreign-owned, especially American, companies. Merrigan nevertheless served on the Irish Congress of Trade Unions (ICTU) Executive Council, 1975-1976, 1977-1979 and 1982-1986, and was President, 1985-1986. In 1989, Merrigan wrote *Eagle or Cuckoo? The Story of the ATGWU in Ireland*, one of the few histories of a British-based union.[6]

Simultaneous to his trade union involvement, Merrigan had joined with support for the Spanish Republic and protests against the Wages Standstill Order and Trade Union Act, 1941. Although he joined the Crumlin Branch of the Labour Party, he was also active in the Trotskyist Revolutionary Socialist Party (RSP) in the mid-1940s. He was influenced by American Trotskyist Max Shachtman and wrote for the International Socialist League journal into the mid-1950s.[7] An avid reader, Merrigan attended the People's College and the Review Group classes of John de Courcy Ireland as well as completing a correspondence course with the British-based National Council of Labour Colleges.[8]

In the Labour Party, Merrigan contested Dublin South West in the 1954 General Election, losing his deposit.[9] He was expelled from Labour in 1957 for supporting the Independent candidate Noël Browne.[10] He was readmitted in 1964 and again contested Dublin South West in March 1970, this time polling 5,004 votes and coming within 262 votes of a seat on the last count. His narrow defeat was blamed on losing votes to Cora Dunne, widow of the late incumbent Labour TD Seán Dunne, and Merrigan's refusal to seek transfers from Fine Gael.[11] ATGWU colleague Des Bonass recalled that some Labour members, from both the right and the left, were opposed to Merrigan standing.[12] He resigned from the Administrative Council in 1970 over the party's failure to expel Limerick East TD Stephen Coughlan for his antisemitic remarks.[13] Merrigan opposed the 1970 electoral pact with Fine Gael and all other Coalition strategies. He also opposed Irish entry to the EEC in 1972, a position at odds with almost all other trade unions.

Merrigan was Chair, Liaison Committee of the Labour Left, 1973-1977, and – objecting to the imposition of a running mate in Dublin Finglas in 1977 – ran as Independent Labour on a joint programme with Browne, his 1,512 votes claimed to have denied Labour a seat.[14] Merrigan was again expelled and from 1977-1982 was a co-founder and Chair of the SLP. Perhaps reflecting the SLP's internal divisions and disagreements with their sole TD, Browne, Merrigan polled poorly in Dublin North West in 1981 and Dublin West in 1982.[15]

Merrigan strongly opposed Partition, called for British withdrawal from Ireland, seeking working-class leadership of the struggle rather than supporting conventional constitutional or physical-force solutions. An internationalist, he supported anti-imperialist struggles in Latin American, Africa and Asia; criticised repressive Communist states within the Soviet orbit; defended Irish Neutrality and championed disarmament and peace; and continuously campaigned for socialist policies to benefit the working class, illustrated by his prominent role in the tax protests of the 1980s. After retirement, Merrigan was active in the Pensioners' Parliament and served on the Irish Labour History Society Committee, 1986-1993.

Matt Merrigan died on 15 June 2000 in the Grand Hotel, Malahide, while attending an ATGWU Conference and supporting calls for the renegotiation of the Social Partnership agreement, Programme for Prosperity & Fairness (PFP), appropriately, as was said at the time, 'with his boots on'. His wife, Rose Cavanagh, had pre-deceased him in 1997. She had been an ATGWU Departmental Representative in Rowntree-Mackintosh when they married in July 1951, honeymooning at the TGWU Conference in Whitley Bay. They had two sons and a daughter. Merrigan was devoted to his family and, in his leisure time, a supporter of St Patrick's Athletic FC.[16]

Rayner Lysaght began his introduction to Merrigan's memoir by stating

> 'What you got was more than what you saw. You saw a small sturdy man with sharp features, unphotogenic and uncharismatic. When he spoke, his voice was harsh, even raucous. Nonetheless, those who would listen heard it stating a realism that went beyond common sense.'[17]

Mick O'Reilly: A Marvellous Legacy

Mick O'Reilly was born in Dublin in 1946. A Shop Steward in the Dublin FIAT car factory, he became an ATGWU Official in 1978; Republic of Ireland District Secretary, 1992, and Irish Regional Secretary in 1996, the first person from the Republic to hold that position: Merrigan was District Secretary for the Republic alone. O'Reilly was suddenly suspended by the ATGWU's London leadership in June 2001, over the admission of the Irish Locomotive Drivers' Association (ILDA) to the union and other issues.[18]

Mick O'Reilly

He was eventually vindicated and returned to work in March 2003 and to his position a little later. His account of this episode, *From Lucifer to Lazarus*, will be published by Lilliput Press in 2019. He retired in 2009, by which time the ATGWU had become Unite. O'Reilly was involved with the Dublin Housing Action Committee (DHAC) in the 1960s and was a member of the Connolly Youth Movement (CYM) and the Communist Party of Ireland (CPI). In 1976, he left the CPI over its position on the Soviet invasion of Czechoslovakia and other issues, joined the Irish Marxist Society and then the Labour Party, eventually drifting out in the new century. He remains active in the ATGWU, Dublin Council of Trade Unions (DCTU) and the National Homeless & Housing Coalition. In 1999, O'Reilly wrote *A New*

Agenda for Economic Power Sharing and gave two long interviews to *Red Banner*, 'Socialist trade unionism, not trade union socialism'.[19]

Writing shortly after Merrigan's death in 2000, O'Reilly recognised that he was

> 'in a variety of organisations, but his consistency is there through the whole lot of them, and that can't simply be explained by the poverty. He made a commitment in his early life to the socialist movement and he never varied from that. He was unusual in the sense that in the 1930s he considered the October Revolution to be the greatest thing that happened in the twentieth century. He was committed to the Left Opposition; he never changed his views on that. Not with the massive advance of the Soviet Union after the war, with the huge advances of all the Communist parties – it never dimmed Mattie's view that the Soviet Union needed more democracy and participation, and this view stayed with him in a variety of organisations through his life.'[20]

When starting work in Rowntree Mackintosh, there were two trade union congresses. The Irish Trades Union Congress (ITUC), founded in 1894, 'split after the war, partially over the influence of Communism in the World Federation of Trade Unions and partly over the existence of what were called British-based unions here – not a term I ever use'. Led by the ITGWU, a breakaway Congress of Irish Unions (Comhar Céard Éireann) was formed in 1945: 'That split lasted fourteen years' and 'as a Shop Steward' Merrigan was involved in 'trying to get an agreement in the other Congress and push that situation forward'.

Merrigan witnessed James 'Big Jim' Larkin speak 'when he was very young' and he 'made quite an impression on him'. Merrigan 'had some of the spirit of the old Larkinites who, if you talked to them, never called a union Official an Official, but ... Delegate. They used that language on the basis that he's someone you can recall and someone you can control ...' For O'Reilly, there was 'no doubt about it, Mattie really enjoyed himself in the ATGWU'. He was

> 'able to advance his own politics: he never found it a detriment, something that held him back. And of course, if the union had a different policy to Mattie, he simply went ahead with his own policy on a personal basis. Indeed, occasionally, he fell out with some of his colleagues ... but basically, I think, the structures of the union allow for a higher level of participation. He had a belief in the Shop Steward system, he believed in empowering them. He pushed that all his life.'

In 1969, Merrigan was 'responsible for the ATGWU re-affiliating' to Labour. He 'didn't agree with non-political trade unionism' and 'even though he was the scourge' of the party leadership, 'he was also very committed to it'. He was expelled twice: 'Most people only manage to do this once, but he was expelled twice'. Once in 1957 when he supplied chairs for a Noël Browne election meeting. Browne was not in the Labour Party then but was not opposing any Labour candidate.[21] He was expelled again over Browne in 1977 when the SLP was formed.

From his appointment as ATGWU Republic of Ireland District Secretary at the 'fairly young' age of thirty-seven, for twenty-six years, Merrigan was in the 'leadership of the union, and [for much of that time] … of the Labour Party', being on the Administrative Council: 'I don't know of any political cause that was going in Dublin, or indeed anywhere in Ireland, at the time that he wasn't associated with'.

One of O'Reilly's earliest encounters with Merrigan was through the DHAC which

'had difficulties. But I remember going around to Abbey Street, and I walked into where the clerks were, and I said, 'Is there any chance of seeing Mattie Merrigan?' and they just picked up the phone. He said, 'Who is it?' They said, 'Someone from the DHAC' and he said, 'Tell them to come up'. It was just as straightforward as that.'

O'Reilly invited him to 'speak on our platform' and he became 'the first trade unionist to do that':

'it was unheard of at the time, and he made no big song and dance about it. He just got up and said his speech, and he supported us, and he was always there at the demonstrations, always around. And, as I say, would find time in a very busy life to associate with a group like that – and I can tell you, it was neither a popular nor a profitable organisation to be in at the time.'

Merrigan 'identified with the women's movement', the 'struggles of Republicans in the North, in the long, long years when censorship took place, when nobody would stand on Sinn Féin platforms'. O'Reilly remembered Merrigan's support for the Hunger Strike in 1981, a difficult position because the ATGWU had 'a big membership in the North'.

'But he never flinched, because it was his view that they were political prisoners, and that they should be treated as such, and he never apologised to anyone for that, and he stood on their platform. I remember … he was chairperson of the National H-Block/Armagh Committee. Now that's not an easy thing to be … He had the courage of his convictions.'

In the 1970s, there were a number of strikes in the motor industry where O'Reilly worked, including in G.H. Brittain's which lasted eight and a half months: 'we not only stopped the company producing cars but we blacked every spare part, every imported car, the length and breadth of this country, and we actually won the strike'. They campaigned over membership of the Common Market and 'we got a Special Protocol which protected car workers' jobs from the time of entry in 1972 until 1984'. Employers were obliged 'to sit down with us and try to develop suitable alternative employment'. In 1981,[22] Chrysler negotiated with Minister for Industry & Commerce Desmond O'Malley, and 'our membership had the right to go and apply for jobs in Semperit', tyre manufacturers in Ballyfermot.

'We rejected this as, firstly, it didn't guarantee that they would get jobs; and secondly, we didn't regard it as suitable employment, because it was already there. Now that would have meant that all the car workers would have been sacked, and they would have been allowed to import cars into this country freely – that wasn't the situation then. So we … made the strike official … There's a famous judgement on this strike which you can't find anywhere because it's not written down. The only person to have written it down was actually the [Industrial Relations] Correspondent from RTÉ, Pat Sweeney, who, as far as I know, has the only record of the Talbot decision …'.[23]

O'Reilly recalled that 'basically, the judge found' that the ATGWU was 'responsible for the sum total of losses of' Chrysler 'for the duration of the dispute'

> 'We refused to accept that judgement. We blacked cars, we occupied the factory, and Mattie was threatened with going to jail. Now, arising from that ... we threatened to bring out our entire membership in the ESB and close the power stations, whereupon the pragmatist of all times, Mr. Charles J. Haughey, intervened in the dispute, and we negotiated an agreement with him [whereby] all our members in Chrysler were made redundant, and each and every one of them were given jobs in the civil service.'[24]

On a visit to the Soviet Union, Merrigan was 'shown around' a museum dedicated to the October Revolution.

> 'Of course, the history of the time notwithstanding, a lot of people would have been airbrushed out ... and Mattie would have had knowledge of the particular photographs concerned because he knew a lot about Soviet history. I wasn't there, but I did speak to people who were and they told me that the curator left the museum when Mattie finished giving his alternative talk – who was Commissar for War and wasn't Commissar for War, and who was in this photograph. He knew all of the Bolsheviks who met their different fates during the Stalinist era ... So he left this man in a very difficult state, and that was his way. You couldn't falsify history with Mattie, because he knew too much about it.'

While many 'certainly regarded Merrigan as a Trotskyite', for O'Reilly this was 'far too narrow a definition': 'I prefer to see Mattie as someone who supported the Left Opposition, not simply the works and position of one person, because he wasn't that kind of a guy.' He was certainly influenced by Trotsky's writings 'but the writings of Connolly just as much' and the influence of Larkin and Lenin. Merrigan 'read fairly widely' and was

> 'not narrow or dogmatic in his analysis. He could read situations. As I said at his funeral, he was a very catholic person, in the sense that he could wake up in the morning, meet the Shop Stewards, talk to other full-time Officials, deal with the bureaucracy of Congress, give a speech on women's liberation, and meet Republicans late at night ... He spread himself widely over a number of movements and causes, and to say that he was simply a Trotskyite is, I think, to misread the totality of his life.'

Merrigan supported the Trade Union Campaign Against Repression and Trade Unionists for Irish Unity & Independence, being responsible for setting that up with Seán Redmond (Irish Municipal Employees' Trade Union/IMPACT).[25] He spoke at meetings on the H Blocks and supported the Good Friday Agreement, 'quite definitely'. As a socialist, he 'respected the Unionist point of view'. In his later life, O'Reilly observed that Merrigan had 'nothing but the highest admiration for' the leadership of Sinn Féin. He 'had a big falling-out with the Workers' Party and those in Democratic Left. He thought they abandoned the nationalist people in the North'. He did not agree with Sinn Féin on everything' but thought the Peace Process 'worth supporting'. He

> 'thought it had the germ of the potential to possibly lessen sectarian tensions, and possibly to bring Catholic and Protestant workers together, a thing he was committed to all his life. And I'm bound to say that, as someone who was a Republican, the Unionist membership of our union had the height of respect for him. Because

whatever else – they might have disagreed with his views politically – they knew that if he was to take up their cause with the employer, you never scratched your head and tried to figure out what side he was on.'

This was 'always abundantly clear when he came into a room'. He 'saw himself as a representative of the workers, not as buffer between workers and employers … and he saw himself as somebody who represented that view – independently'.

> 'Now, like anyone else, if he was in a boat that was sinking, he would quickly tell you to find another way forward. He was no fool. He could handle himself around, be quite pragmatic. He knew that advancement for workers didn't go in a single direction. It wasn't always forward, there were detours sometimes on the way, and he could get very annoyed with people if they didn't accept his advice on what particular detour to take. Nevertheless, in the core of all that was absolute commitment to your cause, and I've seen him numerous times talking to workers and they always understood that. And really, that meant that always he was halfway to a solution, because they believed in him.'

O'Reilly felt that the 'biggest thing I learned from Mattie was his view' that, as well as pursuing a united socialist Ireland, 'make sure you enjoy it as you go through life, because you only get one chance at this'. He had the 'same religion as myself: he was a baptised atheist'. He enjoyed his life and 'left a legacy of unselfish dedication to the working class. At his funeral were republicans, socialists, trade unionists, bureaucrats, women's movement activists and retired workers and O'Reilly knew of few who could have inspired such a disparate crowd. When Merrigan retired, he told O'Reilly that 'he was going to do what he was doing before, as an unpaid agitator for the working class. He carried that promise out'. It was 'a marvellous legacy to leave the world, to basically have a lot of people say, 'He stuck to his principles".

Des Bonass: The Matt Merrigan I Knew

Des Bonass was Chief Financial Officer in the ATGWU Dublin office until his retirement in the late 1990s. He was centrally involved in many solidarity and shop steward initiatives over five decades, including organising some of the Irish support for the National Union of Mineworkersrs during the Great Strike of 1984-1985.[26] Bonass was DCTU President in the early 1990s; served for the ATGWU on the Labour Party Administrative Council in the 1970s; and, after 1977, became National Treasurer, SLP. He continues to be active in the ATGWU and DCTU.

Des Bonass

Bonass was a close confidante and the 'eyes and ears', of Matt Merrigan.[27] Bonass knew him 'all my trade union life … I believed in what he was doing. I always admired him. I suppose he took me under his wing to some extent. I was a very close colleague of his right through his career'. For

Bonass, Merrigan 'never believed in these senior or top-level committees'. Trades Councils and Shop Stewards 'were the people who should have the support' and the ATGWU 'called ourselves 'the members' union''. Merrigan supported the Dublin Shop Stewards' Committee when it was formed, in the early 1970s, 'unofficially encouraging our Shop Stewards to become involved'.

The huge tax marches of the late 1970s, were triggered by workers in Esso 'who were on very big wages'. The ATGWU proposed tax protest marches before the DCTU. It 'would have been democratically decided' as Merrigan would run everything 'through the delegates, through the Shop Stewards'. Bonass 'was new' on the DCTU Executive when Mai Clifford (Irish Women Workers' Union) was President and Fergus Whelan (Ancient Guild of Incorporated Brick & Stone Layers' Trade Union) Vice President. Merrigan 'always attended' DCTU Delegate Meetings and 'spoke at them'. He 'might have been at meetings all day, but he always said the Trades Council was important. As he said, 'If it wasn't there, we'd have to invent it''. It was 'very important' that Merrigan 'had thrown his weight behind' the tax campaign as 'other unions opposed it initially but when they saw it taking off, they actually came in behind it'.[28]

Bonass remembered the Waterford Shop Stewards' tax campaign: 'People would say, people I still know, 'This is getting out of hand, the Shop Stewards are getting too much power''. But Merrigan insisted 'Well, the Shop Stewards are the movement'. At a meeting in St. Anthony's Hall, the 'Dublin Shop Stewards came in behind them, and they had a stoppage'. There was an ESB Shop Stewards' Committee and Merrigan

'always felt the power of the industrial movement could have rested in the ESB, just like now it could rest with Aer Lingus or whatever. He was always battling, not for 'anarchy', but that the unions should use the power they have.'[29]

In the 1970 Dublin South-West bye-election, Bonass remembered 'a phone call from a printing press up in Camden Street'. The young printshop Shop Steward was involved in the campaign and reported that 'Labour Party people had been in getting election literature printed, twenty thousand leaflets; which claimed that Merrigan was a member of the Communist Party'. Dublin South-West's other sitting Labour TD, John O'Connell, 'was paying for it'. Told they were being collected at four o'clock, Bonass sat outside the printers but 'they were never collected'. At a meeting next morning in Dáil Eireann, the 'first question O'Connell asked Labour Party Secretary Brendan Halligan was, 'Is Matt Merrigan a Communist? I don't want a Communist in my constituency'. A row ensued.[30]

In 1971, when Bonass recalled that 'we were all in the Labour Party, Young Socialists, Republicans or whatever', attempts were made 'to bring the left closer together with the Liaison Committee of the Left'. Among those involved were 'great people' like Brendan Scott, Frank Butler, Billy Keegan, Noreen Byrne, and Tony Dunne. Browne was 'on the fringes of it, as was

Michael D. Higgins.' and Ruairí Quinn. Liaison were 'very strong within the Labour Party' and meetings had 'anything up to 60 or 70 people attending'. Labour's Executive

> 'brought in a constitutional change: you couldn't have an organisation within an organisation. We weren't an organisation: we were loosely grouped, we had no constitution, we didn't call ourselves anything, we had no headed paper. We were all expelled anyway. There was a vacuum on the Left. You hear a lot about left unity now. The Liaison Committee of the Left was actually bringing some people from outside the Labour Party into some kind of left unity. The Labour Party didn't want it.'[31]

In 1970, Bonass was on Labour's National Executive when at the Cork Conference, Party Leader Brendan Corish proposed that the party consider Coalition, a complete reversal of existing policy.[32]

> 'We had a terrific campaign [against]. We had a third of the votes, and we won the debate. We planned to swing other people. But they actually brought – I saw it happening – busloads from Kerry. Dan Spring, Dick Spring's father, and Stevie Coughlan organised it. The busloads never attended conference until the actual vote was taking place, and we were outvoted ... Typical of the Left, we never planned what we were going to do afterwards.'

Browne 'got up and walked out' and Merrigan said 'I've had enough of this, I'm going'. Bonass followed him and

> 'the thing snowballed ... People just got up and walked out. There was no planned walkout, I can assure you. Even though history is saying, 'There was a walkout in Cork', there was nothing planned. We were in the foyer and the press were looking for a good story. They gathered around us and were taking photographs. They turned to Noël Browne as he came out a doorway, and said, 'Noel, you were organising this walkout'. 'No, I wasn't ... I was only going to the toilet.''

The SLP came out of this disillusionment. The new party 'took off terrifically'. Merrigan wanted 'to broaden it out'. The Socialist Workers' Movement, League for a Workers' Republic, and Socialist Republicans 'would have been in it'. This 'could have been explosive, but it was just like the Shop Stewards', Merrigan 'felt that if you're afraid of what they're doing, you should not have been there'.

The SLP contested local elections and Browne was elected TD in Dublin Artane. Dublin Central Branch protested about Summerhill's slum housing, sitting down at the corner of Parnell Street, Among those whose names were taken by the police were Mick Rafferty, Merrigan, Fergus McCabe, and Tony Gregory. They were 'fined £50 or twenty-two days' imprisonment and bound to the peace for a year. 'We wouldn't pay it'. After McCabe was arrested, Merrigan 'got everyone he could out of the union to support the protest and a thousand marched from the GPO to Mountjoy'. The seven charged went to a packed court 'convinced they were 'going down''. Merrigan 'said, 'It doesn't look good. I'll make a few phone calls'. To this day, I don't know who he was calling'. When the court convened after lunch, the justice said, 'After full consideration during the lunch break, looking at the evidence, I'm dismissing all these cases'. To this day no one knows what was behind it'.

The SLP had branches in Belfast, Derry and Newry. Bonass recalled that 'some people' were 'Two-Nationist' and were not 'as Republican socialist as some of us'. These 'different individual sections and factions' created difficulties but 'even if the different sections had gone back to their different constituent organisations, it should have continued in some form' and 'might have pulled people in'. Labour had 'moved so far to the right that there was a vacuum on the Left'.[33] Merrigan

> 'got a bit upset about the different factions not pulling together. He wouldn't have blamed the far Left more than anyone else, although he might have been annoyed at the way they wanted to do it. He would have thought, 'Let's get the big picture together, and then move forward'.'

Disillusion set in with activists saying, 'There's no role, we're not getting anywhere, we're in a cul de sac, we would be better off going back into' Labour. Merrigan and Bonass 'did not believe that' and 'would have been for keeping it going. If people had only thought it out, and history has shown this, we should have stayed where we were. Some people aren't for the long haul, though'.[34]

Closing the SLP in 1982 was 'a weird day'. As 'all the Left groups had gone', they 'were practically down to the old Liaison Committee of the Left'. Dermot Boucher's 'simple proposal' was 'that we should all go back into' Labour. There was 'no suggestion that you would go anywhere else or re-form the Liaison Committee of the Left'. Merrigan was 'disillusioned … that it had come to that'. They 'wrapped up the funds, donating them to the Rape Crisis Centre, to whatever campaigns were going on, to *Gralton* magazine. We had £50 left for a few pints'. Browne 'had a big influence' in the SLP's demise after he began 'telling the press he was Independent Labour'. Browne's 'position on the National Question' differed from Merrigan, and other activists were 'kind of putting a lid on'. Although often twinned politically, Merrigan and Browne, certainly in later years, did not get on, personally or politically. The day Browne died Merrigan turned down an invitation to speak about him on RTÉ.

When a DCTU delegation visited Cuba in 1999, Merrigan was 'the star of the show'. At the Cuban Transport Union, he asked 'How many hours does a driver drive in this country before he gets a rest? Would he have a helper?' He wanted to know did they have tachograph? Bonass, who chaired meetings as DCTU President, reflected that 'Of course they never heard of tachographs'. Merrigan asked similar awkward questions at the University of Havana.

Merrigan opposed Social Partnership, 'but it was not just a case of being against partnership'. His position 'was thought out'. He 'saw the power in the unions drifting away to the centre', unions 'losing control'. He was 'not an old-fashioned trade unionist [but] a modern trade unionist'. He opposed pay roll deductions of union dues, preferring one-to-one contact with members. He 'ended up' as ICTU President: 'It must be 'Muggins' turn'. Bonass did not consider, as some did, that Merrigan was 'a thorn in the side for the sake of being a thorn in the side. Anyone that thought that didn't know him'. For those 'who said, 'Ah! Here's Mattie, there's going to be a row tonight!' It wasn't true. It was thought and belief'.

Raynor Lysaght's Political Assessment

D.R. O'Connor 'Rayner' Lysaght was born in Cardiff in 1941 and educated in Cheltenham and at Trinity College. Living in Ireland since the 1960s, he has been active in a number of Trotskyist organisations and is currently a member of People's Democracy.[35] He is widely published on labour history and political theory and practice.[36] In reflecting on Merrigan's death, Lysaght acknowledged that he never 'lost sight of the international working class wood from the Irish trees.[37] In principle, he was an international socialist'. Lysaght quotes Merrigan:

Raynor Lysaght

> 'In spite of the damage of Stalinist reaction to the theory and practice of socialism, the objective economic circumstances that put socialism on the world agenda 150 years ago are still there – only more so. The underdeveloped countries in the world are now in the neo-imperialist grip of the developed world and their people stagger under the burden of foreign debt interest. In their inability to invest in their own agriculture and industry, millions starve and succumb to all the diseases that are heir to poverty; while to salve their consciences the same forces that create these conditions send a pittance to them as emergency aid which does nothing for sustained growth of wealth and further development.'

Lysaght recognised that while Merrigan 'rejected the Republican dogma of armed struggle, he was firm in recognising the need for a single Irish state, independent of Britain'. The 'minimum required', Merrigan wrote, was 'for the [British] Labour Government to declare its intention to work for Irish unity with the Irish Government and all the parties in Ireland and to disengage from Ireland at the beginning of the process'.

Lysaght says Merrigan 'recognised that the struggle for socialism could not be helped by National Wage Agreements supervised by capitalist states' accepting that, as Merrigan himself wrote, 'economic and social consensus is not possible in a society riven by property and class differences'. However, for Lysaght the problem was that

> 'These insights remained those of an individual. At the level of industrial work, the basic needs and common interests provided a common platform for him to build around himself a group of radical Officials of diverse political backgrounds but all opposed to state pay controls. What he could not do was build a lasting movement, whether party or front, to lead the Irish workers to set up state power that would be theirs.'

When Merrigan was admitted to the Labour Party in the spring of 1942, the Communist Party had recently entered too, mixing 'with the existing left wing that had developed under the inspiration of the Trotskyist intellectual, Patrick Trench'.[38] In August 1942, Merrigan worked for Labour in the Dublin Corporation elections that made it the biggest party on the Council, 'a feat it has never repeated'.

In July 1944, Merrigan helped found the Revolutionary Socialist Party (RSP), becoming Dublin Branch Secretary. He had doubts about the RSP's prospects, however, and 'they were soon fulfilled'. With the war's end, international Trotskyism was in dispute over the nature of the Soviet Union and the RSP split, surviving until 1948 in Dublin with two members, Merrigan and John Byrne, before disappearing'.[39] During the 1950s, Merrigan and Byrne continued to work through the Dublin Trades Union Council and in the Labour Party, 'but they were never able to reform a revolutionary nucleus'.[40] It appeared that Byrne and Merrigan had come to take from their RSP experience

> 'an abiding mistrust of small organisations striving for programmatic clarity and sought to build the working class vanguard by individual participation in broad-based organisations: the Labour Party or a left variant of it. The trouble with this was that it depended too much on individual or organisational manoeuvre rather than on raising consciousness. In the 1960s, a new generation of potentially revolutionary socialists were offered little guidance from Byrne or Merrigan. When Mattie Merrigan [organised] the nucleus of what became the Liaison Committee of the Left, he gathered its members together on a vague platform as a sort of Left ginger group defined by little more than opposition to a possible Labour orientation to Coalition. The result was that those who wanted political clarity entered one of the emerging Trotskyist groups. This might have happened anyway, but a clearer lead from Merrigan might have prevented internecine warfare between them. His base became limited to left social democrats.'

Such criticism 'should not deflect attention from' Merrigan's

> 'personal ability and dedication to his class. As an individual, he fought as much as any single person could to advance the interests of the workers. What he could not do was build a political organisation that would share his burden and shoulder even larger ones. He had a lot to give his fellow workers and he gave them a lot. It may seem ungrateful to say he might have given more. It happens to be true.'

Fourteen years after Merrigan's death, Lysaght concluded his introduction to *Eggs & Rashers* by reflecting, as O'Reilly and Bonass did, on his personal warmth, generosity and good-humour. Lysaght regarded the memoir as

> 'valuable partly because, almost despite its author, it describes how this happened: how an individual with his gifts could achieve in his movement major responsibility without enjoying any real power to change matters. Programmatically, Mattie Merrigan's positions were correct and are even more correct today. Equally, the need to supply political leadership to deal with them is even more pressing.'

In Merrigan's 'personal narrative', Lysaght hailed the fact that 'he never surrendered':

> 'If he failed politically, he did not die disappointed, but with the comfort of one who had never sold his soul, and the personal loyalty of his family and his many friends.'

Eggs & Rashers 'describes what was essentially a happy and supportive home life rounding off the picture of the whole man'.[41]

Cuckoo or Eagle?

Did Merrigan move away from revolutionary Marxism or just adjust his modus operandi, perhaps as forerunner, to what he thought could be done, at the level it could be done? Lysaght's assessment is often acute but finally too harsh. On the one hand the objective situation appears to have been against the building of the revolutionary party from 'a revolutionary nucleus', which Lysaght chides Merrigan for failing to do. On the other hand, there were plenty, including Lysaght himself, who had offered 'political clarity' and who gave it a go and built nothing more particularly earth-shaking than Merrigan did. Look at where the far Left is today, TDs and all. How much of Merrigan's broad approach has it embraced, willy-nilly, to get there? Lysaght points to Merrigan's failure to lay a direct bridge to the new revolutionaries. Possibly, but the far Left's errors from the other bank are as regrettable, not least its encounter with the very bridge that Merrigan did throw out, the SLP. As an active member of the Socialist Workers Tendency in the SLP, I accept some of the responsibility for that and for the eventual body blow of the Tendency's withdrawal. A different and patient perspective from the Left *might* have meant a stronger SLP three decades before the United Left Alliance (ULA) attempted something uncannily similar.[42] Three decades before, even as the ULA failed, the far Left grows in proportion to how it employs some of Merrigan's methods.

In 1983, Merrigan's short piece on an Alternative Economic Strategy (AES) was also a brief exposition of a radical political strategy, a Merrigan Manifesto with merit and meaning, to be critiqued and renovated sure, but one we would do well to meditate on today.[43] Was this British Left Labour reformism, or something more? Is it Left reformism or the 'revolutionary reformism' sometimes used to describe the more transitional approach being taken on the radical Left today? Merrigan's response to chary objections to AES is not just to defend an AES but to propose a more radical one, and to point to the extra parliamentary conditions necessary to accompany it. In these more welcoming days on the Left (less so since SYRIZA) for joint formations of revolutionaries, radicals and left social democrats, and for notions of elected workers' governments, as escalating steps on the road perhaps, can Merrigan's riotous AES be read in those terms? He wrote [my emphasis added]:

> 'A sine qua non of developing an AES is that *you must have a mass organisation of working people, politically aware and conscious of historic tasks and capable of overcoming and defeating the forces of bourgeois reaction alluded to above.* It is possible that the fragmented forces of the Irish left, inside and outside the Labour Party, together with the Trade Unions, could put together a political Congress or Alliance that would re-group around, *and struggle for – as a minimum programme –* the AES put forward by Alan Mathews and the ICTU.'

Perhaps it is best to leave the last word with Bonass, in a remark that did not make it into the *Red Banner* final edit: 'He was a revolutionary leader of his time. On the grounds of Connolly or whoever. That's what I would call him'.

Postscript: Matt Merrigan's Writings

Merrigan detailed his life in *Eggs and Rashers,* published in 2014, and, among many obituaries was that by his fellow ATGWU official Ben Kearney in *Saothar.*[44] A surprising amount of Merrigan's writings can be disinterred from the internet. From 1955-1957, he wrote a series of reports on Ireland for *Labor Action,* the US paper of the Independent Socialist League of Schachtman and Hal Draper.[45] They were collected in *Workers' Liberty.*[46] Much earlier, in March 1947, with Spanish Civil War veteran Bob Armstrong, Merrigan wrote a document in support of the bureaucratic collectivist theory of the Soviet Union titled 'In Defence of Revisionism'. It, and a lot more, can be found in the rich online store on Irish far left history, *Arguments for a Workers Republic.*[47]

Notes

1   In 1901, Matthew, 20 and a general labourer, lived at 15 Cameron Street, Merchant's Quay with his father Patrick, 48, general labourer; mother Eliza, 43; and siblings John, 22, van driver; Annie, 18, general servant domestic; Patrick, 16, messenger to grocer; and Christopher, 11. All were born in Dublin except Patrick who was born in Wicklow, www.census.nationalarchives.ie/reels/nai003713438/ [retrieved 27 February 2019]. In 1911, Matthew, 33 and a general labourer, lived at 1 O'Neill Cottages, Usher's Quay, with his wife of eight years Anne, 28, and children Elizabeth,6; Daniel, 3, and Evelyn, 2. Michael Barnes, 30, labourer, lodged in the house. Matthew was registered as having been born in Wicklow, www.census.nationalarchives.ie/reels/nai000170430/ [retrieved 27 February 2019].

2   Matt Merrigan, *Eggs & Rashers: Irish Socialist Memories,* edited and introduced by D.R. O'Connor Lysaght, (Umiskin Press, Dublin, 2014), pp. 1-11.

3   Francis Devine. 'Socialist trade unionist: Matt Merrigan's political formation', *Saothar 12,* 1987, pp. 94-106.

4   Lawrence William White, 'Merrigan, Matthew Paul ('Matt') (1921-2000)' in *Dictionary of Irish Biography, vol 6,* (RIA/Cambridge University press, Cambridge, 2009), pp. 486-487.

5   Devine, *op. cit.*

6   Matt Merrigan *Eagle or Cuckoo? The Story of the ATGWU in Ireland,* (Matmer, Dublin, 1989). See also Francis Devine & John B. Smethurst, *Historical Directory of Trade Unions in Ireland,* (ILHS/WCML, Dublin/Salford,2017), pp. 68-70, 522-534.

7   For a discussion of Merrigan and Schachtman see Lysaght's 'Editor's introduction: Matt Merrigan, Irish socialist' in *Eggs & Rashers, op. cit.,* pp. xiii-xviii.

8   White, *op. cit.,* p. 486. Merrigan would 'liken to have gone to university. I would have liked the privilege and the benefit of a university education. I think it is important for yourself and sometimes the two go together, you know, revolutionary views can always be enhanced by the groves of academia, if you have commitment!', Devine, 'Socialist trade unionist', *op. cit.,* p. 103. He eschewed the commonest educational route for trade unionists as 'I always had a strong ideological antagonism to the Catholic Workers' College'. de Courcy Ireland, 19 October 1911- 4 April 2006, was born in Lucknow, son of a Kildare-born British Army officer, and was educated at Marlborough College, Oxford University and Trinity College Dublin. An outstanding scholar, he taught in Dublin, Drogheda, Bandon and, finally, Newpark Comprehensive School, Blackrock. With his wife Betty Haigh, he supported the Spanish Republic and was active in the Irish Anti-Apartheid Movement and Ireland-China Friendship Society. Politically, he was a member of the NILP (when based in Derry during the war), Labour Party, CPI, Democratic Socialist Party, Workers' Party, Democratic Left and SWP, as well as Irish CND [now PANA – Peace & Neutrality Alliance]. He was a founder, Maritime Institute of Ireland; closely associated with the

National Maritime Museum of Ireland; and Secretary, Dún Laoghaire Lifeboat, See Francis Devine, 'John de Courcy Ireland', *Saothar 31*, 2006, pp. 8-14.

9   He polled 631 votes. Neither running mate, Barney Colgan, 1,924, and Dick Deasy, 1,617, were elected and Irish Workers' League candidate Mick O'Riordan managed only 375. Briscoe, Butler and ffrench-O'Carroll (FF) and O'Higgins (FG) were returned with Seán MacBride (Clann na Pobliachta) who polled 6,151. Brian M. Walker, *Parliamentary Elections Results in Ireland, 1918-1992*, (RIA/Institute of Irish Studies QUB, Dublin/Belfast, 1992), p. 186.

10   Browne, born Waterford 20 December 1916 and educated at Beaumont College and Trinity, qualifying as a doctor. He was active in Clann na Poblachta, 1946-1954; Fianna Fáil, 1953-1954; National Progressive Democrats. 1958-1963; Labour, 1965-1977; and SLP, 1981-1982. He was TD, Dublin South East, 1948-1954. 1957-1965; Dublin Artane, 1969-1973; and Dublin North Central, 1977-1981; and Senator, University of Dublin, 1973. He died in Baile na hAbhann, Galway, 21 May 1997. See his *Against the Tide*, (Gill & Macmillan, Dublin, 1987, 2007) and John Horgan, *Noël Browne: Passionate Outsider*, (Gill & Macmillan, Dublin, 2000).

11   Merrigan's 5,004 left him behind Sherwin (FF) elected with 7,678 but ahead of Jim Mitchell (FG), 4,062; Laurence Corcoran (Non-Party), 4,481; and Dunne, 2,062, Walker, *Parliamentary Elections Results op. cit.*, p. 220. For Dunne see 'Seán Dunne (1019-1969) in Charles Callan & Barry Desmond, *Irish Labour Lives: A Biographical Dictionary of Irish Labour Party Deputies, Senators, MPs & MEPs*, (Watchword, Dublin,2010), pp. 91-94, 275-276, and Henry Cairns & Owen Gallagher, *Seán Dunne, Bray, 1918-1969: The Story of Seán Dunne's Journey From Militant Socialist Republican to Labour TD*, (The Authors, Bray, 2007).

12   Bonass added that an attempt was made to get the National Executive to select the candidate. That failed and the Regional delegates gave him the nomination 'by 90% of the votes'. Then some canvassed Cora Dunne to stand and there were direct attempts to sabotage Merrigan's campaign. See Des Bonass, 'The Matt Merrigan I knew', *Red Banner*, issue 9, March 2001.

13   See 'Stephen Coughlan (1910-1984) in Callan & Desmond, *Labour Lives, op. cit.*, pp. 56-57, 269.

14   Tunney, 7,963, and Bertie Ahern, 3,729, (FF) and Belton, 3,896, (FG) were returned. Halligan and Billy Keegan (Labour) polled 3,055 and 1,174 respectively; Merrigan, 1,512; and de Rossa (SFWP), 1,317; Walker, *Parliamentary Elections Results op. cit.*, p. 231.

15   In Dublin North West in 1981, Merrigan polled 473, his SLP running mate Billy Keegan, 209. Other left candidates were: Labour, Pa Dunne, 2,293 and Halligan, 1,729; Kenny (SFWP), 289; and Éamonn Farrell (SPI), 236. In the Dublin West by-election, November 1982, Merrigan polled 334 behind Tomás Mac Giolla (SFWP), 6,357; Brendan O'Sullivan (Labour), 703; and Michael Connaghan (Democratic SP), 667, Walker, *Parliamentary Elections Results op. cit.*, pp. 240, 252.

16   See Merrigan, *Eggs & Rashers, op. cit.*, pp. 39-48. The couple's children were Maurice, Olga and Matt who became a senior Official in the FWUI/SIPTU associated in particular with health service workers.

17   Lysaght, 'Editor's introduction', *op. cit.*, p. xiii.

18   Brendan Ogle, *Off the Rails: The Story of ILDA*, (Currach Press, Dublin, 2004).

19   See his 'Socialist trade unionism, not trade union socialism', *Red Banner 3*, November 1998, and 'Organise or die', *Red Banner 21*, March 2005. An index of all articles can be seen here - https://redbanner.webs.com/indextoarticles.htm [retrieved 10 March 2019].

20   Mick O'Reilly, 'Matt Merrigan: a marvellous legacy', *Red Banner*, issue 8, November 2000

21   O'Connor Lysaght, letter, *Red Banner* 9 March 2001.

22   In the original, the date was given as 1984.

23   The Talbot plant, owned by Chrysler, was in Santry. For the judgement, see *https://app.justis.com/case/orourke-v-talbot-ireland-ltd/overview/c4Gtm1CJnYWca* [retrieved 27 February 2019].

24   In Bonass, *op. cit.*, he recalled that Merrigan was 'injuncted and 'committed' to jail. He was supposed to go to jail. ... [until] they called them in and a deal was done. It was Bonass's 'responsibility, in the union offices, to pay out all the car workers their wages every week, which were sent from the Department of the Taoiseach'.

25 See Tom Redmond & Francis Devine, Francis. 'Seán Redmond', *Saothar 39*, 2014, pp. 123-124.

26 Bonass, 'Ireland and the miners' strike', *Red Banner 22*, pp. 54-61. For a wider view of Irish support, see Jonathan Saunders, *Across Frontiers: International Support for the Miners' Strike (1984-1985)*, (Canary Press, London, 1989).

27 Bonass, *op. cit.*

28 For the DCTU view see Séamus Cody, John O'Down & Peter Rigney, *The Parliament of Labour: 100 Years of the DCTU*, (DCTU, Dublin, 1986), 'The Tax Campaign', pp. 231-240. For argument see, Paul Sweeney. 'The PAYE sector's perspective on taxation and trade union demand for reform', *Journal of the Statistical & Social Inquiry Society of Ireland*, vol. xxv, no..1, 1983-1984, pp. 27-35, *www.tara.tcd.ie/bitstream/handle/2262/7828/jssisi VolXXV27_35.pdf?seq* [retrieved 27 February 2019].

29 Bonass made this observation in 2001.

30 For Halligan see the Corish essays in this volume. O'Connell, 20 January 1927- 8 March 2013, qualified as a doctor in the Royal College of Surgeons and in 1960 founded *MIMS Ireland* and in 1967 the *Irish Medical Times*. He was Labour TD for Dublin South West, 1965-1981, but expelled for refusing to stand in Dublin West. He was returned as Independent in Dublin South Central, the split vote costing Cluskey his seat. An MEP for Dublin from 1979, O'Connell became Ceann Comhairle, 1981-1983, before joining Fianna Fáil. He lost his seat in 1987 but, after two years in Seanad Éireann, regained it in 1989 and was Minister for Health, 1992-1993, 'Dr John O'Connell: Colourful politician with strong commitment to the poor', *Irish Times*, 16 March 2013, www.irishtimes.com/life-and-style/people/obituary-dr-john-o-connell-1.1327690 [retrieved 13 February 2019].

31 Nearly a thousand people gathered in the Mansion House in February 1976 for the formation of the Left Alternative and to hear speakers from the Communist Party, Sinn Féin the Workers' Party, and the Liaison Committee of the Labour Left, *Socialist Voice*, February 2011, *www.communistpartyofireland.ie/sv2011-02/16-letter.html* Liaison was extant until 1977 when Merrigan was expelled and the majority of members were involved in the formation of the SLP, Irish Left Archive, *www.clririshleftarchive.org/organisation/1442/ #documents* [retrieved 27 February 2019].

32 For Corish see the accounts by Tony Brown, Niall Greene and Brendan Halligan elsewhere in this volume.

33 The far left 'Tendencies' departed in 1979 and 1980.

34 In the 1981 General Election, Browne was elected in Dublin North Central, but of the other six SLP candidates only Merrigan and Dermot Boucher polled more than 1%.

35 Lysaght was in the Irish Workers' Group, 1967; Socialist Labour Alliance; Revolutionary Marxist Group, 1972; Movement for a Socialist Republic, 1976; and Socialist Democracy, 1978. Lysgaht details his life here *https://cedarlounge.wordpress.com/2013/05/20/interview-with-rayner-lysaght/* [retrieved 1 March 2019].

36 See *The Story of the Limerick Soviet*, (Limerick Soviet Commemoration Committee, Limerick, 2003) and *From the GPO to the Winter Palace*, (Studies in Irish Labour History 15, ILHS, Dublin, 2016).

37 D.R. O'Connor Lysaght, 'Matt Merrigan: a political assessment', *Red Banner*, issue 8, November 2000. Quotes here from Merrigan are from the first draft of his memoirs.

38 Trench was born in Galway, son of Wilbraham Trench, Professor of History, English and Mental Science, at Queen's College Galway, and Mary Cross. A talented artist, a poet, and an engaged journalist, he was a prominent figure in bohemian Dublin in the late 1920s. Chronic ill-health obliged him to cut short his involvement in the Spanish Civil War and he was the driving force behind the Workers' International League, Ireland's first Trotskyist movement, while active in the Labour Party. He died in a Swiss sanatorium in 1948, aged 43, see Lawrence William White, 'Trench, Patrick Mackenzie FitzJohn ('Paddy') (1905-1948), Trotskyite socialist', *DIB, op, cit.*, vol. 9, pp. 466-468.

39 Ciarán Crossey & James Monaghan, 'The origins of Trotskyism in Ireland', *Revolutionary History*, vol. 6, nos 2/3, Summer 1996, p.7. They remark (p. 47): 'In Dublin the two comrades carried on for a while, but after a period of isolation they also moved away from organised Marxism. Both ended up as left-wing individuals in the Labour Party who

continued to read the material sent to them by the British and American organisations, but who had nothing to which to recruit anyone'.

40 In 1939, Byrne – Dublin Organiser for Fianna Éireann – began to meet with the small group of Trotskyists (effectively a branch of the equally tiny British-based Workers' International League, WIL) in Dublin and 'went over to the Socialist ideas'. The Dublin group joined the Labour Party and wrote for *The Torch*. Byrne moved to London and WIL activism until deported back to Ireland in 1945. In March 1944, Byrne attended, as did Merrigan, the fusion conference in London of various Trotskyist groups which formed the Revolutionary Communist Party (RCP). He reported being arrested while selling Trotskyist papers in O'Connell Street, at the instigation of 'the Stalinists', and being fined. The RSP launched *Workers' Republic* in May 1947 but by the following year emigration had devasted the group. In August 1948, Byrne visited Belfast (the larger RSP centre) for the Fourth International. His report said that the situation there is 'rather hopeless'. He suggested concentrating on Dublin – where there are two members! He wrote, 'There are two comrades left, one in the Socialist Youth (Stalinists) [Mattie Merrigan] and the other, myself, active in the trade union movement. I am a member of the National Executive Committee of the Workers Union of Ireland ... a member of Dublin Trades Council, was a delegate to the Irish Trade Union Congress for the last two Congresses and am on the Branch Committee of my own union (Corporation Workers). I am in the Irish Labour Party, but it is very dead, and there is no prospect of quick returns'. Byrne remained active in the Labour movement for the rest of his life and Lysaght recalls his isolation, even from a new generation of revolutionary Marxists: 'The present author remembers the pleasant surprise he got, after knowing Johnny Byrne for nine years, as he thought, when Johnny remarked that the workers' seizure of state power would not be simply a matter of electing a Labour Government; he had never heard him suggest previously that electoralism would be insufficient', Crossey & Monaghan, 'The origins of Trotskyism' *op. cit.*, p. 7; D.R. O'Connor Lysaght, 'Matt Merrigan: a political assessment', *Red Banner*, issue 8, November 2000

41 Lysaght, 'Editor's introduction', *op. cit.*, p. xvii.

42 The ULA was formed in November 2010 and included the People Before Profit Alliance, the Socialist Party until March 2013, and the Workers & Unemployed Action Group until October 2012. Five of its candidates were elected in February 2011 – Clare Daly, Dublin North, and Joe Higgins, Dublin West, SP; Joan Collins, Dublin South Central, Richard Boyd Barrett, Dún Laoghaire-Rathdown, PBPA; and Séamus Healy, Tipperary South, W&UAG. In March 2013 Collins left the PBPA and, with Daly and Declan Bree (Sligo), formed United Left which was registered in May. Though never formally wound up, the ULA ceased to function in 2013.

43 Matt Merrigan, 'Developing an Alternative Economic Strategy', *Gralton*, no.7, April/May 1983., *www.clririshleftarchive.org/document/2106/* [retrieved 27 February 2019].

44 Merrigan, *Eggs & Rashers, op. cit*; Ben Kearney, 'Matt Merrigan', *Saothar 25*, 2000, pp. 13-16.

45 Draper, born in Brooklyn as Harold Dubinsky son of Ukrainian Jewish immigrants, 19 September 1914-26 January, 1990, was active in the *Young People's Socialist League* of the *Socialist Party of America* before being a founder of the (US) Socialist Workers' Party, 1937. He left the (US) International Socialists in 1971, concentrating on producing a succession of scholarly works on Marxism.

46 *Workers' Liberty*, vol.3, no.45, October 2014, *www.marxists.org/history/etol/newspape/wl/index.htm* [retrieved 27 February 2019].

47 *International Information Bulletin*, SWP, March 1947, *www.workersrepublic.org/index.html* [retrieved 27 February 2019].

CONAL PARR

'Left From the Margins' –
Paddy Devlin, 1925-1999

It speaks much of my grandfather Paddy Devlin that even in this, my fourth published piece on him,[1] there are new interpretations to take and stories to tell. All historians approach their work with their own set of views, assumptions and partialities, and so I am often caught between thinking of him as a grandparent and an historical figure. Though he has wandered into my work, I tend to minimise his role unless writing specifically about him (as now). Generally, Devlin still resonates through his impact from the margins, as the antithesis of almost every other major northern Irish politician of his generation. His political life may not be considered 'relevant or appropriate enough for the two dominant ideologies',[2] Irish nationalism or Ulster Unionism, but he interacted profoundly with both and left an imprint through his sustained non-sectarian Left-wing politics.

Devlin was born on 8 March 1925 and grew up in the Catholic working-class Lower Falls area of Belfast known as the 'Pound Loney'. By the age of seventeen he had progressed through the ranks of Na Fianna Éireann, and after coming to the attention of the Unionist authorities and going on the run, Devlin was apprehended and interned in the Crumlin Road Gaol in 1942. He explained that as a youngster in West Belfast, 'Elderly people would tell us stories about various Catholic gunmen who defended the areas against Protestants or Orangeman. When you're only three or four years of age and you've been regaled with these stories … those things do come through'.[3] Nevertheless Devlin seized the prison experience, debating with seniors and reading the works of James Connolly and other figures.[4] At the end of his life Devlin confessed that he essentially 'grew up in jail'.[5] On his release Devlin buried his IRA ties, joined the Irish Labour Party – who organised in the city at the end of the decade – and gained a seat on Belfast City Council, before shifting to the Northern Ireland Labour Party (NILP) in 1958. A Secretary of the latter party believed Devlin saw the Labour movement through a cultural prism:

> 'Paddy really wanted to create a Labour tribe to stand alongside the Protestant tribe and the Catholic tribe. You know the Labour movement, it's where you meet your girlfriend, it's where you marry, it's where you socialise, it's where your mates are – it's where your life is. It doesn't exist in Northern Ireland like that. I remember Labour clubs in England and people would all go out on a Saturday night and they'd have a few beers and sing songs and a dance, and the odds are that they'd met the girl they married or the fellow they'd married in the Labour Club. So you would create kind of a tribe – and Paddy wanted to create a Labour tribe.'[6]

An enduring theme was his focus on socio-economic issues in an era of relentless constitutional crisis. In 1984, Devlin remarked

> 'Our difficulty is that we have no real politics. In any other area of the UK you would find people involved in the redistribution of wealth and income. It doesn't happen here because our politics are all about waving flags so everybody ignores the division in society.'[7]

The SDLP and John Hume

On Saturday 28 October 2018 the Northern Ireland Civil Rights Commemoration Committee staged the inaugural Paddy Devlin Memorial Lecture in St. Mary's University College on the Falls Road. The present writer spoke on a panel with former Workers' Party councillor Séamus Lynch, publisher Anne Tannahill, and former Ulster Unionist Westminster MP and Councillor John Carson.[8] At this event, I remarked that I mostly welcomed Devlin being reclaimed by the Social Democratic & Labour Party (SDLP), who are prominent in the civil rights commemorative activities and had essentially organised the lecture. His relationship with the SDLP had often been strained[9] (though Devlin had run-ins with most political groupings in Northern Ireland over the years), with his resigning as the party's Chairman of Constituency Representatives in August 1977 and being officially expelled the following month.[10] What was striking about the seventy to eighty people present was their reflection of the various incarnations of Devlin's life. Members of the old NILP (such as Douglas McIldoon and Brian Garrett) rubbed shoulders with past and present SDLP representatives (Alban Maginness, Tim Attwood and Mary Muldoon), and there was a sizeable Workers' Party contingent, as well as a few Unionists. All are symbolic of different parts of Devlin's life, but most significant for our purposes are those from Catholic working-class political backgrounds that do not subscribe to the current largest nationalist party, Sinn Féin.

The event on the Falls allows us to consider Devlin's ambivalent relationship with the SDLP: the party Devlin co-founded in 1970 with John Hume, Gerry Fitt, Austin Currie, Ivan Cooper and Paddy O'Hanlon. We need to begin by recognising that his relationship with John Hume was far more complex than has often been maintained. To do this it is worth probing Devlin's autobiography *Straight Left*, which was published by the Belfast-based Blackstaff Press in 1993 and remains the critical book for his self-image and later political career. Like many memoirs, it contains vivid recollections of his childhood and Belfast upbringing, but was also one of the first memoirs released by a political player of note from the 1970s. It won the *Irish Times* Irish Non-fiction Prize in 1995 and is still cited by historians of The Troubles. It was orated by Devlin into a microphone (by this point he had lost his sight to a serious diabetes condition); a spoken-word aspect that lends it a peculiar quality, reflecting the gut instincts and colour of the man. However, it was written up – 'ghost-written' is the phrase used by Blackstaff's Managing Editor – by journalist Chris Ryder, based on a 'substantial amount of autobiographical material' prepared by Devlin.[11] Ryder did a fine job of condensing Devlin's memories into a stand-alone book, but this process also allowed some of Ryder's partiality and polemic to enter *Straight Left*, at times preposterously. Several reviews of the book picked up on an unbending hostility to fellow SDLP-founder John Hume,[12] and this can unquestionably laid at Ryder's door. The giveaway is the foreword penned by Ryder himself, which, in an extraordinary moment lists all the 'talented politicians' who founded the SDLP except John Hume.[13]

Though critical of Hume, Devlin was more conflicted and ambiguous than hostile about his former colleague. Certainly, Devlin disliked Hume's centralism; the latter's sleeked 'solo runs' that saw him take decisions over the heads of party colleagues, as also attested to by other SDLP heavyweights such as Séamus Mallon and Eddie McGrady over the years.[14] Politically, Hume was always more of an Irish nationalist and – secondly – a social democrat. Devlin, on the other hand, was always more Labour and republican (in the word's literal meaning). There were political differences between the two along these lines. In 1995 Devlin commented that

> 'the thing about Hume is that he's a good Catholic representative, he's not a socialist. And a Catholic party is not a solution to our problems ... our problems stem from the failure of Protestants and Catholics to merge and deal with their problems as a single people.'[15]

Hume was famously pro-European; Devlin was strongly anti-European Economic Community.[16] Devlin was gruffer and blunter, Hume much more subtle and behind-the-scenes in his achievements, as his efforts in the United States and Europe prove.[17] Nonetheless, there is no evidence to suggest that there was any chasm between the two men, and, if anything, on a personal level Hume and Devlin got on very well, sharing a warm and friendly rapport. Hume provided the foreword for Devlin's first book *The Fall of the N.I. Executive* (1975), and in the late 1990s, Hume travelled to the Devlin family home in the Oldpark Road, in what was their last meeting, to present his old colleague with a portrait painted by Thomas Ryan, dated 22 February 1974. It was composed during the period of the Sunningdale Executive, when Ryan often caught Devlin on trips to Dublin for meetings between the SDLP and Irish Government. Hume handed Devlin this paining and simply told him, 'You were right'. On Devlin's passing in August 1999, Hume of course paid tribute to 'an outstanding lifetime of service to the people of Northern Ireland'.[18]

Both were in their differing ways able negotiators and often acted as the SDLP's first-choice mediators, firstly in talks with Unionist politicians and then in brokering the first Provisional IRA ceasefire in June 1972, gaining among other demands the concessions from Secretary of State for Northern Ireland William Whitelaw that amounted to 'political status' for Republican prisoners.[19] Devlin had been in the IRA in his youth and knew how to talk to the new militants who emerged at the start of The Troubles, leading him to being described by journalist Mary Holland as 'the one SDLP member whom many Republicans would trust to watch over their interests'.[20] As well as being the only two SDLP MPs with a reputation for lending a hand to Republican prisoners in the 1970s – despite being informed on more than one occasion that they were on a Provisional IRA assassination list – both Hume and Devlin welcomed political movement in the Loyalist paramilitary groups throughout the 1980s, especially as it emerged through the Ulster Defence Association (UDA).[21]

A recent account of the Sunningdale negotiations in December 1973 allied them together at the conference, with Devlin noted to have supported Hume when he spoke to say that it was 'our aim is to end politically-motivated violence in Ireland for all time'.[22] However, one of the principle ways Devlin differed from Hume – and, by extension the wider SDLP – was during the same negotiations over the Council of Ireland provision of the Sunningdale Agreement. An Irish diplomat praised Devlin, Fitt, and Currie in a recently-published memoir for their efforts during these negotiations, but singled out Hume for 'far-sighted political thinking, sustained over decades'.[23] This is ironic because, by all accounts, Hume's insistence on the Council – in an 'almost theological' obsession with what was a relatively toothless body[24] – eventually doomed Sunningdale by making it too difficult for Brian Faulkner to sell to his Unionist base. Devlin was credited with recognising this ahead of his colleagues and was quoted as saying that the Council of Ireland ensured that Faulkner was being 'nailed to a cross'.[25] Intriguingly, both Hume and Devlin were mentioned by Faulkner in the speech announcing his retirement from politics, with his experience of working in the Executive issuing him with 'a new and lifelong respect for men like John Hume and Paddy Devlin. I can quite truthfully say that I will trust them to my dying day'.[26]

Devlin joined Hume in opposing the MacBride Principles during the 1980s, though once again for different reasons. This corporate code of nine fair employment principles had been drafted by veteran nationalist Seán MacBride and was being pressed on United States companies through state legislatures in the US. In Devlin's view the terms of the Principles would eventually be skewed and used against Protestant workers,[27] while Hume had the far rounder view that they were an Irish-American initiative designed to encourage disinvestment and thus cripple Northern Ireland's already weak economy, then straining under a particularly high level of unemployment. 'We can't have fair employment unless we have employment', was Hume's famous quip,[28] though his general recognition was of an old nationalist bent that if one made Northern Ireland so barren and depressed, it would speed up the demand for Irish unity. Broadly speaking, Hume privately shared Devlin's view that the Irish National Caucus, the main advocates for the principles, was little more than a 'flat-earth society of Irish immigrants'.[29]

Devlin's political career ended in 1985 when he lost his seat on Belfast City Council. As the Devlin family had moved to north Belfast from Andersonstown, Devlin switched to run for the Oldark Ward. With no 'power-base' in that northern district of the city, he polled only 472 votes and was eliminated on the fourth count.[30] Devlin was one of four candidates for a new Labour grouping he helped to found: the Labour Party of Northern Ireland (LPNI), an initiative so apparently minor he did not mention it in his autobiography.[31] However, archival sources reflect an under-rated local working-class Labour initiative, with Devlin declaring at its launch event that its aim was 'to re-align political forces in Northern Ireland behind the issues of high unemployment, low pay, social deprivation and anti-trade union laws'.[32] The LPNI confirmed it was anti-sectarian, 'unequivocally' opposed to violence, constitutionally independent of other political parties, and was based on 'democratic socialist principles'.[33] At the LPNI's first Annual Conference a matter of weeks after the Anglo-Irish Agreement was signed, it passed a motion confirming support for the accord – still the cornerstone of UK-Irish relations. As Chairman of the new party, Devlin stated that the alternative to the agreement 'was that the North would be turned into a West European Beirut with a consequent toll of death and destruction'.[34] If Devlin's hostility to Hume was so great, he could never have presided over immediate support for an accord so indelibly associated with the brain and acumen of John Hume.

Temperament, Republicans, and Loyalists

Though Devlin was an intellectual and well-read politician, he was often ruled by his emotions. A former NILP colleague noted

> 'that the danger with Paddy was that he was so big-hearted that he'd believe the last man he met. He was a man of emotion, not always of wisdom in that sense. That sounds like a criticism which is unjust, but I think it was a problem in terms of where he was going at any time because these were dramatic events.'[35]

This was particularly the case on 16 August 1969 when Devlin called for arms outside the GPO in Dublin: 'The only way we can defend ourselves is with guns, and we haven't got them. We need them'.[36] He was completely unrepentant when confronted about his statements during the Scarman Tribunal, which investigated the violence of 1969. Devlin justified that he was 'in a highly emotional state; if I had got guns in Dublin I would have brought them up to the Falls Road to get the people to protect themselves'.[37] Then, in a meeting with civil servant Seán Donlon at Iveagh House shortly after Internment without trial was introduced in August 1971, Devlin 'arrived unannounced and asked to see anyone available. Joe Small (I think) and myself saw him and he gave us the very simple message 'we want guns. We want them now. I have my car outside. Where will I go to collect them?"[38] To call for guns during August 1969 may be regarded as unfortunate; to request them again two years later looked like carelessness, though those who lamented such appeals believe they had to be understood in light of the 'terrible pressures' Devlin was under in West Belfast.[39]

The point about the danger of events being driven by the 'politics of the last atrocity' is an important one in light of Devlin's position as a representative for west Belfast. Towards the end of his evidence to the Scarman Tribunal, Devlin lost patience with one of his cross-examiners ('I am getting browned off listening to this'),[40] lashing out: 'You are terribly ponderous – sure as God will strike me dead you are'. Scarman pleaded, 'Mr Devlin, you have done very well indeed for well over five hours. Do not spoil the whole performance now by losing your temper', to which Devlin displayed all the exasperation of the MP for Belfast Falls in 1970: 'My Lord, I should have been away to a funeral today. There is (*sic*) people dead and I did not get the opportunity; and these things are dragging on and on and on. I will answer any question, but for God's sake come to the point'. The rage snap is reflective of Devlin's then-undiagnosed diabetes, though things ended amicably with Scarman calling a halt to the 'long ordeal' and thanking him for his testimony, prompting Devlin to joke, 'My Lord, I noticed that you looked at the calendar when I came in yesterday and I'm thinking it moves quicker than that clock!'[41]

Devlin's Republicanism was later the subject of conjecture by those he clashed with in Sinn Féin, but the questioning of these credentials hardly stands up. Initially, Devlin had been viewed as one of the stronger republican representatives of the NILP by the British Labour Party, who apparently resented being given a 'fierce Republican thrashing' by Devlin at conference.[42] Devlin consistently called for British troops to be withdrawn from Northern Ireland, including in a motion at the 1976 SDLP Annual Conference. The move was marginally defeated (with Hume and Fitt opposed), but it was not the last time Devlin's Republican background re-surfaced. Devlin blamed the killings of the Irish National Liberation Army's Ronnie Bunting and Noel Lyttle on British security forces and, speaking during the 1981 Hunger Strike, he was adamant that 'the British should get the hell out of it. The worst mistake they have made is staying too long'.[43] This may explain why Devlin was confident enough to write the same year how 'The definition of being a republican in Northern Ireland owes little to that found in the *Oxford Dictionary* and even less to that applied by the earlier forms of the Republican movement that I knew in Belfast.'[44]

Nonetheless, his rejection of the Provisional IRA was also sustained and consistent. He sided with the Official IRA in the 1969 split, and blamed 'the Provos' for hijacking the peaceful civil rights movement, creating 'a new and even greater need for basic civil rights in Northern Ireland'. Much of his attitude to the outfit stemmed from broader fears he had about the Catholic community's relationship with the rule of law. On Thursday 6 December 1973, at the Sunningdale Conference, Devlin stated:

> 'We are talking about our constituents. We are intelligent men. We believe that the approach you [the British and Unionists] are pursuing is not right. What happens on the Shankill and the Falls is symbolic. People feel these people [paramilitaries] are patriots – in fact they are thugs and gangsters. During the ceasefire last year, the Provos came on to the streets and acted as a police force. If you don't change the title, people will continue to see the RUC as a paramilitary force. The rumours and stories of fifty years are still in their minds ... Regardless of the reform in 1969 leading to more diverse recruiting, people still see the police as 'black bastards'. We are talking about areas where violence is endemic.'[45]

Throughout the 1970s, Devlin also talked with Unionist politicians and more militant Loyalists, winning the regard of Protestant working-class leaders like Glen Barr. There was even speculation the two mavericks would one day launch a socialist party.[46] 'We were two of a kind in many ways', Barr later recalled: 'It just so happened we were born on different sides of the track'. He knew he would be able to cultivate a relationship with Devlin when he attended Stormont debates in 1974, and 'you could see the divisions starting to emerge, political and social divisions within the Executive itself. You could see the potential for a good, strong opposition'.[47] UDA leader Andy Tyrie recognised the importance of cross-communal links Devlin had built up in the mid-to-late 1960s, with people 'really living and working together, exchanging ideas, mixed couples and mixed company' in pubs 'on the Shankill Road where Paddy Devlin used to hold his trade-union meetings. All this flow between the communities really was breaking it down'.[48] Devlin encouraged the UDA's proposals for an American system and constitution, and praised prominent UDA strategists in an interview with two American senators who travelled on the back of the Carter Administration's increasing desire to become more involved in Northern Ireland in 1978:

> 'Glenny Barr and myself, we would want to break all the Catholic-Protestant alignments up and create new alignments on the way in which wealth and income is distributed. You know, social democracy stuff, and Western European. We believe in treating everybody in the community equal. One of the reasons I left the SDLP is over their attitude to the Protestant sector of the community and that is the reason why Glenny Barr and I are so friendly and that is the reason why I have an in with the UDA and with all of the paramilitaries who talk to me.'[49]

The episode that won Devlin most Loyalist respect occurred during the Ulster Workers' Council (UWC) Strike in May 1974 when he dispensed unemployment benefit 'three weeks in advance' because 'he 'didn't want to have any hardship with the dole offices being closed'.[50] This was a self-defeating gesture in that it sustained the strike but was something Devlin considered a matter of integrity. His socialism prohibited him squeezing the Protestant working-class who directed the stoppage. 'Had he not been the man that he was', commented UVF leader Gusty Spence, 'he could really have put the boot into the working people of the Shankill Road and Sandy Row and east Belfast, but he didn't'.[51] Devlin had an affinity with Spence as a man similarly broadened by the prison experience who emerged – after Devlin had helped to secure his release in December 1984 – to play a progressive role: 'That happened to me, I mean I was in the IRA and I was jailed and when I got out, I headed to the middle of the road, and headed off to deal with politics in the economic and social sense'.[52]

Trade Union Highs, Hunger Strike Lows

After the collapse of Sunningdale via the UWC Strike of May 1974, Devlin immersed himself in his Irish Transport & General Workers' Union (ITGWU) activities. In late 1974 he got a job at the ITGWU as a union consultant, in large part thanks the good offices of its General Secretary Mickey Mullen:

> 'In time I was to become Secretary of the North East Region of the Union. I was elected on a number of occasions to the NIC (Northern Ireland Committee) of the ICTU (Irish Congress of Trade Unions). I was successful in recruiting large numbers of new members from the City Council workers, catering and shop workers.'[53]

Devlin's other major preoccupation at this time was Belfast City Council. His result in the May 1977 local council elections – when he polled a record 7,087 first-preference votes – emboldened his socialist maverick credentials. The ensuing period on Belfast City Council (1977–1981) is something of a lost era, a time when representatives from opposing constitutional platforms united on socio-economic issues, described by Devlin as 'one of the most rewarding periods of my life, for the co-operation we effected in the Council demonstrated that there was a lot of common ground to be ploughed and harvested despite the bigger issues that still divided the community'.[54] Some Republicans revelled in the fall of this chamber, accompanied as it was by a burgeoning Sinn Féin organisation,[55] but other Councillors who allied with Devlin referred to it as 'the most progressive, productive council in years'.[56] An 'unofficial caucus' including Devlin, the Workers' Party's Séamus Lynch, Independent Unionist Hugh Smyth, and liberal Unionists like John Carson was considered to have 'made real progress on socioeconomic issues…on the whole threat of redundancies'.[57] Smyth called the time a 'golden period' with collaboration on 'issues in working class areas, housing, education, health', Left-leaning representatives voting across sectarian lines for 'a better deal for our people. We would have said 'Right Paddy, what way will we vote?'"[58]

This spirit was curtailed by the 1981 Hunger Strike. Matters came to a head for Devlin when he publicly challenged claims that those on hunger strike were members of the ITGWU (they were not). In the municipal elections which took place the month of Bobby Sands' death, Devlin narrowly retained his West Belfast seat on the final count – Gerry Fitt was not so lucky, losing his – and compared the atmosphere to the period following the execution of the leaders of Easter 1916.[59] Sands had personally disparaged him in his diary: 'I see Paddy Devlin is at his usual tricks, and won't come out and support the prisoners. He is not, nor ever has been, a trade unionist, more likely a Unionist!'[60] Always more complicated than the rigid certainties of Ulster politics, and more nuanced than condemnatory during the hunger strikes, Devlin told reporters, 'The five simple reforms the prisoners are asking for should be granted. It would not amount to political status. They are reforms I myself enjoyed when I was in prison'.[61] When he began speaking out against the 'serious sectarian development' of a 'Defence Committee' and the reductionism of every political concern to the sole issue of the prison protest, he and his wife and children found themselves the target of H-Block activists. Devlin's rejection of the Provisional IRA's more sectarian violence, along with his own individualist brand of socialism and working-class politics, meant he was 'just the sort of independent voice within the nationalist community which brought out the Provos' most fascist tendencies'.[62]

An interview Devlin gave to an American academic is worth quoting to give a sense of what he and his family faced at the time:

'My most vivid memory is of being up all night, all the family up and water all over the house, in basins and buckets and the bath, while they made petrol bombs outside your window and threw them from forty or fifty yards down the road or from ten yards under my front window. Then they'd blow the whistle and go, and then they'd blow the whistle again in the middle of the night, maybe about four o'clock, and come dashing around with hurleys and beating the doors shouting, 'Paddy, come out, you bastard'. They'd keep that going for half an hour and away they'd go again and then another whistle went. Once the whistle blew again you knew they were going away.[63]

One of Devlin's fears in this situation was that if anyone did gain entry to his house, he would probably have had to use his firearm to protect his family. His widow Theresa recalled him saying 'The heavies will be round shortly and we'll be out for I'm not shooting anyone',[64] while another friend, the historian Bob Purdie, conversely remembered an image of Devlin 'sitting with his pistol in his hand in his home in Andersonstown, while a mob raged outside and hammered on the front door'. If they had broken through, 'he would have used it', Purdie claimed.[65] Rather than put this to the test, Devlin and his family vacated their west Belfast home and moved to the north of the city.[66]

Devlin retained a stoic commitment to his trade union activities throughout the tumult and death cycles of late-1970s and early-1980s. At a time when Bobby Sands was incarcerated, Devlin led a takeover of glass workers in the Antrim Crystal Plant in Andersonstown. The ITGWU co-ordinated the occupation following a management decision to lay off 170 employees. A committee was set up to run the plant, continue production and pay the workers.[67] More generally, Devlin saw trade unionists as key to providing the main oppositional force to paramilitary influence, as evidenced by their opposition to the failed Loyalist strike – or the attempted 'coup d'état', as Devlin phrased it – of 1977.[68]

Literature

Though Devlin was an emotional and occasionally rambunctious figure, he was also extremely well-read. During the Sunningdale period Devlin swiftly formed 'a close rapport' with civil servant Norman Dugdale 'a reserved Lancastrian, a poet and a Greek scholar. What brought them together was their concern for the casualties of society and their love of literature'.[69] One of Devlin's favourite pastimes had been 'to browse in the book stalls at Smithfield, the old second-hand market in the centre of Belfast which was a haven for bibliophiles and record collectors. Among the treasures I picked up there was an old copy of Victor Gollancz's Red Book Club, which had been published during the war, bringing socialists together in a movement to 'open the second front'.[70]

In January 2007, Devlin's papers were handed over in an official ceremony to the Linen Hall Library in Belfast. However, a set of books as part of a personal library remained in the Devlin family house on the Oldpark Road. As we can find out much about characters from the books they read and valued, it is instructive to compare what Devlin says he read in *Straight Left* to the titles found in his personal library. The names mentioned in his autobiography are: A.J. Cronin (who 'introduced me to the unique life and drama of a mining community'); Emile Zola ('especially *J'accuse*, his defence of Alfred Dreyfus, the French soldier falsely accused of being a traitor'); H.G. Wells (who 'converted me to the Fabian Society's view of rational politics'); and the short stories of Guy di Maupassant, Seán O'Faolain and Liam O'Flaherty.[71] Other books referenced are biographies of Peter Altgeld, a Governor of Illinois at the end of the nineteenth century who freed an innocent man who had been fitted up for the bombing of Haymarket, and the lawyer Clarence Darrow – a particular hero Devlin read about with 'unabated delight' for defending 'labour against capital, the individual against state tyranny, the under-privileged against the privileged'.[72] Devlin also admired G.D.H. Cole and Harold Laski, providing a British theoretical framework to his political outlook.

There is a distinctly more philosophical tone to Devlin's personal library than conveyed in *Straight Left*. Bertrand Russell (a 1960 edition of *Power*) and an introduction to Hegel feature. Seán O'Casey is represented by a soft pamphlet of *The Story of the Irish Citizen Army* (1919) rather than by his plays. Devlin's predilection for political biography is confirmed: two on the aforementioned Darrow – *Attorney for the Damned* (1957) and *A Sentimental Rebel* (1987), both by Arthur Weinberg – while John Hume, Gladstone, Hemingway, Thomas Johnson, and 'High Tories' like Harold Macmillan also appear as subjects, as does Noël Browne's *Against the Tide* (1987). Surveying this private collection, aside from the numerous British and labour histories, pamphlets on socialism and Marxism, names we might expect to find – David Bleakley, Aneurin Bevan, Anthony Crosland, William Morris, Engels – there are titles as diverse as Che Guevara's *Guerilla Warfare* (1961) and Frank Kitson's *Low Intensity Operations* (1971), respective architects of the dialogue Devlin witnessed on the streets of West Belfast; insurrection and counter-insurgency, the handbooks of war. Devlin read material widely and open-mindedly, from pugnacious tracts compiled by Fathers Denis Faul and Raymond Murray outlining British Army brutality, to the Grand Orange Lodge-published *The Battle for Northern Ireland* (1972) by the Reverend W. Martin Smyth.

Curiously, despite its 'faithful picture of working-class life',[73] Devlin omits Robert Tressell's *The Ragged Trousered Philanthropists* (1914) from *Straight Left*. In another article Devlin describes the work as 'a revelation', a story 'in which painters were working together talking as they did so, and the hero began to argue, even provoke his fellow workers, and in doing so tried to make them question the nature of the society in which they lived'. He relished the tale of Brendan Behan sending shipyard painter and Protestant working-class playwright Sam Thompson a glowing telegram invoking Tressell and coming north during the original run of Thompson's *Over the Bridge* to spend the day with Thompson in a Sandy Row pub. Behan, Thompson and Tressell were 'all painters by trade and angry dissenters against the prevailing system. Each in his own way used the pen as sword in the pursuit of change'.[74] Though unmentioned in *Straight Left*, Tressell's masterpiece resided in Devlin's personal library.

A book of essays edited and published by American socialist Upton Sinclair, *The Cry for Justice: An Anthology of the Literature of Social Protest* (1925), was also found among Devlin's books. Extraordinarily it had controversial Belfast Labourman and Unionist Harry Midgley's name inscribed in biro on the opening page, presumably as the first owner. Lodged inside is a list of Devlin's favourite writers and page numbers in his own handwriting, headed with his West Belfast address on the Shaw's Road in 1977 (evidently Devlin scoured this book for quotes to use in speeches). The list of Devlin's writers is extensive, but the names here also offer an insightful glimpse: Hugo, Johnson, Burns, Paine, Swift, Wilde, Shaw, Lincoln, Browning, Mazzini, London, Pankhurst, Gorky, Dickens, Mill, Morris, Moore, Wagner, Tressell and Sinclair himself. The same book also had inside its pages a newspaper cutting referring to Robert Tressell, headlined 'Forgotten Irishman was a Socialist hero'.[75]

The episode for which Devlin was 'most proud' in his Council career concerned the honouring of a literary figure. This was the award of the Freedom of Belfast to poet and man of the Left John Hewitt in March 1983. Hewitt's forced exile at the hands of Belfast's establishment in the late-1950s caused Devlin to resolve, 'if the occasion arose, to bring John Hewitt back to haunt them'. By the early 1980s the Unionist members had indeed 'forgotten', and as Devlin's own political life as an independent socialist was drawing to an end, 'It was a great consolation to me that Belfast City Council in my time had recognised the achievements of our great poet'.[76]

Conclusion

Devlin expressed constant scorn whenever the SDLP was described as a 'mainly Catholic party', and, in hindsight, his fears of the SDLP's turn 'towards Dublin' following the failure of Sunningdale appears to have been well-founded, especially following the recently-announced partnership between Fianna Fáil and the SDLP. In one of his final interviews Devlin commented:

> There was no way I was going to be a Fianna Fáiler, or a Catholic representative. Obviously the SDLP took a turn in that direction ... The like of Hume and (Séamus) Mallon were going off to meet Charlie Haughey and I felt that was the wrong direction for us and was bringing us into nationalism ... once you allow society to divide on green and Orange nationalism you have lost everything because they turn on each other.'[77]

In January 2019 it was announced that Devlin and fellow trade unionist campaigner Inez McCormack had been put proposed as new permanent statues in the grounds of City Hall by a Belfast City Council committee tasked with addressing the under-representation of certain groups – namely, nationalists and women – amongst the existing statues. Developments are ongoing, but a brief controversy arose when the largest party on the Council, Sinn Féin, objected to the plan and issued a 'call in' when the Council was due to debate and vote on the motion. At this session, on 4 February 2019, Sinn Féin's Leader of the Council Ciarán Beattie challenged Devlin's Republican credentials – for his accepting a CBE award in the last year of his life[78] - and drew attention to Devlin's public criticism of militant Republicanism (in 1978), and his refusal to back Republican prisoners in the Hunger Strike period. Sinn Féin's ultimate preference for a statue was for Winifred Carney, the suffragist, secretary to James Connolly, and veteran of the Easter Rising of 1916.

Tellingly it was reported that Councillor Beattie and Sinn Féin 'had no objection to Ms McCormack, but felt that Mr Devlin did not represent the republican community in Belfast'.[79] Two things are notable about this resurrection of Devlin's political profile. Firstly, in a social media age, normally Sinn Féin's political strength is mobilised into vigorous online denunciation and comment, as its activists (many cruelly dubbed 'Shinnerbots') pile in to back their party and/or denounce their opponent(s) on a given issue. This did not happen here. Online attacks on Devlin have been minor, confined mainly to 'Tweets' (online comments) from Alex Maskey, who pointed out that Devlin was 'rejected' with '410 votes' [*sic*],[80] and current Belfast Councillors Séanna Walsh and Ryan Murphy, both of whom voiced their preference for a Winifred Carney statue and expressed regret that a certain type of Republican needed to be acknowledged. By the standards of normal political competition this was mild and reflected in few online engagements or interactions with the said Sinn Féin representatives. The second observation to be made is that the criticisms were a back-handed compliment: an acknowledgement that Devlin still rattles Sinn Féin, and, by extension, a narrow Irish nationalism. Devlin pinpointed Sinn Féin's historic anti-abortion policy ('They're very right wing. On women's issues they're a disaster'), and always separated the Provisionals from the 'traditional IRA' for 'deliberately attacking the Protestant community. Old Republicans washed their hands of the Provos for this reason'.[81] Given his lifetime of opposition to them, it would have been strange if Sinn Féin had not objected to the nomination of Devlin as a potential future statue. 'I was always anti-Provo', Devlin told the *Irish Times* in 1995. 'A lot of the reforms had already been introduced by the time the Provos arrived on the scene. A lot of their violence was unnecessary'.[82] None of this altered his view that militants of all shades, including those associated with Sinn Féin, should always be talked with and included in political negotiations.[83]

Following the Belfast Council session, the DUP's Council Leader Lee Reynolds commented in the local Northern Irish media that 'Another reason Sinn Féin is motivated to do this is they want to write Paddy Devlin out of history'.[84] There is much truth in this statement. Devlin precedes Sinn Féin's hegemony in west Belfast, representing very different historical currents: non-sectarian, Labour socialism. One man who worked with him launching the LPNI in 1985 remembered Devlin being 'always willing to give time and energy to help people in trouble. Benefits claimants, the homeless, people being intimidated'.[85] These underdogs were his abiding constituency.

Notes

1 Connal Parr, 'Managing his aspirations: the labour and republican politics of Paddy Devlin', *Irish Political Studies*, vol. 27, no. 1 (2012), pp. 111–138; 'Paddy Devlin', in John Cunningham & Emmet O'Connor (eds), *Studies in Irish Radical Leadership: Lives on the Left*, (Manchester University Press, Manchester, 2016), pp. 175-185; 'Paddy Devlin, the Labour movement and the Catholic community', in Thomas Paul Burgess (ed), *The Contested Identities of Ulster Catholics*, (Palgrave Macmillan, Basingstoke, 2018), pp. 111-126.

2 Neil Fleming, 'New Ireland, same old heroes', *Fortnight*, no. 405 (June 2002), p. 33.

3 Quoted in Martin Dillon, *Killer In Clowntown: Joe Doherty, the IRA and the Special Relationship*, (Hutchinson, London, 1992), pp. 3-4. See also Paddy Devlin, *Straight Left – An Autobiography*, (Blackstaff Press, Belfast, 1993), pp. 27'49.

4 *Guardian – G2*, 20 November 1995.

5 *Irish News*, 8 January 1999.

6 Douglas McIldoon, interview with the author, Belfast, 27 January 2012.

7 Quoted in *Fortnight*, no. 209 (November 1984), p. 22.

8 While the present author suggested the names, the SDLP made the arrangements for all to speak, with credit especially due to a young party activist named Gerard McDonald. Lynch, Carson and Devlin were all contemporaries on Belfast City Council.

9 An SDLP spokesman once remarked that the party had 'never been more united than in its opposition to Mr Devlin' (*Guardian*, 29 August 1977).

10 *London Times*, 26 August 1977; 19 September 1977.

11 Anne Tannahill, letter to Paddy Devlin and Chris Ryder, 18 June 1992. Paddy Devlin Papers. Linen Hall Library – Personal Archive, Box 4.

12 Terry Cradden, 'Biography', *The Linen Hall Review*, vol. 11, no. 1 (Spring, 1994), p.21.

13 Chris Ryder, 'Foreword' to Devlin, *Straight Left*, p. vi.

14 Sam McBride, 'Declassified files: SDLP under Hume lacked 'unifying policies'', *Belfast News Letter*, 27 August 2018.

15 *Guardian – G2*, 20 November 1995.

16 *Guardian*, 24 April 1972; Gerard Murray, *John Hume and the SDLP: Impact and Survival in Northern Ireland*, (Irish Academic Press, Dublin, 1998), p. 215; Devlin, *Straight Left*, p. 283.

17 Maurice Fitzpatrick, *John Hume in America: From Derry to DC*, (Irish Academic Press, Dublin, 2017).

18 *Irish News*,16 August 1999.

19 *Guardian*, 20 June 1972. See also Patrick Bishop and Eamonn Mallie, *The Provisional IRA* (London: Corgi, 1988), p. 225.

20 *Observer*, 18 June 1972.

21 *Guardian*, 20 February 1976; Murray, *Hume & the SDLP, op. cit.*, p. 169.

22 Quoted in Noel Dorr, *The Search for Peace in Northern Ireland*, (Royal Irish Academy, Dublin, 2017), p. 429.

23 Dorr, *Search for Peace, op. cit.*, p. 6.

24 Maurice Hayes, *Minority Verdict: Experiences of a Catholic Civil Servant*, (Blackstaff Press, Belfast, 1995), p. 175.

25 Quoted in Barry White, *John Hume: Statesman of the Troubles*, (Blackstaff Press, Belfast, 1984), p, 152. Conor Cruise O'Brien was reportedly the Irish Government figure most attuned to Unionist concerns. Dorr notes in his memoir that Devlin (and Gerry Fitt) were 'less enthusiastic' than Hume about the Council of Ireland (Dorr, *Search for Peace*, p. 335). See also Hayes, *Minority Verdict, op. cit.*, p.178.

26 *Guardian*, 19 August 1976.

27 *Irish Times*, 1 October 1987.

28 Kevin McNamara, *The MacBride Principles: Irish America Fights Back*, (Liverpool University Press, Liverpool, 2009), pp, 192-200.

29 *Guardian*, 29 October 1976.

30 Devlin, *Straight Left, op. cit.*, p. 287. The other LPNI candidates were Stanley 'Bumper' Graham (Balmoral, Belfast), T. Blackman (Coleraine, Coleraine Town), and Tony McMullan (Ards, Newtownards). My thanks are due to Mr McMullan for providing me access to LPNI material and newspaper cuttings.

31 The influence of Chris Ryder may also be a factor in consciously overlooking this part(y) of Devlin's career.

32 *Belfast Telegraph*, 21 January 1985.

33 LPNI advert, *Irish News*, January 1985. Privately held archive of Tony McMullan.

34 *Irish Times*, 9 December 1985. The conference, attended by forty delegates, endorsed a party constitution confirming that the constitutional position of Northern Ireland could only be changed by a majority vote.

35 Brian Garrett, interview with the author, Belfast, 28 March 2011.

36 *Irish Times*, 18 August 1969.

37 Scarman Report, 'Paddy Devlin evidence, 2nd Day' (Day 99–19 November 1970), p. 48.

38 University College Dublin Archives, Garret FitzGerald Papers (P215/189), 'Seán Donlon visit to NI – Meetings with Paddy Devlin', 6–7 January 1976. Donlon confirmed that when he saw Devlin a few days later in Belfast he was back to 'his moderate best. The subject of guns was never mentioned'. I am grateful to Dr Brian Hanley for alerting me to this document.

39 Garrett interview.

40 Devlin Evidence (Day 99), Scarman Tribunal, p. 59.

41 *ibid.*, pp. 65, 75.

42 *Guardian*, 22 August 1970.

43 Liam Clarke, *Broadening the Battlefield: The H-Blocks and the Rise of Sinn Féin*, (Gill & Macmillan, Dublin 1987), p. 118; *Irish Times*, 6 December 1976; *Guardian*, 6 July 1981.

44 Paddy Devlin, 'Socialism: The Real Issue', *Fortnight*, no. 184 (December 1981-January1982), p. 11.

45 Devlin foreword to Bob Purdie, *Politics in the Streets: The Origins of the Civil Rights Movement in Northern Ireland*, (Blackstaff Press, Belfast, 1990), p. ix; Dorr, *Search for Peace, op. cit.*, p, 433.

46 *Observer*, 11 March 1973; *Irish Times*, 8 July 1976; *Guardian*, 28 November 1977.

47 Glen Barr, interview with the author, Derry, 28 November 2012.

48 Barre Fitzpatrick, 'Interview with Andy Tyrie', *The Crane Bag*, vol. 4, no. 2, The Northern Issue (1980/81), p. 16.

49 *Northern Ireland: A Role for the United States?* Report by two members of the Committee on the Judiciary, Ninety-fifth Congress Second Session – based on a fact-finding trip to Northern Ireland, the Irish Republic and England, August/September 1978, introduced and compiled by J. Eilberg & H. Fish, Jr (US Government Printing Office, Washington DC, 1979), p. 128.

50 Barr interview.

51 *Irish News*, 23 August 1999. See also Ian S. Wood, *Crimes of Loyalty: A History of the UDA*, (Edinburgh University Press, Edinburgh, 2006), p. 41. Future UDA leader Jackie MacDonald recalled the continuance of social security benefits: 'We were out of work but we got them all the same. That was thanks to Paddy Devlin on the Executive, who authorized payments through employers. I remember going in to one of my bosses wearing UDA combat kit and he stood up at his desk to salute me before he handed over my giro'.

52 Roy Garland, 'Interview with Paddy Devlin', April 1996. My thanks to Roy Garland for providing me with the transcript of this interview.

53 Paddy Devlin, draft notes for use in *Straight Left* entitled 'Some activities in late 1974' (Devlin, n.d.c). Paddy Devlin Papers. Linen Hall Library, Personal Archive – Box 2.

54 Devlin, *Straight Left*, p. 273.

55 Máirtín Ó Muilleoir, *Belfast's Dome of Delight: City Hall Politics, 1981–2000*, (Beyond the Pale, Belfast, 1999), p. 213.

56 Séamus Lynch, interview with the author, Belfast, 19 January 2012.

57 *ibid.*

58 Hugh Smyth, interview with the author, Belfast, 15 February 2012.

59 *Guardian*, 26 May 1981.

60 March 1981 entry, *The Diary of Bobby Sands: The First Seventeen Days of Bobby Sands' H-Block Hunger Strike to the Death*, (Sinn Féin Publicity Department, Dublin, June 1981), p. 40. There has been speculation that Sands's diary was in fact authored by another high-

ranking member of Sinn Féin, who was politically-prominent in the 1980s and is still associated with the party.

61 *Guardian*, 26 May 1981.

62 Clarke, *Broadening the Battlefield, op. cit.*, p. 131.

63 Pádraig O'Malley, *Biting At the Grave: The Irish Hunger Strikes and the Politics of Despair*, (Blackstaff Press, Belfast, 1990), pp.155–6. See also Clarke, *Broadening the Battlefield*, pp. 151–2, 166.

64 Theresa Devlin, interview with the author, Belfast, 22 July 2010.

65 Bob Purdie, 'I remember Paddy Devlin', Facebook memoir post, 3 December 2013. Available at: *https://www.facebook.com/bob.purdie.3/posts/546236042133499 [retrieved 20 February 2019]*.

66 *Irish News*, 26 May 1981.

67 *Guardian*, 10 December 1977.

68 *Guardian*, 9 September 1977.

69 Hayes, *Minority Verdict, op. cit.*, pp. 170, 174.

70 Devlin, *Straight Left, op. cit.*, p. 63.

71 A battered original dark-red edition of O'Flaherty's 1937 novel *Famine* was included in Devlin's personal library.

72 Devlin, *Straight Left, op. cit.*, , p. 63.

73 Robert Tressell, 'Preface' of *The Ragged Trousered Philanthropists*, (Lawrence and Wishart), London, 1955, p. 11.

74 Paddy Devlin, 'The *Over the Bridge* Controversy', *The Linen Hall Review*, vol. 2, no. 3 (Autumn, 1985), pp. 4, 6.

75 The article has been cut in such a way as to obscure the date and name of the paper, though the information indicates the year is also 1977. Paddy Devlin Papers. Privately held archive of Theresa Devlin. Only Wells and Zola are mentioned in both *Straight Left* and the handwritten list.

76 Devlin, *Straight Left, op. cit.*, p. 274; Paddy Devlin, 'John Hewitt – The Ulster Poet' (undated), Paddy Devlin Papers. Linen Hall Library, Theatre – Box 4. Hewitt was said to be especially pleased 'that Paddy Devlin was prime mover in the matter'. Edna Longley, 'John Hewitt, 1907–1987', *Fortnight*, no. 254 (September 1987), p.23.

77 Paddy Devlin, 'Letter: Party label', *Guardian*, 23 February 1976; *Irish Independent*, 24 January 2019; *Irish News*, 8 January 1999.

78 *Irish News*, 6 January 1999. Devlin insisted he was accepting the title as a 'socialist' and a 'labour man'.

79 *Belfast Telegraph*, 5 February 2019.

80 The 'rejected' phrase was also used by Beattie in the Council session, suggesting Maskey was coaching the Sinn Féin team in their approach to this issue. In neither case did the Sinn Féin representatives point out that Devlin had contested this last election in north Belfast, not west Belfast. Ironically, Maskey once questioned the 'marked revision' of Devlin's position, pointing out how he was unconvinced by Devlin's later moderation: 'Paddy Devlin was an outright Republican for some considerable time' (Murray, *John Hume and the SDLP*, p. 68). See also Tim Attwood, 'Letter: Yet again Sinn Féin displays out-of-date strategy of ourselves alone', *Irish News*, 13 February 2019.

81 *Guardian – G2*, 20 November 1995; Paddy Devlin, 'A plain-spoken preacher' of Catholic alienation, *Fortnight*, no. 224 (September 9-22, 1985), p. 14.

82 *Irish Times*, 16 November 1995.

83 *Irish Press*, 15 July 1992.

84 *Irish News*, 5 February 2019. Devlin had a reputation from his Council days of being a trail-blazer on working-class issues, meaning that the DUP – then of a more working-class character – used to follow his Left example on economic issues.

85 Bob Purdie, 'Paddy Devlin 1925–1999', *Fortnight*, no. 380 (September 1999). p. 9.

'A Tenacious Campaigner' for Equality: Sylvia Meehan, 1929-2018

Sylvia Meehan, who died on 6 September 2018 was a remarkable woman and her achievements in the field of equality were trail-blazing. However, if the magnitude of her contribution to the struggle for equality is to be truly appreciated, she must be viewed through the prism of her time. Of course, while full equality has yet to be achieved, the Ireland of Meehan's youth was an entirely different country than the one she recently departed. When she joined the workforce the position of women was still largely shaped, as in other Catholic countries, by the Church. The Irish Constitution, the brainchild of de Valera, who was heavily influenced by church conservatism, still contains Article 41.2 which states 'the State recognises that by her life within the home, woman gives to the State a support without which the common good cannot be achieved'.[1]

As feminists such as Meehan frequently pointed out, the State did not assist women by giving financial support for this aspiration but merely provided shackles to keep them there. This was the reason that women actively opposed this article during the enactment of the constitution. While the 1916 Proclamation had proudly supported equality for women, who played a prominent role in the Rising and in shaping the first Government of Ireland, once the dust settled they were swiftly relegated to the background. In 1925 the Local Government Act was introduced, which was effectively to preserve male jobs. Government further limited women's opportunities in industry through the Conditions of Employment Act 1936, again seeking to protect male employment, with the blessing of the major unions.[2]

Younger women are frequently shocked when they hear what the position of women in Ireland and beyond was prior to this third wave of feminism. For instance, on marriage, women were forced to vacate jobs in the Civil Service, banks, trades such as printing, and even within trade unions. They might, in some cases, be hired on a week-to-week basis at a lower grade and with consequent lower pay, but with no certainty around tenure. Of course, this ban did not apply to women who worked in laundries, catering, domestic service, or other tasks that men felt beneath them. A Government Memo of 1936 specifically stated that the rule did not apply to subordinate posts such as office cleaners.[3] So the ban effectively put limits on middle class women's aspirations. The taxation system also discriminated against married women and marriage wiped out a woman's commercial identity as she could not open a bank account, take out insurance or borrow money without her husband's signature. If a woman left her husband, she had no right to a share of the family assets, including the family home, and there was no divorce. Contraception was illegal, another major factor in the limitation of women's choices.

The Marriage Bar and the consequent paucity of women in senior positions in the public sector meant that women's voices were not heard. Public policy was largely shaped by male mores, which had major implications for policy decisions on a raft of issues that affected women such as health, housing, transport, childcare, education, and pensions. Yvonne Galligan illustrates that the very 'societal attitudes that place women in the home exert a powerful influence on women's own attitude towards political involvement'.[4] These attitudes meant that some women were happy to leave work on marriage as they did not feel rewarded in the workplace because women were frequently relegated to the more mundane tasks and overlooked for promotion. The perception was that they would eventually marry and leave.

Often the fight for equality is viewed as merely about tangible rights but living in a society that virtually discounted the views and aspirations of half its population was deeply frustrating and damaging for the half being ignored, and intellectually and socially damaging for society as a whole. So, the equal society that Sylvia Meehan envisaged was a more rounded and inclusive one. This is the historical backdrop through which Meehan's tenacity, her courage and her outstanding achievements must be viewed.

Early Days
Sylvia Mary Shiel was born on 2 April 1929 in Drumcondra, Dublin, daughter of Dr John Shiel and May Lennon. The middle of five children, Meehan was educated in the Loreto, North Great George's Street, and University College Dublin where she studied legal and political science. While she was undoubtedly fortunate to come from a middle-class background and supportive family that valued women's education, she still entered a university system where barely a quarter of the population was

female.[5] Despite this, Meehan was the first woman to win the Gold Medal for Oratory at the UCD Literary & Historical Society in 1949. The Gold Medal was awarded not for any one debate but on the participant's track record over their time in the Society.[6] This portrayed a woman of sharp intellect, who could hold her own in a predominantly male world, a presage of things to come.

Following her graduation, Meehan obtained work in the Law Library in Earlsfort Terrace, but when she married Denis Meehan in 1954 she was forced to leave her employment because of the Marriage Bar. Denis worked in RTÉ as a broadcaster and later Station Supervisor. He was a trade union activist and was instrumental, along with James Plunkett Kelly, in ensuring that RTÉ staff joined the Workers. Union of Ireland.[7] The Meehan family homes, first in Glasnevin and then Cabinteely, were lively places full of debate and humour. Denis Meehan was rather bohemian, like many of his compatriots in RTÉ, and his collection of cars, in various states of repair, was legendary, not least because they were prone to breaking down.[8] With such parents, life in the Meehan household was never dull for the five children – John, Níall, Sarah, Richard and Rosa. They all recollected a home that was full of life, books, chat and cats. Remarkably, while the children were aged two to twelve, their mother managed to return to further education in 1967 and completed a Higher Diploma in Education.

Meehan presumably chose this profession partially because the ban on married teachers had been lifted in 1957, not for reasons of equality, but because there was a shortage of qualified teachers.[9] She began teaching in 1968, securing a job in the Ursuline Secondary School, Cabinteely, now Cabinteely Community School, teaching English and History. In January 1969, Denis Meehan died of cancer aged forty-four. Now widowed, Meehan came under great pressure to cope with all her work and family responsibilities. She struggled to make ends meet while holding down a teaching job and raising her children. She did much more, however, than just 'hold down' a job, as a former colleague from Cabinteely Community School, where Meehan was Vice Principal, recollects: 'She believed in talent and the encouragement of it and she expected the girls to work hard, study and read, and do well in exams too'.[10]

As someone totally committed to her work, Meehan was incensed to discover that a separated male colleague was being paid more than her as he was entitled to a Married Man's Allowance. This was because in that era,

> 'the evaluation of wages was not based on gender, but on a consideration of the 'family factor' and the thinking that a man with dependents needed to be on a higher wage rate than the average woman, and that, whatever the real value of a woman's job was, it was calculated solely on gender.'[11]

Of course, apart from being discriminatory, this also overlooked the fact that a married man might not have dependents and that a woman might not have a husband, be she widowed or single, but may still have dependents. The realisation of the inequity of the teaching pay scale was a

'call to arms' for Meehan and other women in the 1960s, bearing in mind
that the gender pay gap at that time was around 40%.[12] Meehan reflected
that while the man received a Married Man's Allowance,

> 'There was no married woman's allowance. All over Ireland there was a male and
> female rate for the job …The 'stronger sex', so-called, received a bulkier wage packet,
> I resolved to do something about that, with other women in the post 1960s women's
> movement.'[13]

Union Involvement

Despite the daily juggling acts Meehan had to perform daily, she still made
the time to become involved in her union, the Association of Secondary
Teachers, Ireland (ASTI), and though that activity, the Irish Congress of
Trade Unions (ICTU) and in the fledgling women's movement. She
became ASTI Vice President, even though she was not afraid to publicly
challenge the leadership. She proposed a motion of censure after the
Executive negotiated a pay offer, which was narrowly accepted in 1971.
Despite this willingness to challenge the union hierarchy, Meehan remained
a firm believer in the power of collective action and her ongoing quest for
equality saw her become Chair of the ICTU Women's Advisory Committee
(WAC). This was to prove pivotal both for trade union women and for the
wider women's movement, as unions had become a major influencer of
Government policy on pay and working conditions generally. Trade union
density had grown to around 60% of the workforce, with major dominance
in the public sector, where policies were shaped.[14] This coincided with a
change in Government policy with a transition of leadership of Fianna Fáil
from de Valera to Lemass, who, at the conclusion of the 1964 National Wage
Agreement, opined that it marked 'the passing of the class war conception
of society and the emergence of a new and much more intelligent
partnership era'.[15]

This was not to say that women in ICTU were suddenly given a major role
in policy formulation. The trade union movement had been male
dominated since its inception and, apart from a small minority of left-wing
thinkers, was almost as conservative as Governments of the time. This meant
that women's voices were largely ignored whenever possible. Despite the
WAC's establishment, they were not directly consulted on the writing of the
Congress submission to the Commission on Status of Women and their
request for a woman representative on the National Pay Tribunal was
denied.[16] However, the fact that the WAC had become an ICTU Standing
Committee meant that they had a section in the *Annual Report*, thus
ensuring that their concerns were at least aired at the annual Congress.[17]
Women trade unionists involved at that time, such as Betty Purcell who later
served on the Board of Equality Agency, recount a constant and wearing
battle to progress issues in what was, after all, a patriarchal institution.[18]

True to form, Meehan was not prepared to sit quietly by and in 1974 spoke
on a motion looking for a 'National Steering Committee to re-draft

proposals for apprentice training', to 'include craft and teacher union representatives'. This was to prove controversial as she criticised the lack of reference to girls' access to apprenticeships. She also stated that the current system did not create craft workers but rather an obedient operative.[19] Meehan's debating experience was undoubtedly an advantage as she was able to calmly and cogently argue any point, making it hard for opponents to dismiss her as a hysterical female, a taunt then often used against women to belittle their contributions. In 1976, Meehan spearheaded the launch of the ICTU Working Women's Charter which was widely used in the fight for workplace equality. The Charter demanded progress on issues such as childcare, family planning, pensions and equality of educational access. Over fifty years on some of these issues remain on the table for resolution.[20]

Commission on the Status of Women & the Irish Women's Liberation Movement
The 1960s had also marked a resurgence of the feminist movement which had been largely side-lined after the enactment of the 1937 Constitution. The movement had been kept alive, almost underground, in unlikely sounding organisations such as the Irish Housewives Association (IHA), Irish Countrywomen's Association, Althrusa Club and the Dublin University Women Graduates' Association. Irish women were, nevertheless, keenly following the re-emergence of women's movements worldwide, especially in America and Britain. Meehan was one of the many women influenced by writings such Betty Friedan's *The Feminine Mystique*, which blasted the myth of the 'ideal wife' in the home.[21] The growth of the civil rights movement in Northern Ireland also challenged the status quo. These were undoubtedly exciting times for those seeking progress on civil rights issues and women's organisations kept sustained pressure on Government to look at the issue of gender equality. Their hand was greatly strengthened by a UN Directive on Women, with its stated aim

'To raise the status of women, irrespective of nationality, race, language or religion, to equality with men in all fields of human enterprise, and to eliminate all discrimination against women in the provisions of statutory law, in legal maxims or rules, or in interpretation of customary law.'[22]

In 1968, following a meeting in in Dublin's Cental Hotel of the ad hoc grouping of the IHA, ICA, Althrusa DUWGA and invited women's groups, where a committee was established, who eventually persuaded Taoiseach Jack Lynch to establish the first Commission on the Status of Women on 31 March 1970. The Commission of seven women and five men was chaired by Thekla Beere, first woman to become Secretary of an Irish Government Department.[23] The Irish Commission's terms of reference were;

'To examine and report on the status of women in Irish society, to make recommendations on the steps necessary to ensure the participation of women on equal terms and conditions with men in the political, social, cultural and economic life of the country and to indicate the implications generally - including the estimated cost - of such recommendations.'[24]

It is interesting to note that costs featured prominently in these terms of reference, a recurring theme whenever equality was/is discussed. Of course, it was not just the patriarchy that progressive women had to confront in the struggle for equality. Meehan must have been incensed by the comments of a teacher from the ASTI, a Miss N. Kelleher, their representative at an ad hoc meeting of women's groups called by the IHA prior to the setting up of the Commission, who said;

> 'Speaking personally, she was not in favour of a Commission, in fact we have equal rights except in pay for equal work, it is mostly traditional, as Shakespeare said 'the fault dear Brutus, lies not in our stars but in ourselves that we are underlings'. Women should show in sufficient numbers what they need, equal pay is pretty certain to come, but no need for a Commission.'[25]

The Commission issued an *Interim Report* in 1972 and the *Final Report* was sent to Government in 1973. The findings were far reaching though, as RTÉ reporter Olivia O'Leary concluded, how far the 'recommendations would go to becoming a reality depends not only on Government readiness to implement them, but it also depends on a change to public attitudes and an end to centuries of prejudice'.[26]

While the more established women's groups and the trade union women were working on lobbying, a new and radical group was forming. This began with informal discussions in Bewley's Café and latterly in Mrs Gaj's Restaurant in Baggot Street and became the Irish Women's Liberation Movement (IWLM). Founder members were Margaret Gaj, Mary Maher, Máirín Johnston, Moira Woods and Máirín de Burca.[27] Others rapidly joined the IWLM which was a mix of radical left women of various hues and middle-class women. Several journalists became prominent, including Maher and fellow journalists Mary Kenny and Nell McCafferty. This gave the IWLM an advantage in highlighting their cause, not least securing a *Late Late Show* devoted to its aims. The *Late Late Show*, as the most watched show on TV, was a major influencer and often caused heated debate in households across the country. The IWLM produced a leaflet, *Chains or Change*, which made six demands: equal rights in law; equal pay and the removal of the Marriage Bar; justice for widows, single mothers and deserted wives; equal education opportunities; the right to contraception; and one family one house.[28]

Realistically speaking, Ireland but more especially the Dublin of the 1970s, was a relatively small place so women from different organisations were collaborating on many issues while having different methodologies and political outlooks. Meehan moved with ease between the groupings and because of her intellect, coupled with her understanding of the need for careful strategic planning gained from her work in the trade union movement, was able to keep campaigners on track.

Ireland's Entry to the European Economic Community

1973 was also the year that Ireland entered the European Economic Community (EEC), which proved to be a further advantage for women in pursuit of equality. Article 119 of the Treaty of Rome stated that governments must introduce equal pay on joining the European Commission. The first hurdle knocked down was the Marriage Bar. Its abolition did not, however instantly mean equality for women in employment as most of the senior jobs were already held by men who had had years of advantage in the race to the top.

An even bigger hurdle was that of equal pay. The 1972 National Wage Agreement (NWA) incorporated much of the Commission on the Status of Women *Report* but attempted to rely on negotiation rather than legislation to introduce equal pay. Employers, of course, were not anxious to negotiate on this issue. While the trade unions supported the issue in principle, many male members were concerned that equal pay would mean less jobs for men. The majority still felt that married women were working for luxuries, like an extra holiday or a new kitchen, disregarding the fact that many women were supporting families. Indeed women such as Sheila Conroy, who was a member of the Commission, had long argued that the family wage did not always benefit the family, with money being spent in pubs and at race tracks.[29] Women trade unionists were also concerned that the NWA only recognised equal pay for equal work, rather than equal pay for work of equal value. This meant that unless a male and a female were doing the same tasks, even if the female was doing a task equal to or of greater value than the males, they were not necessarily entitled to equal pay. So, after all the pressure and lobbying the Anti-Discrimination (Pay) Act 1974, was finally passed! This was not without some very smart political manoeuvres behind the scenes, as Meehan recounted in an interview with Yvonne Galligan;

'I'm also told that it (the Bill) came before Cabinet in the absence of the Minister for Finance, Richie Ryan, who at that time was attending a meeting of the World Bank in New York. Michael O Leary had always pressed very much for the setting up of the Agency, and so did the Irish Transport and General Workers Union, at that time, and that view prevailed.'[30]

Galligan also recounted that the Bill passed through all stages of the Dáil the night before the Fine Gael-Labour Government left office in May 1977, its speed partly facilitated by Senator Evelyn Owens, who was Chair of the Seanad at the time and a long-term supporter of Equal Pay.[31]

Just when celebrations should have been happening, the new government bowed to pressure from employers to delay its implementation, again two steps forward one back. However, not to be beaten it was decided to organise a 'Save the Equal Pay Act' pressure group. The women lobbied, sought publicity and organised a meeting in Dublin with over 1,000 attending. Sylvia was naturally one of the speakers along with Evelyn Owens and Eileen Desmond. Pressure was put on the Labour party members of the then FG/Labour Coalition and a delegation went to Strasbourg to lobby Paddy Hillery, the EU Commissioner for Social Affairs.

Employment Equality Agency

In 1977, enactment of equality legislation created the Employment Equality Agency (EEA). Meehan was the obvious choice for the leading role of Chair and Chief Executive. While for any feminist this would have been a dream job, the reality was that the EEA faced several major issues from inception. Firstly, as this was a new departure, a whole new infrastructure had to be set up, without any blueprints, and this structure had to be able to hit the ground running. Secondly, and perhaps just as significantly, there was a tension between the EEA and other Government Departments such as Finance and Public Service where senior Civil Servants and Ministers would have seen the agency as usurping their power. Despite all this, Meehan fought tooth and nail to ensure that the equality agenda did not falter. The EEA had many successes, not least because Meehan utilised her network of allies gained though her battles in the trade union and women's movements. She acould not have achieved much of what she did in the EEA without the support of some of the Board nominees such as Hilda Tweedy, Monica Barnes and May O Brien, then WAC Secretary.[32] One of Meehan's powerful allies was the then Senator Mary Robinson. In the 10th Countess Markievicz Lecture, she outlined the role of the Agency as follows;

'It was established for three main purposes: to work towards the elimination of discrimination in employment, to promote equality of opportunity in employment and to review the working of the 1974 and 1977 Acts. To carry out these general functions the Agency has been given a number of specific powers. For example, the Agency has a discretion to provide assistance to any party to a dispute before the equality officer or the Labour Court who applies to the Agency and that assistance 'shall be in such form as the Agency at its discretion thinks fit'.

However, unlike its counterpart in Britain, the Equal Opportunities Commission, the Agency has neither the statutory authority nor the budget to retain legal representation as part of that assistance.'[33]

Robinson further argued that the EEA had been consistently underfunded meaning that it was unable to properly discharge its functions. Lack of funding was reiterated by the European Foundation for Working and Living conditions who stated;

'It has in many ways been a very effective monitoring and enforcement body. However, inadequate staffing and financial resources appear to have been a feature since the establishment of the Agency, and this has prevented it from being as effective in certain areas as it might wish.'[34]

There were tensions between the EEA and the Labour Court, arising partially because when the Court's understanding of its role, from its establishment in 1946, in dealing with industrial relations issues. Court decisions were primarily based on what was necessary for a settlement in the individual employment case presented, which might depend, amongst other things on the employer's ability to pay, However, cases brought under the Anti-Discrimination (Pay) Act 1974 and Employment Equality Act 1977 were to be decided on points of law, not subject to tailoring to a particular employment. Usually appellants in industrial relations cases had union representation but the EEA was anxious that there should, in more technical cases, be legal representation. Meehan was often accused of 'mothering' individual appellants, which may have been partially true, but it was vital that if cases were taken they were keenly argued as this was new legislation and precedents would be set. Ailbhe Smith, in paying tribute to Meehan stated

> 'One of the things that always struck me about Sylvia was that she was not only highly intelligent and strategic in everything she did, but that she was always very practical and wanted to see specific, named real workable results to improve women's equality. And she absolutely did that especially in the EEA. I remember her time there very well of course and worked with her often. I respected her enormously and I liked her, I really liked her. She wouldn't hesitate to challenge you, mind you, or to let you know if you weren't up to the mark, but that was part of her strength. She stood in awe of no man (that I ever saw) - nor any woman.'[35]

Meehan recounted receiving a letter explaining that it would be psychologically damaging for one particular group of men to receive a wage packet the same size as a woman's. She replied that she was not aware that men had weaker intellects (though sometimes, as in this case, I had my suspicions) and proceeded to apply the legislation to the group concerned.[36] Meehan always saw equality in the round, and while in the EEA argued that more legislation was needed to widen the grounds of the Acts to cover areas such as race, religion, age and so on, what in the subsequent legislation became the nine grounds. In addition, Meehan argued cogently for legislation regarding sexual harassment.[37]

While Meehan could be rightly proud of the pioneering work she did, she must have found it very frustrating to be shackled by the constraints of what was a quasi-government agency, with all the resultant politics. She undoubtedly retired with mixed feelings about her time there. The EEA was replaced by the Equality Authority in 1998. Níall Crowley, who became its CEO, had many battles with the Department of Justice, including one where the then Minister Michael McDowell altered legislation to remove cases taken by Travellers against public houses who refused admission from the jurisdiction of the Tribunal to the District Court. This was bowing to the publicans' lobby, but again shows cherry-picking, however this was the Minister who infamously stated that he saw 'inequality as an inevitable part of the society of incentives that Ireland has, thankfully, become'.[38]

Crowley subsequently resigned his position claiming that an attempt was made to remove him four and a half years before he eventually resigned in protest at the halving of the Authority's budget.[39] Again what price equality? In 2014, the Authority was subsequently merged with the Irish Human Rights Commission to form the Irish Human Rights & Equality Commission. Many feminists and trade unionists argue that this is a retrograde step in that it subsumes gender into one of the nine grounds, where in fact women still make up 50% of the population and can be subject to discrimination on other grounds too. To amalgamate the work on human rights and equality further dilutes the issues and spreads the financial resources ever more thinly.

Life after The Employment Equality Agency

Meehan was of course not someone who understood the term 'retirement'. After her retirement from the EEA in 1992, she moved on to tackle another inequality, that of age, becoming one of the founder-members of the Senior Citizens' Parliament. Máiread Hayes, the CEO of the Parliament, stated

> 'Sylvia was committed to ensure that the voice of older people was heard in all areas which affected their lives. She was determined that the mantra 'Nothing about us without us' would apply to all older people ... She served two terms as Chairperson of the Irish Senior Citizens' Parliament and was a driving force in the organisation of the Protest in 2008 against the withdrawal of the Medical Cards for those aged over 70. She stepped down from active service in 2010 but was always available at the end of the phone for advice and inspiring conversation.'[40]

Meehan had an amazing capacity to serve during her lifetime and was a member of the Advisory Commission of European Community, 1977-1992, acting as Chair in the 1980s; Irish, EU & United Nations Consultative Committees on Employment Rights; National Economic & Social Council (NESC); and the National Council on Ageing & Older People. She undertook two overseas assignments through APSO (Agency for Personal Service Overseas) as advisor to the Namibian Government on gender policy, 1997-1999. She was actively involved in Cherish, campaigning for the first Unmarried Mother's Allowance which was introduced in 1973. She was a founding Committee member of the Irish Labour History Society, serving from 1973-1978. She received many awards for her work. In 1997, the University of Limerick awarded her a Doctor of Laws; in 2009 she was presented with a Quinn-Healthcare/Rehab/RTÉ People of the Year Award for asserting the rights of Older People; in 2010 Dublin City Lord Mayor Emer Costello presented her with an award in recognition of her Advocacy of Older People; and in 2014, Griffith College awarded her a Diploma in Professional Excellence.

At the Griffith College award ceremony, Meehan again showed that she was still very much abreast of the issues facing women when citing the death of Savita Halapanaver, saying 'I hope a woman may come here as a refugee is never again forced to give birth against her will'.[41] In 2015, addressing the National Women's Council of Ireland (NWCI), she stated

> 'Irish women must utilise the great strides in equality we've achieved to drive for social justice for all. For too many years, girls have grown up in Ireland with limits placed on what options they might have in life. We don't want girls who are LBTQ to still grow up with those limitations. A yes vote for marriage equality will remove one of these obstacles and be one step on the way to ensuring all girls can live their life the way they want to.'[42]

Meehan suffered a debilitating stroke in 2015 after which her health gradually deteriorated. On her death on 6 September 2018, many tributes were paid. President, Michael D. Higgins said her pioneering work on equality in education and employment had left a lasting legacy.

> 'In her life, Sylvia Meehan overcame many challenges, becoming a tenacious campaigner for workers' rights, determined to promote the inclusion and empowerment of women, older people and all vulnerable sections of society. Her energy, vision and dynamism were directed at making Ireland a more empowering, informed and welcoming society.'[43]

ICTU General Secretary Patricia King said Meehan's 'pioneering work paved the way for a generation of feminists'. She had 'believed that woman must demand their place at the negotiating table and encouraged greater participation by women in the trade union movement, in civic society and in politics'.[44] Orla O'Connor, Director, NWCI, said Meehan 'will be a great loss not only for her family but for the women's movement in Ireland'.[45] At her mother's funeral, her children reflected on their loss. Rosa said that her mother 'believed in equality and human rights that left nobody behind'; Níall observed that 'my mother looked conventional but was not. She grew old but never had an 'old' idea'; Richard said she was 'great fun, a teller of stories, a natural teacher, a great supporter, a very positive influence and in 1970s Ireland, very 'unusual'. She was everything that Ireland was not, but she 'was' of an emerging Ireland that she helped shape'; and John spoke about her being 'unorthodox, an unorthodox mother? She was great'.

Postscript

To appreciate the life and achievements of Sylvia Meehan, the mountains that had to be climbed by women from the 1960s onwards to achieve equality need to be understood. She was not just an intelligent woman who, through adversity, had to fight her own corner, she was much, much more. She was a true believer in equality and was prepared to fight like a lioness to achieve it. She understood the power of networking, especially with other women. She passionately believed that women needed to seize more power, especially in politics, in order to bring about a more equal society. It is fitting that this chapter concludes with Sylvia Meehan's own words,

> 'We older folk, therefore, put a lot right in this country. We are passing on the baton to you, the younger generation. There is still a lot wrong and it will be your job to put it right.'[46]

Notes

I am indebted to John Meehan for several articles and e-mails and to Francis Devine who gave me his obituary for Meehan that will appear in Saothar 44, 2019.

1 Article 41 is headed 'The Family', www.irishstatutebook.ie/eli/cons/en/html#article41 [retrieved 10 March 2019].
2 Mary E. Daly, 'Women in the Irish workforce from pre-industrial to modern times', *Saothar* 7, 1981, pp. 74-83.
3 National Archives of Ireland, DT S9248, Government Memo 1936. [title of memo needed]
4 Yvonne Galligan, *Women and Politics in Contemporary Ireland*, Pinter, London, 1998), p. 39.
5 CSO, *That Was Then, This Is Now. Change in Ireland, 1949-1999: A Publication to Mark the 50th Anniversary of the Central Statistics Office*, (CSO, Dublin, 2000), www.cso.ie/en/media/csoie/releasespublications/documents/otherreleases/thatwasthenthisisnow.pdf [retrieved 10 March 2019].
6 UCD L&H Secretary 164th Session email 4/3/2019
7 Kelly, 21 May 1920-28 May 2003, worked in the Gas Company and, as a great admirer of Jim Larkin and his son Young James, became a Workers' Union of Ireland Official before his writing career saw him become an award-winning Producer in RTÉ. His play, The Risen People, eventually became *Strumpet City*, the literary embodiment of the 1913 Lockout. See Francis Devine, 'James Plunkett Kelly', *Saothar 28*, 2003, pp. 14-16.
8 John Meehan notes on his father Denis Meehan, 11 May 2017.
9 See Éoin O'Leary; 'The Irish National Teachers' Organisation and the Marriage Bar for women National Teachers, 1933-1958', S12, 1987, pp. 47-52.
10 Memoir written by Emer Ní Rónáin a colleague from Cabinteely Community School September 2018.
11 Irish Labour History Society Archives (ILHSA), *Irish Women Worker's Union, Annual Report, 1949-1950*.
12 CSO, Historical Earnings 1938 to 2015, www.cso.ie/en/releasesandpublications/ep/p-hes/hes2015/ [retrieved 10 March 2019].
13 *In Her Own Words*, commemorative brochure published by the Meehan family for their mother's funeral.
14 Mary E. Daly, 'Women and trade unions in Donal Nevin, *Trade Union Century*, (Mercier Press, Dublin, 1994), pp. 113.
15 Martin Mansergh, *'The political legacy of Seán Lemass, Études Irelandaises*, 25-1, 2000, pp. 141-172.
16 ILHSA, ICTU, WAC 1969 Review.
17 Daly, 'Women and trade unions', *op. cit.*, p. 114 .
18 Purcell, a trade union, human and global rights activist, was a staff member of RTÉ Authority and member, FWUI General Executive Committee until 1990. In 1991, she took a landmark case to the Europe Court of Justice on Section 31 of the Broadcasting Act to Europe. See her *Inside RTÉ - A Memoir* ,(New Island, Dublin, 2014).
19 ICTU, Report of the Proceedings of the 16th Annual Conference Dublin, July 1974, pp. 403-414.
20 The Charter is reproduced in full in Francis Devine, *Organising History: A Centenary of SIPTU, 1909-2009*, (Gill & Macmillan, Dublin, 2009), pp. 643-645.
21 See https://nationalhumanitiescenter.org/ows/seminars/tcentury/Feminine Mystique.pdf [retrieved 10 March 2019].
22 Title of UN document needed and source
23 Beere, born near Granard, County Longford, was the daughter of a Church of Ireland Minister and educated at Alexandra College and Trinity College. In 1924, she began as a Grade III Temporary Clerk in the Statistics Section, Department of Industry & Commerce, before, in 1925-1927, spending two years studying in the United States where she supported the campaign to reprieve Sacco & Vanzetti. She served on many Commissions before and after her retirement in a distinguished career, see Frances Clarke, 'Beere, Thekla (June) (1901-1991), Civil Servant and first Chairwoman of the Commission on

the Status of Women', *Dictionary of Irish Biography, vol 1*, (RIA/Cambridge University Press, Cambridge, 2009), pp. 414-415.

24 *Commission on the Status of Women Report*, 1972, (Stationery Office, Dublin, 1972), p.7.

25 June Levine, *Field Day Anthology of Irish Writing, vol 5*, (New York University Press, New York, 2002), p. 190.

26 Olivia O'Leary, www.rte.ie/archives/exhibitions/1666-women-and-society/370227-status-of-women-report [retrieved 10 March 2019].

27 Margaret Dunlop, born in Edinburgh in 1919 to Irish parents, as a pacifist joined the Red Cross as a nurse during the Second World War and married a Polish RAF member Boleslaw Gaj, the couple moving to Dublin and opening a restaurant in Molesworth Street and then Baggot Street. She was active in the Dublin Housing Action Committee and the Irish Women's Liberation Movement. She died on 26 June 2010. Mary Maher, a reporter with the Irish Times and prominent member of the National Union of Journalists, has been involved in the women's and socialist movements since the 1960s. Máirín Johnston, born in the Liberties in 1931, was active in the Communist Party of Ireland and socialist politics, campaigning particularly on women's issues, peace and disarmament. She has written widely on feminist and socialist history, see her *Dublin Belles: Conversations With Dublin Women*, (Attic Press, Dublin, 1989). Woods, born in London in 1934, daughter of British Catholic Civil Servant and an Irish, studied medicine at TCD, winning medals for psychiatry, surgery and medicine. Active in the DHAC and Irish Voice for Vietnam. Strongly pro-choice, her involvement in the anti-amendment movement led indirectly to the creation of the Sexual Assault Unit in the Rotunda Hospital, Emily O'Reilly, 'Woods: zealous campaigner who has lived with controversy', *Sunday Business Post*, 3 February 2002, www.irishsalem.com/individuals/accused/eddie-hernon/moirawoods-zealouscampaigner-03feb02.php [retrieved 10 March 2019]. de Burca, born 1938, writer, journalist and activist, with Mary Anderson, forced a change in law to enable women to serve on juries. She was Secretary, Official Sinn Féin for eleven years; a founder IWLM member; and DHAC, Irish Voice on Vietnam, Irish Anti-Apartheid Movement, Prisoner's Rights Organisation and Right to Die Ireland activist.

28 http://womeninhistory.scoilnet.ie/content/unit6/lberation.html [retrieved 10 March 2019].

29 Irish Trades Union Congress, Report of Proceedings 1951. Sheila Williams, born in Bantry on 22 April 1918, was a hotel worker and ITGWU Dublin No 4 Branch activist, serving on the National Executive Council, 1955-1959, until, having married the union's General President John Conroy, she was forced to retire. After Conroy's death in 1969, she became Secretary, 1960-1988, and President, 1988-2012, People's College, and served on the Commission for the Status of Women, 1972, and RTÉ Authority, 1973-1979. She died on 11 May 2012, see Marianne Heron, *Sheila Conroy: Fighting Spirit*, (Attic Press, Dublin, 1993)

30 Galligan, *Women & Politics*, op. cit., p. 81.

31 Owens, 22 January 1931-26 September 2010, worked in Dublin Corporation and was active in the Irish Local Government & Public Services Unions , leading the campaign for equal pay and treatment for women. Active in the Labour Party, she served in the Seanad, 1969-1977, her last term as Leas-Chathaoirleach. From 1984, she was a member of the Labour Court and was its Chair, 1994-1998. She died on 26 September 2010, see Sheila Simmons & Francis Devine, 'Evelyn Owens: equal rights campaigner, Labour Court Chair' in Francis Devine & Jack McGinley, *Left Lives in Twentieth Century Ireland*, (Umiskin Press, Dublin, 2017), pp. 199-210.

32 Tweedy, born Anderson in Clones, County Monaghan, 26 August 1911, and educated at Alexandra College, Dublin and the University of London. She married Robert Massy Tweedy in 1936. In 1941, with four friends – Andrée Sheehy-Skeffington, Marguerite Skelton, Nancy Simmons and Sheila Mallagh – she drew up a 'Housewives' Petition' leading to the creation of the Irish Housewives' Association, which she represented on the Commission on the Status of Women. She died in 2005. See her *A Link in the Chain: The Story of the Irish Housewives Association*, 1942–1992, (Attic Press, Dublin, 1992); Alan Hayes (ed), Hilda Tweedy & the Irish Housewives Association: Links in the Chain, (Arlen House, Baldoyle, 2011). Barnes. née MacDermott, 12 February 1936-3 May 2018, was Fine Gael TD for Dún Laoghaire-Rathdown, 1982-1992 and 1997-2002. O Brien, born in

Donnybrook, 30 May 1932, from 1947 she worked for the ITGWU as a Clerk/Typist and then Branch Assistant, 1972, Dublin Nos 6/8 Branch (Clothing & Textiles). From 1982-1992, she was the ITGWU's first Women's Affairs Official, winning many precedent-setting equality and equal pay cases. She served on the EEA and ICTU WAC. See her *Clouds on My Windows: A Dublin Memoir*, (Brandon Books, Dingle, 1994).

33 Mary Robinson, The Tenth Countess Markievicz Lecture – Women, Work & Equality, (Irish Association of Industrial Relations, 1985), www.ul.ie/iair/sites/default/files/1985%20Lecture%20by%20Mary%20Robinson.pdf [retrieved 10 March 2019].
34 'Employment Equality Agency', www.eurofound.europa.eu/efemiredictionary/employment-equality-agency [retrieved 10 March 2019].
35 Ailbhe Smyth e-mail to John Meehan, 7 September 2018.
36 In Her Own Words, op. cit.
37 *ibid.*
38 David Quinn Irish Independent, 15 October 2004.
39 Carol Coulter, Irish Times, 10 May 2010.
40 Mairead Hayes Irish Senior Citizens publication September 2018
41 In her own words, Notes published by the Meehan family for Sylvia's Funeral
42 NWCI Publication: Tuesday, May 05, 2015.
43 https://president.ie/en/media-library/news-releases/statement-by-president-higgins-on-the-death-of-sylvia-meehan [retrieved 10 March 2019].
44 www.ictu.ie/press/2018/09/06/the-general-secretary-of-the-ictu-patricia-king-ha/ [retrieved 10 March 2019].
45 www.nwci.ie/index.php/learn/article/nwci_pays_tribute_to_sylvia_meehan [retrieved 10 March 2019].
46 In Her Own Words, *op. cit.*

SÉAMUS DOOLEY

'The Accidental Official':
Jim Eadie, 1929 -

James (Jim) Eadie might well be described as 'an accidental union official'. His appointment as the first Irish Organiser and later Irish Secretary of the National Union of Journalists, UK and Ireland (NUJ) arose from the decision of the appointed candidate to decline the job in a curious dispute over the funding of the post. Eadie was the first of only three Irish Secretaries and is a legendary NUJ figure.[1] Yet he maintained a relatively low profile within the wider trade union movement while consistently delivering results for his members. Much of the NUJ's impact on employment, education, training and media policy can be credited to Eadie and the team he managed to build around him during his long period at the helm.

Formation of the NUJ
The NUJ's foundation meeting was held in the Acorn Hotel, Birmingham in March 1907 but it took many years before it was established on a formal footing in Ireland.[2] From its formation, Dublin, with its strong concentration of newspapers, was in the NUJ National Executive Council's sights. However, the revolutionary turmoil in Ireland during the union's formative years served as a barrier to expansion across the Irish Sea.[3] F.J. Mansfield in *Gentlemen, the Press* refers to what he describes as 'The Invasion of Ireland' in 1909 during which twenty people attended a meeting in Dublin. NUJ Secretary William Newman Watts went on, with mixed results, to visit Waterford, Derry and Cork ('a fruitless meeting') and held a successful meeting in Newry, returning to London with 100 recruits.[4] In 1910 Ireland was represented at the Annual Delegate Meeting (ADM) held in Ireland but in those formative years the

159

organisational focus was mainly on the establishment of a strong industrial presence in England.[5]

In 1927, the NUJ General Secretary and President attended a Dublin Branch meeting where it was confirmed that, through unofficial channels, the Dublin newspaper proprietors were willing to talk to the NUJ but they would only do so in joint talks with the rival Institute of Journalists (IOJ), a move which would have been contrary to policy as determined by the union's ADM.[6] The foundation of the *Irish Press* strengthened the union and Dublin Branch Secretary James O'Farrell, as Night Editor, played a key role in ensuring that staff were immediately recruited to the NUJ.[7]

At the 1942 ADM, Dublin delegate R.M. Fox accused the NEC of seeking to abandon members in Ireland and proposed a motion calling on the union to register as a Negotiating Body under the 1941 Irish Trade Union Act, contrary to union policy in relation to State control of unions.[8] Conference accepted an amendment from the Treasurer supporting the status quo with a compromise of sort – Dublin could remain as present but 'in the event of circumstances requiring it, the NEC was authorised to deposit £1,000 for a trial period' with provision for a review at the next ADM.[9] The NEC subsequently accepted a request to register under the Act but the entire episode led to rows, ructions and even the resignation of the President in a dispute over collective responsibility.[10]

The NUJ stand taken by the Irish membership was vindicated when Dublin Branch, as part of the then Dublin Printing Trades Group (DPTG), secured two pay rises in 1943 and secured full-scale agreements on terms and conditions.[11] That success laid the foundations for new branches and an expansion of the NUJ's membership despite competition from the Guild of Irish Journalists (GIJ), founded in 1949 with support from the Catholic church and the Irish Government.[12] Managing such conflicts was to become a regular feature of the Cross-Border union and provides an intriguing backdrop to Eadie's appointment as the first full time paid official of the NUJ in Ireland.

Table 1: NUJ Irish Membership, 1926-2017, Select Years [Northern Ireland membership within total]							
1926	80	1950	397	[95]	1990	2,858	[646]
1930	68	1960	608	[208]	2000	3,873	[734]
1940	95	1970	1,202	[302]	2010	3,933	[850]
1945	203	1980	2,138	[561]	2017	2,274	[749]

Source: ITUC & ICTU, *Annual Reports*
Note that female membership was 1950, 95; 1960, 208; 1970, 302; 1980, 561; 1990, 646; 2000, 856; 2010, 990; and 2017, 1,096

Early Years & Joining the Union

James 'Jim' Eadie was born in Stonepark, Roscommon town on 4 June 1929, son of James and Mary Eadie (née Farrell), in the shadow of Moat Park, seat of the Crofton family. He was the second eldest in a family of three boys and two girls 'My father was a small farmer, so were my mother's people – there were only small farmers, except Lord Crofton, and I never saw him'.[13] Eadie was educated at Roscommon Christian Brothers' School and earned a reputation as a tough, uncompromising half forward when lining out on the school Gaelic football team in the Connacht Colleges Cup Final in 1947-1948 school year against Summerhill College, Sligo. Such was his prowess on the sports field that he was encouraged by the Christian Brothers to repeat his Leaving Cert the following year but a successful objection by St Jarlath's in the season's first game saw Eadie disqualified. He instead acted as umpire alongside future All Ireland winner Frankie Stockwell of Tuam. The partisan Eadie provoked controversy as he and Stockwell disagreed on every score: 'We lost that game despite my best efforts. I abandoned secondary school, leaving college football and umpiring behind me'.

Eadie decided to pursue a career in journalism, joining the female dominated secretarial course at Roscommon Vocational School, 'sitting in the back row learning shorthand and typing'. Keeping up his interest in football with St Coman's club he got to know *Roscommon Herald* sports journalist and future editor Michael O'Callaghan who encouraged the youthful Eadie's interest in journalism. O'Callaghan's advice was direct and sensible, 'Keep on reading, keep on writing. Stick at it'. O'Callaghan's colleague Jim Flanagan was equally encouraging. In 1950, *Roscommon Herald* shareholder and County Surgeon Dr Jock O'Hanrahan was sufficiently impressed to offer Eadie the opportunity of a probation, with the approval of his partners, Paddy Nerney and C.E Callan. Probation meant long hours and hard work.

> 'Two pounds and ten shillings a week … Ten shillings for smoking, pictures and dancing and the rest on digs in Boyle. On Monday morning my mother gave me cash for the bus from Roscommon and Boyle.'

As a General Reporter, Eadie was also required to tout 'for sales and advertising'. He recalled hearing of the advances made by the NUJ in the National Wage Round of 1947 and decided to apply for union membership to the now defunct Athlone & District Branch. He was admitted to membership on 1 April 1951, but not without a dispute.[14] He was at first refused admission to the branch, on the basis that he was only a probationer. The logic applied was that the union was for permanent staff and if they took on probationers they would have to defend them if they were not taken on permanently. It was an experience which shaped his attitude to trade unionism and as a full-time union Official Eadie was always committed to the welfare of young recruits. He was especially alive to the use of union rules to unfairly restrict entry to the profession. Coincidentally his successor as Irish Secretary, Éoin Ronayne, was also refused membership of the union first time round, because he had been working on an illegal pirate radio station. In turn the author, Séamus Dooley, succeeded Ronayne having also suffered the indignity of rejection by Athlone & District branch in 1981 on the basis that he was 'a communications student masquerading as a journalist', the 1980s equivalent of a probationer![15]

Western Adventures

Eadie arrived in the *Roscommon Herald* at a time of company expansion. The owners were committed Fianna Fáil supporters who saw the propaganda value of owning local papers. Michael O'Callaghan moved to Mullingar to set up a local paper, being succeeded by a future national columnist and *Irish Independent* critic, Des Rushe. Eadie was sent to Ballinasloe to work on the *Western Herald*, later moving to work on a new Athlone edition. However, failure to provide adequate resources meant that the *Herald's* expansion plans failed, despite the sterling work of Eadie, Rushe and O'Callaghan to shake the dominant titles like the *Connacht Tribune, Westmeath Independent* and *Westmeath Examiner.* The established papers, Eadie recalls, were inclined towards Fine Gael and gave coverage to that party's Councillors. O'Hanrahan and his colleagues were trying at local level what Dev did nationally with the *Irish Press.*

Eadie has fond memories of Ballinasloe, where at twenty-one years of age he recalls removing his pioneer pin and taking his first drink at a reception attended by the Tanaisté and Labour Leader William Norton.

> 'I'd never drank before and did not like the smell of beer so Jimmy Spollen (*Westmeath Independent*) recommended sherry. I drank sherry all day and never again.'

Athlone was 'not a happy place' since he was required to work long into the night, typing up reports of Urban District Council meetings which he had to send next morning on a bus to Boyle. It was soul destroying work, made more so when the paper frequently appeared with some of his copy missing. In Athlone he formed a friendship with a young up and coming barrister, future Minister Brian Lenihan. On Sunday mornings Eadie headed for a football match, Lenihan to Cumann meetings in South Roscommon as he sought to build a political career. Through his work, Eadie got to know his football hero Jack McQuillan, whom he would later report on in Dáil Éireann as a Clann na Pobhlachta TD.[16] As a socialist, one of his regrets was that he never got to vote for McQuillan as he never qualified to vote in the constituency. Football dominated Eadie's leisure time and being what he described as 'an itinerant reporter', he lined out – not always legally – with Gaelic football teams in Westmeath, Roscommon and Galway all in the one season. He cast his first vote when he moved to Dublin.

Back in Boyle after his Athlone sojourn Eadie was a victim of what became known as the Battle of Castlerea when he lined out for Boyle against Owen Rua's junior team, a breakaway club founded by Roscommon GAA legend

Owensie Hoare. Eadie, a Roscommon town native, was seen as something of a traitor and heavily marked – 'in every way' during the game. Jack McQuillan's brother Bill, a Locum due to do medical exams the next day, was, in Eadie's words, 'floored, flattened, knocked out'. After a bloody game, a mob attacked Eadie. There were so many trying to attack him, that they were falling over one another and he escaped with damage to one tooth! Bizarrely Eadie wrote 'a reasonably objective' match report for the *Roscommon Herald* but also filed a formal complaint to the County Board which led to disciplinary action against his opponents. His team declined the offer of a replay. It was his last GAA match. From then on, Eadie devoted his energies to journalism and trade unionism but he retains his passion for Roscommon football.

Dublin Bound & Not Playing the Gallery

Equipped with a natural curiosity and strong political nous, Eadie was never going to stay too long in Roscommon but it was his girlfriend, Bridie Reynolds, a secretary in the *Roscommon Herald* from Mantua, Elphin, who encouraged him to apply for jobs in the national press. On 17 March 1956, the young couple boarded the excursion train to Connolly Station, Dublin. As they stood outside Wynn's Hotel on Lower Abbey Street, Reynolds noticed Independent House and prodded Jim to call in. On arrival, Eadie met a journalist whom he recognised, John Healy, later Tourism, Aviation and Diplomatic Correspondent and a highly regarded News Editor. There and then he secured a job with the *Irish Independent, Sunday Independent* and *Evening Herald*, as a Group Reporter, 'subject to three editors, three deputies and a lot of news editors and subs'. He had 'left the Bohemian life of Boyle. It was time to go in a different direction. We got engaged and I could save, leaving money in the GPO, £5 or £6 a week'. Eadie and Reynolds married on 17 June 1958 and set up home in Dublin. They had four children, Deirdre, Caroline, Colm and James.

It did not take long for Eadie to make waves as a reporter. As part of the Oireachtas Press Gallery he was required to join the 'pool system' whereby journalists from different titles took turns at shorthand reports of Parliamentary Debates, providing carbon copies known as 'blacks' to colleagues. Eadie broke ranks by recording the contributions of backbenchers and Independents such as McQuillan and Noël Browne 'because they were saying interesting things'.[17] Senior Parliamentary Reporters objected to his decision to break with the then convention that backbenchers were not reported. Frustrated, Eadie submitted his version of a particular debate only to the *Irish Independent*, to the consternation of the Press Gallery: 'If you don't behave, we will have you put off the gallery', he was warned. Looking back on it, Eadie says he won and lost battles: 'I did toe the line, sometimes, sometimes I got my own way'.

Eadie looks back on his *Independent* years with mixed emotions. He was disappointed at the lazy approach to journalism in Independent House and not slow to make his views known. 'Why can't we write our own stories, we are spending too much time re-writing', he argued as the News Desk ordered re-writes of stories from rival papers. He viewed with concern the failure to counter the rise of the Press Group but reporters were not encouraged to give opinions. With the opening of RTÉ television, the early 1960s saw an exodus to broadcasting but Eadie failed to get an interview for the Newsroom. A tentative offer to move to the *Irish Times* did not bear fruit. Despite his admiration for the *Press* – 'the best newsroom in Dublin' – Eadie rejected an overture to work in Burgh Quay, having strong reservations about the management style of the man who was keen to recruit him.

There was limited NUJ activity in Independent House. Political journalist Maurice Hickey was Dublin Branch Chair and ran the union in the *Independent*. Where other unions have Committees, print unions have Chapels, and while unions have Shop Stewards, print unions traditionally elected Fathers of the Chapel (FoC). When the legendary Mary Maher was elected head of the union at the *Irish Times*, she became the first Mother of the Chapel in Dublin Branch. Eadie recalls that Hickey, as FoC, was 'a bit easy going with a *laissez faire* attitude' at a time when journalists were getting frustrated and cranky. When Hickey stepped down Bill Shine re-formed the Chapel and Eadie took his first steps in active union involvement as a Collector of dues: 'We were young: we felt we should and could be doing better. The job was unsatisfactory for the work and so was the money'.

For Eadie, Shine's achievement was to bring the Chapel to a point of militancy in the early 1960s. NUJ organisation was made complicated by the presence of the Institute of Irish Journalists (IIJ) and GIJ and in any negotiations on pay claims both were involved.[18] The 'employer exploited that situation' with the IIJ 'being more compliant than the NUJ'. In many ways it was a pay dispute which consolidated Eadie's Chapel involvement. At a Labour Court Conciliation conference, Shine and NUJ Assistant Secretary Ron Hallett accepted a pay offer of thirty shillings but the Chapel rejected the claim as inadequate and a sell-out. Eadie recalls, 'we told them to keep their thirty pieces ... We thought Shine was the Messiah and he had let us down'. Hallett, in the fashion of the time, led the negotiations and travelled back to London without consulting the Chapel. Throughout the 1950s and early 1960s, union negotiators dropped in from Acorn House, the NUJ's London Head Office, while routine administration, organising and Chapel negotiations were carried out by lay Officials, including Michael McInerney, *Irish Times* political reporter.[19]

The Chapel rejected the deal at a meeting, but the NUJ's Executive insisted that there must be a secret ballot and despite Eadie's best efforts the deal was passed by a narrow margin. Once again, he was in trouble with the Press Gallery when he canvassed support for a 'No' vote in Leinster House.

Forced to live with the outcome the *Independent* Chapel embarked on a new mission. McInerney, NEC member for Ireland and de facto leader of the NUJ in Ireland, was ousted, replaced by Pat Nolan of the *Irish Times* Chapel. Shine was ousted as FoC replaced by future broadcasting legend Frank Hall, with Eadie as his Deputy. Hall had a fraught relationship with the Murphy family. Eadie recalls him as erudite and cultured but unsuited to the Social Diary column which he was supposed to write: 'He was not a name dropper and did not have the personality for what they wanted to compete with the *Evening Press* diary. He wrote the most beautiful prose and was very gifted'. Hall could also be impulsive and his decision to write to the Chairman of the company above the heads of local management soured relations. It led to what Eadie terms 'a cold war' and his Chapel Officers felt strongly that Hall was badly treated. In time Hall secured a job in RTÉ and Eadie found himself as FoC.

Reluctant Official

The NUJ NEC had been resistant to moves for a full-time office in Dublin but in 1964 ADM delegates defied their NEC by voting to appoint a full-time Organiser based in Dublin. Pat Nolan was offered the job. Nolan was a conscientious Chapel and Branch Officer, and a man of firm religious convictions but refused to follow the Catholic Church line on Communism and stuck with the NUJ when others left to join the GIJ.[20] Nolan tentatively accepted the NEC offer but with a characteristic twist placed a condition on the appointment. He proposed that Irish members pay a levy to cover his salary as a means of ensuring that he – and those he served, would not be 'beholden' to Acorn House. Having decided to appoint an Irish Organiser and make financial provision for the post, the NEC would not accept Nolan's pre-condition.[21] It was to fall to Eadie

'I never wanted the job. We wanted Pat to take it, but he agonised about the levy idea and the importance of independence. At that stage none of us cared about anything except getting the job filled before the NEC changed its mind. One night in the Pearl Bar I told Pat, 'You have to make up your mind. If needs be, I will go for it myself, but we cannot lose the chance'.'

Nolan stayed firm, the post was advertised and Eadie emerged as the successful candidate. He went on to work well with Nolan, who remained a loyal lay activist. Eadie recalls getting a call during the 1965 Printers' strike from London official Ron Hallett telling him to go to London for an interview. On one occasion when Nolan and Eadie were returning from an NEC meeting in London, Nolan expressed the desire to drop into Brompton Oratory to pray. Eadie expressed surprise that he felt the need to do so as he had conducted himself very well over the weekend. Pat responded: 'But I found myself voting with the communists a little too often'.[22]

The creation of a full-time post was a baptism of fire for the FoC of the *Irish Independent* whose appointment coincided with a print industry dispute which saw the entire Dublin NUJ membership being laid off and dependant on union benefits for ten weeks. The 1965 strike by the newly styled Irish Graphical Society was long and difficult but among the positive developments was the establishment of the DTPG, subsequently the Dublin Printing Group of Unions.[23] Eadie worked assiduously to develop links with sister unions and through the DTPG secured a seat on the Irish Congress of Trade Unions (ICTU) Executive Council on four occasions.[24] Seats were contested on a rotational basis, ensuring that the print industry would be consistently represented.

Appointment of a full-time Official coincided with the opening of a NUJ office in Liberty Hall, newly-opened headquarters of the Irish Transport & General Workers' Union (ITGWU). Office administration fell under the remit of Patsi Dunne who, in 1982 succeeded Eadie as Organiser when he was appointed as Irish Secretary or, to give him the correct but seldom used title, Assistant Secretary (Ireland). In 1982, Dunne's appointment was significant. She was the first member of the clerical staff to be appointed to an industrial organising role. Dunne and Eadie had complementary skills and talents and forged an impressive partnership.

In an interview with Patrick O'Connell and Lelia Doolan, Eadie gave an insight into his own attitude to the work of a journalist and Official. He had gone into journalism because 'I could not contemplate myself sitting at a desk from nine to five every day, for six days a week – [as] it used to be one time'.[25] Although an Official, Eadie confessed to not being fond of paperwork: 'Now I have this job, and 50% of the time I'm out – I don't like desk work, or administrative work, neither do most journalists'.[26] Dunne, on the other hand, was a born administrator with a keen eye for detail. Eadie's gregarious nature endeared him to members. Overnight visits might lead to revelry, but woe betide any Chapel Officer who failed to turn up ready for battle the next morning.

The foundation of RTÉ presented significant organisational challenges but, as in the national newspaper sector, Eadie was blessed with strong, lay activists. In 1963, NUJ members in RTÉ conducted a nine-week strike which led to pay increases of over 10%. RTÉ and the national newspapers were already closed shops, with the NUJ and print unions controlling access to employment. National agreements were reached with the Provincial Newspapers Association of Ireland, (PNAI) a management group drawn from mainly family owned newspapers. Eadie's intimate knowledge of the sector proved invaluable and was reflected in the agreements, which included far seeing national procedures for dealing with disputes. All agreements covered freelancers as well as staff.[27] Eadie took pride in the fact that the NUJ was the first union in the Republic to lodge a maternity pay claim to a group of employers. Afterwards, Eadie told *Studies*, he had discovered that the employers had conceded a claim for twelve weeks on full pay in the belief that it would not be a substantial burden 'because we won't be employing many women anyway'.[28]

The NUJ made significant gains in the badly paid regional press sector. Eadie was especially adamant that the job's anti-social nature should be recognised and in a Labour Court claim in 1978 argued that 'provincial journalists are based in rural areas where they are well known and are, therefore often required to attend to varied work matters outside office hours'.[29] The Court refused full parity with the national press but recommended that the basic rates be increased by 5% at each point of the scale to bring basic pay rates for provincial journalists closer to those of their colleagues in the national press. A nationwide work to rule was called off in January 1979 after settlement talks which saw the PNAI, under the redoubtable Úna Sheridan concede 5% increases backdated to 1 March 1978.[30] In the 1978 Labour Court case the PNAI stated that twenty-eight of the thirty-nine newspaper houses in the regional sector had local agreements providing for rates from £10 to £40 above the minimum national rate.[31]

Training Champion

Always interested in education, Eadie was directly involved in moves to establish the first full-time journalism course in Ireland at the College of Commerce, Rathmines. He served as Chairman of the Irish Committee of the National Council for the Training of Journalists (NCTJ) and his address to the 1968 NCTJ AGM reflected his direct approach to training, as well as his tendency to shoot from the hip in a manner which inevitably made an impact on his intended target. Calling for the appointment of full-time professional tutors or training officers by newspaper publishers he declared:

'For too long the practice of journalism in this country has been too much under the control of management boards and individual proprietors whose interests in journalism were purely a secondary nature.'[32]

He berated proprietors, whose representatives would have been present at the meeting, for their failure to invest in editorial resources, recalling that an unidentified company had resisted the installation of a direct telephone line to their newsroom on cost grounds 'although the switchboard was clearly unable to cope with the traffic'. In a typical Eadie aside, he declared himself puzzled at reading a newspaper report in which 'the opening sentence had 72 words, the second had 74; the fourth had 79; the fifth had 79 and the seventh sentence had a record 93 words!' He went on to express sympathy with the sub.[33] Eadie remained critical of the industry. Drawing on his experience on various AnCO and print industry training committees he complained that employers were 'terribly negative' when it came to training.[34]

A natural contrarian, Eadie was always uncomfortable with the idea of unions becoming too close to powerful figures. This extended to branches and he staged a very public protest at the presence of Minster for Justice Seán Doherty at an NUJ dinner in Roscommon organised by the West of Ireland and Athlone & District Branches. Given Doherty's record, Eadie's response was understandable. Protocol never prevented him from expressing his views, often in a trenchant fashion.[35]

A far more distinguished Minister, Donogh O'Malley, used an NUJ event to announce a significant breakthrough in Irish education policy.[36] O'Malley spoke at a dinner in Dún Laoghaire on 12 September 1966 to announce free access to second level education. Eadie recalls the dinner was part of a training event run by the NUJ's UK-based Training Officer George Viner. Eadie had no direct involvement in preparations 'but was on the podium when O'Malley spoke'.

> 'I was told in advance by Séamus Brady, who was some sort of advisor to O'Malley and had been an *Express* reporter, that the Minister was going to say something 'significant'. In the question and answer session, O'Malley was asked 'how can this be afforded?'. I was struck by his answer: 'I will tell you what I told the Minister [of Agriculture or Finance], if we can afford to spend millions on the eradication of Tuberculosis in cattle, surely we can educate the children of the nation.'[37]

London Calling

Travel to London often exposed Eadie to the cultural differences between the two islands. During his induction period as an Official, he was invited for a drink by General Secretary Jim Bradley. It was four o'clock in the afternoon and they could not find any pubs open. On their way back to the NUJ office, then in Soho's notorious Great Windmill Street, Bradley pointed to a billboard poster portraying scantily clad performers at Raymond's Revue Bar and said: 'You wouldn't get that back in Ireland'. Eadie responded pithily: 'No, but you could get a fucking drink'.[38]

Eadie was never afraid to challenge the consensus and his interjections at union conferences were inevitably blunt and to the point. At the 1989 ICTU Annual Delegate Conference, he caused consternation when proposing a motion calling on affiliates to 'consider' withdrawal from the Programme for National Recovery (PNR), pressing a vote in circumstances which sent the top table into a spin. The NUJ wanted a Special Delegate Conference within six months. They had proposed a similar motion the year before, 'unwisely in our view but perhaps because it was premature'. Eadie repeatedly emphasised the word 'consider', counselling that 'if you do not accept the motion, it will be interpreted as complacency'. He added concerns that the PNR was worsening employment and emigration, not improving the plight of the low paid and witnessing an outflow of capital. When asked by ICTU President Gerry Quigley (INTO) was the NUJ prepared to consider remission, Eadie said, 'No, we are not'.[39] The motion passed by 139 votes to 125 leading to a Special Delegate Conference which in turn narrowly accepted continuation of the Social Partnership programme by 180 votes to 140, the narrowest margin on any national agreement.

Billy Attley then Federated Workers' Union of Ireland and later SIPTU General Secretary, subsequently explained the defeat:

'It was the only sunny day of the week and they [the delegates] were all down in the pub. It was Peter Cassells's [ICTU General Secretary] first Conference and he was trying to reply to the debate. I looked around and I knew we were fucked. So, I said to him 'I am going to reply to the debate. This is your first Conference and your first speech, and you can't be defeated. It won't damage you as much as me. All the people who would have voted for us were in the pub and we lost narrowly.'[40]

The NUJ always prided itself on being a lay-led union and Michael Foley – who served as Chair of the then Irish Industrial Council and NEC member from Ireland – recalls Eadie's strong encouragement to young activists whom he trusted to assist with Chapel negotiations.[41]

'His style suited the NUJ. He was good at getting Irish Area Council members and the NEC members from Ireland to take responsibility for negotiations. There were a lot of activists who he would call on. When he addressed you as 'Chairman' or 'NEC member' you knew Jim had a job for you to do.'

Former NUJ President, the late Eddie Barrett, recalled long, enjoyable car trips around Ireland with Eadie carefully working out his negotiating strategy. Future President Barry McCall had the honour of proposing Eadie as NUJ Member of Honour in 1992. He strongly believed that Eadie had not always got the credit he deserved for his pioneering work:

'Jim's work over the years was akin to that of a missionary. He frequently ventured into hostile territory and usually emerged with new recruits and improved conditions for members. The risks to personal safety were possibly more due to the requirement to socialise rather than any actual physical threat – but these did arise from time to time, and not from the sources you might expect. At one set of negotiations at a fledgling newspaper in Kilkenny which had been established as a rival to the *Kilkenny People* the news editor threatened to bring firearms to bear to gain leverage. Jim was having none of it and responded with a verbal volley of his own.'[42]

As with most British based unions in Ireland, there were tensions between HQ and the 'regional' offices. Eadie ably navigated such difficulties, mainly because he enjoyed excellent relations with fellow Officials and left the politics to be played out by well briefed NEC members. He had an especially good relationship with Bob Norris, Assistant General Secretary and one of the most influential figures in the union over many decades. Eadie's tribute to him when Norris died in 2018 is instructive. Norris was a member of the NEC which appointed Eadie as Irish Organiser and on visits to Dublin they combined business with pleasure. Rule 18 complaints [allegations of a breach of union rules] inevitably landed on Norris's desk and Eadie admired his knack for problem solving and diplomacy: 'After some fraught sessions at these hearings a little relaxation was in order, and Bob was always ready for a good party'.[43]

Eadie and Norris were involved in setting up an unsuccessful Irish copyright licensing system aimed at emulating a copyright licensing system operating in some European countries where newspaper and magazine publishers, journalists and authors combined to form an agency that would issue licences to outside parties to use published material for agreed fees. To Eadie's disappointment, while the 'NUJ, SIPTU and some others registered such an agency in Dublin … the publishers did not come on board, so the initiative failed, sadly'.[44]

The evolution of Eadie's role and consequently the development of the union's autonomy in Ireland was slow. Then, as now, funding new posts was a challenge.

> 'Following requests from the Irish membership for more union autonomy in Ireland, the NEC set up a committee to study the issue. George Findlay was chairperson. Eddie Barrett was also a member. Among recommendations was the upgrading of the Irish Office. Eventually, it was the delegate meeting in Portrush that agreed to the recommendations despite strong opposition from the NEC, which was in no hurry to carry out DM wishes.'

At a policy level, Eadie found himself caught between the wishes of the wider membership and elements of the union in Ireland, North and South.

Press Freedom

Section 31 of the Broadcasting Act 1960 presented a challenge to the NUJ. Eadie strongly opposed Section 31 and press censorship generally and had no difficulty with the NUJ policy. The 1972 ADM heard the NUJ General Secretary promise support to any branch planning industrial action to protest the ban.[45] In September 1972, as the first anniversary of the directive approached, NUJ members in RTÉ in Belfast staged a token two-hour work stoppage in protest. Spokesman, Kevin Myers insisted the Chapel's decision to move from private to public protest was because, 'our credibility with a considerable section of the Northern population had been steadily eroded'.[46] Dublin Broadcasting Branch, drawn largely from RTÉ, was at times more ambivalent than the wider union about Section 31. Charlie Bird noted,

> 'Many people in the RTÉ newsroom took the view that Section 31 was the law of the land, we had no choice but to work within the restriction. It was the more moderate view. Others argued that we should fight the censorship head on. That was the opinion of the leadership of the National Union of Journalists in Dublin and London.'[47]

Bird described as 'ludicrous' the 1986 ADM resolution which committed to supporting any member disciplined for refusing to work within the limits of Section 31.[48] Eadie was steadfast in defending NUJ policy while seeking to keep RTÉ members on side. As always, he drew on lay activists, to steady the ship and many RTÉ journalists supported his stance. Unchartered waters were entered in March 1988 when a young journalist, Jenny McGeever, faced disciplinary action over broadcasting the voice of Martin McGuinness as part of a Morning Ireland report on the obseques of three IRA members shot dead in Gibraltar. A ballot for industrial action was taken in RTÉ but interrupted by McGeever's decision to seek independent legal advice and a judicial review. Bird expressed his disagreement publicly:

> 'The NUJ adopted a position on Section 31 which we oppose. This policy affects only our branch, and we think it is ludicrous that other branches are adopting a policy which we have to implement. We opposed that resolution at last year's annual conference.'[49]

Former Athlone and District Branch members Eddie Rogers, left, and Geoff Oakley in conversation with Jim Eadie at the 2007 Irish Delegate Conference in Tullamore.

Eadie replied, 'Members in RTÉ are governed by union authority. Do Charlie Bird and his members want to defy us?'.[50]

The NUJ asserted its authority and in December that year the NEC decided to take a test case to the European Court of Human Rights in Strasbourg. Eadie confirmed the initiative at a Dublin press conference. Bird, resigned from his position but remained a union member.[51] The Broadcasting Branch, under its new Chair Ian Corr, subsequently endorsed the NEC's position and the Irish Office but Eadie was disappointed at the damage done to the unity of the union, always his first priority.

Barry McCall believes Eadie's role in Northern Ireland deserves special mention.

> 'Jim had the often difficult and indeed dangerous job of representing journalists throughout the whole island during a time when The Troubles were at their height. The mere act of crossing the Border in a southern registered vehicle was to take a risk. NUJ members in Northern Ireland worked under constant threat to their personal safety as they endeavoured to carry out their duty to report the news without fear or favour. Representing them industrially required a high degree of sensitivity to the political context in which they worked. Any hint of bias could have had the most terrible consequences for all involved.'

Section 31 tensions were mirrored, perhaps with greater intensity, by internal debates in Ireland over union policy on abortion. On this Eadie declined to publicly take sides but worked hard to retain in membership those who opposed the official Pro-Choice position adopted at the NUJ ADM in 1979.[52]

Politically, Eadie was a lifelong socialist in the Labour Party tradition. He was founder of the Party's Churchtown Branch through his close association with ICTU Official Barry Desmond.[53]

'Barry needed a branch and I was involved with his wife Stella and himself in setting up a small branch. That gave him a nomination to conference. They appointed me branch treasurer, but I really had nothing to treasure.'

Jim Eadie retired as NUJ Irish Secretary on 1 July 1994. During his tenure, NUJ membership in Ireland increased from 788 to 3,456, testimony to his diligence, organising abilities and capacity to work with and inspire others.[54] In retirement Eadie was instrumental in setting up the Senior Citizens' Parliament and NUJ Retired Workers' Committee. He and his wife Bridie continue very active lives in Grange Road, Rathfarnham, Dublin.

The NUJ is a niche union which, despite many challenges, has maintained its independent identity. Journalists are, by definition, independent-minded, informed and well-connected and treat with scepticism the advice of Officials. This was never a problem for Eadie. He was never afraid to present the unvarnished truth, even if that made him unpopular with the full-time union leadership, Chapel Officers, members or what he regarded as the trade union establishment. The rotation system among print unions deprived the ICTU of his consistent participation at Executive level and may have contributed to Eadie's qualities being underestimated outside the NUJ and sister unions in the industry.

Underestimating the Roscommon man was always a mistake, as many employers also found to their cost. Eadie commanded affection and loyalty among members across the union: his genuine interest in and commitment to the welfare of members and their families earned him enormous respect and was his hallmark. His appointment coincided with the emergence of strong lay activists but there can be no doubt that the evolution of the union, the development of its structures in Ireland and ultimately its ability to punch about its weight owes, much to the legacy of Jim Eadie.

Notes

Note that unattributed quotations from Eadie are from an interview with Séamus Dooley on 4 February 2019. My special thanks to Barry McCall for his assistance in seeking to capture the spirit, of Jim Eadie, to Michael Foley, and of course to Jim himself for sharing his memories, only a handful of which are recalled here.

1   Eadie was succeeded in 1994 by Éoin Ronayne and in 2002 by Séamus Dooley. Martin Coffey in 1944, B. Malin 1947 and Michael McInerney 1948 had been part-time Irish Secretaries.
2   For brief outline of Irish press trade unionism see Francis Devine & John B. Smethurst, *Historical Directory of Trade Unions in Ireland*, (ILHS/Working Class Movement Library, Dublin/Salford, 2017), pp. 275-287 and for NUJ in Ireland, pp. 508-510.
3   Clement Bundock, *The National Union of Journalists, a Jubilee History*, (NUJ, Oxford, 1957), p. 1.
4   F.J. Mansfield, *Gentlemen, the Press*, (W.H Allen, London, 1943), p. 57.
5   *ibid.*
6   The IOJ was founded as the National Association of Journalists in Birmingham in October 1884, changed its name to the IOJ in 1888. It received a Royal Charter in 1890 and an

additional Charter in 1990, becoming the Chartered Institute of Journalists. In 1910, disaffected members left into form the NUJ. There were unsuccessful attempts to merge the two bodies in 1921, 1928, 1943, and 1966, see https://cioj.org/history-of-the-cioj/ [retrieved 7 February 2019].

7   *ibid.*

8   Richard Michael Fox, 1891-December 1969, was born in Leeds, second of four sons to a schoolteacher mother and engineering workman father. His parents were active in the Co-operative Movement, and as a young man Fox joined the Socialist Party of Great Britain and Industrial Workers of the World (IWW). In 1914, Fox denounced the Imperialist War and refused Conscripted leading to several terms of imprisonment. Released in April 1919, he enrolled at Ruskin College in Oxford. Fox married children's author Patricia Lynch and they spent time in London, Paris, Brussels, and Germany before eventually settling in Dublin. In addition to a prolific journalistic career and literary works, Fox wrote a number of labour history works: *Rebel Irishwomen* (1935); *Green Banners: The Story of the Irish Struggle* (1938); *The History of the Irish Citizen Army* (1943); *James Connolly - The Forerunner* (1943); *Years of Freedom: The Story of Ireland 1921-48* (1948); *Jim Larkin: The Rise of the Underman* (1957); and *Louie Bennett: Her Life & Times* (1958). He died in Dublin. Peter Berresford Ellis, 'An influential historian of Irish labour', www.irishlabourhistorysociety.com/pdf/R%20M%20Fox.pdf [retrieved 5 February 2019].

9   Mansfield, op. cit., pp. 490-493.

10 *ibid.*

11 *ibid.*

12 The GIJ was formed in March 1949 and affiliated to the Congress of Irish Unions and, from 1959, ICTU. It never declared more than 50 members and in 1970 was reduced only to eight, Devine & Smethurst, *op. cit.*, p. 283.

13 Interview with Dooley, 4 February 2019. Note, all other unattributed Eadie quotations are from this source.

14 Tim Gopsill & Greg Neale, *Journalists, 100 Years of the NUJ,* (Profile Books, London, 2007), p. 206.

15 Interview with Éoin Ronayne, November 2018

16 McQuillan, 1920-1998, from Ballyforan, won All-Ireland Championships with Roscommon in 1943-1944. He was TD for Roscommon, 1948-1965, being returned for Clann na Poblachta, 1948; Independent Republican, 1951; National Progressive Democratic Party, 1958; and Labour, 1968. He served as Labour Senator, 1965-1969 and was a founder, with old ally Browne, of the Socialist Labour Party, 1977. In 1966, he was appointed General Secretary, Irish Post Office Officials' Association, a breakaway body, non-ICTU affiliated body from the Post Office Workers' Union. See Lawrence William White, 'McQuillan, John ('Jack') (1920-1998), Gaelic footballer and politician', *Dictionary of Irish Biography*, vol. 6, (RIA/Cambridge University Press, Cambridge, 2009), pp. 179-181.

17 Browne, 20 December 1915-21 May 1997, was born in Waterford and educated in England and Trinity College where he qualified as a doctor. He suffered from TB and lost both his parents and some siblings to the disease. He became Minister for Health, 1948-1951, on his first day in the Dáil as a Clann na Poblachta TD, resigning over the Mother & Child Scheme debacle. After a brief time in Fianna Fáil, he led the National Progressive Democrats, 1958-1963, before joining Labour, 1963-1973, and the Socialist Labour Party, 1977-1982. He served in Seanad Éireann for the University of Dublin, 1973-1977. See his *Against the Tide,* (Gill & Macmillan, Dublin, 1986, 2007) and John Horgan, *Noël Browne: Passionate Outsider,* (Gill & Macmillan, Dublin, 2000).

18 It is likely that the IIJ was the Irish branch of the IOJ.

19 McInerney, 1906-1980, was born in Limerick and joined the Communist Party of Great Britain while working as railway clerk in London where he was co-founder of the Connolly Club. He contributed to the *Daily Worker* and edited *Irish Front,* 1939 -1941, when a clerk for the Great Northern Railway, Belfast. An active trade unionist and editor of the Communist Party of Ireland's *Unity,* in 1946 he joined the *Irish Times* becoming Political Correspondent, 1951. He was President and Organiser, NUJ Irish Branch and elected an

Honorary Life Member, 1974. Among his many writings is *Peadar O'Donnell: Irish Social Rebel,* (O'Brien Press, Dublin, 1976).

20 Gopsill & Neale, *op. cit.*, pp. 207-208.

21 *ibid.*

22 Recalled by Barry McCall in correspondence with Dooley, 5 February 2019.

23 Owen Curran, *Two Hundred Years of Trade Unionism, 1809-2009,* (Irish Print Group, SIPTU, Dublin, 2009). For the Dublin Typographical Provident Society/Irish Graphical Society/Irish Print Union, see Devine & Smethurst, *op. cit.*, 280-282.

24 Eadie served annual terms from 1982-194 and 1993-1994.

25 Patrick O'Connell & Lelia Doolan, 'Meet the press: interview with the Assistant Secretary of the NUJ Jim Eadie', *Studies*, vol 73, no 291 (Autumn 1984), pp. 185-205, www.jstor.org/stable/30090577 [retrieved 5 February 2019].

26 *ibid.*

27 NUJ Archive.

28 O'Connell & Doolan, *op. cit.*

29 NUJ Archive.

30 NUJ Archive.

31 NUJ Archive.

32 Speech by Jim Eadie, NUJ Archive.

33 *ibid.*

34 *ibid.*

35 The author was a member of the Athlone and District branch and attended the function with colleagues from the Tullamore/Midland Tribune chapel and witnessed Eadie's intervention.

36 O'Malley, 17 January 1921-10 March 1968, was Fianna Fáil TD for Limerick East, 1954-1968, and Minister for Health, 1965-1966, and Education, 1966-1968. He represented Shannon, Munster, Connacht and Leinster at rugby.

37 Eadie is unclear whether the Minister meant the Minister for Finance or Agriculture but either way it confirms the belief that far from being a solo run O'Malley's announcement was signalled to colleagues.

38 As recalled by Barry McCall, in correspondence with the author.

39 ICTU, *Report of Proceedings of Annual Delegate Conference, Bundoran, 1989*, pp. 50-54.

40 Tim Hastings, Brian Sheehan & Pádraig Yeates, *Saving the Future, How Social Partnership Shaped Ireland's Economic Success,* (Blackhall Publishing, Dublin, 2007), pp. 45-46.

41 Eadie in conversation with Dooley, January 2019.

42 Eadie in correspondence with Dooley, 5 February 2019.

43 Eadie in correspondence with the author, 19 October 2018.

44 *ibid.*

45 NUJ Archive.

46 John Horgan, *Broadcasting and Public Life, RTÉ News and Current Affairs, 1926-1997,* (Four Courts Press, Dublin, 2004).

47 Charlie Bird with Kevin Rafter, *This is Charlie Bird,* (Gill & Macmillan, Dublin, 2006), pp. 157-160.

48 *ibid.*

49 *ibid.*

50 *Irish Times*, 27 March 1988. In conversation with the author on 5 February 2019 Eadie recalled the interview: 'I was livid, so much so that the interviewer, Geraldine Kennedy told me to calm down!'

51 Bird with Rafter, *op. cit.*, p. 161.

52 Interview with Dooley, 5 February 2019.

53 Desmond, born in Cork on, was an ITGWU and ICTU Official, and Labour TD, Dún Laoghaire-Rathdown, 1969-1989, and MEP, Dublin, 1989-1994. He served as Minister for Health & Social Welfare,1982-1987, and member, European Court of Auditors,1994-2000. See his *Finally & In Conclusion: A Political Memoir,* (New Island Books, Dublin, 2001) and *No Workers' Republic! Reflections on Labour and Ireland, 1913-1967,* (Watchword, Dublin, 2009).

54 ICTU, *Annual Report, 1965*, and *Report of the Executive Council, 1993-1995.*

BRIAN KENNY

'A Long March':
Sam Nolan, 1930 -

Veteran Dublin Council of Trade Unions (DCTU) Correspondence Secretary Sam Nolan was a third generation carpenter. In 1911, Nolan's father, Samuel Senior, lived with his parents James and Elizabeth and five siblings at 25 Back Lane, Naas, County Kildare.[1] He joined the British Army in 1914 and survived the conflict, although it had a 'profound impact on him'. He moved to Dublin in 1924

Sam Nolan addressing a protest march in O'Connell Street, Dublin

and, in 1928, married Annie Kavanagh from Rathangan, County Kildare. Their only child Samuel James 'Sam' was born in 23 September 1930 in the Rotunda Hospital. In 1930s Dublin, the Nolan family was different. Nolan Senior was left wing, a carpenter by trade and active in the Irish National Union of Woodworkers.[2] Many other families had up to ten children, whereas young Sam was an only child. Neighbours could leave their front door open during the day and Sam Senior defiantly had a large picture of Stalin hung in his hallway. As people passed, they would look in and quickly bless themselves.

Initially young Nolan attended the Damer School run by the Unitarian Church and then the local Christian Brothers School – a much tougher world: 'There was legs of chairs and leathers and you got bet for anything'. Nolan, however, was one of the lucky ones – 'word came down that I was a convert and to go easy on me'. Nolan finished in the CBS in 1942 and the next step was Synge Street Secondary School. By the time, Nolan got to his Inter Cert year he was recognised as a bright student and the Brothers in Synge Street were encouraging him to do his Leaving Cert. His mother, scarred by 'the horrendous effects of widescale unemployment', 'had other ideas and the lure of immediate and steady employment … cut short Nolan's education'.[3]

175

Guinness's was the obvious place for her only son. It was among the city's largest employments, with good conditions. Nolan's job was 9 to 5 which left him with lots of free time. He began to read the left-wing literature in the house. His father had made a mahogany book case which he filled with communist and left-wing books. Nolan asked his father for guidance and only then learned that Sam Senior had never read a book in his life.

Undaunted, Nolan began to find his own way by reading 'all about working class and labour history'.[4] As he read, he realised that

> 'around me there were rich and poor and I began to think that society needs to be changed and I began to get interested in socialism. By the time I was sixteen I decided I wouldn't change things within Guinness's so I said to my dad that I would like to serve my time as a carpenter.'

Nolan joined the Amalgamated Society of Woodworkers (ASW), a British-based union. Fortnightly branch meetings were held and even as a young apprentice, Nolan became actively involved.

Socialist Politics

In 1947, Nolan joined the newly formed Socialist Youth Movement (SYM) and remembers it fondly: 'It had about 30-40 members, many being students, and it was a great centre of debate ... people like Roy Johnston[5] and Justin Keating[6] were involved. Most members were sympathetic to the USSR. We knew nothing of Stalin and his abuse of power in those days'. At this time, there were huge levels of hostility in Ireland towards anything that smacked of socialism. In an attempt to counteract this, the SYM changed its name to the Democratic Youth Movement (DYM). Among its members were Brendan Behan's brothers, Dominic and Brian, who lived on Kildare Road in Crumlin.[7]

At a DYM meeting one evening in early 1948, it was decided to hold a public meeting on the need for public swimming pools at the church on Clogher Road, Crumlin. A platform was set up and as people emerged from their sodality, the DYM speaker started his appeal to the youth of Crumlin. The people listened for a few minutes but the mood quickly changed. Suddenly, stones and sods were being flung, along with cries of 'communist bastards'. DYM members were chased down Sundrive Road all the way to Rialto. As Nolan recalls, 'It shows you how naïve we were, but also what we were up against'. The DYM began to peter out in 1949. Brian Behan went to England and others, including Nolan, decided to join the Communist Party, then called the Irish Workers' League (IWL). Nolan's seventy-year long career in left wing politics was now fully underway

The Irish Workers' League (IWL) was launched in1948 in Dublin and Nolan joined in 1949. He and his comrades 'began to really embrace socialist ideas. We believed that everything had a history, everything is in motion ... Capitalism had not always existed ... Capitalism would then change to socialism ... with workers in control'. It was a fervent Marxist analysis, which helped maintain the small IWL membership in conservative Ireland of the 1940s and 1950s: 'It put us apart from other workers … we had a vision and were part of the future'. IWL activity revolved around education classes and selling the party paper the *Irish Worker's Voice*. In 1951, the IWL began to hold public meetings in Dublin city centre on Sunday mornings. It was a 'mini Hyde Park corner' type event and speakers included Michael O'Riordan,[8] Joe Deasy[9] and Mick McCarthy, who later went on to run 'The Embankment' pub near Saggart.[10] Again, there was hostility and abuse from onlookers, but this did not deter Nolan or the IWL.

While the going was tough in Ireland, the Communist movement in Eastern Europe generated hope. In 1951, Nolan attended the large Third World Festival of Youth & Students organised by the World Federation of Democratic Youth in East Berlin: 'We thought it was quite wonderful. We met all these other young people from different countries … There were huge big banners of Stalin …he had saved the world and was a world leader'. Trips like this kept Nolan going: 'I was very involved and a member of the National Executive from 1954 until 1975. I was also part of a very good Education Committee, which included Joe Deasy, Paddy Carmody and George Jeffares … it would take three or four nights per week and my only social life was a few drinks after meetings'.[11]

In the early 1950s, Nolan remembers heading off up into the Dublin mountains on his motorbike and looking down over the city:

> 'I said to myself, in fifty years time we will have socialism in this city. We were convinced. We had the USSR and the 1949 Chinese revolution and socialism in the eastern European states. Nearly one third of the world was socialist. So why wouldn't it come to Ireland.'

The IWL seemed almost blissfully unaware of the realities of the Stalin régime, but Soviet Party Leader Nikita Khrushchev changed all that. At the 20th Congress of the Communist Party of the Soviet Union (CPSU) on 25 February 1956, Khrushchev spoke at length about the cult of the person of Stalin 'who practiced brutal violence … and who often chose the path of repression and physical violence'.[12] Khrushchev's speech was unprecedented. Nolan was 'upset of course but felt it was a chance of a new start … now that it was exposed we can improve'.

However, the following year the uprising in Hungary was suppressed quickly and the IWL viewed it as a counter-revolution, which they did not support. This was not a view which held sway among the general public in Dublin. A few days after the Russian invasion, 3,000 people marched in protest through the streets and the 'New Books' shop in Pearse Street was attacked.[13] There seemed to be no hiding place for IWL members. One night they were due to meet at their Pembroke Road office. On arrival, there were about fifty people there with their rosary beads and praying loudly. Leading the prayers was Kevin O'Kelly, who went on to become RTÉ's Religious Affairs Correspondent. IWL members decided it was best to keep on going and ended up having their meeting on Sandymount Strand.

1957 and the Unemployed Protest Committee

Through all this, Nolan had to earn a living. He finished his apprenticeship in 1951 and ended up on a site in Walkinstown. Here he met Jack Murphy, later to become the 'Unemployed TD', for the first time. In late 1954, Nolan found employment with Collen Brothers and soon became ASW Shop Steward. The company was 'Protestant', run by brothers Lyle and Standish Collen. Standish had been a Captain in the British Army during World War Two and, according to Nolan, 'still thought he was directing his troops in El Alamein'. A dispute over a thirty-minute lunch break led to Nolan being sacked and then victimised when he sought work on other Collen sites. The message had gone out that he was not to be employed. While Nolan picked up work for a couple of months, by the end of 1956 he faced the dole queue.

Nolan and some IWL colleagues decided to fight back. Early in January 1957 at the Werburgh Street Labour Exchange, they held an impromptu, outdoor meeting. Nolan, Packie Early, Johnny Mooney and Jack Murphy spoke.[14] The Unemployed Protest Committee (UPC) was set up soon afterwards. The first of the UPC's many protest marches took place in January 1957. It was led by Murphy and only 100 people attended. At the front of the march was a large banner, which read 'Support Us In Our Demand For Work'. Despite its small start, the UPC grew in numbers:

> 'We organised demonstrations and marches and after a month we had about two or three thousand people marching'. At one march Nolan declared that 'it would have to be impressed on the trade unions and Government and Dáil members that we were not prepared to endure the plight of 95,000 unemployed in the country any longer.'[15]

The political situation changed not long after the UPC was set up, with the collapse of the second Inter-Party Government in February 1957. The UPC decided to run a candidate and with the help of long-time republican and socialist Peadar O'Donnell, they managed to get backers for the deposit of £100. O'Donnell was told that Nolan was the favoured candidate. However, a couple of days later a problem emerged:

> 'We met with Peadar again who told us that his friends were happy to give money for the deposit but not if Sam Nolan was the candidate. They all knew I was a Communist and didn't want to be associated with that. This led to some soul searching on my part. I said that if I run the whole focus would be on me as a Communist and not the unemployment issue. The alternative was Jack Murphy. I was disappointed to step down but it was the right thing to do.'

So, Murphy became the candidate in Dublin South Central, a constituency with high unemployment and with the Werburgh Street Labour Exchange right at its centre.

The campaign got great support: 'All sorts of people came in to help from the 'Labour', delivered leaflets, made posters, helped with the canvas around the flat complexes ... we ran a great campaign and got a good response'. Murphy's campaign slogan was 'Give the Unemployed a Voice in the Dáil'. His demands were direct and to the point. 'We have one demand – Work; We have one ambition – To live and work in Ireland'. Nolan remembers it as being a great campaign: 'Jack's message was obviously striking a chord. People were enthusiastic, but it wasn't until the last week that we thought we had a chance'. And all this in a campaign that cost just fifty pounds, which included money spent on fish and chips and packets of cigarettes for the canvassers.[16] Murphy got just over 3,000 first preferences and beat Labour's Roddy Connolly for a seat.[17] His victory rally was held in Abbey Street and Nolan proclaimed that 'a spirit of revolt was rising in Ireland ... the Committee intended to fight for the unemployed men in Dublin and would keep up its pressure until every man in Dublin and in Ireland was in employment'.[18]

Murphy's election gave a huge boost to the unemployed movement in Dublin and elsewhere: 'We had about 5,000 people at an outdoor meeting in Cork and over 2,000 in Waterford. Then we had similar groups in Galway and Sligo'. Looking back Nolan saw that the 'unemployed movement became the rallying point for all the radical and left wing forces in the country'.[19] However, in their Budget that year the Government abolished food subsidies for bread, butter and milk. The UPC decided to hold a number of protest meetings and it was agreed that Nolan would write to Archbishop John Charles McQuaid asking for his help. Then, out of the blue, events took an unexpected turn.

> 'About a week after I wrote to McQuaid I arrived at our office in Werburgh Street to find Jack Murphy with two other Committee members, Jimmy Byrne and Thomas Canavan, lying on camp beds and saying they were on hunger strike over the food subsidy issue ... Jack was very religious and he had his rosary beads wrapped around his fingers. There had been no consultation and Jack told us we wouldn't have agreed if they had asked us.'

Some other members were unhappy at being upstaged, with one of them telling Murphy he 'should be leading the unemployed and not sitting there on his butt'.[20]

The UPC were in a dilemma but clearly could not disown Murphy and his fellow hunger strikers. Public meeting were held in Abbey Street and after one of these meetings, the protestors marched to the Dáil. The *Irish Times* reported that the 'crowds stood back in orderly fashion while three men – Messrs Sam Nolan, William O'Meara and Patrick Earley – presented themselves at the gate and sent a message into the House'.[21] They met with Labour TD Denis Larkin, along with Jack Murphy, after which Murphy emerged and told the waiting crowd, 'I would ask you all to disperse now and go to your homes. Tomorrow night at Abbey Street there will be a public meeting and myself and the two other hunger strikers will make a statement'.[22]

While the nightly meetings continued, behind the scenes the UPC were trying to find a way of ending the hunger strike without losing face. They went to meet trade union leaders in the Provisional United Trade Union Organisation (PUTUO) and following this, an appeal was issued urging the men to come off the strike.[23] They were assured that their protests had the support of the trade union movement.[24]

A rally announcing the end of the four-day protest was held in Abbey Street where 4,000 people marched to the UPC headquarters in Werburgh Street. Murphy and his colleagues were received enthusiastically. Nolan chaired the rally and declared 'that never before had the Irish people voiced their opinion so strongly ... he appealed to all who were in employment to urge their trade unions and their TDs to take action to end mass unemployment'. The same day as the newspapers reported the end of the hunger strike, they also reported that the Government had re-imposed control on bread prices, so the efforts of Murphy and the UPC seemed to bring some immediate change.[25]

Despite this concession, the UPC continued their protests. On one occasion, Murphy reluctantly led a large march of women and children on the food subsidy issue. Three thousand people, mainly mothers and their children, marched on the Dáil but the Gardaí stopped them from getting near Leinster House: 'It was a great demonstration, plenty of women with their prams. When we got near the Dáil we were met by a phalanx of police outside, but the women bet them with the stale bread they had hidden in their prams'. No Government members were prepared to come and meet the protestors and Murphy called on the marchers to return to College Green. There, Nolan thanked the marchers for their restraint: 'you came out from your tenements and slums tonight to show your hungry children to Dáil Eireann and have no doubt they knew you were there alright'. As the meeting ended, a large number of children pressed against the railings of the Bank of Ireland and chanted 'we want bread, we want bread'.[26]

Despite these impressive marches, all was not well within the UPC. Murphy had been a reluctant participant in the 'women and children' march, telling his UPC colleagues he needed time to find his feet in the Dáil. The situation was further exacerbated when the UPC Committee found out that Murphy had been to see Archbishop McQuaid on his own: 'One Monday morning Jack didn't turn up for our normal meeting until 11 o'clock and told us he had been to see the Archbishop'. UPC Committee members were annoyed, which was added to when Murphy reported on McQuaid's comments:

> 'Jack told us that the Archbishop made three points. Firstly, that he would arrange to get the Merrion Square railings painted which would create some work. Secondly, that he couldn't interfere in Government policy about food subsidies. Thirdly, that he wanted it understood that Sam Nolan was one of the most dangerous men in Ireland.'

Left: Sam Nolan, aged 25, on his motorbike, 1955.

Below: Sam Nolan, Audrey Herrity and Paddy Carmody on their way to Bucharest to attend a youth festival organised by the World Federation of Democratic Youth, 1953.

McQuaid had obviously decided that Nolan was the mastermind and was manipulating Murphy. For his part, Murphy now seemed to suggest that he would have to cut his ties with the UPC and its Communist elements. It spelt the beginning of the end.

By the beginning of June, there had also been an upturn in the building trade and some of the IWL members involved in the UPC began to pick up work. By August 1957, Murphy had broken with the UPC and set up a separate group, which did not get public support. Murphy was very upset and in March 1958, he resigned his Dáil seat, emigrating to Canada with his family soon afterwards.[27] Murphy said he was resigning 'as a protest against the appalling indifference of the main political parties to the plight of the unemployed'.[28] His resignation created bitterness, as he did not consult with his former colleagues who had worked so hard to get him elected.[29]

To Moscow ... On a Sick Note

Despite the sour end to the UPC campaign, it was time for Nolan and his colleagues to move on. During most of 1957, not only was Nolan unemployed, he and his wife Audrey were expecting their first child and living with their in-laws. Fortunately, as the protests began to fizzle out, Nolan managed to find work with Dockrell's, the builder providers.

As the 1950s drew to a close, Nolan had moved on from Dockrell's and found work with John Sisk & Company. His involvement in the IWL was still strong and it seemed, for a change, that his political views were gaining some support.

> 'There was a great buzz at the time in left wing circles about the USSR. They had put the first man into space, Yuri Gagarin, and they seemed to be leading the way technologically. Khrushchev was beginning to emerge as a significant public figure on the world stage.'

It was not surprising then that Nolan and his IWL colleague, Seán 'Johnny' Nolan [no relation], were happy to accept an invitation to attend the 22nd Congress of the Communist Party of the Soviet Union in October 1961. Nolan's problem was how to get off work. A sick certificate covering him for three weeks was produced and Nolan warned all his comrades, both at home and in the USSR, that he did not want to see his name published anywhere. At the Congress, the two Nolans had time to visit the Space Museum, shake hands with Gagarin and meet delegates from all the other countries – Britain, New Zealand, Canada, India. This helped Nolan believe that the IWL was part of a powerful world movement

A shock awaited Nolan when he returned home. His name had appeared in one of the Irish papers as a delegate to the Congress. Sisk's promptly told him his job was gone. Nolan was out of work at a bad time, as he had just bought a house in Finglas. However, he managed to find work again and, indeed, apart from that long period of unemployment in 1957, Nolan was never again out of work for more than a couple of weeks. The enthusiasm Nolan brought back from Moscow was not dampened. In the party paper, he described the Congress as an event, which 'will be spoken of in history in the same breath as October 1917'. He welcomed the fact that all Stalin's misdeeds had been exposed and described him as someone who had 'lost contact with real life and in his later years began to believe himself infallible'.[30]

In March 1962, at their first Congress in eight years, the IWL was re-named the Irish Workers' Party (IWP). The party launched a major policy document *Ireland Her Own* which argued that the 'transition from an Ireland divided and dominated by capitalism and imperialism to an Ireland united, free and socialist could be – indeed had to be – affected by a long series of peaceful stages, utilising the existing parliamentary and other state institutions in Belfast and Dublin'.[31]

The 1964 Builders' Strike

Nolan also continued to be an active trade unionist. At this time, most workers in the building trade had a 44-hour week, which included four hours on a Saturday morning. In early 1963, in one of his regular contributions to the *Irish Socialist*, Nolan noted there were 70,000 people unemployed and he suggested that a central demand of the trade union movement should be 'to share the work' and they could start by fighting for a 40-hour week.[32]

Negotiations with the various employers continued through the first half of 1964. By July, the building unions had got frustrated and eventually served strike notice, to come into effect after the builders' holidays. The employers did not respond, perhaps thinking it was just a bluff. The strike commenced on 18 August 1964 and although it was confined to Dublin, it involved approximately 20,000 workers. Sites were shut down right across the city with immediate impact. By the second day, the *Irish Times* reported that 75 contractors had called to the Central Strike Committee's office to commit themselves to the 40-hour week.[33]

A key feature was the Strike Committee's ability to cover all the different sites: 'we used send out squads of cars to check out the different sites and chase off anyone still working'. The strike was largely controlled by the rank-and-file, which 'showed the new confidence of an aggressive working class operating in a buoyant economy'.[34] With the pressure on, some of the smaller builders began to give in. Before the end of the first week, approximately 300 hundred contractors were prepared to sign up to the 40-hour week. On 25 September, a large demonstration, attended by about 15,000 people, was held in Dublin, marching from Saint Stephen's Green to Parnell Square. A large banner with '40 Hour Week' emblazoned on it was unfurled from Nelson's Pillar as the many thousands of marchers passed through O' Connell Street.

With both sides 'digging in', union Officials continued to 'tic tac' with the various employers to see if a settlement could be negotiated. Eventually, with the strike in its seventh week, an agreement was reached. The 'deal allowed for the introduction of the 40-hour week in the winter, with the hours in the summer to be examined by a commission. This eventually led to the introduction of the 40-hour week all year round'.[35]

Housing Action

The 1960s was a decade of dramatic change, with demonstrations happening around the world. It was the era of mass student protests with those in France almost leading to the collapse of De Gaulle's Government. In Ireland, student protests while on a smaller scale were still important. Nolan remembers 'Ruairí Quinn, who became known as 'Ho Chi Quinn', was one of the leaders and they occupied the College Hall in Earlsfort Terrace. I remember Kevin Myers was also one of the leading figures and at that time he would have regarded the likes of me as a moderate'. The IWP attempted to build on this more sympathetic environment. Well written pamphlets on Pearse and Connolly were produced in 1966. The party also initiated the Connolly Youth Movement (CYM), of which Nolan was a founding member.

Within this decade of protest, the plight of Dublin's homeless became a major issue. In response to this crisis, the Dublin Housing Action Committee (DHAC) was set up in 1967. Some leading members, like Proinsias De Rossa and Mairín de Burca, were members of Sinn Féin, others were in the IWP.[36] Dennis Dennehy, a Dublin bus worker, became Secretary.[37] The DHAC was a radical movement believing in direct action. It encouraged homeless people to squat in empty properties and it forcibly resisted evictions. Dublin Corporation meetings were interrupted and DHAC members chained themselves to the railings of condemned houses.[38]

Nolan and other IWP activists became involved. The DHAC held a number of street protests and eventually Dennehy was jailed for squatting in a house in Mountjoy Square.

> 'One Saturday after Dennehy was jailed we had a march from Parnell Square. A scuffle broke out on O'Connell Street and the guard's baton charged. My head was split open and blood was pouring down my back. We retreated to the GPO and I remember standing up on one of the plinths there, addressing the crowd on behalf of the Trades Council.'

Shortly after that, there was a march to the Dáil.

> 'When we came to the Bank of Ireland in College Green everyone sat down. I got up and spoke on behalf of the Trades Council, but after a couple of minutes, I was arrested and lugged off to Pearse Street Garda Station. There was only one person in the cell ahead of me – a young and enthusiastic Vincent Browne who was active in Young Fine Gael. He must have been on the demo and had obviously kicked up along the way. In the end, there were twenty of us in the cell. We were charged but got off with a caution.'

Later that year, as is the way of many such protest movements, the DHAC campaign began to peter out. Amongst other factors, Dublin Corporation was developing thousands of new housing units in Ballymun and this eased the crisis.

Communism & Change

However, while the Left in Ireland expanded and the trade union movement grew, the IWP was changing and beginning to move toward a substantial split. International developments proved to be hugely challenging. Reforms in Czechoslovakia introduced by President Alexander Dubček were suppressed. These reforms, known as 'The Prague Spring', were welcomed by the IWP, which saw Czechoslovakia as taking 'the lead in the democratisation of life in the socialist countries'.[39] Nolan recalls 'the vast majority of our members supported Dubček. It was socialism with a human face – personal freedom, foreign travel and so on ... There was no obvious tension in Ireland as only Mick O'Riordan and a few others were in favour of the Soviet stance'.

In the 1969 General Election, Nolan ran for the IWP in Dublin Central. He pledged 'to use my abilities to fight for the real interests of the working people. My life has been one of struggle for the upliftment of my class. The building sites and trade union meetings have been my universities'.[40] Nolan ran a strong campaign with good support, although he did run into a bit of bother with the Catholic church in Meath Street for painting campaign slogans on the local school wall. However, Nolan ended up with only 242 votes. 'The response was good but it looked as if Labour were going to do well and people wanted to give them their vote'. Nolan was not disillusioned: 'Having come through the 1950s, you wouldn't be disillusioned with that result'.[41]

Amidst the turmoil in Northern Ireland, moves to unite the IWP and Communist Party Northern Ireland into one party had been gathering pace. Eventually, in March 1970, the third Communist Party of Ireland (CPI) was created to represent the movement in the whole country. The new CPI experienced what was for them considerable growth. In the 1974 Dublin City Council elections, the Party ran four candidates, including Nolan in Finglas. His campaign, under the slogan of 'Power to the People', was unashamedly left wing. Unfortunately, his enthusiasm was not matched by the voters and he ended up with the 'the usual 200 votes ... However, the overall response was quite good. I remember that as the high point for the CPI in Dublin'. By the following year, the CPI claimed it had thirteen branches nationally, most in the Republic, and it seemed to be on the up and up.

Despite this level of activity, the outlook of the CPI was changing and moves were afoot to bring it back more under the direction of Moscow. The Party Congress in 1975 brought matters to a head. General Secretary Michael O'

Riordan wanted to reverse the decision made in 1968 to condemn the Soviet invasion of Czechoslovakia.

> 'The centrepiece of the Congress was to be the 'political resolution' from the Executive Committee. O'Riordan had inserted into it support for the 1956 invasion of Hungary and the 1968 invasion of Czechoslovakia. In addition, the resolution made clear 'that there is only one kind of socialism ... that will guarantee the new society ... that confirmed by the experience of the socialist countries'.'[42]

The resolution made clear that the 'Moscow line' was the only line for the CPI to follow. Debate became tense and acrimonious and the resolution was eventually carried.

Nolan and some other comrades were aggrieved: 'And then soon after this there was a kind of mini purge. Paddy Carmody, who edited the *Irish Socialist* under the pseudonym of 'A. Raftery', lost his position and other people were dropped from various committees'. A number of members met and decided there was no point in carrying on. Over thirty resigned, including some of the best and most active members in Dublin such as George Jeffares, Carmody, Mick O'Reilly, Joe Deasy and Nolan himself. In their letter of resignation, the group claimed the party was abandoning democratic socialism and going back to old style Stalinism.[43]

> 'None of us wanted to leave; it was a way of life. My whole adult life had been taken up with the Party. It was tough, but we couldn't stay. We were being smothered and you felt you couldn't develop ideas.'

Joining Labour

Having initially formed the Irish Marxist Society, some of those resigning joined the Labour Party, with Nolan becoming active in his local branch in Finglas East.[44] It was quite a culture shock: 'I had been in a party all my life where, at branch level, we discussed world issues – Russia, the 'Cold War', America. Labour was quite different. There was some politics talked, but the whole emphasis was on getting a TD elected'. Nolan had to adjust to this new reality and he found that whatever political debate there was usually took place in the pub after branch meetings. In the 1979 local elections for Dublin Corporation, Nolan was a Labour candidate, which was certainly easier than running for the CPI. While the election gave him a great insight into how local politics worked, perhaps it was not surprising that he ended up with his 'usual 250-300 votes'.

Since 1967, Nolan had worked with Sisk and that continued until he left in 1982. On one occasion, he was even asked to do some work at the home of a Sisk director: 'He was very pleased with me and the day I finished he poured me a glass of whiskey. As I was about to leave he asked 'where's your tool box? I want to carry it out to your car as a mark of appreciation – and he did'. Nolan eventually ended up working in the Sisk headquarters in Tallaght, where one of his jobs was to prepare a new office for Mr. Sisk Senior – all the special work in wood panelling was left for him to complete.

While they talked regularly, there was never any mention of the time Nolan was sacked after his Moscow 'sick leave'.

Sisk obviously trusted Nolan and even confided in him about the terrible problems he was having with his neighbour, notorious crime figure, Martin Cahill ['The General'], whose house overlooked the Sisk's. According to Sisk, Cahill made a habit of standing on his garden shed shouting and roaring in at the Sisk family. Nolan thought it 'a most strange relationship – the daily mass goer and the former Communist – regularly chatting together. He shook my hand and wished me well when I left'.

Tax Marches

Throughout his career, Nolan maintained an active involvement in the DCTU. The DCTU-led 'tax campaign took place when the country had changed fundamentally. Joining the EEC in 1973, along with Lemass's economic policies of the 1960s, did open us up to the influence of the wider world'. In the 1978 Budget, Government backtracked on a move to increase taxes for farmers. To the hard-pressed PAYE workers, who were paying over 85% of all income tax at this time, this was too much to take. By early 1979, the Craft Group of Unions had requested the DCTU to organise a one-day work stoppage for 20 March. This approach did not readily find favour with the Irish Congress of Trade Unions (ICTU) 'hierarchy'.

In contrast to the ICTU, the DCTU leadership was quite left wing, including forceful personalities such as Ben Kearney, Mai Clifford, Fergus Whelan and Nolan.[45] By mid-March, the DCTU Executive had formally approved the March stoppage and a full delegate meeting was called to endorse the move. Just before the delegates assembled, the ICTU leadership tried to persuade the Executive to back down: 'It was a right ding-dong and at one stage the ICTU people were accusing us of leading people on the road to anarchy'. However, the Executive stood firm and the motion, when put to the delegates, carried almost unanimously.

As they prepared for the big day of protest, Nolan and his colleagues were shocked by the untimely death of DCTU Secretary Paddy Carmody on 18 March: 'He was very intelligent, had a sharp mind and was an excellent lecturer. Paddy had been one of the people at the heart of the CPI's education work and was sorely missed'.[46]

The day before the march, in an obvious effort to regain leadership on the issue, the ICTU pledged to launch a nationwide campaign for tax reform. In its more optimistic moments the DCTU hoped for a turn out of 40,000 people in Dublin. In the event, it was reported that 'upwards of 150,000 PAYE workers took to the streets of Dublin today to demand tax reform in the largest demonstration in the history of the State'.[47]

The march and demonstration were a huge success.

'We went from Parnell Square, down O'Connell Street to the Dáil and Government Buildings where we handed in our petition. Then we went back to O'Connell Street where the rally and speeches took place. I spoke along with Mai Clifford and Fergus Whelan. I remember looking down O'Connell Street and it was packed all the way from the bridge at one end up to the Parnell monument.'

Nolan told the assembled crowd, 'on this day at least, the trade union movement is the supreme power in the city ... [the strike] puts pressure on the Government to reform the tax system. For this we make no apologies to anyone'.[48]

Both the ICTU and Government were rattled. Congress decided to set up a commission to examine the whole tax question, with representatives of the DCTU taking part. Suspicious of this being just a delaying exercise, the DCTU called for another public demonstration on 1 May. Despite ICTU opposition, the protest went ahead on a wet and windy day and estimates of the attendance varied between 15,000 and 50,000 people.

The work of the Congress Tax Commission dragged on: 'We were very unhappy at the progress being made and at the end of 1979 the DCTU started to agitate for another nationwide stoppage early in 1980. This time we had a number of other unions supporting us and eventually Congress rowed in behind us as well'. The demonstration took place on 22 January 1980 and once again the turn out was huge. The next day the *Irish Times* reported that 'In the biggest demonstration of organised labour in the history of the State, an estimated 700,000 people in 37 centres throughout the Republic took to the streets yesterday to impress on the Government their demands for reform of the PAYE tax system'.[49] In his address to the marchers, Nolan warned Taoiseach Charles Haughey that 'he must choose between justice and equality for the PAYE wage and salary earners and the protection of the wealthy in our society ... Our marching feet have spelt out the message loud and clear – reform the tax system'.[50] It was only that night as he watched himself on the BBC news that Nolan began to realise just how big an event the march had been.

Congress met with the Government to push for tax reform. Government offered to set up its own Commission on Taxation but this was rejected as the ICTU sought immediate concessions in the Budget. The response was very disheartening, with only minor changes introduced on Budget day. It was a salutary lesson for Nolan, the DCTU and the trade union movement.

Labour Left

After the 1977 General Election, when Labour resumed their 'normal' role in opposition, further attempts to develop 'the Left' in Labour emerged. This was a fraught time in Irish political life with three General Elections held between June 1981 and November 1982. More than anything else, whether to enter Coalition Government with others, primarily Fine Gael, dominated debate with the Labour Party during the 1980s – and the party was hugely divided on the issue.

The aftermath of the June 1981 election saw a heated Labour Party Conference, decide in favour of Coalition by a very small majority: 'It was a very contentious debate. Even before the election, there had been a fierce battle as to whether two candidates should run in the constituency where Party Leader Frank Cluskey, was running. In the event John O'Connell ran there as well and Cluskey lost out'. In the end, it was decided that a Special Party Conference would have to be held before any commitment to Coalition could be made. Party Leader Michael O'Leary did not agree with this approach and the extent of his unhappiness was revealed five days later when he resigned both as Leader and as a party member. Soon afterwards, he crossed the floor of the Dáil to join Fine Gael.

Given this level of political volatility, it is not surprising that Labour Left (LL) emerged and became a significant force within the Labour Party during the 1980s. Nolan recalls this period well: 'The big lesson of the tax marches a few years earlier, despite the massive street demonstrations, was that political change was also needed. The Labour Party, by developing socialist policies, could be that party'.

By 1984-1985, LL was a strong presence within Labour. At the Party's 1985, Annual Conference a motion calling on Labour to renegotiate the Government's economic plan was defeated by just a handful of votes, out of over a thousand delegates.[51] Because of the strength of feeling about Coalition, a Commission on Electoral Strategy was set up with Nolan one of its members. The Commission reported the following year and recommended that the party fight all elections on the basis of independent policies and 'remain independent of all governments save in those circumstances where national conference decides that exceptional national circumstances dictate otherwise in order to defend the vital interests of our own electorate'. This, in Nolan's view, was a high point in the influence of LL who were now confident enough to argue that the debate within the party on Coalition was over.[52] While the Commission's recommendations were formally embraced by the party at its 1987 Annual Conference, the commitment of the leadership was unclear.

Labour's 1987 Conference provided an initial boost for LL. Under pressure from the membership, Party Leader Dick Spring had to propose setting up a Leadership Commission, which would consider a more democratic way of electing the Party Leader.[53] It had been a bad weekend for the leadership and Spring knew it. As the Conference came to an end, Fergus Finlay, Spring's Special Advisor, recalled an angry Party Leader telling him 'Never again ... Next time we take the fight to them. And they won't know what hit them'.[54]

The leadership was determined to ensure that their 1989 Conference would not be a repeat of 1987. It was held in Tralee, in the heart of Spring's constituency, and the party hierarchy was determined this time it would be different. When the key votes were called, the leadership had the numbers.

Emmet Stagg was beaten decisively for the position of Vice Chair. An appeal to reinstate three 'Militant' branches was also well beaten, although Nolan recalls LL supporting it on the basis of 'freedom of expression'.

After the 1989 Conference, Nolan and LL faced a bleak future: 'The general membership was less inclined to support us, possibly wondering 'what was the point?" LL faded away. Despite its demise, Nolan saw it as being a positive influence within the party.

> 'We promoted discussion and debate about the big issues of socialism and economic policy ... the party was alive at that time and LL with its debates, discussion and agitation helped to bring it alive. In my view this all contributed to the 'Spring Tide' in 1992'.

UCATT

In 1982, Nolan was appointed as a full-time Official with UCATT (Union of Construction, Allied Trades & Technicians). He organised building sites around Dublin:

> 'A lot of my work was getting in new members or trying to get the lapsed members to re-join. All the time you were trying to organise the casuals and then more often than not you were trying to reorganise them when they moved on to another site and another job.'

While conditions on the big sites were usually good, the way the industry operated was changing: 'What began to creep in via England was more sub-contracting and self-employment. That caused huge problems for us'. The practice began to spread to carpenters and other trades and the end result was workers starting to say that they did not need a union as they were now self-employed. There was a real resistance to Nolan, UCATT and unions generally.

In this changing environment, Nolan's role and approach also had to change.

> 'Out in the big housing schemes in Tallaght and Clondalkin, fellows were asking me to negotiate prices for them. I became one of the few Officials in our union who understood this whole pricing system and I became quite successful in negotiating these agreements.'

Having covered construction for a number of years, Nolan moved to deal with large State and Semi-State bodies – Dublin Corporation, Eastern Health Board, Aer Lingus, and Aer Rianta. These employments had a high level of union organisation, which on occasion led to some strange disputes. On one occasion, a Dublin Corporation carpenter refused to work when he was asked by his foreman to carry a small glazing strip 500 yards onto the site. The carpenter contended that he should have a labourer with him for that job and fought his suspension: 'I did my best to argue his case but when the Corporation produced this small, four-ounce glazing strip we were laughed out of it. The carpenter in question left the union afterwards and gave out yards about me'. On another occasion, one of the site foremen arrived back after lunch but could not find one of his tilers who eventually appeared an hour later. A row ensued. The foreman claimed that when he came back from lunch at 1.45, the tiler was not to be found. To which the tiler memorably replied, 'you weren't back at 1.45 it was 1.55, sure wasn't I sitting in the pub across the road watching you'. Incidents like these made life interesting for Nolan in his job as workers' representative.

Throughout his years with ASW/UCATT, Nolan was actively involved with the DCTU, holding the position of Correspondence Secretary continuously since 1979. While the DCTU did not again reach the influential heights of the mass tax marches of 1979-1980, it continued to be active on a range of issues. In the early 1990s, DCTU initiated a campaign for a National Minimum Wage. It got the ICTU involved and eventually the issue was raised as part of the Partnership 2000 agreement, culminating in the introduction of the National Minimum Wage Act in April 2000.[55]

Nolan worked for UCATT from 1982 until he retired in 1995 aged sixty-five. As a worker and Official, he was involved in the building industry for close on fifty years and had fought for, and secured, a range of improvements for workers. It was not surprising that the *Irish Times* marked his retirement with an article, which described him as 'one of the most colourful figures in the Irish trade union movement'.[56]

Retirement and Reflections

Nolan was never someone who liked to be idle and when he retired, he had plenty to do. He was nominated to serve on the Employment Appeals Tribunal (EAT), a position he held for nine years. This was combined with serving on the board of DION, the government body providing support to Irish emigrant groups. He was Chair of the Finglas Cabra Partnership, a local development body set up to tackle problems of unemployment and social inclusion, and remains involved.

In 2010, Nolan was presented with a Special Award at the Labour Party Annual Conference in recognition of his long years of service to the party, and the Lord Mayor of Dublin, Councillor Emer Costello, presented him with an award to acknowledge his contribution to the working people of Dublin. However, Labour's participation in Government with Fine Gael in 2011 was a bridge too far for Nolan and he moved away from the party:

> 'I disagreed fundamentally with them about the bail out of the banks and the whole austerity agenda. If they had stayed out of Government in 2011 they would have won the subsequent election.'

Instead, Nolan involved himself in various grass root struggles such as the 2011 'Occupy' movement and addressed young participants on the history and role of trade unions. Indeed, part of Nolan's challenge in recent years has been to get the trade union movement more involved in campaigning.

Nolan continues as DCTU Correspondence Secretary, attends monthly meetings and is active in its various campaigns, such as the water charges protests, the housing crisis and Repeal of the 8th Amendment. In 2017, he produced his thirty-eighth consecutive Trades Council Annual Report and in May 2018 spoke at what he reckons was his fifty-eighth consecutive May Day demonstration in Dublin.

As Nolan moves toward his ninetieth year, he remains an active, committed trade unionist and socialist striving to galvanise the Left. While not able for as many 'long marches' as before Nolan is active on social media engaging in debates and discussions. Twenty-five years in the CPI, thirty plus years in the Labour Party, seventy years an active trade unionist, thirty-eight years as DCTU Secretary, over a half century of May Day marches … Nolan has led a very full life. So why did he do it over all those years?

> 'By my early teens I felt I should devote my life to fighting injustice and inequality in a world which kept the many poor and the few very rich. This was not a good career move, but it led to a fulfilling life … As I continue to engage in the immediate struggle I have not lost the long-term vision. I am always optimistic but I know that I am unlikely to see any fundamental change in my lifetime. However, we must remember that a central truth of socialist theory is that economic or political determinism does not exist. People have choices and people make history.'

Notes

This study of Sam Nolan's life is drawn on and developed from Brian Kenny, Sam Nolan: A Long March on the Left, *(Kenny Personal History Publishing, Dublin, 2010). That work was based heavily on interviews between Kenny and Nolan in 2010 and Nolan's own words, frequently cited in this text, are in italics / or single quotation marks*

1   James, 48 and a house carpenter; his wife Elizabeth, 40; and their children John, 20, plasterer; Samuel, 17, carpenter; and scholars Frances, 15; Elizabeth, 14; Matthew, 12; and James, 6, *www.census.nationalarchives.ie/reels/nai002580901/* [retrieved 16 September 2018].
2   The INUW was founded in 1921 as a breakaway from the ASW. See Francis Devine & John B. Smethurst, *Historical Directory of Trade Unions in Ireland*, (Irish Labour History Society/Working Class Movement Library, Dublin/Salford, 2016), pp. 211-220, 519-520.
3   Brian Kenny, *Sam Nolan: A Long March on the Left*, (Kenny/Personal History/Publishing, Dublin, 2010), pp. 17-18.
4   Nolan cites Jack London, *The Iron Heel*, (Macmillan, London, 1908) as particularly impacting on his thinking, Kenny, *op. cit.*, p. 19. See *www.gutenberg.org/files/1164/1164-h/1164-h.htm* [retrieved 16 September 2018].
5   Johnston, born 1929, a physicist, worked in Aer Lingus and Trinity College Dublin. He was active in the Irish Workers' League, Connolly Association whilst in Britain, Wolfe Tone Society and Sinn Féin. He was IRA Director of Education, went with the Officials after the split, and was active in the CPI, 1972-1977 before joining Labour and finally the Green Party. See his *Century of Endeavour: A Biographical & Autobiographical View of the Twentieth Century Ireland*, (Tyndall Books/Lilliput Press, Carlow/Dublin, 2006).
6   Keating, 1930-2009, was born in Ballymore Eustace and, after activity in the Communist movement, became Labour TD for Dublin County North, 1969-1977, serving as Minister for Industry & Commerce, 1973-1977. He was elected to the Senate on the Agricultural Panel, 1977-1982 and as MEP for Leinster, 1984. See Francis Devine, 'Justin Keating', *Saothar 35*, 2010, pp. 100-102.

7   Brian, 1926-2002, was active in the CPGB, Socialist Labour League and Workers' Party in Britain, For Dominic, see Michael Halpenny, 'The patriot game – Dominic Behan, 1928-1989' in Francis Devine & Kieran Jack McGinley (eds), *Left Lives in Twentieth Century Ireland*, (Umiskin Press, Dublin, 2017), pp. 169-184.

8   For O'Riordan, 1917-2006, see Michael Quinn, *The Making of an Irish Communist Leader: Michael O'Riordan, 1938-1947*, (CPI, Dublin, 2011); and Francis Devine, 'Michael O'Riordan', *Saothar 31*, 2006, pp. 5-8.

9   For detail on Deasy, 1922-2013, see his *Fiery Cross: The Story of Jim Larkin*, (ILHS, Studies in Irish labour History 9, Dublin, 2004); Evanne Kilmurray, 'Joe Deasy: the evolution of an Irish Marxist, 1941-1950', *Saothar 13*, 1988, pp. 112-119: Francis Devine, 'Joe Deasy', *Saothar 38*, 2013, pp. 181-184 and Brian Kenny, *Joe Deasy: A Life on the Left*, (Hugh Geraghty-Crumlin, Drimnagh and Walkinstown Branch, Labour Party, 2009)

10 McCarthy, 1918-2004, was a bricklayer and political activist before his life in music and theatre, see his *Early Days* and *London Years*, (Kildanore Press, 1990).

11 See Joe Deasy, 'George Jeffares', *Saothar 20*, 1995, pp. 12-14. Jeffares died in 1995.

12 Khruschev, *Speech to 20ᵗʰ Congress of the CPSU*, February 1956.

13 Mike Milotte, *Communism in Modern Ireland: The Pursuit of the Workers' Republic Since 1916*, (Gill & Macmillan, Dublin, 1984), chapter 10.

14 Mooney from Ballyfermot and Earley from Leitrim were long-standing CPI stalwarts.

15 Evanne Kilmurray, *Fight, Starve or Emigrate: A History of the Irish Unemployed Movement in the 1950s*. (Larkin Unemployed Centre, Dublin, 1988).

16 *ibid.*

17 Connolly, 1901-1980, was James Connolly's son. He was President of the first CPI in 1921 and edited the *Workers' Republic*. He then helped form the Workers' Party of Ireland before joining Labour. He was LP Secretary, 1941-1949; Labour TD for Louth, 1943-1944 and 1948-1951; and Senator, 1975-1977.

18 *Irish Times*, 14 March 1957. The full result was: elected (first preference vote), Seán Lemass (Fianna Fáil), 8,136; Maurice Dockrell (Fine Gael), 4,607; Celia Lynch (FF), 2,704; Philip Brady (FF), 3,236; and Murphy, 3,036. Also rans were Joseph Barron (Clann na Poblachta), 2,049; Roddy Connolly, 1,932; Thomas Finlay (FG), 1,906; Tomás Ó Dubhgháill (Sinn Féin), 1,734; Anthony Morney (FF), 1,621; and Edward Hosey (FG), 966.

19 Sam Nolan, 'Unemployed Struggles: 1920s to 1950s' in Seán Nolan (ed), *Communist Party of Ireland Outline History*, (CPI, Dublin, 1975). P.60

20 Kilmurray, *op cit.*, p. 37

21 *Irish Times*, 15 May 1957.

22 *Irish Times*, 15 May 1957. Larkin, 1908-1987, a son of Big Jim Larkin, was Labour TD, Dublin North East, 1954-1961 and 1965-1969; Lord Mayor, 1955-1956; and General Secretary, Workers' Union of Ireland, 1969-1977.

23 The Irish Trades Union Congress was split in 1945 with the creation of the Congress of Irish Unions. On 5 January 1956, ITUC and CIU formed the Provisional United Organisation of the Irish Trade Union Movement, which became known as the PUTUO) which worked out a new constitution for the united Irish Congress of Trade Unions in 1959.

24 *Irish Times*, 17 May 1957.

25 *Irish Times*, 17 May 1957.

26 *Irish Times*, 22 May 1957.

27 Murphy left with his family but they returned to Ireland in 1964. He died on 11 July 1984. In the bye-election the seat was won by Patrick Cummins (FF), 6,014; beating John Hegarty (FG), 3,389; Seán MacBride (Clann na Poblachta), 3,030; Roddy Connolly (Labour), 2,762; and Noel Hartnett (National Progressive Democrats), 2,688.

28 Kilmurray, *op cit.*, p. 41

29 Kilmurray, *op cit.*, p. 41.

30 *Irish Socialist*, January 1962.

31 Milotte, *op cit.*, chapter 10.

32 *Irish Socialist*, March 1963.

33 *Irish Times*, 19 August 1964.

34 Séamus Cody, John O'Dowd & Peter Rigney, *The Parliament of Labour: 100 Years of the Dublin Council of Trade Unions*, (DCTU, Dublin, 1986), p. 218

35 For full discussion of the strike see Charles Callan, *50th Anniversary, 40-Hour, 5-Day Week Building Workers' Strike, 18th August-19th October 1964*, (Irish National Painters' & Decorators' Craft Group – SIPTU & ICTU Construction Industry Committee, Dublin, 2014).

36 de Rossa, 1940-, was WP/DL/LP TD in Dublin North West, 1982-2002 and Minister for Social Welfare, 1994-1997. He was MEP for Dublin, 1989-1992 and 1999-2012. de Burca, 1938-. Is best known as a journalist but was Secretary, Official Sinn Féin for eleven years.

37 For biography of Dennehy, 1938-1984, see Bill McCamley, *Dennis Dennehy – Socialist Agitator*, (Labour History Workshop, Dublin, 1985).

38 *Irish Times,* 17 June 1968.

39 *Irish Socialist,* May 1968.

40 Sam Nolan, *Election Pamphlet,* 1969.

41 Elected were Vivion de Valera (FF), 7,493; Frank Cluskey (LP), 5,413; Maurice Dockrell (FG), 4,364; and Thomas Fitzpatrick (FF), 2,619. James Mooney, 1,714ll; Griff Cashman, 1,574; and James Downey, 895, also ran for LP. Nolan garnered 0.7% of the First Preference vote.

42 Milotte, *op. cit.,* 'Epilogue', pp. 293

43 *ibid.* pp. 295.

44 See Paddy Carmody, *Socialism and Democracy,* (Irish Marxist Society, Dublin, 1977).

45 Kearney was active in the ATGWU and Whelan then in the Ancient Guild of Incorporated Brick & Stone Layers' TU before becoming an ICTU Official. Clifford, an Irish Women Workers' Union activist, was the first woman to serve as DCTU President, 1978-1981.

46 Carmody, 1927-1979, was Secretary, Rathfarnham Branch, LP, 1946-1948, before involvement in the IWL/IWP/CPI. He edited the *Irish Socialist.* 1961-1975, and was active in the Amalgamated Transport & General Workers' Union.

47 *Irish Times,* 21 March 1979.

48 *ibid.*

49 *Irish Times,* 23 January 1980.

50 *ibid.*

51 Paul Dillon, *Explaining The Emergence, Political Impact and Decline of Labour Left; 1983-1992,* Masters in Politics Thesis, University College Dublin, 2007.

52 *ibid.*

53 *Irish Times,* 26 September 1987.

54 Fergus Finlay, *Snakes and Ladders,* (New Island Books, Dublin, 1998), chapter 3.

55 Similarly, DCTU initiated a campaign to have May Day declared as a Public Holiday. Congress got involved and the May Public Holiday was introduced by then Minister for Employment and Enterprise Ruairí Quinn, in 1993.

56 *Irish Times,* 26 September 1995.

DAN O'NEILL

Leader, Activist, Encourager:
Rodney Bickerstaffe, 1945-2017

Rodney Bickerstaff led the National Union of Public Employees (NUPE) from 1982-1993 before it merged with the Confederation of Health Service Employees (COHSE) and National & Local Government Officers' Association (NALGO) to create UNISON.[1] Bickerstaffe was UNISON General Secretary, 1996-2001; President,Trades Union Congress (TUC), 1992-1993; President, UK National Pensioners Convention (NPC), 2001-2005; and President, War on Want, 2006-2017. This writer's interest in Bickerstaffe was heightened in September 2013 when, in the company of a young UNISON National Officer Colm Porter from Wexford, I shared a conversation with Bickerstaffe in a café across from UNISON's London offices on Euston Road. He was charismatic and an overwhelmingly friendly man. He spoke about his labour activism; getting his first trade union job; trips to Liberty Hall; and his close relationship with Tony Benn. He spoke about Ireland, his sense of profound connection only becoming fully comprehended in middle age when he met his Irish family for the first time.

I DID BUT SEE HIM PASSING BY...

Artist: Ken Gill

Early Life & Elizabeth Bickerstaffe

Paul Routledge said Bickerstaffe would often tell the curious claim that 'I'm a bastard'. When listeners were shocked at his frankness, believing it to relate to his no-prisoners leadership style, he would add: 'No, I mean a real bastard'.[2] For almost half a century, Bickerstaffe had wondered who his real father was. Bickerstaffe was born on 6 April 1945 to a single working-class mother, Elizabeth 'Pearl' Bickerstaffe (later Topham). Born in 1920, she was the eldest of ten children. Her grandfather's ironmonger's business was ended when the premises were destroyed by fire, driving the family into poverty. For a brief period, Elizabeth Bickerstaff's childhood 'family was so poor that they lived in a railway carriage in a gypsy field'.[3] She became a nurse and subsequently a Child Care Officer and served over forty years as a rank-and-file NUPE member.[4] When she was twenty-four years old and training as a nurse in Whipps Cross Hospital, East London during World War Two, a carpenter from Dublin called Tommy Simpson was admitted complaining of stomach pains. A war-time romance sparked between them. Elizabeth found herself pregnant but, like many war-time romances, it was short lived. Simpson returned to Dublin and they never spoke again.[5] As in Ireland, single motherhood had an associated social stigma in 1940s Britain. According to Bickerstaffe's own account, when Elizabeth told her parents she was expecting a child, her father 'hit the roof'. Charles Alexander Edmund John 'Jack' Bickerstaffe was a mechanic, strong union man, Labour Party member, and chaired the National Unemployed Workers' Movement (NUWM) in South Yorkshire. Though never a declared Communist Party member, his activism in the party-dominated NUWM and his readership of the *Daily Worker* suggested shared ideological leanings.[6] He was, however, a man of his time and unable to come to terms with his daughter's situation, and asked her to leave her family home. Within two months of Bickerstaffe's birth, Elizabeth was a Residential Nurse caring for other people's children so she could keep her son with her. After two years, however, her father relented, and she and her son moved back in with her parents, sisters and brother in the Doncaster home Bickerstaffe described as phenomenally happy.[7] In 1956 Elizabeth married Norman Topham, a local man whose marriage had ended in divorce and who Bickerstaffe considered 'as good as gold. He was a wonderful guy'.[8] Although Elizabeth and Norman had no children of their own, he had custody of a son, Peter, from his first marriage. Peter and Bickerstaffe were good school friends.

Elizabeth was political. When sixteen, she began keeping newspaper cuttings about the Spanish Civil War and Japan's invasion of China. She amassed hundreds of cuttings, filling more than 170 pages of her scrapbook during the eighteen months leading up to February 1939 when, with the fall of Catalonia, the Spanish Republic disintegrated.[9] According to Bickerstaffe's friend, colleague and archivist James Sutherland, Elizabeth was a massive influence on her son's political formation. Bickerstaffe recalled how his mother took him on NUPE marches or brought him to her workplace and introduced him to colleagues. She was a very committed NUPE member, providing her son with a left apprenticeship. Among Bickerstaffe's papers were handwritten letters between his mother and then NUPE General Secretary Sydney Hill.[10] They clearly indicate that his mother saw a trade union career for her son. When Bickerstaffe went to college and graduated at twenty-one years of age, Elizabeth wrote her first letter to Hill wondering if there was any possibility of there being some kind of a job in NUPE for him? Ultimately, he was invited along for an interview and appointed.[11]

Employed by NUPE

In 1966, after education at Doncaster Grammar School and graduation with a sociology degree from Rutherford College of Technology, Newcastle-upon-Tyne, Bickerstaffe was appointed NUPE Area Officer in Yorkshire. He had found his calling. He soon discovered the movement's unusual workings. According to his Press Secretary for many years, Mary Maguire, 'Bickerstaffe told of how he had to travel the region by bus, until a colleague died and he was told 'you can have a car now'. 'So, that's the way of the union', he replied taking the car'.[12] In 1974, Bickerstaffe became Deputy Divisional Officer, North East Division, and then Divisional Officer in the newly-created Northern Division a year later. In 1977, with his wife Pat (née Bennett) and a young family, Bickerstaffe moved to London to take up the National Officer's role at age thirty-six.[13]

Universally known as 'Bick', Bickerstaffe was instantly recognisable by his black, heavy-framed NHS spectacles and a haircut that many compared to Buddy Holly's. Self-deprecating and humorous, he mocked his own hairstyle. On BBC's *Question Time*, when asked to respond to the question 'Does the panel tip, and if so whom and how much?', he responded, 'I don't like the concept of tipping because I believe that people should be paid a reasonable, living wage. But yes. I do tip. I tip my barber (pointing at his head) and that's the result'. Mark Seddon, writing in the *Guardian*, observed:

> 'His tough, uncompromising oratory often held Labour and trade union conferences spellbound, but behind these rhetorical masterpieces, ferociously denouncing inequality and poverty wages, was a highly thoughtful, pragmatic and strategic union leader who could be mixing it with Arthur Scargill one day and Tony Blair the next.'[14]

UNISON North West Regional Secretary Kevan Nelson noted the respect Bickerstaffe garnered across the political spectrum 'for his consistency, principles, decency, sense of humour and oratory skills. He had integrity. He had been consistent over many decades as a leader on the left'.[15] Nelson said he had a 'division of labour around internal Labour Party affairs that enabled him to not get too hands on in the internal machinations of that era when Labour moved to the right'. He had 'people like Tom Sawyer' who represented NUPE within the Labour Party 'so he kind of kept out of that'. Bickerstaffe was 'consistently there at all the major disputes … prominently supporting workers'. He was 'a big presence at the Durham Miner's Gala' where his 'magnificent oratory … brought respect because he could convey the movement's message very well'. He impressed on programmes like *Question Time* where 'he championed the low paid' and 'won the Minimum Wage': 'He wouldn't settle for half'.[16]

For Bickerstaffe, many of NUPE's achievements were 'often only achieved after years of struggle, frequently including many setbacks and disappointments along the way'.[17] NUPE had one of the fastest continuous histories of membership growth amongst contemporary British unions; and organised more women workers than any other, including substantial numbers from the black and ethnic minority communities, dedicating organisation, resources and representative facilities to such members.[18] Bickerstaffe's office as leader of NUPE, coincided with Thatcherism in full swing. It was a challenging environment for trade unions. For some, 'defeat in the 1982 health dispute ... acted as a curtain-raiser for the miner's humiliation less than three years later and gave the Government the green light to introduce competitive tendering in the NHS'.[19] However Bickerstaffe's leadership ensured that NUPE remained a strong fighting force, eventually merging with other public sector unions to create a synergy capable of defending that sector, its services and workers.

UNISON

Bickerstaffe was integral to the merger between NUPE, NALGO and COHSE which created UNISON in 1993.[20] According to former UNISON North West Regional Secretary Frank Hont, he was not solely responsible for the merger but was one of the main catalysts. There had been innate distrust between some members in the various unions and Bickerstaffe's helped overcome the division as he 'was able to instil confidence between officials and create personal relationships between senior lay activists'.

> 'There was suspicion because, say for instance you were a dinner lady, your boss was a NALGO member. If you were a cleaner in a hospital, your boss might be an administrator in the hospital who was in NALGO, so there was a natural suspicion between white and blue-collar workers. It's hard to imagine now in some ways but at that time, twenty-eight years ago, that's where the suspicion came from, I think. We also negotiated separately, so NALGO would do a deal in a local authority and then NUPE would do their own deal with the same employer. There was quite often a suspicion that one side was getting a better deal than the other. So, there was a real need to bring unity and to bring solidarity.' [21]

Kevan Nelson identified key factors that led to the mergers, referencing Thatcherism and the need to build unity to respond to it more effectively:

> 'What drove the merger forward ... was the impact of privatisation in the public services and the general decline that set in during the Thatcher Government with cuts and anti-union laws. The unions were on the back foot and there was significant membership decline. That's often a key factor in mergers and it has to be acknowledged as a fact in the UNISON merger. COHSE's base was affected by policy changes. A lot of their members were in mental health services which were being decentralised and closed, so their industrial base was changing. NUPE's membership was ravaged by collective tendering and privatisation. NALGO had more continuity at that time, but the changes would affect them later.' [22]

It was a generally seen as a successful merger and Bickerstaffe was proud of it. Having achieved his mission, however, he served only one term as General Secretary. This disappointed many activists and Officials because it was felt that he had a lot more to offer and he was only fifty-five years of age. He had his own reasons.[23] Perhaps, to paraphrase his friend Tony Benn, Bickerstaffe left to 'dedicate more time to politics', as stepping down certainly did not represent the end of his political and social activism.[24] Looking back on UNISON's formation, Bickerstaffe observed that it markedly strengthened union democracy, not least by pioneering the special representation of women members at all levels.[25]

Minimum Wage & the Labour Party

One of Bickerstaffe's most notable UNISON campaigns, was his uncompromising battle for the introduction of a Minimum Wage. Although the concept is now accepted, before it was introduced by the New Labour Government, there were quite a lot of objections to it from all sides of the political spectrum. According to Jim Sutherland, although the Conservative Party was 'its most vociferous opponent, most of the large trade unions' also opposed 'believing it would undermine the process of collective bargaining if Government was involved in setting pay levels. As well as this, some wanted to protect the wage differentials between skilled, semi-skilled and unskilled workers'.[26]

Hont remembers 'a difficult battle' because many other trade unions representing craft and skilled workers

> 'opposed it because they saw it as reducing the differential between their grade and the manual workers grade. So it wasn't a popular cause inside the trade union movement or inside the TUC. It was seen as levelling out something that had existed for many, many years, going back to the guilds. It took a bit of impetus when Labour took power in '97.'[27]

From the early 1980s, Bickerstaffe made waves in the Labour Party, pushing it to support the cause. His first breakthrough came in 1985 when he successfully moved a composite motion calling for the introduction of a Statutory Minimum Wage. Speaking on the motion, Bickerstaffe proclaimed:

> 'It has been a historic, long march to get to today. We have been trying for 20 years to get this Labour Party Conference to pass by a two thirds majority a resolution that commits our party to set up when in power a statutory, national, minimum wage. I shall not be long this morning, because I think that we have got it in the bag. I think that you all know that although we have had trade unionism for these past 150 years, we have never been able to do what we should have done for the low paid of our nation, have we? Of course we have not.'[28]

The following year, he moved a similar motion at the TUC Annual Congress which was carried overwhelmingly although opposed by the TGWU (Transport & General Workers' Union) and Electrical, Electronic, Telecommunications & Plumbing Union.[29] In early 1991, future Labour Leader John Smith met Bickerstaffe to discuss the Minimum Wage, acknowledging the fact that Labour, although supportive of the concept, had to consider the formula. Bickerstaffe wanted it to be set at two thirds of male median earnings. Smith thought it wise to view this as a medium-term goal as opposed to an immediate objective.[30]

According to Bickerstaffe, Smith 'said this in the most supportive and friendly basis believing the Tories would try to rip us apart during the election period. John asked whether it might be possible for us to meet for a long evening to discuss the matter thoroughly on a private basis'.[31] The meeting that followed involved Bickerstaffe and Peter Morris, UNISON Senior Research Officer, on one side of the table and Smith and Shadow Employment Secretary Tony Blair on the other. Bickerstaffe recalled how the formula was abandoned after Smith's death.

> 'In the wee small hours, we concluded with an understanding that to help the return of a Labour Government, I would discuss the possibilities within my own union, NUPE, and then with others, but that we could not guarantee anything. After many discussions within the movement ... all were agreed on a form of wording accepted by NUPE's Executive which was a formula of 50% of male median earnings rising over time to two thirds. When John Smith died on 12 May 1994, everything changed, of course. Tony Blair .... decided that although he knew well of the bargain struck, firstly at Oxford, and then in the various meetings between trade unions and the Labour Party leadership, he did not want to have any formula at all put before the British electorate during the next General Election campaign. So, the formula was murdered before it could do any good in the land.'[32]

Despite this, progress was made on the issue when New Labour came to power due to the influence of the trade unions. Bickerstaffe thought that

> 'what was achieved in 1998, and what we still have in 2015, is a Low Pay Commission, with good, intelligent and good-intentioned people, but who are not totally independent. Thus the previously agreed level of a 'Plimsoll Line for labour', below which workers would not sink was replaced by a series of small pay rises from a very low beginning now challenged by many as being nowhere near the Living Wage that we had been envisaging for a hundred years.'

Although Bickerstaffe was a lifelong Labour supporter and fostered a working relationship with the New Labour Government, relations were often fraught. According to Alistair Campbell, on 1 May 1995 Bickerstaffe warned him that Blair would need the unions once in power: 'I reported back to TB who said they can just fuck off'. Indeed, Campbell notes the difficulty Blair had disguising his 'contempt' for the unions.[33] According to Nelson, when the diary came out, Bickerstaffe made a virtue of the quote, using it in his speeches: 'During the New Labour era there was some antagonism towards Rodney but nobody would go out of their way to be seen to be his enemy because of his stature and his decency. So whilst Blair would have resented his persistence and his support to retain Clause 4, Rodney thrived on the resentment. He made a virtue of it'.[34] Bickerstaffe was, however, a pragmatist and understood that he had to work with New Labour. He believed that there were people in Cabinet who could advance progressive policies and get things done.[35]

When in 2012 the Minimum Wage was named as the most successful Government policy of the past thirty years in a survey of British political experts, Bickerstaffe referenced the fact that the Irish Government had reduced the minimum wage claiming it was as an emergency measure in response to the financial crisis, making an 11% cut from €8.65 to €7.65 per hour.[36]

> 'From self-made men and women who worship their creators, to the jawless wonders who can barely hold in their mouths the silver spoons planted there at birth, once

more the old game is afoot,' proclaimed Bickerstaffe. 'Whether it is natural greed or genuine fear of the economic times and the globalised 'need' to race down wages to the bottom, the new and old right wing are saying the same things. 'A job at any price is better than no job at all.'[37]

Bickerstaffe fought for decent, living wages for workers of all backgrounds until his final days. His association with the cause of the Minimum Wage can be evidenced in a tweet posted by former Deputy Prime Minister John Prescott on hearing of Bickerstaffe's death: 'Without Rodney Bickerstaffe there'd be no minimum wage, which improved the lives of millions. When you met Rodney you made a friend for life'.[38] Mary Maguire said Bickerstaffe could be

> 'downright awkward at times. He'd never give up. He'd keep coming back to the argument and worry away at his opponents, like a dog to a bone ... It was that tenacity that gave millions of workers a pay rise in 1998 with the introduction of the statutory National Minimum Wage. It was no easy achievement. But, Bick, as he was known, knew he was right – all he had to do was convince the rest of the world.'[39]

The Union in Ireland

Through NUPE and UNISON, Bickerstaffe had a direct link with Ireland as both organised in Northern Ireland. Although the union's Irish membership was never numerically significant, reaching 2.2% at its highest in 1992, what was remarkable was how the Irish tail often wagged the national NUPE/UNISON dog on equality issues.[40] UNISON Irish Regional Secretary Patricia McKeown remembers that Bickerstaffe was 'always tremendously supportive of us and the membership in Northern Ireland'. While 'the smallest part of the union' could 'be regarded as the most insignificant part', it was 'never the case with him'. He provided 'tremendous support during all of the conflict and supported the kind of work we were trying to do, like the early work around equality, human rights and trying to move towards some kind of a Peace Process'. He had a 'particular passion for the lowest paid women workers, and that is one of the reasons he was such a champion of the Minimum Wage, before it was an accepted policy' across the movement. He 'backed us when we started off pushing for the minimum wage inside the Irish Congress of Trade Unions (ICTU)' and the 'ICTU took that position in advance of the TUC and Rodney was delighted about that'.[41]

Writing in the *Morning Star*, TUC General Secretary Frances O'Grady echoed Bickerstaffe's special hunger for women's rights: 'Rodney will be remembered as a great champion for equality and social justice, especially for low-paid women'.[42] On UNISON's creation, the union adopted green white and purple, the colours of Emmeline Pankurst's Women's Social & Political Union, as their own at the suggestion of NUPE President Anna McGonigle from Omagh.[43] McGonigle was full of trepidation when becoming President in 1992. On the advice of Regional Officer Inez McCormack, McGonigle, approached Bickerstaffe during a delegation at Westminster and he immediately produced his diary and gave her his home and private telephone numbers. Accroding to McGonigle, the day after he became General Secretary, he came into a School Meals Working Party in London, introduced himself and 'promised the dedicated, encouraging leadership that followed'. McGonigle thought 'he did not like anyone who was there for the wrong reasons' and 'demanded the same selflessness from others'.[44]

In the battle for equality and low paid women, Bickerstaffe's ally was Inez McCormack.[45] She campaigned to organise and re-value the contribution of the 'forgotten', predominantly women, young workers and immigrants in low-paid jobs'.[46] Under her stewardship from the mid-1980s, NUPE successfully fought for equal pay and in-house contracts to supply cleaning and catering services in Northern Ireland hospitals at a time when, under Tory pressure, services were being outsourced.[47] During The Troubles, union organisers worked in a highly challenging environment. Under McCormack and Bickerstaffe, NUPE Northern Ireland rejected attempts by others to impose policies based on false dichotomies of religion, opting instead to support members in workplaces and communities grappling with issues identified as important to them.[48] Unlike some other British leaders, Bickerstaffe was respectful of the nuances of the Irish situation, and never tried to push his own ideology onto those who had to live within the day-to-day reality of conflict. The contradictions of attempting to sperate trade union issues from the political situation in Northern Ireland met him face on during an industrial dispute in the Royal Victoria Hospital, Belfast in 1986 when, in Bickerstaffe's own words, the workers were treated like 'enemies of the state.' According to Bickerstaffe,

> 'the strikers, joined by 100 women workers, were confronted by a convoy of 17 police and military Landrovers complete with personnel carrying machine guns. In another terrifying scene, the divisional Mobile Support Unit was drafted in... Such provocation and intimidation... must be condemned by all who share civilised values, regardless of their views in Northern Ireland. Ancilliary workers at the Royal Victoria do not want to be dragged into a political battlefield.'[49]

For McKeown, 'when it came to The Troubles, Rodney took his lead from Inez and the lay structures in Northern Ireland. He listened to what we had to say and supported us. There was never any question of imposing a view. He took a very democratic approach to it and he trusted us'.[50]

Travellers
Bickerstaffe's respect for Ireland did not stop there. According to McKeown, he had 'a particular passion for the rights of Irish Travellers'. Irish Travellers 'had supported him through a difficult period and he paid that support back in spades by becoming a champion for their rights'. NUPE Northern Ireland were 'the one part of the union' that ran 'a campaign that was trying to get a real voice out there for Travellers'. There was 'real and deep racism on this island'. NUPE worked 'with Traveller organisations' and 'tried to get the issue onto the trade union agenda and backed by ICTU' finally succeeding 'in making that a very visible cause'.[51] According to Andrew Ryder, former Policy Officer, Gypsy & Traveller Law

Reform Coalition, Bickerstaffe was one of the few public figures to stand in solidarity with the Travelling Community. This commitment sprang from his Doncaster childhood where he grew up with and befriended local gypsies and Travellers. He had vivid childhood memories of 'Gypsy friends being evicted and moved on'.[52] In the 1980s and 1990s, Bickerstaffe was President, Labour Campaign for Travellers' Rights (LCTR), which fought to reverse the Conservatives' Criminal Justice and Public Order Act, 1994 which had abolished the statutory duty on local authorities to provide halting sites. When Labour were in Government, Bickerstaffe was instrumental in getting them to include Gypsy and Traveller accommodation needs in regional spatial strategies, later dismantled by the Coalition Government, weakening the drive for more sites.[53]

Bickerstaffe recalled then Conservative Leader Michael Howard – who had been seeking to cash in on anti-Traveller sentiment in the tabloids – while addressing the National Federation of Gypsy and Traveller Liaison Group in 2006.

> 'Just before he stepped down as leader of the Conservative Party, I and Irish Traveller activist Kathleen McCarthy met Michael Howard. Michael had been good enough to call on the Dale Farm Travellers' Site to canvass during the General Election. Well, what I should say is that he stood in the garden of someone opposed to the site and forgot to speak to the Travellers. We attempted to put that right by seeking a meeting with him to which he graciously agreed. He was a lawyer specialising in planning law before becoming an MP, so we offered him a job for when he retires from parliament.'[54]

Finding His Irish Father

In 1997, Bickerstaffe began searching to find his father. His mother had told him who his father was from a very young age and provided him with an address in Cabra where he had lived with his parents.[55] That autumn, while visiting Dublin, Bickerstaffe knocked on the door of that address. There was nobody in, but an elderly neighbour told him of another family member who occupied the house who lived a few kilometres away. The man, Bob Hartigan, told Bickerstaffe that he thought they might be related and put his daughter Ann in contact with him by telephone. Ann Hartigan proved to be Bickerstaffe's first cousin. Bob Hartigan was married to Bickerstaffe's father's deceased sister. Ann told him that his father had three other children in Ireland, Liam, Francis and Tommy Simpson.[56]

Bickerstaffe's brother Tommy Simpson was a trade union and political activist; long-time SIPTU FÁS Branch member; President, Dublin Council of Trade Unions, 2014-2016; and Green Party candidate in a number of Local and General Elections. Simpson recounts first finding out that he had a half-brother:

> 'My aunt Maureen called me and invited me over to her house. She told me 'a man has come from England and he says that he's your brother'. I asked her what his name was and she said, 'Well his name is Rodney and he's a Union Official'. I thought to myself, there must be a thousand Rodneys in the trade union movement, then she said, 'he's on *Question Time* with David Dimbleby next week'. I asked if he was in the

audience or on the panel because that makes a big difference and she told me that she thought he was on the panel. I said that there was one Trade Union Official in England by the name of Rodney Bickerstaffe that I've been following for years. That he was a really radical guy and a good trade union leader. Of course, I went out and I bought a copy of the *Radio Times* in the first shop I came to. I looked at *Question Time* for the following week. It said 'Rodney Bickerstaffe, leader of Britain's largest trade union UNISON'. At ten or eleven the following Monday night, Rodney rang me and he said who he was. He was calling from the Labour Party Conference in England but he said he wanted to come over to meet me and his other two brothers. He knew at this stage that his father was dead and that he had three half-brothers. He arranged for himself, his wife Pat and his son Phillip to come over the following Sunday and we all got on like a house on fire.'[57]

Regarding his newly found family, the *Daily Mirror* reported 'It's wonderful', declared a Bick holding back the tears. 'I've got a whole new family and they're such lovely, friendly people'.[58] The story received widespread press coverage and Bickerstaffe was invited to announce the National Lottery winners on television, making the most of his thirty-nine seconds by talking about a living wage.[59] His mother Elizabeth died in January 1999 during the making of the short film the BBC made for the National Lottery. Ironically, she died in London at the precise time Bickerstaffe entered his father's Dublin house for the first time.[60] He never had the chance to meet his father, Thomas 'Tommy' Simpson, in person as, unaware to Bickerstaffe, he had died in a nursing home in Lemington Spa in 1989 and was buried in Oscott Cemetery, Sutton Coldfield, near Birmingham. Bickerstaffe later visited the nursing home and spoke to those who cared for his father.[61]

Retirement & Death

Bickerstaffe remained an activist long into his retirement, most notably as President, NPC, 2001-2005. Hont recounted that Barbara Castle rang him up to ask 'Would you fancy being the President of the NPC?'[62] Bickerstaffe replied,

> "Oh yeah? I wouldn't mind that'. She said, 'the thing is, Jack Jones doesn't want you to do it'. Then a couple of hours later he got a phone call from Jack Jones saying, 'How do you fancy being President of the NPC? I'm pushing for you, but Barbara Castle doesn't want you'. That's the old shit you get in any movement. The 'I'm the one who's promoting you mate, no one else' attitude.'[63]

From 2005, Bickerstaffe focused more on world matters. He chaired the Global Network working with organisations in Asia, Africa and Latin America; was President of War on Want; and chaired the Ken Gill Memorial Fund.[64] He was Patron of the Dalit Solidarity Network UK, campaigning against the oppression of India's caste system.[65] He was awarded Honorary Doctorates from Keele University, University of Hertfordshire and Sheffield Hallam University, and the Freedom of the Borough from Doncaster Metropolitan Borough.[66]

Bickerstaffe's death in October 2017 caused shock and grief. Hont recalled being with him the previous February.

'We went to an exhibition about the International Brigade together ... We knew he was really ill but he wasn't taking visitors towards the end, so it was still a shock when he died. I tweeted immediately and the way I described him was 'mentor, comrade, and friend', because for me, that's what he was. He mentored me. He convinced me that I should be a Regional Secretary ... the best ten years of my life. It was a dream job and it was him who said, 'of course you've got to go for it!' So he was encouraging ... supportive. He'd ring you up at seven o'clock in the morning, that was the only other bloody thing about him. The phone would go and you'd know it was him making four or five calls to people at the start of his day. You'd never forget that! But they were always helpful phone calls.'[67]

Hont described Bickerstaffe's extensive personal network

'One day I was down in London having a drink outside a pub just off Euston Road. He'd long retired but he walked past the pub so we called him over ... 'Come and have a drink with us!' we said. He wasn't a big drinker, but we were ... So he had a glass of red wine and sat down. 'What are you up to?' asked Rodney, so I said, 'Well we're putting a play on at the Labour Party Conference about Paul Robeson'. He said, 'That's interesting. I just spoke to Paul Robeson Junior'. I said I didn't know there was anyone called Paul Robeson Junior. He said, 'Oh, it's his son. He lives in Manhattan. I'll ring him'. This is like ten o'clock at night ... So he gets his little mobile phone out. He never had an iPhone. He had one of these little Nokia things. And he rings Paul Robeson Junior in Manhattan and passes me the phone. I said 'Hello Paul, I'm sitting with Rodney Bickerstaffe'. I told him about the play. I gave Rodney the phone back and said, 'Who the fucking hell would have Paul Robeson Junior's number in his phone?' It's surreal isn't it! It didn't stop there. He probably had the Prime Minister of Denmark's phone number in his phone book.'[68]

Bickerstaffe contracted cancer of the oesophagus. In his final days, he was cared for by members of the union he helped create. On 3 October 2017 Rodney Bickerstaffe died, aged seventy-two. Paying tribute to Bickerstaffe, British Labour Party Leader Jeremy Corbyn said, 'He was a warm, decent and principled man, an outstanding trade unionist and socialist, and a great friend and support to me over many years ... Rodney was always global in his views and perspectives, a real internationalist'.[69] Bickerstaffe's brother, Tommy Simpson, echoed this sentiment saying, 'he was immensely admired by his members ... He was one of the most humble people you could meet. No pretentiousness at all'.[70]

To paraphrase Nelson Mandela, Bickerstaffe was a campaigner for the poor, fighting oppression and exploitation throughout the world.[71] He was a warm spirited man who took a genuine interest in the lives of those he met. He was husband, father, brother, son and to many, a working class hero. Speaking on his retirement from UNISON, Bickerstaffe reflected:

'It all goes so quickly doesn't it. It doesn't seem like a few months ago that I was in a little Anglia car. It was January 1967. I had a little Perdio Radio on the back seat. It was playing 'Penny Lane is in my eyes'. I thought the world was my oyster. What I wasn't going to do ... The trade union movement, the labour movement, the world, the cosmos didn't know what I was going to do! Then suddenly you realise that they never found out because although you try, you can only do a little. And that little you have to do as a collective. The collective, our collective, is called the trade union movement.'[72]

Bickerstaffe was regarded as 'one of the most important trade union leaders of the 1980s and 1990s in Britain.[73] He held to his working class values, was inspired by his mother's sacrifices on his behalf and her struggle with low pay and continuous under-valuation of her and other women's work, and determined in his desire to involve members and communities in campaigns to resist attacks on public services. His discovery, late in life, of his Irish family enriched his understanding of who he was, and although his life's work may not have felt complete while austerity and Toryism diminished working class existence, global migration and exploitation spiralled, and intolerance and injustice denied so many the basic necessities. However dissatisfied Bickerstaffe may have felt, those observing his efforts to change things for the better could only conclude that it was a full life lived to great purpose on behalf of the many rather than the few.

Notes

1   Dan O'Neill, 'A warm and principled man', *Liberty, vol. 16. no. 4*, October 2017
2   Paul Routledge, *The Bumper Book of British Lefties*, (Politicos, London, 2003), p. 19.
3   Routledge, 'Bickerstaffe hunts for father and uncovers a family', *Independent*, 16 December 1998.
4   Stephen Williams & R.H. Fryer, *Leadership & Democracy: The History of the National Union of Public Employees, Volume 2, 1928-1993*, (Lawrence and Wishart, London, 2011), p. 392.
5   Routledge, 'Bickerstaffe hunts for father and uncovers a family', *op. cit.*
6   Jim Jump, *A Spanish Civil War Scrapbook: Elizabeth Pearl Bickerstaffe's Newspaper Cuttings of the Wars in Spain and China from August 1937 to May 1939*, (Lawrence & Wishart, London, 2015), p. 7.
7   Pat Thane & Tanya Evans, *Sinners? Scroungers? Saints?: Unmarried Motherhood in Twentieth-Century England*, (Oxford University Press, Oxford, 2013), p. 94.
8   John Boy, Blog Post entitled 'Britain is a country which once made and has now lost and says 'Goodbye' to an old giant of the Trade Union Movement called Rodney Bickerstaff.,' http://britainisnocountryforoldmen.blogspot.com/2017/10/britain-is-country-which-once-made-and.html [retrieved 4 January 2019].
9   Jump, *op. cit.*, p. 8.
10 Hill, 29 October 1902-17 August 1968, grew up in Dudley in the English Black Country. He left school at fourteen; completed an engineering apprenticeship; and was President, Dudley & District Trades Council, 1928-1935, and Labour Councillor in Tipton,1937-1947. He became NUPW Midlands Organiser in 1935; National Officer, 1945; Chief National Officer, 1960 and Assistant General Secretary, 1962. He served on the TUC General Council, 1963-1967.
11 James Sutherland interview with Dan O'Neill, 2 August 2018.
12 Mary Maguire, 'One of the Greats', *Union Active! The Magazine for Members in Yorkshire and Humberside,* Winter 2017.
13 Williams & Fryer, *op. cit.*, p. 392.
14 Mark, Seddon, 'Rodney Bickerstaffe Obituary', *Guardian*, 3 October 2017, www.theguardian.com/politics/2017/oct/03/rodney-bickerstaffe-obituary [retrieved 15 December 2018].
15 Kevan Nelson interview with Dan O' Neill, 3 August 2018.
16 Nelson, *op cit.*
17 Williams & Fryer, *op. cit.*, p7.
18 Williams & Fryer, *op. cit.*, p7.
19 Williams & Fryer, *op. cit.*, p15.
20 Williams & Fryer, *op. cit.*, p392.
21 Frank Hont interview with Dan O' Neill, 5 August 2018.
22 Nelson, *op. cit.*
23 Nelson, *op. cit.*
24 Tony Benn signalled the end of his parliamentary career in 1999, when he announced he would not be standing for re-election at the next General Election so that he would

have 'more time to devote to politics and more freedom to do it'.

25 Williams & Fryer, *op. cit.*, p6.

26 Jim Sutherland, e-mail to Dan O'Neill, National Minimum Wage/Living Wage, 2016.

27 Hont, *op. cit.*

28 Rodney Bickerstaffe, Speech to the Labour Party Conference in Bournemouth, 1985.

29 Sutherland, *op. cit.*

30 Sutherland, *op. cit.* Smith, 13 September 1938-12 May 1994, was born at Baddarroch, Dalmally, Argyll, eldest of Sarah Cameron [Scott] and schoolteacher Archibald Leitch Smith's three children. He was MP Monklands East, 1970-1983; Minister of State for Energy, 1975–1976; Minister of State for the Privy Council Office, 1976–1977; and Secretary of State for Trade and President of the Board of Trade, 1978–1979, in Jim Callaghan's Government. After Neil Kinnock resigned following Labour's loss in the 1992 General Election, Smith was elected Labour Leader in July 1992. In 1993, he abolished the trade union block vote at Labour Party Conferences, replacing it with 'one member, one vote'. After Smith's sudden death, he was succeeded by Blair. Gordon Brown & James Naughtie, *John Smith, Life and Soul of the Party*, (Mainstream Publishing, Edinburgh, 1994); Christopher Bryant (ed), *John Smith, An Appreciation*, (Hodder & Stoughton, London, 1994); Andy McSmith, *John Smith: A Life 1938–1994*, (Mandarin Publishing, e-book, 1994); Mark Stuart, *John Smith – A Life*, (Politico's Publishing, London, 2005).

31 Sutherland, *op. cit.*, p. 8.

32 Sutherland, *op. cit.*, p. 8.

33 Alastair Campbell, *The Blair Years: Extracts from Alastair Campbell Diaries*, (Hutchinson, London, 2007), p. 58.

34 Nelson, *op. cit.* Clause 4 was a part of the 1918 text of the Labour Party constitution which set out the aims and values of the party. It was revised in 1995 by Blair.

35 Tommy Simpson interview with Dan O' Neill, 11 July 2018.

36 BBC, 'Minimum Wage 'most successful government policy', 10 September 2018, www.bbc.com/news/uk-politics-11896971 [retrieved 15 December 2018].

37 Rodney Bickerstaffe, 'Minimum wage should be a living wage – Bick', http://unisonactive.blogspot.com/2010/12/minimum-wage-should-be-living-wage-bick.html [retrieved 22 September 2018].

38 John Prescott, Twitter post, 3 October 2017 [retrieved 12 July 2018].

39 Maguire, 'One of the Greats', *op. cit.*

40 Francis Devine, 'Mistress of her own history: UNISON's Anna McGonigle of Omagh' in Seán Byers & Francis Devine (eds), *William Walker, 1871-1918, Belfast Labour Unionist Centenary Essays*, (Umiskin Press, Dublin, 2018), pp. 151-152.

41 Patricia McKeown, interview with Dan O'Neill, 8 August 2018.

42 Frances O'Grady, 'Rodney Bickerstaffe: in tribute to a legend', *Morning Star:* 4 October 2017, https://morningstaronline.co.uk/article/rodney-bickerstaffe-tribute-legend [retrieved 4 January 2019]

43 Devine, *op cit.* p. 159.

44 Devine, *op cit.* p. 159.

45 Tommy Simpson, e-mail to Dan O'Neill, 16 January 2019

46 Francis Devine, 'Changing everything: Inez McCormack, 1943-2013' in Francis Devine & Kieran Jack McGinley (eds), *Left Lives in Twentieth Century Ireland*, (Umiskin Press, Dublin, 2018), pp. 211-234.

47 Devine, 'McGonigle', *op cit.*, p. 2

48 Williams & Fryer, *op. cit.*, p. 528.

49 Rodeny Bickerstaffe, as quoted in Rosemary Sales, *Women Divided: Gender, Religion and Politics in Northern Ireland*, (Routledge, New York, 2002)

50 Patricia McKeown interview with Dan O'Neill, 8 August 2018.

51 McKeown, *op. cit.*

52 Andrew Ryder, 'Tributes to Rodney Bickerstaffe', *Travellers Times:* 11 October 2017, www.travellerstimes.org.uk/news/2017/10/tributes-rodney-bickerstaff [retrieved 11 September 2018].

53 Ryder, *op. cit.*

54 Sutherland, *op. cit.*

55 Tommy Simpson, e-mail to Dan O' Neill, 16 January 2019.
56 Tommy was born in 1949, Liam in 1951 and Francis in 1953.
57 Tommy Simpson interview with Dan O'Neill in SIPTU College, Dublin, 11 July 2018.
58 Kevin Maguire, 'Remembering Rodney Bickerstaffe: A trade union titan who changed our lives for the better', *Daily Mirror*, 3 October 2017.
59 Maguire, 'One of the Greats', *op. cit.*
60 Simpson, e-mail to Dan O'Neill, 16 January 2019.
61 Simpson, e-mail to Dan O'Neill, 16 January 2019.
62 Castle, 6 October 1910-3 May 2002, was born Barbara Anne Betts in Chesterfield, youngest of three children to Frank Betts, a Tax Inspector, and his wife Annie (Ferrand). She grew up in in an Independent Labour Party household. Although prohibited from formal political activity as a Civil Servant, her father edited the *Bradford Pioneer*, the city's socialist newspaper, and Annie was elected a Labour Councillor. Castle was MP for Blackburn, 1945-1979; MEP, Greater Manchester, 1979-1989; and, as Baroness Castle, sat in the Lords from 1990. She was Minister for Overseas Development, 1964-1965; Minister of Transport, 1965–1968; Secretary of State for Employment and First Secretary of State, 1968–1970; and Secretary of State for Health and Social Services, 1974-1976.
63 Hont, *op. cit.* James Larkin (J.L. or 'Jack') Jones, 29 March 1913-21 April 2009, was born in Garston, Liverpool. He left school at fourteen and became a docker. He was converted to socialism by reading Robert Tressell's *The Ragged Trousered Philanthropists* and joined the TGWU becoming Shop Steward and Delegate, National Docks Group Committee. In 1936 he served with the British Battalion, XV International Brigade as Political Commissar, Major Attlee Company. He was seriously wounded at the Battle of the Ebro in 1938. After the war, he became a full-time TGWU Official in Coventry as Midlands Secretary. As a Labour Party Executive member, he chaired the policy group on Industrial Democracy. He was elected TGWU General Secretary, 1968-1978; strongly opposed the 1966-1979 Labour Government's Prices & Income Policy; and, within the TUC, was instrumental in creating the Social Contract, ACAS (Advisory, Conciliation and Arbitration Service) in 1975, and campaigned for Britain to leave the EEC in the 1975 Referendum. He was President of the NPC and International Brigade Memorial Trust. See Jack Jones, *Union Man: An Autobiography*, (Harper Collins, London, 1986).
64 Gill, 30 August 1927-23 May 2009, born in Melksham, Wiltshire, became a draughtsman and Merseyside/Northern Ireland Official for DATA (Draughtsmen's and Allied Technicians' Association). He was General Secretary, Technical, Administrative and Supervisory Section (TASS), 1974-1988, until it merged with ASTMS (Association of Scientific, Technical & Managerial Staffs) to form the Manufacturing, Science & Finance Union (MSF) He was MSF General Secretary, 1988–1992. He maintained a strong interest in Irish affairs and expanded DATA/TASS/MSF membership in Ireland considerably.
65 David Haslam, 'Caste discrimination law would be a fitting tribute to Rodney Bickerstaffe', *Guardian*, 9 October 2017, www.theguardian.com/politics/2017/oct/09/caste-discrimination-law-would-be-a-fitting-tribute-to-rodney-bickerstaffe [retrieved 22 September 2018].
66 https://en.wikipedia.org/wiki/Rodney_Bickerstaffe [retrieved 1 October 2017].
67 Hont, *op. cit.*
68 Hont, *op. cit.*
69 Tributes paid to Bickerstaffe: *Daily Mail, 1 June 2018*, www.dailymail.co.uk/wires/pa/article-4944172/Tributes-paid-death-former-trade-union-leader-Rodney-Bickerstaffe.html; Paul Routledge, 'Bickerstaffe hunts for father and uncovers a family', *The Independent*, 16 December 1998. www.independent.co.uk/news/bickerstaffe-hunts-for-a-father-and-uncovers-a-family-1191663.html [retrieved 1 June 2018].
70 Tommy Simpson interview with Dan O'Neill in SIPTU College, Dublin, 11 July 2018.
71 Nelson Mandela, video message recorded for the 2001 UNISON Conference, supplied to O'Neill via email by James Sutherland. 8 August 2018.
72 Rodney Bickerstaffe, 'Retirement Speech to UNISON Conference as featured in the Rodney Bickerstaffe Tribute Film, 2001, www.youtube.com/watch?v=DP_zuVKe3p4 [retrieved 1 June 2018].
73 www.theguardian.com/politics/2017/oct/03/rodney-bickerstaffe-obituary [retrieved 1 June 2018].

FRANCIS DEVINE & HELENA CLARINGBOLD

'That All Around May Plainly See …'
A Triptych of Banner Artists:
W.L. Reynolds, 1842-1881;
Thomas Kain, 1886-1948; and
Jer O'Leary, 1945-2018

'Bring out the banners once again, You union women, union men,
That all around may plainly see The power of our unity'
John Warner, 'Bring Out the Banners'[1]

Walking behind or watching banners pass can be stirring but few ever ask of their creators. The death in December 2018 of Dublin actor and banner artist Jer O'Leary generated widespread grief. As actor, he had become the personification of Big Jim Larkin in stage productions and street demonstrations. As banner artist, his instantly recognisable work defined the labour movement's iconography from the 1980s. He will be remembered together with other artists who left their mark on our trade union banners, among them W.L. Reynolds and Thomas Kain.

John Gorman, art historian and pictorial cataloguer of British working class experience, considered that the Irish banners he reviewed in Belinda Loftus's catalogue for the *Marching Workers* exhibition in 1978 were 'deeply rooted in the heraldry of the medieval guilds' and 'displayed a curious

Thomas Kain

Jer O'Leary

blend of the masonic, religious with craft pride and a shameless sentimental nationalism'.[2] There was a 'general absence of socialist imagery' with, perhaps surprisingly, James Connolly, James Larkin – in the north even William Walker, 'not appearing with the regularity that might be anticipated.[3] The 'millennium, as a concept' – in Britain the socialist dawn, at home the Workers' Republic – was 'almost entirely absent'. Gorman thought, in the last analysis

> 'The iconography of the organised Irish working class seems at times to struggle for identity, its true purpose obscured ... by religious and nationalist symbolism, yet the true spirit and strength of the grip of brotherhood the world o'er repeatedly asserts its independence.'[4]

Loftus noted that whereas banners in England 'went out for' the Jarrow miners in 1831, Tolpuddle Martyrs in 1834, Chartism in the 1840s, Reform in the 1860s, the London Dock Strike of 1889, and May Day from 1890, in nineteenth century Ireland, banners attended more nationalistic events for O'Connell, 1830, 1864 and 1875; Amnesty demonstrations, 1860s; Manchester Martyrs, 1870s; Land League, 1870s-1880s; and centenary celebrations, 1798 and 1803. Those banners reflected their trade guild origins or were replete with shamrocks, round towers, wolfhounds, saints and heroes, with overtly Catholic religious references.[5] John Swift and T.P. O'Neill provide illustrations [line drawings] of typical designs.[6]

W.L. Reynolds and the Boyne Fishermen

Drogheda artist W.L. Reynolds's trade banners are displayed in Drogheda Millmount Museum. His Boyne Fishermen banner, painted in oils, Gorman contended was 'worthy of exhibition in any gallery in the world'.[7] William Reynolds was born in Dowth, Slane, County Meath on 22 September 1842. He was a classmate of John Boyle O'Reilly, the Fenian transported to Australia before escaping to America.[8]

Reynolds 'etched in wood for some of the Dublin weekly prints, who discovered his talents', the *Weekly News* and *Dublin Star* being 'enriched by many of his etchings'. In the years before his death he began 'experimenting in etching with acids on steel and the incautious use of the chemicals he used resulted in blood poisoning'. The *Drogheda Argus* noted that he

> 'had all the temperament of the child of genius retiring and unobtrusive, working at his ease out there at Oldbridge comparatively unknown and not over blessed with the world's wealth, but yet rich in his love for art and the admiration of his many friends. Two perfections were very conspicuous in his character; he was a most sincere Catholic and an equally sincere Patriot. He was also a wonderful linguist, self-taught and read with avidity.'[9]

On Reynolds' untimely death on 30 December 1881 at thirty-nine years of age, the *Argus* recorded – in sentiments that might apply to O'Leary – that 'a bare line or two in the obituary column last week recorded the passing away' of Reynolds, 'whose talents and patriotism deserved a prominent and more than a passing tribute to his genius and worth of nationhood': 'records of his genius are emblazoned on the trade banners of Drogheda'. The paper added:

> 'So long as those banners are carried aloft, the admiring eyes of his countrymen will be reminded of this self-taught, highly gifted artist, the creation of whose pencil they are. They are works of art, as we have often said, that would be worthy of any great painter.'

Reynolds's funeral to Donore Churchyard was the 'largest seen in that part of the country for many years past' and, again in echo of O'Leary, the

> 'Trades of Drogheda trouped their banners around the grave of the artist ... a graceful and well merited tribute, worthy of the Trades and of the Dead. The funeral was a most impressive demonstration, the significance of which could not but strike the most casual observer and drew crowds of admiring friends from all parts of the neighbourhood and some from Dublin.'[10]

Reynolds's gravestone is inscribed thus:

> 'Pray for the soul of William Reynolds, Oldbridge, to whose memory this cross has been raised by his friends at home and abroad, who admired him for his many virtues, sterling patriotism and great and varied gifts and as an artist, who successfully illustrated the religious and national glories of his native land.'

Reynolds's banners included those of the Brick & Stonelayers Drogheda – Henry Grattan and the motto 'Ireland A Nation' on the reverse of a display of trade imagery; and the Drogheda Labourers' Society. Painted in very primitive style, this banner shows a family group with sickles gathering corn. A boy is dressed as a girl, local folk belief being to deceive faeries who had the practice of stealing boys. O'Connell and Wolfe Tone peer down from the corners while the reverse shows Adam and Eve, modestly dressed in grass skirts, being expelled from the Garden of Eden.

The trade banners were first drawn to public attention by the newly-formed Old Drogheda Society in an Industrial Exhibition in 1965 organised by the Drogheda Junior Chamber of Commerce.[11] Reynolds's Boyne Fishermen banner had 'pride of place' as a 'splendid nine by seven-foot, oil on canvas, depicting three fishermen on the Boyne, at Tom Roe's Point, downstream from Drogheda'. It was discovered in an

> 'outhouse, at Miss Murphy's residence in Francis Street ... rolled up in Irish Linen and stored in a metal cylinder, suitable for carrying to the various parades, protests and public demonstrations during the turbulent years of two decades, towards the end of the nineteenth century, when people showed their nationalistic aspirations.'

The banner depicts a method of salmon fishing still in use today with Spanish canoe and a 'priest' [a wooden club] used to despatch fish caught. Reynolds's models were identified as Owen Quigley, grandfather of Moira Corcoran, a founder, with Harry Fairtclough and Jim Garry, of Millmount Museum in 1974 and mother of noted folk singer and collector Seán Corcoran; Brocki Gordon, the man with beard and pipe; and either a Heeney or Bannon. Corcoran knew that her grandfather was twenty-three when the banner was painted, so it can be securely dated. Drogheda landmarks of the Boyne Viaduct, Saint Peter's Church, Tholsel, Millmount and Magdalene Tower decorate the background. The town's Meath bank is telescoped down to the Maiden Tower, Mornington. Medallions on each side of the scroll depict Saint Brigid and Saint Patrick. On the reverse, Saint Peter stands on a globe, key in hand, pointing to the Church of Rome. The Book and Keys, a hound, harp and shamrocks illuminate three corners. Loftus noted that the banner was 'unusual in that there was no existing guild or trade union symbolism to draw on', giving Reynolds s free hand. She regarded it as his masterpiece.[12] The banner, with that of the Brick & Stonelayers, can be seen here.[13]

In 1873, Bernard Finglas, Francis Street, and brothers Matthew and Edward Murphy, Scarlet Street, commissioned Reynolds to paint the banner. He was 'regarded by many as the greatest Irish banner painter of all time'. The banner took eight persons to carry it and was last paraded on St Patrick's Day 1975. In addition to banners, Reynolds painted thirty portraits of saints for the Guilds of the Holy Family Confraternity in Saint Peter's Church, West Street. A 'Mrs Tierney and Miss Madden of Tullyallen said that Reynolds was in poor health all his life and that the poison 'only hastened the end of the poor man".[14]

Thomas Kain

Thomas Jeremiah Kane was born at Maryhill Barracks, Glasgow on 5 June 1886, son of Thomas Jeremiah Kane, a tailor and Private, G Company, 1st Royal Scots, born in Hamburg, Germany, and Catherine Browe.[15] The couple had married in the Curragh on 15 August 1883. Thomas was the eldest of four: Kathleen born c1888 in County Clare; Mary Teresa born c1890 and Christopher born c1892, both in Dublin. In the 1901 Census, Kain is recorded as Tomás Ua Catháin, 14, Irish and English speaker and Telegraph Manager. He resided at 26.3 Charlemont Street, Fitzwilliam Dublin, with his mother Catherine Kane, 40, widow and charwoman; sister Kathleen, 13; Mary, 11; and Christopher, 9. The gaelicisation of Kane's name raises interesting questions about possible involvement in Conradh na Gaeilge [Gaelic League] or the level of Irish he received at school. Kathleen is also listed as having Irish and English.[16] It is not known when the spelling of his surname changed to Kain.

In the 1911 Census, Kain, 24, lived at 6.5 Charlemont Street, Fitzwilliam, Dublin, with his mother Catherine, 50, charwoman and widowed, and brother Christopher, 19, an 'apprentice artificial print making', both Dublin-born. Kain himself was a carpet fitter, raising the question as to whether he was a member of the Carpet Planners of the City of Dublin Trade Union, an active Dublin Trades Council and Irish Trades Union Congress affiliate before 1916 which merged into the Irish Transport & General Workers' Union (ITGWU) in 1919.[17] Kain spoke Irish and English and was listed as married for a year, although no wife was recorded in the house. Kain had married Maria Smith on 24 November 1909 in St Kevin's Church, Harrington Street, Dublin.[18] All were Catholic. His mother died on 26 May 1924 and brother on 7 May 1935 and both are buried in Mount Jerome. In October 2013, through the efforts of his relatives Nuala Gilsenan and Helena Claringbold, the National Graves Association and Technical, Engineering & Electrical Union, a headstone was erected.[19] Kain attended the Royal Hibernian Military School in Dublin.[20]

On 6 October 1934, Kain made application for a Military Service Pension from his address at 15 Old Camden Street. He claimed to have joined the Irish Citizen Army (ICA) in 1913 'on its formation', the membership card he produced for 1914 listing him as Number 3.[21] With Connolly and Mallin, Kain was involved in asking members to declare their willingness to fight, an exercise carried out towards the end of 1915.[22] Before the Rising he was involved in 'occasional mobilisation and training' and he 'removed and stored ammunition from Liberty Hall'. He stated that he was 'Secretary to James Connolly' and was 'responsible for all mobilisations' holding the rank of Lieutenant. Frank Robbins corroborated this by recalling that 'all men received their instructions from the Chief Mobilisation Officer of the Army, Lieutenant Thomas Kain', his orders in turn coming 'directly from' Connolly or Michael Mallin.[23] Kain 'gave up his job' after a military raid on Liberty Hall and was 'full-time … day and night, from that until Easter Sunday'.[24]

In Easter Week, Kain went from Liberty Hall to Dublin Castle. He was 'in charge of five men' and, 'instructed by Seán Connolly' was ordered to 'take the Guard Room'. They fired in and 'threw in one bomb which did not explode'. They 'succeeded in rushing it and over-powering and disarming the sentries'. They barricaded themselves in until Monday night when they were forced to retreat to Lahiff's plumbing shop, 12 Castle Street, remaining in the cellar until discovered on Wednesday night and brought to Ship Street Barracks. Kain was removed to Kilmainham and thence to Richmond Barracks, Wandsworth Prison and finally Frongoch. He was among the last batch of prisoners released before Christmas 1916. Kain is named on a commemorative plaque for the ICA at City Hall.[25] Before capture, Kain secreted the ICA membership books, returning with Frank Robbins in 1927 to reclaim them.[26]

Writing in 1923, Kain reflected that Connolly's intention at Easter week was not

'immediately attaining a Republic but rather to bring about a resurrection of that revolutionary thought and action in Ireland which, he calculated would lead ultimately to the emancipation of the Irish working class.'[27]

Kain's socialist values were unswerving. In his pension application, Kain commented that

'on my release from Frongoch I found it impossible to gain employment owing to my activities in 1916. I received the Commandant's permission to absent myself from ordinary parades in order to attend night classes to equip myself for another [unreadable].'[28]

Kain's brother, 'who had a place on the Quays was boycotted and we had to clear out ... I was practically doing nothing at that time, Murray and Frank Kelly and myself were running the Frongoch Studio at 50 Blessington Street'.[29]

Kain continued to be active in the ICA, however, being involved in an attack on police at the corner of Dawson Street and St Stephen's Green on 5 June 1919 after a Connolly Commemoration, firing a few shots from his revolver. He was 'engaged on work for Mr Collins' on other occasions but his activities were mostly confined to moving arms and making alterations to premises. In addition to those attesting to his evidence, his pension application was witnessed by ITGWU General President Thomas Foran, Peace Commissioner, on ITGWU headed paper.[30] Matthews does not include Kain in her list of ICA members active in the War of Independence.[31] Kain's explanation was that

'I never relinquished my membership. At one time I was asked to resign my commission for I was not turning up at the meetings, but I did not do so. Although O'Neill gave me permission [to attend art classes] he may have not mentioned it to any of the Army Council.'[32]

On 22 December 1937, ITGWU General Secretary William O'Brien wrote on Kain's behalf having been 'personally acquainted' with him 'for about thirty years'. O'Brien said Kain was 'associated with' Connolly 'from 1910, having been in fact, a member of the Committee (of which I was Secretary) which arranged for the return' of Connolly from America. O'Brien, from 'my own knowledge' attested that he 'personally saw his [Kain's] Commission as Lieutenant, being made out on Saturday April 22nd when he reported to' Connolly to make 'arrangements for taking certain buildings commanding the Upper Castle Yard'. Kain showed Connolly a 'newly-manufactured key' for access purposes. O'Brien was interned with Kain in Frongoch.[33] On 25 May 1938, Kain was awarded a pension at Grade E for a period of 130/179 years amounting to £23 12s 8d. After his death in 1948, William 'Billy' Oman, an old ICA comrade from 1916, wrote on behalf of Mrs Kain.[34]

Kain worked for Boileau & Boyd as an artist and French polisher. The National Irish Visual Arts Library documents that Kain attended the Metropolitan School of Art, later the National College of Art & Design, from October 1918-July 1924.[35] He kept illustrious company in the Radical Club in the 1920s, fellow members being F.R. Higgins, Seán Keating, Maurice McGonigal, Frank O'Connor, Liam O'Flaherty, Seán O'Sullivan and Cecil Salkeld.[36] In 1925, at the Royal Hibernian Academy he completed portraits of T. Magee, TD, and of James Connolly. Kain exhibited with distinction. In 1926, in the Daniel Egan Gallery, two of Kain's works hung among modern art from Paris. His lacquer work won him First Prize for painted furniture at the Royal Dublin Society Aonach Tailteann. His portraits of ITGWU General Presidents Thomas Foran, 1926, and Thomas Kennedy, 1942, hang in Liberty Hall and it is known that ITGWU General

Secretary William O'Brien and Cork Official and Labour TD Thomas Nagle sat for him. A portrait of Ina Connolly Heron, 1923, sold at auction for £2,400 in 2008 and his image of Connolly was lent, on occasion, by the ITGWU to the Royal Hibernian Academy and National Gallery of Ireland. His 1925 painting of Countess Markievicz was presented to the Irish Labour History Society by Kain's grand-niece Nuala Gilsenan in 2008 and briefly graced the Markievicz Executive Room of Connect. It is inscribed on the back, 'Portmarnock T Kain 15 Old Camden Street 27/7/1925'.[37] He also painted James Mallon, 1916 Volunteer and internee in Frongoch and Ballykinlar,[38] and the socialist trade unionist Walter Carpenter.[39]

As 'KN', Kain's cartoons appeared in ITGWU publications and, from January-March 1924, the *Voice of Labour* carried his small block advertisement for 'Banners & Flags Painted in Oils' and 'Illuminated

Thomas Jeremiah Kain, his wife Kathleen (née Browne) and their son Thomas, c1887
(photograph courtesy of Nuala Gilsenan and the Doyle family)

Addresses (Special Terms to Trade Union Members'.[40] It is thought that not all of Kain's banners survive but his bannerette for the ITGWU Band, 'established Dublin 1919', in dark green edged with golden tassels, bears a beautifully painted oval portrait of Connolly wreathed with laurel.[41] This was similar to his banner for the ITGWU Belfast Branch made in 1930, 'James Connolly 1916' again the central image. On the obverse is a bust of 'James Hope 1798'. The material is Elliott's Irish poplin. Loftus considered that this 'elegant banner' must have been expensive. William McMullen, then Belfast Branch Secretary and later ITGWU General President, said that whilst Connolly was an obvious choice, 'it was difficult to decide who should go on the other side'. Hope was chosen as a 'good blend of Catholic and Protestant'. When the union tried to repair it in the early 1960s a 'man from Corry's' thought he was receiving an Orange banner and 'refused to do the job when he discovered Connolly and Hope were on it'. The union had a former Worshipful Master in their ranks who 'showed them how to carry the banner and lent them straps and strings' from Clifton Street Orange Hall. Loftus concluded: 'It is interesting to compare the bold vulgarity of the re-placement made for the union in 1966 by the English firm of Tutill'.[42]

Kain's 1920 banner for the ITGWU No 1 Branch Carters' Section is regarded as a 'very fine piece of painting. The scene on the back is very apt and well executed and the scroll-work is exquisite'. Connolly's bust adorns the front while on the reverse, the four provincial emblems in each corner, there is an 'oval scene of a carter on Custom House Quay, with the Custom House behind and a ship beside'. At top is 'THE CARTERS' and below 'THE OLD RELIABLES'. Kain signed and dated his work of oil on Irish poplin with a shield bottom trimmed with a gold and green woollen fringe.[43] The carters or quay labourers had a lengthy tradition and strong associations with O'Connell.[44]

Kain took commissions from other unions, as for the Electrical Trades Union (ETU) in 1930, explaining the TEEU, now Connect, involvement in his headstone. In an oval, flanked by provincial emblems, 'Mercury/Lugh is running carrying a torch in his left hand, sword in his right, naked except for a belted skirt, most improbably arrayed with Celtic ornaments on the border'. A scenic collection of lakes, mountains and fields is behind. On the back is a dark blue background is a 'silver torch picked out in bronze with red flames', again with provincial emblems. Presumably under ETU instruction, Loftus comments that 'here he [Kain] departs from the revolutionary idealism of the English certificate', a reference to the British ETU emblem of a French revolutionary woman standing on a globe hailed by the workers, an image close to those of Walter Crane. Instead, Kain painted a 'half classical-half Irish mythical figure, a light-bearing messenger'. As different poplin was used for each side, this 'must have been quite an expensive banner'.[45]

A self-portrait of Kain appears in a memoir about fellow ICA man Tom

Daly.[46] The painting substantiates his relatives' description of him as being five feet ten inches tall of heavy build with deep auburn hair and moustache. Another described him as being a 'very jolly person with a big strong voice and distinguished'. Thomas Kain died in hospital after a short illness in 9 October 1948, his address 368 Kildare Road. The *Irish Press* recorded that attendees at Kain's funeral included his widow, Mrs A. Kain and her son and daughter, Seán and Nuala, and his sisters Mary Doyle and Kathleen O'Byrne. Three volleys were fired over Kain's coffin draped in the tricolour and flag of the ICA.

Jer O'Leary – The Great Only Appear Great

Connolly would not again appear on a Dublin banner until Jer O'Leary's work in the 1980s. Jeremiah James Dominic 'Jer' O'Leary was born in Holles Street Hospital, Dublin on 4 August 1945, one of Denis O'Leary, a barman, and Sarah 'Sadie' Healy's four children.[47] Raised in Upper St Columba's Road, Drumcondra, O'Leary was educated at St Vincent's CBS, leaving at fourteen years of age to become a messenger boy with the Irish Yeast Company in College Street and then RGDATA (Retail Grocery, Dairy & Allied Trades Association). When sixteen, he emigrated to Birmingham, working in the Bull Ring development, before returning and working as a porter in Brunswick Street Hospital and thence the Eastern Health Board.[48] He was an active member of ITGWU Dublin No 5 (Building) and No 18 (Public Services) Branches, SIPTU Health Services, Irish Equity and, most recently, SIPTU Region 1 Retired Members' Committee. In February 2019, he was to receive his Fifty-Year Membership badge.

O'Leary joined the Republican Movement in 1967 and, from 1970, served three years in Mountjoy Jail 'for activities associated with his membership of the Official IRA'.[49] Prison proved, in his sister Margaret's words, to be a 'huge turning point in his life'. He took art classes, discovering a talent for graphic design and winning an ITGWU Members' Art Competition three years in a row, the judging panel chaired by Noel Sheridan, Director, National College of Art & Design.[50] This led to ITGWU General Secretary Michael Mullen commissioning O'Leary to design new banners for the union. After the appearance of his first banner, commissions flowed and the colour, imagery and politics of his work transformed Dublin labour's street presence. In 1976, O'Leary joined the Communist Party of Ireland and, with Margaret, joined 18,500 at the Eleventh World Festival of Youth & Students in Havana under the banner 'For Anti-Imperialist Solidarity, Peace and Friendship'. The O'Learys helped organise an Irish pageant.

Before his sentence, O'Leary had met Eithne O'Brien, a shipping clerk with Bell Lines, from Mulhuddart, County Dublin, and active in the ITGWU Dublin No 2 (Clerical) Branch. They married in 1975 after his release, enjoyed a deeply happy marriage and had three children, Norah, Clare and

Diarmuid.[51] The family were dealt a severe blow on 10 May 1998 when Diarmuid, then aged twenty-two, died in a fire in a guesthouse in Glasgow having travelled to see Celtic win the Scottish Championship. O'Leary shared a celebratory hug with his son as they unexpectedly met each other outside Parkhead. Diarmuid's loss had significant impact on Eithne's health and neither parent fully recovered from their grief.[52] O'Leary was close, politically and personally, to his brother Denis, suffering another blow when he died 3 December 2009. When Eithne died on 12 December 2017, his 'world collapsed'.

On 29 March 1975, O'Leary appeared as Big Jim Larkin in Margaretta D'Arcy and John Arden's *The Non-Stop Connolly Show*, a twenty-four-hour piece of radical agit-prop theatre produced by Jim Sheridan in Liberty Hall.[53] The play was described as 'probably the most ambitious attempt in English to dramatise working-class and socialist history'.[54] D'Arcy and Arden can be seen discussing their project with some excerpts in the RTÉ Archive.[55] O'Leary's personification of Larkin's power and charisma – in this and a 1977 Project Arts Theatre production of Plunkett Kelly's *The Risen People* – lifted the audience from their seats and began his career as an actor. Theatre director and writer Peter Sheridan recalled that O'Leary's Larkin was 'probably the greatest example in my lifetime of taking an audience on a journey they never suspected they were going on'. This was particularly so in Jim Sheridan's adaptation of *The Risen People* in the Gaiety Theatre for the centenary of the Irish Congress of Trade Unions in 1994.[56] O'Leary, playing Larkin for the ninth time, can be seen in a 1979 production in the Amalgamated Transport & General Workers' Union Hall.[57] At the State Commemoration of the 1913 Lockout, who else but Jer O'Leary performed Larkin's speech from Cleary's window – what was once, on Bloody Sunday, William Martin Murphy's Imperial Hotel?[58] In February 2011, he delivered Larkin's words on 'The Day of Shame' protests against the cutting of the Minimum Wage.[58]

O'Leary became the personification of Larkin to a generation of Dublin activists and never tired of the role.

> 'Playing Larkin is a pleasure and an honour. Some parts are just performance tasks but Larkin was one of the finest specimens of humanity, a wonderful mind, great courage and heart of a lion, unusual vision, and a voice like rolling thunder.'[60]

All this led to a career in film and theatre. In 1977, O'Leary performed in Donald Taylor-Black's interpretation of Bertolt Brecht's *The Mother*, a highlight of that year's Dublin Theatre Festival. From 1979, he appeared in forty-two film and television productions including *My Left Foot*, *The Field* and *In the Name of the Father*, all directed by Jim Sheridan; *Michael Collins* as Thomas Clarke, directed by Neil Jordan; and most recently, *Game of Thrones*.[61]

Although O'Leary had no professional art training, he had intrinsic skills for portraiture and graphic design and brought these gifts to his banners. He acknowledged that the banners were 'only made possible due to the huge support and active participation of Eithne ... not only did she advise with the creative visions of designs of the early banners but they were stitched by her on a very basic old-fashioned Singer sewing machine with a foot pedal, and in many instances embroidered by hand in our small living room.'[62]

For O'Leary, as in Warner's song, they were 'moving murals'. They were displayed in exhibitions in places as disparate as Sligo, Islington, New York, Moscow and Havana as well as fulfilling their main purpose in demonstration. Art historian Seán Oliver observed that

'some bourgeois members of the artistic fraternity' considered that O'Leary's work in banner art did 'not constitute true artistic effort, because he works neither in stone, bronze or oils, but uniquely in cloth, they claim that he is not, aesthetically speaking, an artist in the true sense of the word.'

Oliver acknowledged that O'Leary worked 'within an artisan tradition' but one with 'deep roots', tapestries dating back to the thirteenth century and representing 'some of the highest forms of artistic expression in European art'. O'Leary's work, drawn from his own experiences of working class deprivation and struggle, expressed 'the revolutionary aspirations and yearning for political emancipation of the class he comes from'. Oliver concluded that O'Leary's 'banners are works of art'.[63]

Banners in the twentieth century experienced leaner times. Trade unions had few resources and circumstance, cost, the want of occasion, all conspired to drive banners to basement decay and their carriers to emigration or disgruntled oblivion. The dominant influence in the banner revival from the 1980s was O'Leary. In his banners, Celtic patterns and insignia mixed with the striking revolutionary murals of Mexican artists Sigueras, Orozoca and Rivera.[64] There was a 'concern for historical accuracy' – both of image, iconography and language – and a 'desire to retrieve the ordinary from obscurity'. Connolly quotations abound – many for the first time on Irish banners – 'hammering home the message that social and political questions are but ends of the same stick'. Pavement observers could not fail to understand the essential politics of the slogans and vibrant images. National imagery was still present – and rightly so for his were Irish banners – but it was part of an overdue internationalism, everything underpinned by the concept of class struggle. Such overt socialist messages did not endear O'Leary to begrudging critics.

'For many of us in the labour movement, however, such criticism does not matter. Jer O'Leary's true gallery is O'Connell Street and a Trades Council demonstration; a smoke-ridden hall gathered to hear a Dunne's Stores striker challenging racism; a windswept picket line in Leixlip, County Kildare, as young women fight for the right to join a union; or a provincial union hall on the occasion of the feting of veterans.'

For Francis Devine, reviewing an exhibition of O'Leary's work in the Project Arts Centre in 1994,

'O'Leary's traditions are not self-created, they are part of our collective inheritance. We are indebted to him for re-awakening our sense of the past as others are fearful that this may lead to the revival of our hope for the future. Irish labour iconography was deadened by the pursuit of respectability and succeeds now in its challenge to the respected and its uplift of the respectful.

The great only appear great because they hang in the National Portrait Gallery. Banners will one day announce the masses clamouring for admission.'[65]

For O'Leary's true gallery was 'O'Connell Street, rain-sodden and windblown, banners heading the narrowing throng'.[66] Among the many marching ITGWU banners were those for Cavan; Cork No 4 Branch with Tadhg Barry; Dublin No 19 with Lockout Martyrs James Nolan, John Byrne and Alice Brady; Limerick No 1; Newry with James Fearon; and Sligo. He made other banners for the Ancient Guild of Incorporated Brick & Layers & Allied Trades Union; Irish National Painters' & Decorators' Trade Union; MANDATE, National Organisation for the Unemployed; Postal & Telecommunications Workers' Union; Irish Anti-Apartheid Movement; Communist Party of Ireland; and Connolly Column, International Brigade. He made a replica of the ICA's Starry Plough for Second Age's production of Seán O'Casey's *The Plough & the Stars* in 1993.[67] A banner for the Dublin Council of Trade Unions Centenary in 1986, in the county's sky and navy blue, depicted Bloody Sunday on one side and Pádraig Pearse's words on the reverse: 'Heroic Dublin! / Redeemed from a thousand shames / And her name made splendid / Amongst the cities of the world'. Perhaps O'Leary's most iconic banner is that for the Federated Workers' Union of Ireland with Joseph Cashman's dramatic 1923 photograph image of Larkin, arms aloft over his iconic words 'The Great are not Great, The Great only appear Great because we are on our knees. Let us arise!' against a scarlet background. This image inspired Óisín Kelly's Larkin Monument, a location for many an O'Leary homage.[68]

O'Leary was gregarious, compelling company, raconteur, wit, balladeer, a 'great character' whose popularity was reflected in the Wake held for him in the Mansion House and the huge attendance at his funeral.[69] His interests were wide and he insatiably sought details on international struggles, historic and contemporary.[70] On 21 June 1977, he inserted a memorial notice in the *Irish Times* personal column for 'Maguire, Molly', a tribute to the Molly Maguires executed on that day in 1877.[71] He was fascinated by Native American culture, Geronimo a particular hero. He was a sports fan, particularly football with passions for Drumcondra, Bohemian (after Drums' demise) and Celtic. Heroes included 'Bunny' Fullam, Charlie Tully and 'Jinkie' Johnstone. Many in O'Leary's circle will miss the regular post of a collection of photocopied pages from the socialist press and *Ireland's Own*, intriguing football memorabilia, poems and songs – many self-penned, postcards of his film parts and, always, himself, Eithne and the kids.

Jer O'Leary died peacefully in his home on 26 December 2018. President Michael D. Higgins observed that 'all those who love and appreciate Irish art and theatre will have been immensely saddened by the news of the death of Jer O'Leary, activist, actor, orator' who 'will forever be remembered for his unstinting political activism'.[72] His coffin left Saint Agatha's Church to a recording of 'Streets of Laredo'. The massive attendance reflected O'Leary's varied worlds of socialist and republican politics, trade unionism, community activism, theatre and art. Famous rubbed shoulders with infamous, illustrious with obscure, this unusual concoction being O'Leary's everyday.

O'Leary's sister Margaret concluded her address by citing one of her brother's favourite sayings, 'If you have not been involved in the passions of your time you have not lived'. Like Reynolds and Kain before him, O'Leary was passionately involved in his times not least, through his theatrical performances and his banners, in hopes of inspiring others to follow the same progressive path and 'that all around may plainly see, the power of our unity'.

Notes

In compiling this article, we are grateful to Norah and Margaret O'Leary; Brendan Byrne (Irish Labour History Society); Seán Heading (Connect); Scott Millar (SIPTU); Joe Mooney (East Wall History Group); and Matt Doyle (National Graves Association) for their assistance.

1   The song may be heard at *http://unionsong.com/u034.html*. Francy Devine re-worked the song for the Musicians' Union of Ireland, 'Strike Up That Chord', *https://francydevine.bandcamp.com/track/strike-up-that-chord* [retrieved 25 January 2019].

2   Belinda Loftus, *Marching Workers*, (Arts Councils of Ireland, Belfast/Dublin, 1978) and John Gorman, 'Banners and ballads', *Saothar 5*, 1979, pp. 80-82.

3   Walker in fact had graced an Amalgamated Society of Woodworkers' banner unveiled in Belfast in 1935 and adorning the front cover of Seán Byers & Francis Devine, *William Walker 1870-1918: Belfast Labour Unionist Centenary Essays*, (Umiskin Press, Dublin. 2018).

4   Francis Devine, 'Re-awakening our sense of the past' in *Jer O'Leary's Banners of Unity*, (North Inner City Folklore Project, Dublin 1994), pp. 35-37.

5   Loftus, *op. cit.*, p. 19.

6   John Swift, *A History of the Dublin Bakers & Others*, (Irish Bakers', Confectioners' & Allied Workers' Amalgamated Union, Dublin, 1948), pp. 238-304; Timothy P. O'Neill, 'Irish trade banners' in Caoimhín Ó Danacháir, *Folk & Farm: Essays in Honour of A.T. Lucas*, (Royal Society of Antiquaries of Ireland, Dublin, 1976), pp. 193-214. Neil Jarman, *Displaying Faith: Orange, Green & Trade Union Banners In Northern Ireland*, (Institute of Irish Studies, Queen's University Belfast, 1999).

7   Gorman, *op. cit.*

8   O'Reilly, 28 June 1844-10 August 1890, was born in Dowth, the son of a headmaster. He moved to Preston, Lancashire, when fifteen as a teenager and became involved in the 11th Lancashire Rifles Volunteers. Returning to Ireland in 1864, he joined the IRB, was arrested, spent time in Pentonville and Dartmoor before transportation to Western Australia in 1867, escaping in 1869, eventually to Philadelphia. He settled near Boston and became a journalist. He died in Hull, Massachusetts, on 10 August 1890.

9   Brendan Matthews, 'William Reynolds and trade banners', *Drogheda Independent*, 10 August 10 2011, *https://www.independent.ie/regionals/droghedaindependent/ news/william-reynolds-and-trade-banners-27158828.html* [retrieved 24 January 2019].

10 Drogheda 'flags' had famously paraded at a massive Amnesty rally at Tara in 1843, an event recorded in the broadside ballad, 'The Tara Monster Meeting', *https://digital.nls.uk/broadsides/view/?id=20795*. This has been recorded by Francy Devine on his forthcoming CD *An Ownerless Corner of Earth*. For full description see Gary Owens,

'Structure and symbol in the O'Connellite 'Monster Meetings'', *Journal of the Old Drogheda Society 18*, 2011. In April 2016, artist Michael McLoughlin conducted a conversation in Drogheda Millmount Museum's Banner Room in April 2016 about the banners and their public appearances, forming the basis of an installation in the Highlanes Gallery, *http://mmcloughlin.org/index.php/starry-plough/* [retrieved 24 January 2019].

11 Moira Corcoran & Peter Durnin, *The Drogheda Banners: Aspects of the History of Drogheda, No 5*, (Old Drogheda Society, Drogheda, 2001); Harry Fairtlough & Jackie Rooney, 'In our museum: the [Trade] Banner Room', *Journal of the Old Drogheda Society*, no. 3, 1979, pp. 16-22; and 'The guild and trade banners', *http://www.millmount.net/node/42* [retrieved 24 January 2019]. For trade unionism at the time Reynolds painted his banners see Frank Gallagher, 'Drogheda's early trade unions', *Journal of the Old Drogheda Society*, no. 13, 2001, pp. 7-22, and Charles Callan, 'The painters of Drogheda', *Journal of the Old Drogheda Society*, no. 13, 2001, pp. 149-166.

12 Loftus, *op. cit.* p. 79, colour illustration between pp. 40-41.

13 *http://slanehistoryandarchaeologysociety.com/index.php/famous-people/12-william-reynolds-the-banner-artist* [retrieved 24 January 2019].

14 'Banner artist William Reynolds', *Drogheda Independent*, January 9 2004, *www.independent.ie/regionals/droghedaindependent/localnotes/banner-artist-william-reynolds 27105422.html* [retrieved 24 January 2019]. He also designed the Celtic cross, with sword intertwining a harp, over the grave of Colonel Patrick Leonard, a Fenian buried in Monknewtown Cemetery, Slane. Reynolds' brother worked as carpenter on the Oldbridge Estate.

15 It is not certain that Thomas Senior was born in Germany – information from Helena Claringbold.

16 Information from Helena Claringbold and *www.census.nationalarchives.ie/reels/ nai003724859/* [retrieved 4 February 2019].

17 www.census.nationalarchives.ie/reels/nai000185797/ [retrieved 24 January 2019]. Devine & Smethurst, *Historical Directory of Trade Unions in Ireland*, (ILHS/WCML, Dublin/Salford, 2017), p. 292. The ITGWU had 57 carpet planners in membership on 31 January 1920, *Watchword & Voice of Labour*, 25 September 1920.

18 Information from Helena Claringbold.

19 Brendan Byrne, Labour Lives no 14: Thomas Kain, 1886-1948', *Saothar 37*, 2012, pp. 99-101.

20 Byrne, *op. cit.*, 2012, pp. 99-101; Theo Snoddy, *Dictionary of Irish Artists: Twentieth Century*, (Merlin Publishing, Dublin, 2002), p. 295. The grave is No 2-0369, *www.igp-web.com/IGPArchives/ire/dublin/photos/tombstones/1headstones/mt-jerome137.txt* [retrieved 25 January 2019].

21 This number is given in membership lists in Ann Matthews, *The Irish Citizen Army*, (Mercier Press, Cork, 2014) and Daithí Mac an Mhaistir, *The Irish Citizen Army: The World's First Working Class Army*, (Connolly Books, Dublin, 2017). The latter lists him among those members from a 'skilled' background as opposed to 'unskilled/semi-skilled' or 'petit bourgeois/middle class'.

22 Matthews, *op. cit.*, p. 55.

23 Frank Robbins, *Under the Starry Plough: Recollections of the Irish Citizen Army*, (Academy Press, Dublin, 1978), pp. 55-57.

24 *http://mspcsearch.militaryarchives.ie/docs/files//PDF_Pensions/R1/MSP34REF13912Thomas Kain/WMSP34REF13912ThomasKain.pdf* [retrieved 26 January 2019]. The raid is explained in Rosie Hackett's Witness Statement reproduced in full and annotated in Francis Devine & Manus O'Riordan, *James Connolly, Liberty Hall & the 1916 Rising*, (Studies in Irish Labour History 11, ILHS, Dublin 2006).

25 *www.irishmedals.ie/City-Hall.php* [retrieved 26 January 2019].

26 Robbins, *op. cit.*, pp. 55-57.

27 *Voice of Labour*, 12 May 1923.

28 *http://mspcsearch.militaryarchives.ie/docs/files//PDF_Pensions/R1/MSP34REF13912Thomas Kain/WMSP34REF13912ThomasKain.pdf;http://mspcsearch.militaryarchives.ie/docs/files//PDF _Pensions/R1/MSP34REF13912ThomasKain/W34E3374ThomasKain.pdf* [retrieved 25 January 2019].

29 Murray was most probably James Murray, ICA activist 1918-1923, based in Barry's and Hamman Hotels. Francis Kelly, 282, lived at 152 Parnell Street, a labourer, he was active in Liberty Hall and St Stephen's Green.

30 *ibid.* Those attesting were Seán Byrne, 22 Upper Wellington Street; George Connolly, 13 Buckingham Terrace; M. Donnolly, Islandbridge; Michael Kelly, LH; J. O'Neill, 187 Donnycarney Road; J. Keogh, 6 Hendrick Street; Séamus McGowan, Drumcondra; Phil O'Leary, 4 Mid Gardiner Street; J. O'Shea, 15 Joyce Road; Frank Robbins, 5 Fairview Terrace; and J. Seery, 14A Benburb Street.

31 Matthews, *op,. cit.*

32 *http://mspcsearch.militaryarchives.ie/docs/files//PDF_Pensions/R1/MSP34REF13912Thomas Kain/WMSP34REF13912ThomasKain.pdf* [retrieved 26 January 2019]. James O'Neill was ICA Commandant, 1917-1922, '17 – James O'Neill, The Irish Citizen Army, and reorganisation in the Docklands', *http://eastwallforall.ie/?p=3624* [retrieved 27 January 2019].

33 O'Brien recorded these events in his autobiography, *Forth the Banners Go*, (Three Candles, Dublin, 1969), pp. 284-286 and they are repeated by Thomas J. Morrissey, *William O'Brien, 1881-1968: Socialist, Republican, Dáil Deputy, Editor & Trade Unionist*, (Four Courts Press, Dublin, 2007), p. 102. For O'Brien's letter see *http://mspcsearch.militaryarchives.ie/docs/files//PDF_Pensions/R1/MSP34REF13912ThomasKain/WMSP34REF13912ThomasKain.pdf* [retrieved 25 January 2019].

34 Oman's Witness Statement is reproduced in Devine & O'Riordan, *op. cit.*

35 *www.nival.ie/collections/artists-database/view/artist-items/name/thomas-kain/* [retrieved 25 January 2019]. His attendances were from October 1918-July 1919; October 1920-July 1921; October 1922-July 1923; and October 1923-July 1924.

36 Éimear O'Connor, *Seán Keating in Context: Responses to Culture in Post-Civil War Ireland*, (Carysfort Press, Dublin, 2009), p. 23; *http://mspcsearch.militaryarchives.ie/docs/files//PDF_Pensions/R1/MSP34REF13912ThomasKain/W34E3374ThomasKain.pdf* [retrieved 27 January 2019].

37 Information from Helena Claringbold; Byrne, *op. cit.*, pp. 99-101; Snoddy, *op. cit.*, p. 295.

38 *Mallon's portrait was recently autioned, www.adams.ie/53948/JAMES-MALLON-1916-Volunteer-and-internee-of-Frongach-and-Ballykinlar-A-large-and-interesting-collection-including-a-portrait-of-Mallon-half-length-in-Volunteer-uniform-by-Thomas-Kain-oil-on-canv?ipp=All&keyword=&view=lot_detail* [retrieved 25 January 2019].

39 Carpenter, 1871-1926, born in Kent, was a chimney sweep, moved to Dublin and in 1911 was ITGWU Organiser and Secretary, Socialist Party of Ireland. From 1911, he was Secretary, International Tailors, Machinists and Pressers' Trade Union. His sons, Walter and Peter both fought with the ICA under Connolly in the GPO in 1916. Ellen Galvin, *Walter Carpenter, A Revolutionary Life*, (East Wall History Group, Dublin, 1916) and available as PDF, *https://cedarlounge.files.wordpress.com/2006/07/jm-pamphlet-doc-apr-2016-latest-version.pdf;* D.R. O'Connor Lysaght, 'Walter Carpenter, communist', *http://eastwallforall.ie/?p=3588;* 'Eastwaller arrested for insulting a British Royal – Walter Carpenter (1911)', http://eastwallforall.ie/?p=324; "The man who exposed the slum owners': municipal elections, January 15th 1914', http://eastwallforall.ie/?p=826; '1916: the destruction of Liberty Hall & Walter Carpenter, http://eastwallforall.ie/?p=3365; 'Walter Carpenter: from sweep to revolutionary, a forgotten figure from 1913 Lockout', *http://1913committee.ie/blog/?p=542* [retrieved 25 January 2019].

40 *Voice of Labour*, January-March 1924.

41 This banner was donated to the ILHS by the late John F. Carroll and is currently on display in Liberty Hall.

42 Loftus, *op. cit.*, pp. 89-90, illustrations 59, 68-69. SIPTU commissioned a striking new banner in 2018.

43 Loftus, *op. cit.* pp. 82-83, illustration p. 43

44 Devine & Smethurst, *op. cit.*, pp. 65-90.

45 Loftus, *op. cit.*, pp. 86-87, illustrations pp. 55-56.

46 'The 'Blackguard' Tom Daly, the 1916 Rising and the Frongoch rat catcher!', *http://eastwallforall.ie/?p=2294* [retrieved 25 January 2019].

47 Denis was born on 10 September 1915 and Sadie, 4 April 1919. Margaret was born 3

February 1947; Carmel, 10 May 1959; and Denis, 19 January 1952. Denis Senior joined the RAF just prior to the Second World War in 1939 and worked in the bar trade from 1945-1980, finishing as Manager, Gaffney's of Fairview. His picture famously appeared in the *Illustrated Pictorial Magazine*, November 1943, captioned 'The battle for Italy goes on. Allied guns hammer at German defence lines. Allied planes speed across the glaring sky. Enemy shells whine overhead. Here in this Italian field that yesterday was only stubble bulldozers are hard at work making a new runway for Allied planes. But it is Sunday and late in the afternoon Squadron Leader David Lewis, an Irish Dominican priest and chaplain to an RAF wing, puts vestments over his shirt and shorts to celebrate Mass for the Catholics among the many RAF airmen and operators. The portable altar rests on an ammunition box propped up on petrol tins'. The 'Altar Boy' was Denis, then twenty-eight. On 10 September 1943, he had landed at Salerno, surviving a ten-day German onslaught. Sadie only received this confirmation that her husband to be was alive when the magazine arrived in Drumcondra months later. They married during Denis's brief furlough in October 1944. Margaret O'Leary, *From Serving on WW2 Frontline - to serving Pints in Gaffney's Pub, Dublin 3*. Before marriage, Sadie worked for Bull's of Suffolk Street, religious and church suppliers.

48 His sister Margaret O'Leary's address to his funeral, 3 January 2019.
49 'Jer O'Leary obituary: The actor who brought history to life', *Irish Times*, 12 January 2019, *www.irishtimes.com/life-and-style/people/jer-o-leary-obituary-the-actor-who-brought-history-to-life 1.3753811* [retrieved 24 January 2019].
50 Francis Devine, *Organising History: A Centenary of SIPTU, 1909-2009*, (Gill & Macmillan, Dublin, 2009), p. 638.
51 Diarmuid was born on 10 March 1976; Norah, 6 June 1978; and Clare, 4 December 1982.
52 A poem by Francis Devine, 'Over and Over', (*May Dancer*, Watchword, Dublin, 2007, p. 27) was published in the *Celtic View* and on the club's website. Some years later, O'Leary took pride in the fact that some Irish supporters – who had gathered numerous sets of team strips and brought them over to townships around Johannesburg – photographed Diarmuid's poem framed in a number of the township club premises.
53 'The Non-Stop Connolly Show', *www.irishplayography.com/play.aspx?playid=31126* [retrieved 25 January 2019]. O'Leary is listed in the cast as Gerry.
54 Michael Cohen, 'A Defence of D'Arcy and Arden's Non-Stop Connolly Show', *www.cambridge.org/core/journals/theatre-research-international/article/defence-of-darcy-and-ardens-nonstop-connolly-show/CC9B0677714F1D61B096AA63C9C57D8C* [retrieved 25 January 2019].
55 'Committed to the ideas of James Connolly', *www.rte.ie/archives/2015/0324/689284-the-non-stop-connolly-show/* [retrieved 25 January 2019].
56 'Banks to banners: Jer O'Leary – making trade union banners', *Sunday Tribune*, 5 January 1986.
57 *www.rte.ie/archives/collections/news/21225779-the-risen-people/* [retrieved 25 January 2019].
58 *Jeremiah 'Jer' O'Leary: the Bard of Drumcondra, 4th August 1945-26th December 2018*, commemorative pamphlet produced for his funeral; *www.decadeofcentenaries.com/state-commemoration/* [retrieved 26 January 2019]. He did this once before in 2013 for a North Inner City Folklore Project re-enactment – and on many other occasions.
59 www.youtube.com/watch?v=V1049MOn174 [retrieved 27 January 2019].
60 *The Bard of Drumcondra, op. cit.*
61 *My Left Foot* (1989); *After Midnight, Stephen, The Field, Hard Shoulder* (1990); *The Miracle, The Parent* (1991); *More Bricks Than Bouquet* (1992); *In the Name of the Father* (1993); *Braveheart* (1995); *Michael Collins, The Majesty of the Haunt, Some Mother's Son* (1996); *The Informant, The Boxer, The Butcher Boy* (1997); *Animal Farm, Ballykissangel* (1999); *Borstal Boy, Ordinary Decent Criminal, Angela's Ashes, Rat* (2000); *Disco Pigs* (2001); *Bobbie's Girl, In America* (2002); *Dead Bodies, Headrush* (2003); *Turning Green, Get Rich or Die Tryin'* (2005); *Psych Ward, Paul's Father* (2009); *Marú* (2010); *This Must Be The Place* (2011); *Milo, Game of Thrones* (2011); *Out of Here* (2013); *My Whole Half Life* (2014); *Lost in the Living, Penny Dreadful* (2015); *Banshee Blacktop, An Irish Ghost Story* (2016); and *The Tattoo* (2017), *www.imdb.com/name/nm0641596/* [retrieved 26 January 2019].

62 *The Bard of Drumcondra, op. cit.*

63 Seán Oliver, 'Works of art' in *Banners of Unity, op. cit.*, pp. 19-21.

64 José Clemente Orozco, 23 November 1883 - 7 September, 1949; Diego María de la Concepción Juan Nepomuceno Estanislao de la Rivera y Barrientos Acosta y Rodríguez, known as Diego Rivera, 8 December 1886 - 24 November 1957; and David Alfaro Siqueiros (born José de Jesús Alfaro Siqueiros, 29 December 1896-6 January 1974, were responsible for the Mexican Mural Renaissance and were greatly admired by O'Leary.

65 Francis Devine, 'Reawakening our sense of the past' in *Banners of Unity, op. cit.*, pp. 35-37.

66 'Jer O'Leary, actor, union man and banner artist' in Jack McGinley (ed), *Dear Comrade, SIPTU, 1990-2010*, (Watchword, Dublin, 2010), p. 110.

67 *ibid.*

68 *Banners of Unity, op. cit.*, passim. Cashman, 1881-1969, was for a period Head of the Irish Press Photographic Department, see *www.rte.ie/archives/2013/0130/365262-big-jim-larkin-irish-trade-unionist-died-on-this-day-in-1947/* [retrieved 27 January 2019].

69 A flavour of a pint with O'Leary was captured by the Marino Local History Society, 'Jer & Dan' Featuring Jer O'Leary & Mick Hynes, (2015), *www.youtube.com/watch?v=Q3uUcWVARRc*; and a short tribute from Spanish films, www.youtube.com/watch?v=t5xEKZHuMTo [retrieved 27 January 2019].

70 *https://jerolearyactor.weebly.com/articles.html#PhotoSwipe1548537777420* [retrieved 27 January 2019].

71 Those hung were James Boyle, Alexander Campbell, James Carroll, 'Yellow Jack' Donahue, Michael J. Doyle, Thomas Duffy, Edward J. Kelly, Hugh McGeehan, Thomas Munley and James Roarity. Ten others were hanged over the next two years: Martin Bergan, Dennis Donnelly, Thomas Fisher, John 'Black Jack' Kehoe, Patrick Hester, James McDonnell, Peter McHugh, Peter McManus, Charles Sharpe and Patrick Tully. See Kevin Kenny, *Making Sense of the Molly Maguires*, (Oxford University Press, New York & Oxford, 1998).

72 Patsy McGarry, 'An ordinary bloke with many talents: Remembering Jer O'Leary', *Irish Times*, 3 January 2019, *www.irishtimes.com/news/social-affairs/an-ordinary-bloke-with-many-talents-remembering-jer-o-leary-1.3746979* [retrieved 24 January 2019].

Paddy Devlin at ITGWU Annual Conference, c1980, with Michael Mullen (General Secretary),
Joe Meehan (Belfast Branch Secretary), Fintan Kennedy (General President) and Joe McBrinn (NEC).
Photograph courtesy of Irish Labour History Society

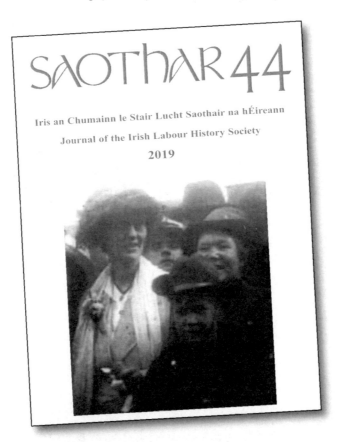